BRICK AND MARBLE
IN
THE MIDDLE AGES

BRICK AND MARBLE
IN
THE MIDDLE AGES

GEORGE EDMUND STREET

ISBN: 978-93-5614-328-9

Published: 1874

LECTOR HOUSE LLP
E-MAIL: lectorpublishing@gmail.com

1.—North Porch, Sta. Maria Maggiore, Bergamo.

Frontispiece.

BRICK AND MARBLE
IN
THE MIDDLE AGES
NOTES OF TOURS IN THE NORTH OF ITALY.

BY

GEORGE EDMUND STREET, RA.,

MEMBER OF THE IMPERIAL AND ROYAL ACADEMY OF
THE FINE ARTS, VIENNA,
ETC. ETC.

SECOND EDITION.

WITH NUMEROUS ILLUSTRATIONS.

1874

𝕿𝖔 𝖙𝖍𝖊 𝕸𝖊𝖒𝖔𝖗𝖞

OF

THE RIGHT REV. SAMUEL WILBERFORCE,

LORD BISHOP OF WINCHESTER,

ETC. ETC.,

IN TOKEN OF THE AUTHOR'S MOST SINCERE AFFECTION,

AND

IN GRATITUDE FOR NUMBERLESS BENEFITS RECEIVED FROM HIM,

THIS VOLUME,

ORIGINALLY DEDICATED TO HIM IN 1855,

IS NOW INSCRIBED.

PREFACE TO THE SECOND EDITION.

THE First Edition of this volume has been so long out of print that I had almost ceased to regard myself as responsible for all that it contains. It was the rapid and fresh summary of a happy journey undertaken in the early years of my artistic career. There were, I knew, many details in which it could easily be improved, and many journeys taken over the same ground might have enabled me to go far more into detail than I was able to do when I published it. I find, however, on reading again what I wrote so long ago, that age and greater knowledge of the subject have generally confirmed my old ideas, and that, as far as regards the principles of my book, I still believe them to be true and just. In revising what I wrote, however, I have found myself obliged to make many alterations and additions, sometimes in relation to towns not visited on my first journey, sometimes in reference to buildings either not described at all or at best insufficiently described before. In doing this I have endeavoured not to increase too much the bulk of the volume, and as far as possible not to interfere with the general character or tone of its contents, though in the process of revision the larger portion of the book has had to be re-written.

I hope, if other occupations admit of it, before long to add to this volume a second, containing notes of tours in the centre and south of Italy, undertaken with the same object of studying and describing the too little appreciated art of Italy in the Middle Ages, which seems to me to be almost equally full of interest in all parts of the Peninsula.

The materials which I have accumulated for this purpose are only too considerable, and the very richness of the subject has made me shy of approaching it; but the necessity of publishing another edition of this volume has revived my resolution to complete as soon as possible the work which I originally proposed to myself, and of which I have never lost sight. But whether I accomplish this or not, the volume which I now republish may, I hope, give a tolerably complete view of Italian Gothic architecture north of the Apennines.

Those who wish for further archæological details as to the age and history of buildings, will not find great difficulty in supplementing what I have written. For myself I confess at once that I have not had time or opportunity for examining the documentary history of the buildings I have described, and that the dates where I have given them are generally obtained at second-hand, though never given save where they accord with the architectural character of the work. It was never for merely archæological purposes that I made my many journeys in Italy. Before I first travelled there I had made myself well acquainted with all the best remains of the Middle Ages in England: I had travelled, sketch-book in hand, through France and Germany, and I knew, therefore, something of the art of our fathers in most districts north of the Alps. But so far I had found no time or opportunity for the study of those early Italian buildings which give the key to the history and style of ours, or of those later works in which, with more or less distinctness, the architects north of the Alps repaid the debt they had previously incurred to the South.

I felt then, as I do now, that no study of architecture was complete which did not proceed exhaustively with the study of all European varieties, and above all of that of Italy. Moreover, there was something in the practice and tendencies of our own day which gave special interest and fascination to such a study. We had gone on in our old paths, studying the works of our own country, which in some respects were deficient in their teaching. We wished to combine the best architecture, the best painting, and the best sculpture in our works. The world seemed to respond to our aspirations, and it is south and not north of the Alps that examples of such a combination have to be looked for. So again it was desirable at any rate to meet the demand which was naturally arising for colour in construction, and here again it was in Italy only that numerous ancient examples of such a combination were to be found. These were the special inducements to me in my earliest journey to Italy, and their influence is as strong as ever upon me. I feel, indeed, even more now than then, the importance of such study to the English architect of to-day. The more men educate themselves by the study of ancient examples, the more is their work likely to become refined and scholarly, whilst at the same time there is no real risk of its becoming less original.

It is quite possible, and one wishes above everything to see it usual, for architects to design all their work without special reference to, or really copying from, any old work. But before doing this they ought at least to put themselves in the same position as to knowledge of what had been done before as that in which their forefathers were. Unless they do so, the desire for originality will only be satisfied by the production of excesses and monstrosities, whose only claim is that they are new—one which, in spite of those who demand a new style, I venture to declare to be their sufficient condemnation.

It remains only to say, that since I first visited Italy two works have been published which add infinitely to our knowledge of the sister arts of painting and sculpture, and enable the artist to travel with a full certainty that he will not lose anything by reason of the ignorance or carelessness of his guide. I need hardly say that I refer to Messrs. Crowe and Cavalcaselle's 'History of Painting in Northern Italy,' and to Mr. C. C. Perkins's admirable volumes on 'Italian' and 'Tuscan Sculptors.' To the latter, indeed, I owe I know not how many acknowledgments for the information I have derived from him. He has done that for the History of Mediæval and post-Mediæval sculpture in Italy which had before hardly even so much as been attempted, and his facts and conclusions are almost always so stated as to command the assent of his readers.

PREFACE TO THE FIRST EDITION.

IN these days of railways and rapid travelling there is scarcely any excuse for ignorance of Continental art. The most busy man finds some short holiday in the course of the year, and, if wise as well as busy, spends it not in quiet sojourn at home, but in active search of the picturesque, the beautiful, or the old, in nature or in art, either in his own country or abroad.

And as the holidays of busy men are short, and therefore to be made as much of as possible, I conceive that I shall be rendering some service, and providing myself with a fair excuse for my presumption, if I venture to shew, by a simple narrative of a tour undertaken in the course of the year before last, how much it is possible to accomplish with pleasure, and, when one has some definite object in view, with profit of no common kind, even in a short holiday.

There are many classes of travellers, and each doubtless flatters itself that its own is the very best of all modes of travelling; and sorry should I be to attempt to disabuse any one of so pleasant a self-deceit. But the more I think of it, the more certain it appears that the reasons and objects which always take me away from home are precisely such as make up the sum of happiness and pleasure to a traveller.

Indeed, without some definite object before him, beyond the mere desire of relaxation and pleasure, few travellers know that thorough joy of heart which an architect feels as he begins the journey which bears him away from home on some ecclesiological or architectural ramble.

Such an one, hard-worked for more than five-sixths of the year, may, if he will, press into the short remainder left to him for a holiday as much both of profit and of pleasure as it is possible to conceive. He goes, sketch-book in hand, with some ancient town or thrice noble cathedral set before him as his goal; and, passing along smiling valleys, or over noble mountains, drinks in all that he sees, not the less gratefully or delightedly in that he views it as the preface only to his more intense enjoyment in the study and pursuit of his own well-beloved art.

If such be my case—and such it is—wonder not, gentle reader, that I desire to shew how much enjoyment may be snatched from time in little more than one short month, nor that I am anxious to put on paper the thoughts that have been uppermost in my mind as I travelled, and looked at and drew the old builders' works in the north of Italy, the more as they seem to bear with much force upon questions debated with more and more eagerness and anxiety every day, by very many of those who take the most lively interest in the progress of Christian art.

In past years I had travelled—rapidly, it is true, but not without learning much, very much, of what was useful—by the noble cities of Belgium, up the church-be-sprinkled banks of the fair Rhine, over the plains of Bavaria, and through much that was most noble and interesting in different parts of France and Germany; I had dreamt of old times and old men in the antique streets of Bruges and Nurem-berg, and under the shade of the still more ancient walls of Regensburg, in the solemn naves of Amiens, of Köln, of Freiburg, of Strasburg and Chartres, and of many more most noble piles; I had paced the ruins of old abbeys, and studied, so far as I could, in all of them the science and the art of my forefathers; but so far all my time had been devoted to the study of Northern art, and I had found no time and no opportunity for the study of that modification of the pointed style which distinguishes the cities and the churches of the north of Italy. No wonder then that, with a prospect at last of a first sight of Italy and Italian architecture before me, I looked forward long and anxiously for the end of summer, for that happy autumn which brings ease and relaxation to so many a wearied heart; and that when at last, at the latter end of August, I found myself absolutely on my way, I was in no common degree disposed for the thorough enjoyment of all that I met with.

It is well here to observe, by the way, that there is much in the present position of architects and the world which may give to these few remarks upon the pointed architecture of the north of Italy—slight and sketchy though they may be—a de-gree of value beyond what they would have had only a short time since.

It is impossible not to feel that the great and general interest in art, created by the revival of true principles within the last few years, is a subject of the greatest congratulation to all true artists. It is not only in architecture, but happily in paint-ing also, that first principles are now studied with some determination by men who command the respect of a world educated hitherto to admire and believe in the falsest and weakest schools of art. It was, therefore, with the desire to see how far these first principles were worked out by the architects of the Middle Ages in Italy, how far moreover they were developed in directions unattempted by their brethren in the North, and how far they have succeeded in leaving us really noble works for our study and admiration, that I undertook my journey.

Let me say, too, at the same time, that I started without either the intention or the desire to examine at all carefully the works of the Renaissance architects. For this there were many reasons—among others my own unfitness by predilection and education for the task, the shortness of my time, and the fact that, as it appears to me, their works have already received as much both in the way of illustration and of description as they deserve.

I should wish also, I must confess, in all my studies of foreign architecture, to confine myself to those buildings in which there appear to me to be the germs at least of an art true and beautiful in itself, and of service to us in our attempts to improve our own work. It does not appear to me that the works of the Italian Renaissance architects really contain this. I see no reason whatever for doubting that if we wish for a purer school of art we must either entirely forget their works, or remember them so far only as to take warning by their faults and failures. I see no reason for allowing that they have succeeded in carrying out true principles, either of construction or ornamentation, to any greater extent than their imitators in England. The same falseness of construction, and heaviness, coarseness, and bad grotesqueness of ornamentation, seem ever to attend their works, together with the same contempt of simplicity, repose, and delicacy which we are so accustomed to connect with them. In short, I see but little reason to differ from the estimate which Mr. Ruskin has given of their merits in the 'Stones of Venice,' and what he has so well said I need not attempt to enlarge upon.

My own feeling is, that as in the pointed arch we have not only the most beautiful, but at the same time incomparably the most convenient feature in construction which has ever been, or which, I firmly believe, ever can be invented, we should not be true artists if we neglected to use it.

I hold firmly the doctrine that no architect can properly neglect to avail himself of every improvement in construction which the growing intelligence of this mechanical age can afford him; but this doctrine in no way hinders the constant employment of the pointed arch; on the contrary, it makes it necessary, because it is at once the most beautiful and the most economical way of doing the work that has to be done.

There are, I well know, advocates for the round arch, whose theory appears to be that we ought to go back for some ages, to throw ourselves as it were into the position of men who knew only the round arch, and from this to attempt to develope in some new direction: this is Mr. Petit's theory, and it is, as appears to me, one which it is not difficult to meet.

Its supporters assert that pointed architecture is so essentially the effort of a particular age, and marked by certain peculiarities so decided, as to be filled, even in its most noble works, with a kind of spirit which in this age it is vain to attempt again to evoke. The old Gothic spirit is, they say, dead; and, glorious as it was, its flight was but meteor-like, and, having passed across the horizon of the world in its rapid course, it has sunk beyond all possibility of revival.

It appears to me that those who so argue confound the accidents with the elements of the true Gothic architecture of the Middle Ages, and mistake altogether the object which, I trust, most architects would propose to themselves in striving for its revival. The elements are the adoption of the best principles of construction, and the ornamentation naturally and properly, and without concealment, of the construction; the accidents are, as it appears to me, the particular character which individual minds may have given to their work, the savageness, or the grotesqueness as it has been called, which is mainly to be discovered in the elaboration of particular features by some particular sculptor or architect, and which in the noblest works—and, indeed, I might say, in most works—one sees no trace of. The true Gothic architects of the Middle Ages had, in short, an intense love of nature grafted on an equally intense love of reality and truth, and to this it is that we owe the true nobility and abiding beauty of their works; nor need we in this age despond, for if we be really earnest in our work, there is nothing in this which we need fear to miss, nothing which we may not ourselves possess if we will, and nothing therefore to prevent our working in the same spirit, and with the same results, as our forefathers.

The mediæval architecture of Italy presents, however, one further practical argument against this theory of the lovers of the round arch which they cannot, I think, meet.

It will be found in the following pages that in Italy there did not exist that distinction between the use of round and pointed arches which did exist for three centuries north of the Alps. They were content there to use whichever was most convenient, and whichever appeared to them to be most effective in its intended position. We therefore find, in most Italian mediæval buildings, round and pointed arches used in the same work, the former generally for ornament, the latter for construction; and the effect of this is in some degree to make us lessen the rigidity with which a study of Northern art might otherwise affect our views on this point. But I think no argument can be used by the lovers of the round arch which would ever go farther than to leave us open to the choice of both round and pointed arches, just as in these old Italian buildings: they have no right to say, "You may not use the pointed arch at all," but they perhaps may be allowed to ask, "Why exclude for ever the round arch?" and then I should refer them to Italy for a proof that as a rule the mixture of the two is neither harmonious nor satisfactory; whilst at the same time I should go on to shew them that, when they talk of the virtues of Roman and Romanesque architecture, of the repose and the simplicity which distinguish them, of their grandeur and their general breadth and nobility of effect—in all these things they do but sing the praises of the best Italian architecture of the thirteenth and fourteenth centuries, and that in studying the style we may well be guided by it in what we do, not to the forgetfulness of the glories of our own land, but to the development in a forward direction of what we inherit from our forefathers of that architecture which, after a lapse of three centuries, we now see on all sides reviving with fresh vigour from its temporary grave, and which requires only prudence and skill on the part of its professors to make even more perfect than before.

My object therefore in the following pages will be mainly to shew the peculiarities of the development of pointed architecture in Italy, and specially to shew in what way the materials so commonly used there—brick and marble—were introduced both in decoration and in construction. All these points are of the very greatest importance to us, for I am persuaded that not only will some reference to Italian models do somewhat towards the improvement of our art, but that in no matter is information more needed, and improvement more easy, than in the use of brick in architecture; whilst working in marble has been as yet so little practised among us, that we may almost regard it as at present unattempted, though, as I hope to shew, there is no longer any reason why this should be the case.

It is impossible to conclude this Preface without mention of the obligations which not only all who travel in Italy, but all who are interested in good architecture, owe to Mr. Ruskin. No man need or can profess his acquiescence in every one of the opinions which he has propounded, but as an architect I feel strongly that a great debt of gratitude is owing to him for his brilliant advocacy of many laws and truths in which every honest architect ought gladly to acquiesce. He may be well content to bear the opposition which he has evoked, satisfied that all that he has written is in the main most certainly for the benefit and exaltation of art of all kinds.

Nor less is a debt of gratitude to be acknowledged by every traveller to my friend Mr. Webb for his most excellent and trusty work on 'Continental Ecclesiology:' it is certainly the most absolutely correct guide-book ever drawn up for ecclesiologists anywhere; and in travelling over the same ground, as I have done in this tour, my excuse for giving what I have in the way of descriptions of the same buildings is, that what I have written has been all with a view, beyond that of merely describing the churches, of shewing the principles upon which their builders worked, and giving, so far as the limits of such a work will allow, drawings of the buildings I have described.

It will depend on circumstances whether I am able at some future day to continue my inquiries among the churches and domestic buildings of Central Italy, a tract at least as rich as that over which the tour described in the following pages took me.

It remains only to say that all the illustrations which I have given are engraved from my own drawings on the wood from my sketches made on the spot, and that I have endeavoured as much as possible to avoid giving subjects which have been before published. It would have been easy to add largely to them, especially from my sketches in Venice, but it seemed to me that, as this could only be accomplished by adding also to the cost of the book, it was much better to omit them. I have avoided therefore giving drawings of any buildings already drawn by Mr. Gally Knight, to whose work I must refer my readers for representations of several of the buildings described, and for illustrations of Venice I must refer to Mr. Ruskin's engravings and to the photographs which have rendered her features so well known to almost all students of architecture.

In conclusion, I cannot speak too highly of the assistance afforded to the architectural student by Murray's Handbook of Northern Italy: it is almost invariably correct, and gives just what one wants to know of nearly all buildings of any interest or importance.

Oxford, 1855.

CONTENTS

CHAPTER XII.

CHAPTER XIII.

CHAPTER XIV.

APPENDIX.

LIST OF ILLUSTRATIONS

Page

(THE FULL-PAGE ENGRAVINGS ARE NUMBERED IN ORDER.)

✿ The engravings marked * are taken from Mr. Fergusson's
'History of Architecture.'

BRICK AND MARBLE
IN
THE MIDDLE AGES.

CHAPTER I.

Routes to Italy—Paris—Strasburg—Rouffach—Basel.

> "Yet waft me from the harbour-mouth,
> Wild wind! I seek a warmer sky,
> And I will see before I die
> The palms and temples of the South."

Tennyson.

AN architectural tour in Italy seems to afford about as much prospect of pleasure and information combined as any which it is possible for an English student to take. He may see, if time allows, so much on his road, that whether one thinks of the journey or the end of it all is, at any rate in the perspective, charming. And in these days when, what with railways, through-tickets, and Cook's and other guides for timid tourists, the journey from one end of Europe to the other is made so quickly and so cheaply as to be within most educated men's reach, it is no wonder if most of us in our turn make the venture.

Many are the ways by which one may reach the North of Italy, but one or two only of them seem now to be commonly used, to the exclusion of all others, and with great loss of pleasure to all travellers who make the journey more than once. The natural, because the quickest, road is now by the Mont Cenis tunnel to Turin, and for the country described in these pages nothing can be more convenient. But when my first journey was made, it was more easy to take one of the passes leading to Milan, and so I went by the Splügen. Since those days I have found my way to and from Italy by other roads which I recommend strongly to others. I pass by such a well-known road as that by railway over the Brenner, in order to suggest three other roads, either of which brings the traveller down upon Venetia in the happiest possible frame of mind if he is at all capable of being moved to pleasure by the sight of exquisite scenery, pleasant and religious people, and roads and country not too much crowded with tourists.

The first of these is by the Lake of Constance, the Vorarlberg, and the Vintschgau to Botzen; the next by the Brenner pass as far as Franzensfeste, and thence by the Ampezzo pass through Cortina and Cadore—Titian's country—to Conegliano, and so by railway to Venice, a road lighted up by the wild beauty of the Dolomite mountains and now unaccountably neglected by English tourists; the third, and perhaps the most charming, though somewhat indirect, and requiring more time, again by the Brenner as far as Franzensfeste, thence by railway to Lienz—stopping to see the fine church and Dolomite mountains at Innichen on the way—and then by country carriages from the Pusterthal into the Gailthal where there is the most charming combination I know of pastoral and picturesque scenery, seasoned by interesting old churches; and thence to Ober Tarvis and by the stern and magnificent Predil pass to the head of the Adriatic at Gorizia, whence—after seeing Aquileja and Grado—the traveller may, with halts at Udine and Pordenone, reach his goal at Venice by railway.

But in this my first journey to Italy, I was sufficiently happy in finding the Splügen prescribed for me as on the whole the most convenient mode of reaching in succession all the spots which had most special interest for me. My scheme was to make myself fairly well acquainted with some of the most interesting Italian cities north of the Apennines, and for this purpose to descend from the Splügen on Bergamo, and from thence to go on to Venice, halting as often as necessary by the way, and then to return by Mantua, Cremona, and Pavia, or by Ferrara, Bologna, Parma, and Piacenza to Milan, and so home. And railways, if they have made the journey somewhat more easy than it was, and have deprived it now and then of the charm which always attends the recollection of impediments and difficulties on the road, have not in any way altered the advantages of such a route for those whose tastes are at all akin to those which I carried abroad with me in those days, and carry still with undiminished strength. Whether, however, one enters Italy by one pass or another, the first part of one's journey is by the well-worn road to Paris, which, by reason, I suppose, of its being the prelude to nearly every holiday tour that I make, never seems to be stale, old, or too well-known.

There is something very novel, and it strikes me more every time it is seen, in the aspect of everything directly you have crossed the Channel; indeed, there is no country in Europe so much as France, and no city, perhaps, so much as Paris, which strikes an Englishman as being foreign in its aspect, and new in all its customs and proceedings. The dress of every one, the arrangements of the railways, the harnessing and character of the horses, the mode of life in hotels, and the ordinary habits and pleasant traits of the middle classes are all quite fresh to the English eye. Nor is the aspect of the country less so: fields cut up into small strips of a dozen kinds of crops; unprosperous-looking cows, each feeding discontentedly and drearily, tethered to a man or woman on a small patch of grass; corn cut and then stacked in small cocks for a month or two of exposure to the pleasant changes of the atmosphere; and the entire absence of hedge-rows and other trees than poplars, all go to make up a thoroughly un-English picture.

After skirting the coast and its dreary expanse of sandhills, reminding one very much of those singular sands on the north coast of Cornwall, which are so often shifting about, covering up new churches, or uncovering the old oratory of some early British saint, we reach the banks of the Somme, and then travel along a poor peaty tract of country until the famous west front and short but lofty nave of Abbeville come in view. Thence by a valley (rather more rich than is common in good churches) we continue our race for Amiens. Among these churches I may instance the hipped saddle-back roofed steeples of Picquigny, Hangest, and Pont Rémy, as very valuable examples of their order; that of Picquigny, indeed, surmounting a central steeple, and finished at the top with some delicate open iron-work, is about as graceful a specimen as I know.

At Longpré is another church with a steeple of some pretension, but not satisfactory. It has a perforated spire of stone much too small for the size of the tower, and ungraceful in the extreme.

At Amiens one always longs to stop again and again to feast one's eyes upon its glorious cathedral, perhaps after Chartres and the Parthenon the noblest and most masculine piece of architecture in the world. But with us this was impossible; our destiny was—come what might—to endeavour at any rate to discharge ourselves in Paris within the shortest possible number of hours from London; and the dusk of the early autumn evening prevented our having more than the very slightest glimpse of the Minster.

The refreshment-room at Amiens is one of the best I have ever been in—reasonable, clean, and good—and placed just at that happy distance from the sea at which the poor wretches who have been in the depths of woe on the passage begin to recover their presence of mind, and with it, of course—as good Englishmen—their appetites; what wonder then if the Buffet at Amiens prospers!

The rest of our journey to Paris was all performed in the dark, relieved only by the sight of the then long-expected comet, and it was almost midnight ere we found ourselves settled at our hotel.

I am never sorry to have a day in Paris. In spite of alterations and reconstructions which have converted an interesting old city into the most spick-and-span place in the world, there are even to the present day parts which are untouched by the improver, and full of a pleasant national character which seems to be little to the liking of the rulers of the French. There is, too, in spite of the changes which a great and rich city must always undergo, a great deal which is interesting to the architect. We may look at old engravings, and wish ourselves back in those old times when the walls surrounded the city where now the Boulevards run round its heart, when the Temple and a number of other important buildings, now wholly destroyed, adorned the country just outside the walls; but the city which has still, among other architectural treasures, such churches as Notre Dame, S. Germain des Près, the Sainte Chapelle, S. Martin des Champs, and a host of lesser lights, and the Chapel of Vincennes, and S. Denis within a short drive, is in quite a different category from such a city as London, and is indeed hardly second to any other in Europe in architectural interest.

To come to much later times and very different work, it is always pleasant to be able to walk down the Boulevard des Italiens to the Madeleine, and for a few minutes to gaze at a church which certainly presents one very grand idea—that of space—clothed in very gorgeous dress. One always feels a certain sympathy for a church in which so many people are ever praying; and I have never yet been into this church without being able to count them by scores. The last time I was at Paris I remember being struck by seeing for the first time a peripteral building made really useful. The walls within the columns were hung with rich draperies, and a long procession coming out marched round the circuit of the church between the columns and the walls, and in again at the west door; the effect was, as may be imagined, very striking.

From the Madeleine we found our way to the new church of S. Clothilde, a large cruciform church, and the last erected in Paris in the Gothic style. Its design is intended to be of early character, but in reality is quite late in its effect; nor do I know when I have seen anything much less successful than the two western steeples rising but a short distance above the nave roof, and looking mean and weak to a degree. In plan the church is not badly arranged; there is just such a choir as might easily be properly used, and a large space for congregational purposes.

How much we want churches, in this respect at least, somewhat like S. Clothilde, in our large cities in England!

There are here a great many windows filled with stained glass, executed, I believe, by Mons. Marischal. His windows are illustrations of a truth which men are very slow to receive and act upon, viz. that in decorating a transparent material, one whose transparency moreover is the sole cause of its use, we have no right to shade it with dark colours so far as to destroy its brilliancy. These windows were elaborately shaded, and, as a necessary consequence, were heavy and dismal in their effect; besides which, most unpleasant mixtures of green, yellow, and ruby, and of ruby and blue—very glaring and very bad—abounded.

The carving of the capitals is, as is usually the case in recent foreign works, all derived from natural types of foliage, and is fairly well done: but the carving of rather elaborate sculptures of the "Stations" did not please me, having none of the severity of ancient examples. When shall we see a school of sculptors rise able really to satisfy the requirements of the times? I confess I despair more on this point than on any other; for I have as yet seen no fair attempt made to recover the style, or work upon the principles, of the best mediæval sculptors. The work of our modern sculptors is nearly all foreign and unreal, and almost always involves the assumption that they are representing the proceedings of the Greeks or Romans, and not of the English: it is impossible therefore that such a school can be healthy, strong, or successful. We lack men who will give us (clothed with as much anatomical correctness as they like, so that they do not leave them lifeless and academical) representations of subjects from English history and national life, illustrations of the Scriptures which we still believe, of the faith which we still profess, conceived in something of the architectonic and yet really dramatic and romantic spirit which marks the best sculpture of the middle ages. The strange thing is that with works near at hand which few living men could rival, they absolutely refuse to study them at all, and I believe if we were to summon all the most eminent sculptors to a conclave and put them to the question, not one in four of them would confess to having ever been to Chartres or Bourges, and four out of five would assert that it would have done them no good if they had. If they would give us anything at all comparable to the great works of the best Greeks the case would be altogether different, but to be served with a réchauffé of the antique when one is crying out for something suitable to the present, is cause enough for the apathy of the English public about sculptors' work. We ask for English history or Bible story, and are treated to nymphs combing their hair; and for figures of our Lord and St. Peter, and get nothing but Musidoras and Clyties. No sculptor would lose much by the study of the best mediæval examples of drapery—and there are among the gothic statues which deck the doors and porches of the churches I have named, some of the most admirable description, such as warrant any one, who is at all troubled with feeling for his art, in using strong language about those who neglect them. In Italy we shall find the same careful shutting of men's eyes to what is good, simply because it belongs to the thirteenth or fourteenth centuries. Orvieto is left on one side in order to spend time over work not possessed of a tithe of the beauty of that on its cathedral façade; and, indeed, just as the French examples, they appear only too often never even to have been so much as heard of!

The study of ancient sculpture in England is not quite so easy, because our old buildings are not so rich in it as are the French; but if one is told—as one is too often—that the art of sculpture in the middle ages was unknown or rude in comparison with its state now, one may fairly refer to some of the modern attempts at its imitation for a proof that this was not the case, as e.g. to the recumbent effigy of Archbishop Howley at Canterbury, or to another, of some more humble individual, in the south transept of Chichester Cathedral; a glance only at which, and a comparison with some of the noble mediæval effigies lying in all the stateliness of their repose by their sides, will at once show any one that it is not merely necessary to put an effigy upon its back with its hands in prayer in order to vie with the effigies of the thirteenth and fourteenth centuries. The position is something, but not all, and requires very much more skill in its treatment than of late years we have had to bestow.

From S. Clothilde we went first to the pleasant gardens of the Luxembourg—gardens which always make one envious for London—and thence to Notre Dame. Here I always feel no slight pride in the success which its architect has achieved. Six hundred years have passed over Paris, one effort after another has been made, vast sums of money have been spent, and still this great work stands supreme and separated by a vast distance from all competition, and greatest beyond comparison of all Parisian buildings, not only in its general scheme, but equally in the admirable design and execution of every detail. There is much to be seen and learnt here in every way. The west doors are superb. The planning and construction are very fine, and the series of sculptures behind the stalls full of interest and well worthy of study.

From Notre Dame one goes, of course, to the Sainte Chapelle. When this journey was undertaken everything about this chef-d'œuvre was gradually growing to perfection: the flèche was being put up on the roof, the painting on the walls was nearly finished, and the altar was in progress. Since then it has escaped, as it were by a special providence (and why not?), from the incendiary fire which destroyed almost the whole of the surrounding Palais de Justice, and it still rises uninjured among the ruins. Of all the chapels of the same kind it is certainly the most beautiful—and whether one names our own St. Stephen's, or thinks of others, such as the Chapel at S. Germer and the other at Riom, the Paris chapel is certainly by far the finest—being in truth a real work of inspired genius.

Altogether, I cannot help thinking that the effect upon the mind of what one sees in Paris is very unsatisfactory; the revival of Christian art seems, as it were, to be only skin-deep; there seems to be no enthusiasm for it. What is done is done in the same way as other public works, as the business of the state, not by the will of the people. The scaffolding, which was just being removed from the avenue leading from the Tuileries to the Barrière de l'Etoile, after having assisted at the fête of Napoleon, was an illustration sufficiently apt of the work which seems to engage too many of the artists of Paris; Parisian fête composers and decorators really appear to be the architects of the day, and of course this fact must mitigate very much against real art in every branch, as its tendency is to make people accustomed to temporary exhibitions, the shortcomings of which are pardoned on the score of their temporary character, and so the artist is lowered in his tone by assisting in the production of works which are not intended—as all great works ought to be intended—to last for ages.

A day in Paris is generally a long and tiring one; and so we found it; but nevertheless we pushed on without delay, and leaving our hotel before the table-d'hôte was much more than half over, we drove to the station of the Strasburg Railway, and in a few minutes we were *en route*. If any one doubts the possibility of really resting one's body in a railway carriage, let him take the same precaution that we took, and he need not despair: a day of sight-seeing in Paris is certainly the best possible recipe for sound sleep in a railway carriage, and I believe that when we arrived at Strasburg, at about eight the next morning, we were very fairly rested. I confess, however, that I did feel a twinge of horror when I found that the train by which we were anxious to reach Basel left again in about half an hour—too long to wait, but not long enough for either breakfast or dressing. There seemed, however, to be no alternative, and so on we went, comforting ourselves as best we might with some sour grapes and bad dry bread—the sole edibles procurable at the Strasburg buffet!

The Railway from Strasburg to Basel is much more enjoyable than iron-ways generally are. There is scarce a cutting during the whole extent of the journey, and the views of the chain of the Vosges are—before one has gazed on real mountains in Switzerland—very delightful.

The railway runs up the broad valley of the Rhine, and within a few miles of Strasburg approaches very near to the mountainous district. The outlines of the hills are bold, picturesque, and well varied; and, as they rise rather precipitously from the valley, are often crowned with ruined castles, and have on their lower slopes large and populous-looking villages, they are at any rate very pleasing neighbours for a railway journey.

A few architectural notes of such churches as are passed on this route (which I travelled not for the first time) will not be out of place, though, with one exception, there is not anything of great value.

At Schlestadt there is a large tower of late date to the principal church, which is rather fine in its effect. It has its two upper stages nearly similar, which is rarer at home than abroad. Another church has an early spire; and there is a smaller church with a good open turret. Opposite Schlestadt the chain of the Vosges is very striking, and some of the picturesque outlines of hills capped with ruined castles remind one of the more famous banks of the lower portion of the Rhine. Beyond Schlestadt we reach Colmar, the cathedral of which is large, and has a late tower capped with an ugly bulbous roof. Another church in Colmar has a good open-work and very light turret rising from the middle of the length of its roof. The effect of this kind of turret, of which we in England have no examples, is always very satisfactory.

But the best church in the whole extent of this journey is that of Rouffach, one on whose merits 'Murray' — whose services all travellers must gratefully acknowledge — is silent. It is of early date, cruciform in its plan, and the crossing surmounted by a good early tower and spire of octangular form. Each side of the tower has a good window, above which a string-course forms the base to a gable on each side. The angles of the spire spring from the bases of these eight gables, and the whole design reminded me somewhat of the only example of the same type in England — the beautiful steeple of Lostwithiel. Rouffach has a good choir terminating in an apse, and a south-western steeple, surmounted by a slender spire too small for the tower. Altogether, the general effect of the church is very fine. Beyond this point there are no features of interest; the Vosges retreat into the distance, and nothing is to be seen but a dead flat of field and wood, relieved occasionally by a village or town, remarkable mainly for the ugliness of its church. The busy manufacturing town of Mulhausen is passed, the number of stations is carefully reckoned, and long before you catch the first view of Basel you are heartily sick of the slow pace at which the Strasburg and Basel Railway Company always arrange to carry their passengers.

Those who know the Hotel of the Three Kings at Basel will understand how grateful was the information given to us, as we mounted its steps, that the table-d'hôte was to be ready in half an hour. Refreshing enough at any time, such an announcement was doubly so to travellers just arrived from a journey from Paris without a stoppage; and in no bad spirit did we enter the salle à manger, whose windows, opening into balconies which absolutely overhang the great and glorious Rhine, flowing strong and quick for ever in the same unceasing current, make it about the pleasantest room of the kind that I know.

There are few things in the world so fine as a mighty river, few rivers so fine as the Rhine, and few spots so favourable for its contemplation as the balcony at Basel. As you look at the deep colour of the water, you think of all the wonders which on its way it has seen. You remember your own exploits and pleasant walks in past times along the lovely valley of the Aar, and over the barren and stony waste of the Grimsel, to the source of this beautiful feeder of the Rhine; or you think of Lake Constance and Schaffhausen, and of the beautiful valley of the Upper Rhine, and of the lakes of Wallenstadt, Lucerne, Brienz, and Thun—every one of which seems to the mind's eye to be represented and brought near by each wave that dashes madly along before your gaze. And then, whither do they all so swiftly wend their way? Down by minsters and by castles, along broad plains, through narrow water-worn chasms, and again through great, dreary, but many-peopled flats, into the sea, there to mix themselves and all their recollections in the great, glorious, but tradition-despising depth of Old Ocean.

CHAPTER II.

Churches of Basel—Storks—Rheinfelden—Frick—Baden—Zurich: the Cathedral—Fondness of the Swiss for Bright Colours—Lake of Zurich—Rapperswyl—Linth Canal—A Wayside Inn—Wesen.

"For pallid autumn once again
Hath swell'd each torrent of the hill;
Her clouds collect, her shadows sail,
And watery winds that sweep the vale
Grow loud and louder still."

Campbell.

AT Basel we engaged a voiturier to take us to Baden, whence the only Swiss railway was to have the privilege of conveying us to Zurich. Our scheme for reaching Italy was to pass by the lakes of Zurich and Wallenstadt, and then, following the valley of the Rhine, to cross over the pass of the Splügen to Chiavenna, and so to reach Lake Como.

We left Basel at two o'clock in the afternoon, hoping to reach Baden by about nine; the weather looked threatening, but we took a cheerful view of this, as of everything else, as all good travellers should, and comforted ourselves with the thought that at any rate we could better afford to have a wet day between Basel and Baden than between Zurich and the Splügen.

The view of the city as you leave it is certainly very striking; the cathedral spires are picturesque in their outline, and the number of churches with turrets and steep roofs combine with them to produce a most ecclesiastical-looking town. Nor need any one interested in architecture despair of finding much pleasure in a more careful inspection of its buildings. They are full of interest, though generally passed too rapidly by people in a hurry to get on to enjoy the pleasures which await them beyond.

The roofing of the cathedral is worthy of notice as being composed of variously coloured tiles, arranged in diamond patterns over the surface of the roof, and giving a degree of richness to the colouring of this generally heavy part of the building which is very admirable.

In another fine church of the early part of the fourteenth century here, I remember being amused to see how quietly the storks possess themselves of all kinds of places for their nests, and think even the ridge of the steep roof of a church a proper place for their abode. The good people at Basel build their chimneys with flat tops for the express benefit of their long-legged friends; who, from their ele-vated and well-warmed abodes, look down sedately, and with a well-satisfied air upon their unfledged brethren below.

Why the people here love storks, the people of Venice pigeons, and the peo-ple of Berne bears, I leave to more industrious inquirers to decide, satisfied only to notice the fact that it is so, as each of these fancies adds one to the list of local peculiarities so valuable in the recollections of a journey.

The road from Basel to Baden is for the first half of the way very pretty; we came in, unfortunately, for rather drenching rain, and so lost all beyond the sug-gestion of some striking views. The towns through which we passed were not of much interest, though there were many picturesque and pleasant-looking subjects for the pencil. The most striking place on the road was Rheinfelden, a largish vil-lage (or perhaps I ought to say small town, as it rejoices in a Rath-haus of some pretension), surrounded by very high walls, and entered by tall stone gate-towers, pierced with pointed arches, and surmounted by upper stages of timber, with tiled roofs of quaint and effective character; and here and at Stein and Baden I noticed that almost all the houses were old and very little altered. I observed particularly the old shop-windows of very simple design, closed with folding shutters, and taking one back to old times most decidedly in their design.

Shop-window, Rheinfelden.

Beyond Rheinfelden the road, which so far has skirted the Rhine rather close-ly, leaves it again for a few miles until it touches it for the last time at the small town of Stein.

From Stein we saw an imposing-looking church on the other side of the river at Sekingen. It has a great western front with two bulbous-topped steeples, and is of very considerable length. The division between choir and nave is marked by a delicate turret, and the whole church, as far as one can judge by a distant view, looks as though it would well repay a visit. There are six bays in the nave, five and an apse in the choir. The former has very simple windows, whilst in the latter they are rather elaborate. There is no aisle to the choir and no transept.

The rain continued incessantly until we reached the long straggling village of Frick, a quaint and antique-looking place, where our voiturier stopped for an hour to bait his horses, who, however, at Rheinfelden had enjoyed a treat in the shape of a loaf of very brown bread, a kind of food second only, in the estimation of foreign steeds, to the precious *morceaux* of lump sugar with which Swiss voituriers are so fond of encouraging and petting them.

We were nothing loth to stretch our legs; and finding that the church was worthless—one of those unhappy bulbous-spired and bulbous-roofed erections so common in some parts of the Continent, and the roof of even the eastern apse of which was twisted into a most ingenious and ugly compound curve—we took up our quarters in the respectable hostelry and "Bierbrauerei" of the Angel, and de-voted ourselves to the consumption of coffee and beer of no bad quality. Our host wished sadly to see us located under his roof for the night, but we were resolute in our determination to reach Baden that night, and so persisted in going, though to our subsequent regret.

It was soon dark, and the new moon, which shone cheerfully upon us, gave us just a glimpse occasionally of the scenery, which about Brugg, where we crossed the Aar, and again at Königsfelden, seemed to be remarkably good.

At last, at about half-past ten o'clock, we reached what we fondly hoped was to be our resting-place. But Baden chose not to take us in, and to our horror, as we drove up to the chief and only available inn, we were met with the dismal announcement from the mouth of the civil landlord, that all the rooms were full.

However, we dismounted, and found that there was no other inn in Baden proper, but that at the Baths there were several; at them our landlord assured us that he knew we should find no room, and so we thought it useless to return and try. Our only course seemed to be to feed our horses again and then go on to Zurich; and as Swiss drivers and Swiss horses never seem to tire of trotting on slowly and drowsily along the road, there was no difficulty in at once coming to an arrangement with our coachman.

Accordingly, at midnight we started again, hoping at some early hour in the morning to reach Zurich. It was sufficiently provoking to be toiling on slowly and sleeplly for nearly four hours almost alongside of a railroad which would have taken us early the next morning in three-quarters of an hour; but there was no help for it, and so we did the best we could, by sleeping whenever we were able, to pass the weary hours away.

At last, just as the day began to dawn, we came in sight of Zurich and its lake, and last, not least, we reached the great hotel. Here we pulled up, knocked desperately, awoke the slumbering porter—but, alas! only to hear again the unwelcome sounds which had greeted our ears at Baden! He suggested, however, that at the Hôtel Belle Vue we should probably find beds, and so on we drove, rather in despair at our prospects, though, happily, unnecessarily so, for the Belle Vue gladly opened its arms for our reception, and ere long we were, oblivious of all our toil, comfortably ensconced in bed. From our windows we had a pleasant view of our quarters; it was broad daylight, and the prospect was—as from such a position, looking up a lake, it always is—very fair and charming.

We were up again soon after eight, and were glad to find the morning fine, though the clouds were low, and we saw, consequently, nothing of the distant view of mountains which lends its greatest charms to Zurich. The town is, however, pretty and striking. The picturesque houses, with wooded hills on all sides beyond them, and very charming views of the lake, if they do not make its attractions first-rate, at any rate make them very considerable.

The main feature of interest for me was the cathedral, a fine Romanesque church, very fairly perfect, but mutilated in its interior arrangements by the Calvinists, in whose hands it now is. In plan, it has a nave with aisles of six bays, a short choir, and east of this a square-ended sanctuary, the aisles having apses, roofed with semi-domes. In the nave two of the aisle-arches make one groining bay. The transverse groining-ribs are of a simple square section, the diagonal ribs having in addition a large round member. The triforium is very large and fine, and is made use of for congregational purposes, being fitted up with seats, which, curiously enough, are all made to turn up as misereres. There are no transepts. The sanctuary arch is loftier than the choir arch, and seems to have been intended to be very distinctly marked. In the clerestory there are two simple round-headed lights in each bay; the choir is arcaded all round internally, and for frigidity of effect cannot be surpassed; the internal fittings comprise an immense pulpit, but, so far as I could see, not even an apology for an altar.

The exterior has two western steeples,[1] and a north doorway, each jamb of which has three detached shafts, standing considerably in advance of the wall, which is entirely covered with diapers. The arch itself is semi-circular, and very simple in its moulding; but this simplicity rather adds to than detracts from its general grandeur of effect. The whole is inserted in an additional thickness of wall, set on, as it were, against the original wall, and the extreme width of the doorway itself is no less than eighteen feet nine inches. The cloisters were remarkable, and very good of their kind; the arches rested on detached shafts, the capitals of which were elaborately carved in a very peculiar manner, but very effectively. The whole design was unlike any Northern Romanesque, and bore much more similarity to the best Lombard work. Unfortunately, the whole of this cloister was rebuilt in

---

[1] In a view of Zurich, published A.D. 1654, these steeples are shown with octagonal spires rising above the gabled sides of the towers; the belfry stages and cupolas now existing must therefore be of a date subsequent to the publication of this view.

1851, the carving having been re-worked, or renewed throughout in imitation of the original. It will be seen, however, that, in spite of alterations, this is a very fine church, of a very early type, and peculiarly valuable in a country which, like Switzerland, has comparatively little left that is really good in the way of architectural examples.

2.—Cloister, of Zurich Cathedral.*

There are other churches in Zurich, but I believe not old, and at any rate I had no time to examine them. One of them is appropriated to the use of the Roman Catholics; and there is one desecrated, rising from the edge of the lake, and forming a prominent object in the general view of the town as you leave by the steamer; this is of good outline, but has no details remaining of any value. The point chiefly to be noticed in the churches of Zurich appears to be the way in which their spires are all painted red, looking in the full sunshine very bright and picturesque.

The Swiss have a great feeling for bright colour, and on our way from Basel to Baden we noticed one of the many instances of this in several turrets covered with brightly-coloured glazed tiles. A light green seems to be the favourite colour, and is commonly used without mixture with any other. They look best with their lower side rounded, and when of small size; and are constantly used in turrets rising out of roofs which are entirely covered with plain tiles. I remember, two years before, noticing with extreme pleasure the beauty of some dark green tiles used at Schaffhausen; and I have already had occasion to mention those on the cathedral at Basel with equal commendation. Unhappily, we have to lament that English people, in their insane hatred of bright colours, if they saw such tiles used in England, would be horrified at such a violation of the correct simplicity and uniformity of colour to which the cheapness of slate has made them accustomed. Some modern attempts, however, at introducing coloured tiles have not been so successful as could be wished; and of all, perhaps the least so is the roof of the new Maria Hilf church at Munich, on which tiles of light blue colour are used in such large masses, that at first sight it seems that half the roof is stripped, and that the pale blue sky is seen instead of roof.

At ten o'clock we left our hotel by the steamer for Schmerikon at the head of the Lake of Zurich. The weather still looked doubtful, though much better than on the previous day, and our host of the Belle Vue, taking a good view of this, as is a landlord's duty, conducted us to the boat with smiling anticipations of fine days to come.

The shores of the lake are, for the greater part of its length, literally fringed with houses all painted white, and contrasting violently with the trees, vineyards, and green hills by which they are backed. On the north the shore is low and gradually shelving down to the water; on the south it is rather more precipitous, but after all not very striking. At the head of the lake heavy dark round clouds hung upon the hills, and left us in pleasant doubt as to whether or no we had fine mountains to discover when they cleared away; a doubt, as it happened, not settled, as far as we were concerned, save by certain lively and not too trustworthy representations which we afterwards met with, in the shape of advertisements of the Zurich hotels, and which showed a line of snow mountains as the ordinary horizon of their visitors.

The churches on the lake are very numerous and very similar. The steeples are almost always gabled, and from these gables rise spires painted red, and very thin and taper in their form. The gabled sides of the towers are generally made useful rather than ornamental by the introduction of enormous clock-dials. The only decidedly mediæval church which I saw between Zurich and Rapperswyl was at one of the villages on the north shore of the lake, I think at Meilen, but I am rather uncertain as to the name. Its design is both novel and very good; the pinnacles on the gable being unusual in saddle-backed steeples, and giving considerable picturesqueness of outline. The accompanying woodcut will show the general character of the design, and it will be seen that the tower is on the north side of the choir. The steeple roof is covered with greyish-red tiles, with a pattern marked on them with yellow tiles.

Church on the Lake of Zürich.

The steamers on this, as on most Swiss lakes, are somewhat tedious in their journeys, as they take a most zigzag course, first calling on one side of the lake and then on the other, until one doubts whether one will ever reach the journey's end. At Horgen of course we discharged a large proportion of our English passengers, who were all bound for the Rigi, but their places were soon occupied by the um-brella-loving natives, who flocked in and out of the boat in great numbers at every station, and by the time we reached Rapperswyl we had no more fellow-country-men in the boat, and perhaps, like many Englishmen, to say the truth, we then first thoroughly realised that we were abroad. Much as one loves one's country, certainly one source of pleasure when abroad is the not hearing too much English spoken or seeing too many English faces.

At Rapperswyl, famous for having the longest bridge in the world, there is a most conspicuous group of buildings on rising ground above the lake, very pic-turesquely thrown together; it consists of a church and a castle; the latter has sev-eral towers capped with pyramidal and saddle-backed roofs, and the former has two towers in the position of transepts, with saddle-back roofs gabled north and south, the southern tower being considerably the larger of the two. Altogether, the group is one of uncommon variety and picturesqueness of outline. Below, in the town, is a small church, with a most happily-conceived though very simple bell-turret rising out of the roof, square in its plan, but capped with an octagonal spirelet. This is a not uncommon plan in this part of Switzerland, and is always most agreeable in its effect. The views from the terrace by the side of this castle are of singular beauty. It is high enough above the lake to command a good view of its whole expanse, and to secure a not too distant view of some of the mountain peaks of Glarus. Rapperswyl is a good point to stop at, for the sake of a visit to the famous pilgrimage church at Einsiedeln, certainly one of the spots in Switzerland most curious and interesting, though its buildings have no claims to our regard on the score of architectural beauty.

Passing under, or rather through, the bridge, we found that it was very narrow and had no side railing of any kind, so that it appears to be far from a pleasant contrivance for crossing the mile or two of shallow water which here scarce serves to keep up the appearance even of a lake; and perhaps it is upon the score of the absence of real danger of drowning if one fell over that they dispense with any protection. At Schmerikon, which we reached in four hours from Zurich, we left our steamer, and immediately embarked on a barge in order to go by the Linth ca-nal to Wesen; but we found that, however expeditious this might be in descending, it was a kind of conveyance not to be recommended highly to any one wishing to ascend the canal, inasmuch as—unlike ordinary canals—this is neither more nor less than the glacier-torrent of the Linth bringing down the melting snow from the Glärnitsch and Todi glaciers, and rushing along at a really tremendous pace; to those, however, who have time, it may be commended as affording magnificent views of the mountains of Glarus and of those which rise so grandly above the Lake of Wallenstadt.

As we entered the canal from the lake we were amused by the unsuccessful attempts of our crew to secure some wild-fowl, two of which they succeeded in shooting, and then, without any kind of regard for the feelings of passengers panting to arrive at Wesen in the promised two hours and a half, they deliberately proceeded—of course in vain—to chase the unhappy birds, which, though wounded, were quite able to dive much deeper than their enemies could reach, and so the only consequence of the chase was a hearty laugh at the expense of the baffled sportsmen, half an hour's delay, and much lost ground to be made up.

The entrance to the canal was very striking; a low hill covered with larch and birch rose from the water's edge, and above this, the mountains, gradually shelving upwards, were terminated in a line of rocky ridges of very grand and rugged character. Whilst we were admiring the view a slight shower passed over us, and the sun suddenly breaking out, produced one of those lovely effects of colour so peculiar to mountain scenery; a rainbow seemed exactly to fill up one of the great basins formed by the undulations of the mountains, and, after bathing a great sweep of mountain-side in the richest and most distinctly marked colours, gradually died away.

The canal, which at first looks more like a river, soon takes a bend to the S.W., and then, passing under a quaint wooden bridge, over which passes the road to Uznach, we found ourselves in what certainly looked sufficiently canal-like. The stream is so rapid that the walls built up on either side are preserved from being washed away by stone groins running out into the stream, and acting as so many breakwaters to keep the water in the centre. Slowly and steadily our horses pulled us up, whilst we, mounted on the top of the cabin, were able to see over the walled sides of the canal, and to enjoy the glorious prospect before us.

Before long our captain blandly informed us that he was going to stop for dinner at a wayside house, so we, anxious to make the same good use of our time, attempted to follow his example. Unfortunately the landlord, though very jolly-looking, had a very badly stocked larder, and we had to satisfy ourselves with bread, honey, and wine. It is true, indeed, that our host did produce some cold meat—portion, as I imagined, of a goat dressed some ten days back—but this was not eatable, and was valuable only as furnishing an opportunity to him of showing his perfect power of making the best of a bad thing. To season the goat he brought in vinegar and oil, and, putting them upon the table, exclaimed with some *empressement*, "Voilà, monsieur; mais le vinaigre n'est pas bon!" just as if this was the strongest recommendation he could give us! We laughed heartily, avoided the vinegar, and parted good friends with our host, thanking him from our hearts for having saved us the painful operation of making the discovery about its quality for ourselves!

Our not very satisfying repast finished, we embarked again upon our barge, and in the occasional intervals, when sudden and heavy storms of rain obliged us to seek shelter in the cabin, we were much amused in watching the proceedings of some men belonging to the boat, who spent the whole of the five hours consumed in the journey in an unceasing game of cards; I must do them the justice to say that they played very good-humouredly, and laughed without ceasing. Under no circumstances could we have seen the scenery more gloriously; occasional bright gleams of sunshine broke in upon and followed clouds of the most inky hue, and then came pelting down heavy showers, accompanied by howling wind and darkness; and as we reached the opening of the valley, looking up beyond Glarus to the great mountains which close in its upper end, I think the effect was really more grand and terrific than anything I have ever seen. The mountains are of very fine outline, and of great height, as we saw by the more than occasional glimpses which we had of snow about their summits. By the time we reached Wesen the wind was so violent that we found it difficult to keep our places upon the top of the cabin; and we disembarked just before dark, in time to see the fine mountains on each side of the Lake of Wallenstadt here and there through the storm-clouds, and its waters beaten by the wind into not insignificant waves. We had to walk through the entire length of the village—a picturesque, quaint little place, sheltered under the almost overhanging rocks at the side of the water—and arrived at last at the capital and thoroughly Swiss inn, the Hôtel de l'Epée, where we were to sleep.

Travellers now speed very differently along this country, and, I fear, see less than they ought of its beauties. Steamboats no longer attempt to pass beyond Rapperswyl, and the railway hurries one along by the beautiful Lake of Wallenstadt to the valley of the Rhine, only earning one's gratitude when one is in violent haste, and because by a branch line it makes a détour to Glarus and Stachelberg much more possible than it was when first I made the journey. On the whole I fear, where railways pass through beautiful scenery, the tourist loses more than he can possibly gain, not only in the views of the country, but equally in the incidents of travel, which are becoming only too monotonous and similar everywhere.

CHAPTER III.

Wallenstadt—Sargans—Gorge of the Tamina—Ragatz—Chur—
Ems—Reichenau—Thusis—Zillis—Andeer—Splügen—The
Splügen Pass—The Custom-house—Cascade of the Medessimo—
Campo Dolcino.

> "Where the mountains
> Lift, through perpetual snows, their lofty and luminous summits."
>
> *Evangeline.*

THE storm of the evening gave no kind augury of sunshine on the morrow, and with rather anxious thoughts we listened as it roared among the mountains which overhung our hostelry. But it seemed that we had suffered enough, and when we woke we found that, though the clouds had not yet cleared off from the sides of the mountains, there was nevertheless every prospect of a fine day.

We were obliged to leave by an inexorably early steamer at half-past five for Wallenstadt, and so lost all but the suggestion only of the magnificence of the mountains which tower up so grandly over the north shore of the lake. Like Goethe on his way into Italy, we might exclaim, "What do we not pass over, both on the right hand and on the left, in order to carry out the one thought which has become almost too old for the soul!" But our time was limited, and our chief anxiety to spend as much of our short holiday as we could in Italy; and so, sad though we were to miss what was doubtless so well worthy of being seen, on we were bound to go without delay.

Before we started I had secured a voiturier whose carriage was at Wallenstadt to take us on to Chur, so that on this score I had no trouble before me. Our voyage was only too soon made. Unlike the Lake of Zurich, where the traveller rather hopes that each place at which he stops may be the last, on this lake, as the tiny steamer ploughs its way rapidly over its surface, with its goal always in view, and with not a place to stop at on its road, he ceases not to long that his pleasure may be prolonged!

By seven o'clock we were in our carriage, and *en route.* The sun began to shine, and every minute the clouds rose higher and higher; so that, before we finally lost—by turning into the valley of the Rhine—the last view of the valley of the lake, we could see the peaks of the mountains which we so wished to have seen before, the Sieben-Churfürsten, which tower so grandly over the lake.

Wallenstadt is but a poor place, its situation being unwholesome, and its inns not much to be commended. It has a church of modern character, with an old-looking tower in the position of a transept, with a saddle-back roof, gabled north and south. On the lower part of the south side of this tower are paintings of the Crucifixion and some other subjects, apparently of some antiquity. Just above the town, on the right, we passed the ruins of an old castle; and at a slight rise in the road had a beautiful view of the calm waters of the lake, looking blue, but very much smaller than it really is. This, no doubt, is owing to the great height of the precipitous rocks on its north side, which we now saw for the first time, the clouds having at last risen and disclosed some of the beauties which they had been concealing from us.

The valley from Wallenstadt to Sargans, just beyond which our route, after crossing the very low watershed, joined the valley of the Rhine, was strikingly beautiful. Its ecclesiological features were not, however, remarkable, if I except the constant repetition of what I have often noticed in the Catholic cantons of Switzerland and in Tyrol—the occurrence, namely, of grated openings on either side of the western door-way, commanding the interior and protected by an open porch, through which passers-by, though not able to enter, might still see the altar. On our journey from Basel to Zurich we passed a church the altar of which was lighted up, and the doors behind these gratings left open very late at night. It was in a lonely place, and when I passed there was no one in or near the church. I never see this arrangement without wishing to introduce it in England. There are so many of our Churches which cannot conveniently be left always open, and where such a provision might suggest to passers-by, as it does here, the propriety of using a church at other times than those of public service.

The cultivation of this valley is not so uninteresting as its ecclesiology. Here we first found the vines trained about in the horizontal Italian fashion, whilst under them great gourds and pumpkins developed themselves to a prodigious size.

Sargans is a very picturesque old town, and has some capital examples of good Swiss carpentry in its houses; in addition to which there is a picturesque and antique-looking castle, rising high above the houses on a rock, guarding the eastern entrance to the town, and commanding the junction of our road with that of the valley of the Rhine leading to the Lake of Constance.

Our coachman was under a bond to travel as fast as a diligence which lumbered on slowly in advance of us, and as far as Ragatz was quite true to his word; there, however, we determined to pause for a few hours, not willing to pass anything so famous as the baths of Pfeffers without a visit. Leaving our carriage, we mounted a light car, and were soon ascending the beautiful gorge of the Tamina to the baths. The road is capitally made, and follows the windings of the mountain torrent so closely as to require some nerve in those who drive rapidly along on their road to or from the baths. The ascent is steep, but in rather less than an hour we found ourselves at the baths. The rocks rise nearly perpendicularly behind the ledge of rock on which they stand, and the only mode of access to the upper and more wonderful part of the chasm was by passing through the long corridors, which betokened the once religious object of the building. These passed, and in charge of a guide, we crossed the torrent by a rude bridge, and then by a rather precarious path made our way, as it seemed, almost into the bowels of the mountain. The gorge is so very narrow that in many parts the light of the sky is no longer visible, the rocks overhanging each other above the head. All the while the torrent is roaring by our sides, and we feel that we are indeed enjoying an excursion into the very heart of the rocky earth. At last we reach the end of the path, are compelled by our guide to ensconce ourselves, one by one, in a small kind of box formed round the source of the spring—to pronounce it very hot and very nasty (its two most eminent qualities)—and then, still admiring the matchless grandeur of the rocky way, we regain our car, and are soon again whirled down the hill to Ragatz.

Our driver is a cheerful, pleasant fellow, talks German much better than the man we brought from Wesen, is communicative, moreover, and seems to enjoy a laugh and a joke uncommonly. Of course we become friends, and with no trouble on our parts, though with some little on his, it is arranged that our old driver shall remain where he is, and that our new friend, proud in the possession of the then very necessary Austrian passport, shall take us on as far at any rate as Chiavenna. A hurried Swiss luncheon—wine, honey, bread and butter—is soon despatched, and again we are on our way under the auspices of our new voiturier.

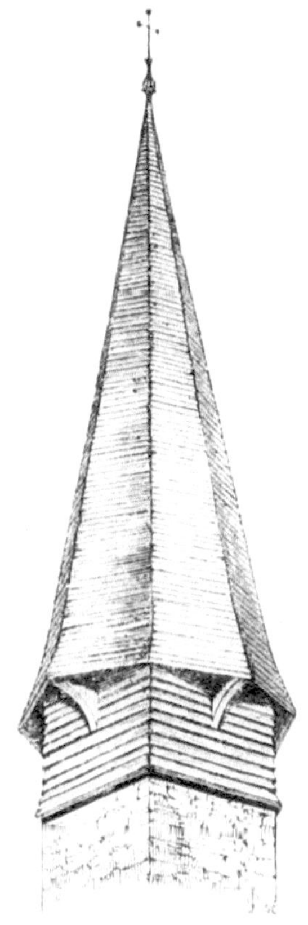

Wooden Spire—Ragatz.

But we must not leave Ragatz without noticing its church, remarkable for its exceedingly good octagonal wooden spire springing in an unusual manner out of a square wooden belfry stage, and another church at (I think) Vilters, close to Ragatz, which has a lofty tower finished on each side with a sharp gable, and a thin octagonal spire rising from the intersection of the cross-gabled roof; both these steeples are in a position which for some reason is very popular in this district— the south side of the chancel.

3.—Interior of Cathedral. Chur.*

From Ragatz to Chur the churches are all very similar; they have tall towers generally in the same position as those near Ragatz, and capped with bulbous roofs, or sharp spires covered with metal. The road is not quite the most agreeable we have travelled; some of the views, it is true, are most lovely, and the mountains—among which towers pre-eminent the grand outline of the Falkniss—are very noble; but, despite all this, the valley is too wide, and the Rhine, by periodical inundations, manages to secure so nearly its whole extent to itself, that there is a waste, desolate, and pestilential look in the foreground which is not prepossessing. We arrived at Chur at about half-past one, and, not sorry that our horses required rest, betook ourselves to the inspection of this very curious town.

It is entered by old gateways, and many of the streets are still full of ancient houses. The curious feature of the place is however its complete division into two quarters—the Protestant and the Catholic—the latter walled off, and entered by its own gates.[2] It occupies the upper part of the town, and contains in the cathedral church of S. Lucius an attraction for architects which has unusual merit and interest. Its plan consists of a nave of three bays, a choir of one bay raised by twelve steps above the nave, and a sanctuary much narrower than the nave and choir, and also of one bay. The steps from the nave to the choir are narrow and on each side, and between them is a very flat wide arch, under which access is obtained to the crypt, the floor of which is a few steps below the nave, and extends under the choir and sanctuary. The plan is, it will be seen, not unlike that of the Cathedral at Zurich, save that here there are no apsidal terminations at all.

A sketch of the interior of so singular a church cannot be uninteresting, and it will be seen from this that the whole is of the very earliest pointed work, and good of its kind; the crypt is supported in the centre by a column resting upon a grotesque animal. Two of the altars have fine shrines of metal of the thirteenth century, and two other altars have ancient pricket candlesticks, and there are some fine brass standard candlesticks also; the choir stalls are old, and there is a late triptych behind the high altar, and a very fine Sakramentshaus with metal doors just below the northern flight of steps to the choir, which reminded me of the very fine example in a similar position in the cathedral at Ulm. The altar is of stone of the thirteenth century, with five detached shafts in front, supporting the slab or mensa. The whole church is groined. It is worthy of notice that the choir makes a great bend out of the straight line towards the north—so much, indeed, that it is impossible to avoid noticing it as one enters the church. The steps from the nave

---

[2] This division is seen clearly in one of the curious prints by Merian, which illustrate a most valuable and interesting book, entitled 'Topographia Helvetiæ,' published at Frankfort-am-Main, A.D. 1654, and full of most picturesque and exact views of Swiss towns; they are valuable, as proving beyond all question their state in the beginning of the seventeenth century, and as being executed with very much artistic feeling. That of Chur gives the whole town in the most complete manner; the castle, the churches, the walls, and the many watch-towers, with the magnificent mountains behind them, making one of the most picturesque *ensembles* conceivable. Many of these views of Swiss towns are remarkable, as proving how very regularly the mediæval towns were planned whenever there was the opportunity, the streets all at right angles, and the great church and marketplace in the centre of the whole.

to the choir lack dignity. But it is true that if they had been in the centre, and the entrances to the crypt on each side, the crypt would not have been seen, as it now is, from the nave, and a striking effect would have been lost. The west end has a fine round-arched doorway with several shafts in each jamb, above this a large window of the same character, and in the gable a small middle-pointed window. About ten feet in advance of the west doorway is a curious remnant of a gateway with piers and shafts resting upon monsters, looking, however, very much as though it had been removed from elsewhere.

Service commenced just as I was obliged to think of leaving the church; the priests wore red cassocks and tippets, and very short surplices edged with lace, and looked unclean and untidy; there was no one in the body of the church, and the sacristan, after the service had commenced, walked backwards and forwards about the choir, down the steps into the nave, and then—after a little attention bestowed on some matter there—out of the church. On a subsequent visit to this church (in 1872) I found repairs in progress, which bade fair to destroy some of its great archæological interest.

Descending from the melancholy and squalid-looking Catholic quarter, we soon came upon the Protestant church, dedicated in honour of S. Martin, which is now somewhat remarkable. It is old, but it has been plastered, whitewashed, and then painted by some original artist over its whole exterior, in an extraordinary imitation of all kinds of inconsistent architectural devices; pilasters, cornices, mouldings, tracery, and the like, are all boldly represented with black paint, and in such style that we all stopped the moment we saw it, struck by the conviction that it must be a scene from some play, so utterly absurd, flat, and out of all perspective did the whole look.

The situation of Chur is very lovely, placed as it is just at the point where the Schalfiker Thal joins the valley of the Rhine, and upon the steep and rugged bottom slope of the mountains.

The weather was every moment becoming more glorious, and just as we left Chur, along the road which leads to Reichenau, we had one of the most lovely views we had enjoyed. It is not always the case, however beautiful may be the scenery, or however lovely the weather, that one finds everything group together perfectly; here, however, it did, and I commend the subject to the pencils of those who follow me on this route.

We soon reached Ems, whose church, situated upon a green knoll above the village, has the peculiarity of a small apsidal building east of the chancel apse. The key was not to be found, so that I could not go in to examine what this building was. This church had an octangular steeple, whilst another church in the same village had one of the bulbous coverings of which I have before complained. At Reichenau it is proper to go to see the house in which Louis Philippe acted in 1793 as schoolmaster under a Monsieur Jost, and I fear we fell rather in the good opinion of our driver when we neglected so proper and regular a custom; but so it was. The garden of the inn is charming, and from its edge you obtain the best view of the junction of the Vorder and Hinter Rhine, and having enjoyed this thoroughly, we passed rapidly through Reichenau, across its two quaint covered wooden bridges, and by the beautiful meeting of the waters, until we found ourselves following the course of the Hinter Rhine and fairly on the Splügen road.

We only wished to reach Thusis by sunset, and so our time was ample for enjoyment; we walked much of the way, detecting eagerly every here and there patches of snow on the mountains in the distance, each of which is hailed as a discovery by every fresh traveller, who feels himself transported with delight by the distant view of the pure white against the sky.

Castles are here as numerous as ever upon the Rhine, and at least a dozen, I should think, might be reckoned perched on every favourable spot between Reichenau and Thusis. As the road advances the valley widens out into a kind of basin, into which flow two streams, the one through the as yet unperceived gorge of the Via Mala rather to the right, the other through an opening in the mountains directly in front of us, which allows us a charming view of the snowy heights above the Julier Pass, drinking in the last red rays of the setting sun, long since passed away from the ground on which we stand; then there is a long ascent, and, passing peasants coming in from hay-making, merrily laughing and singing, we drive up the straight ugly street of Thusis to the Via Mala Hotel. But the evening is too glorious to lose, and in five minutes we are out again on foot to explore the commencement of the black defile; and until we are absolutely turning into it, so narrow is the gorge that it is not seen, but when seen, and by such a light, how grand and beautiful it is! We ascended some distance and then stood and admired. Above us tremendous rocks towered high into the air, riven in two for the narrow chasm in which we stood, at whose bottom we heard the distant roar of the Rhine, and down below and beyond, framed as it were between the grand outline of rocky crag and pine-covered mountain, lay the valley of Domleschg, still retaining, by contrast with the gloom around us, some light upon its fields, and castles, and villages. Rest was well earned after such a pleasant and actively spent day, and, if we were late in starting in the morning, it was as much the fault of our coachman as of ourselves. However, though not so early as we intended, we left soon after six, and in a few minutes were again in the Via Mala. And now by daylight I doubt whether we were not all disappointed; there is so much in a name that one expects something *very* terrific from such a name, and this it scarcely is. It is seldom fair to compare one piece of scenery with another, but still I feel that this was certainly not the most savage I had ever seen, and therefore not justly *my* Via Mala. But beautiful in the extreme it was, and I believe we all regretted that we so soon found ourselves again in the more open valley on the road to Zillis. Here we found a church with a lofty tower, in the same position, and with a spire of the same design, as that at Ragatz; the nave low and ugly, the chancel lofty, with a steep pitched roof and apse; the windows pointed but modernized; the belfry windows of the steeple of three lights, with circular arches, and divided by shafts, which were continued on in blank panels on each side of the windows, so as to form an arcade of five arches on each side. And this I believe was the last noticeable church we saw before we reached Chiavenna, and in its arcaded belfry I fancied that I saw something of an Italian influence at work, which might well have been the fact.

We soon reached Andeer, where we waited but a short time, and then commenced a steep ascent. The lovely scenery, the mountains closing in round us, and the roar of the falls of the Rofla making music in our ears, made our way very enjoyable. There was but little chance, however, of rapid progress, as from Andeer to Splügen the road is almost always on the ascent, sometimes gradually, at others in steep zigzags up the shoulder of some obstructive hill, and constantly overhanging or crossing the rapid, white, foaming mountain-stream, sole representative here of the noble river whose broad waters have been admired at Basel. The air of desolation becomes more decided as one reaches Splügen. Trees and shrubs more scarce, and often blasted by the fierce rush of the wintry wind, or the keen sharp blow of the fallen rock, or the swift sweep of the avalanche, aid in making up the desolate picture. Vegetation has well-nigh ceased, and the eye, though deceived at first by the intensely red colour perceived every here and there on the hill-sides and on the rocks, discovers presently that not to flowers or plants, but to lichen or other such desolate vegetation, is it owing.

By the time we caught the first sight of Splügen the sky was overclouded, the wind rose, and a sudden heavy storm of rain gave us a lesson in the customs of the weather in these regions, to which our driver's quiet assurance that we should probably have a snowstorm on the pass added the few remaining drops required to make up the draught which we saw ourselves doomed to swallow.

Splügen, however, was reputed to have an inn which would give us enviable shelter for a couple of hours, and we entered at once, hoping, if we waited, again to see the blue sky before we crossed the boundary between the North and the South—between Switzerland and Italy.

The table-d'hôte was just about to commence, and in came a diligence from Milan, and out came the passengers: another carriage, which had pursued us relentlessly all the way from Andeer, came in at the same moment, and down we sat, about fifteen English people, not one of whom had been in the house ten minutes before, not one of them stopping for more than their own and their horses' dinners, and all proceeding in different directions, either on their way home satiated with travel, or just about to dive like ourselves in full quest of pleasure and excitement, into a new country. These meetings are always curious, generally amusing, and to the quiet and attentive observer of character not a little edifying. On this occasion there was subject-matter enough, and we found an old gentleman, travelling sorely against his will, under the care of an active and thoroughly vulgar wife, some literary old maids of another party, and the enthusiastic damsel of a third, each in their way amusing, and not the less so in that it was necessary to inspect them and part with them so rapidly.

Splügen, in a soaking rain, is not a pleasant place; and as I employed myself in sketching from the inn window the very picturesque old bridge, which gives[3] all <u>its architectural</u> character to the village, I conceive that I accomplished all that was

[3] I grieve to say it does so no longer. When I last crossed the Splügen, in 1869, this bridge had disappeared, and one of iron had been erected in its place. It was a capital example of the skilful carpentry of the old Swiss bridge-builders.

necessary; and when we got into our carriage again, and, crossing by the bridge, left the Bernardin road to the right, and finally plunged really into the Splügen route, it seemed like a reward for my industry to find the rain cease and the sun again occasionally shine out.

The ascent begins with a series of zigzags, which rapidly carry the road high above the valley of the Rhine, and then, passing through one of the long covered galleries for which this route is famous, it emerges in an upland valley or dip between two mountains, up which it takes a steady course along a road macadamized, by-the-by, mainly with the white marble which abounds here, until, just below the summit, it comes again upon a steep mountain-side, to be surmounted only by a patient unravelling as it were of the intricacies of an endless zigzaging, which at last brings us to the Swiss guard-house and the entrance to the great gallery. The clouds are low and gathering; but still as we see below us white patches of snow every here and there, and above us the blue edge of a great glacier marked with lines of crevasses and fringed with a white edge of snow, we feel that we have really at last achieved the summit. Noisily we trot through the arched gallery, and then, after another slight ascent for a few minutes, we stop and put on the drag, and then down we go rapidly and cheerily, backwards and forwards, occasionally giving a merry tap to some corner post at the turns of the road, in order to let it be known that we, our driver, and our horses, are all of us heartily glad that we are at last on the south side of the pass—no longer the German Splüg*en*, but, as we learn from divers notices along the road, the Italian Splug*a*. A short drive takes us to the custom-house—not looked forward to cheerfully by those who have met, as we had at Splügen, a man turned back by mistake, and after two days' delay again retracing his steps—but happily, in our case, passed easily enough, and with an exhibition of the greatest courtesy and civility from the Austrian officer, the mention of whom reminds me of the great change which has taken place in the political status of this country since first I made acquaintance with it. It is a change of no little importance to the traveller, who now goes without let or hindrance almost everywhere, instead of being worried out of his life by troubles about passports which even Austrian courtesy could not make tolerable.

We are soon off again across a drear and peaty-looking plain, with no view of the neighbouring mountains, and accompanied along the road by a troop of wild smuggler-like fellows, in broad-brimmed steeple-crowned hats, loose jackets, knee breeches, and coarse stockings, riding wildly along on rough horses, without saddles or bridles, but every one of them handsome grand-looking fellows, showing, as they smiled, teeth of the purest white, and more nearly coming up to one's idea of real Italians than any with whom, later in our journey and more in Italy, we happened to meet. Before long, however, we again commenced the descent, and then, after passing through two or three galleries of prodigious length, at last came out upon one of those spots, the view from which, as much perhaps by reason of its associations as for its intrinsic beauty, rests on the mind for ever after, as one of the most lovely ever seen. On our right a steep mountain track slopes rapidly and almost perpendicularly down to a narrow valley, whose opposite and no less precipitous side we are about to descend; below us, far down, we see the village roofs of Isola, with its church and Italian campanile; beyond—and this is indeed the great charm of the prospect—down the valley, where the atmosphere seems redolent of the South, we see a grandly formed mountain, and again to its right another but more distant; between these two dim and distant shades lies the lake of Como—beyond them the broad rich plain of Lombardy; the sun shines forth, and we dream henceforward of that valley, looked down upon from the gallery on the Splügen, as one of the brightest prospects of our lives!

We had not gone far beyond the last gallery before our voiturier made good a boast which he had often repeated, of showing us a real waterfall on a grand scale before we parted company, and, pulling up his horses, made us—not unwilling—dismount to look *down* the cascade of the Medessimo. A passage has been formed from the road to a point which just overhangs the fall, and here, securely parapeted round, you look down over a grand sheer fall of some eight hundred feet, in the course of which the torrent which goes to feed the threadlike Lira down below us in the valley, and just now roaring in bold volume underneath our road, loses itself in soft, delicate, and fairy-like spray, and ere it reaches the rock below, seems like some delicate mist falling from the sky for ever in endless and exquisite change of form. Just beyond the cascade the most wonderful part of the descent in an engineering point of view commences, and the road seems really to descend the perpendicular face of the rock, surpassing in boldness most other roads that I know, and affording very fine and varied views of the cascade on the descent. We soon reached Campo Dolcino, a miserable and most dirty-looking village; and were, sorely against our will, obliged to wait for our horses to bait; and then on we went, the sun some time set, and the night dark and cloudy. Presently a storm arose; and without lights, and travelling along a road turning sharp angles every minute, and never losing the music in our ears of the roaring Lira, our lot seemed more wild than enviable; at last we came to a house and tried unsuccessfully to borrow a light, but presently at another house we succeeded, and then guided by a lantern we pursued our way safely enough. I have seldom been out in so grand a storm; the lightning was vivid beyond all that I could conceive; and as at one minute it played about on the foaming water beneath us, and at another lighted up the whole mountain-side beyond with pale and intensely lovely light, flickering, playing, and dancing about in the wildest fashion, I believe we felt half sad when house after house appeared, and at last we entered the long, narrow, and thoroughly Italian streets of Chiavenna.

Another journey took me to Chiavenna at the same time in the evening, on my way north from Como. It was the night of the 8th September, the Nativity of the Blessed Virgin, and every peasant in his solitary châlet on the mountain-side was burning a bonfire in her honour. There seemed to me to be something very touching in this flaming burst of distant greeting from mountain to mountain, and few circumstances have ever brought home more vividly to me the isolation of these mountaineers, than the compensating power of a sympathetic faith which made them thus bid each other welcome by their flaring fires.

CHAPTER IV.

Chiavenna—Lake of Riva—Colico—Gravidona—Lake of Como—Varenna—Stelvio Pass—Lecco—Bergamo: Broletto—Churches—Castle of Malpaga.

"But now 'tis pass'd,
That turbulent chaos; and the promised land
Lies at my feet in all its loveliness!
To him who starts up from a terrible dream,
And lo, the sun is shining and the lark
Singing aloud for joy, to him is not
Such sudden ravishment as now I feel,
At the first glimpses of fair Italy."

Rogers.

THE situation of Chiavenna is eminently beautiful: in a deep valley surrounded on all sides by mountains whose slopes are covered with soft and luxuriant foliage of oak and chestnut, and where every available open space is devoted to trellised vineyards, it contrasts strongly with the pine-covered hills so lately passed on the northern slopes of the Alps; placed, too, at the confluence of two streams—the Meira and the Lira—it rejoices in the constant rushing sound of many waters.

It was only necessary to move out of the shade of our hotel into the melancholy piazza in which it stands, to discover that an Italian sun lighted up the deep blue sky; and a walk to the principal church, dedicated in honour of S. Lawrence, a stroll through the narrow streets, and a rather toilsome ascent through a vineyard formed upon a rock which towers up behind a kind of ruined castle, and from which a capital view is obtained of the singular and beautiful cul-de-sac in which the town is planted, sufficiently convinced us of its power.

The church of S. Lawrence is entered from a large oblong cloister, in one angle of the space enclosed by which rises a tall campanile, its simple form, and its arcaded belfry full of musical bells, contrasting well with the outline of the hills which overhang and hem it in. On the east side of the cloister are the church, an octagonal baptistery, and a bone-house, all ranged side by side and opening into it, and the latter curious as an example of the extent to which the people of Chiavenna amuse themselves by arranging sculls and arm-bones into all kinds of religious and heraldic devices, and with labels to mark the names of their former owners. The *tout ensemble* is picturesque in its effect, and the cool pleasant shade of the cloister, with the view of the church and its tall campanile, and irregularly grouped buildings looking brilliantly white in the clear sunshine, was very pleasing.[4]

Italian beggars, persevering, and, at any rate in appearance, very devout, did their best to annoy us here and everywhere when we ventured to stop to examine or admire anything; and Italian beggars are certainly both in pertinacity and in filth about the most unpleasant of their class.

My voiturier gave me a lesson worth learning, and not perhaps unworthy of note for other unsuspicious travellers. We had a written contract to Chiavenna, and thence to Colico he had agreed verbally to take us for a certain sum; before we started I found, however, that he intended to charge us three times as much as we had agreed upon, and, as very luckily we found a diligence on the point of starting, we secured places in the cabriolet at its back, from which we had the best possible position for seeing the views, and so left him in the lurch, with divers admonitions to behave himself more honestly for the future.

At ten we left, and had a very enjoyable ride to Colico. The valley, however, bore sad traces of the havoc made by the inundations of the Meira, and of the storm of the previous night. We soon reached the shores of the little Lake of Riva, along whose banks our road took us sometimes in tunnels, sometimes on causeways built out into the water, until at last we reached the valley up which runs the Stelvio road, and then, after passing along the whole length of a straight road lined on each side with a wearisome and endless row of poplars, we were at Colico. Here we prudently availed ourselves of the opportunity of an hour's delay in the departure of the boat for an early dinner, and, then embarking, waited patiently the pleasure of our captain.

The scenery of Lake Como has been so often extravagantly praised that I was quite prepared to be disappointed; but for the whole distance from Colico to Lecco it is certainly on the whole more striking than any lake scenery I have seen. The mountains at its head are extremely irregular and picturesque, and throughout its whole length there is great change and variety. In this respect it contrasts favourably with most other lakes, and I certainly think that not even in the Lake of Lucerne is there any one view so grand as that which one has looking up from within a short distance of the head of Como over the Lake of Riva to the mountains closing in the Stelvio, and rising nobly above the sources of the Meira and the Lira.

Somewhat, too, may be said of the innumerable villages and white villas with which the banks of the lake are studded; they give a sunny, inhabited, and cheerful feeling to the whole scene; and, reflected in the deep blue lake in those long-drawn lines of flakey white which are seen in no other water to such perfection, add certainly some beauty to the general view.

One of these villages—Gravidona—within half an hour's sail of Colico, ought

[4] Probably most travellers who pass by Chiavenna are now on their way to or from the Engadin by the beautiful Maloja pass. They will do well before they reach the top of the pass to notice on their left the ruined remains of a Gothic chapel of the fifteenth century, which may, I suppose, aspire to the honour of being at a greater height above the sea than any other Gothic church in Europe. Its architectural merit is not great, but still it has a certain value, as showing how well a simple little Gothic church looks among the wildest mountain scenery.

not to be left unvisited by any one who cares about architecture.

Close to its little harbour stand two churches side by side, one an oblong basilica, the other a baptistery of, as it seems to me, such great interest that I give illustrations both of its plan and of its exterior. It will be seen that the dimensions are small, the total internal width being less than forty feet, whilst the design of the east end is most ingeniously contrived so as to give no less than five eastern apsidal recesses. There are two stair-turrets in the wall on each side of the western tower which lead up to a sort of triforium-passage which is formed behind an arcade in the side wall of the church, and one of them leads also to the first floor of the tower. The triforium consists of an arcade of seven arches in each side wall. The three small apses at the east have each their own semi-dome, and the chancel as well as all the other apsidal recesses are similarly roofed. All the walls retain more or less traces of old paintings, the Coronation of the Blessed Virgin occupying the principal apse, and the Last Judgment the west wall. The whole church is built in white marble and black lime-stone used in courses, or stripes, with extremely good effect.

The roof of this Baptistery is of wood. The exterior is best explained by reference to my drawing of the west front. It stands on a charming site with a background of lake and mountain, such as one seldom enjoys. There is a contrast here, which strikes one very much, between the ingenious skill of the planning of such a building as this and the rudeness of the execution of the details. I know nothing as to the history of Gravidona; but it looks as though the plan came from the hands of men who knew something of the Church of San Vitale at Ravenna, whilst its execution was left to the rustic skill of the masons of the country.

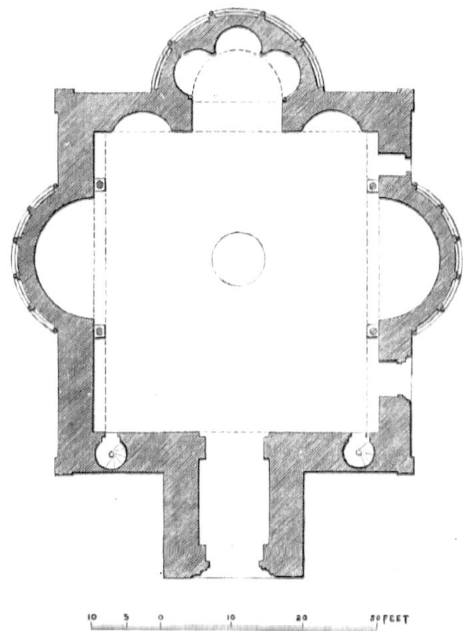

Ground Plan—Baptistery, Gravidona.

4.—Baptistery. Gravidona.

The Baptistery is dedicated to S. John the Baptist. Close to it, as I have said, stands the Church of San Vincenzo, which though Romanesque in its foundation has been much modernized, and is now mainly interesting on account of the exquisite examples of late fifteenth century silversmiths' work which still enrich its sacristy. Conspicuous among these is a silver processional cross. This cross is nearly two feet across the arms by three feet in height from the top of the staff. There is a crucifix on one side and a sitting figure of Our Lord on the other; figures of SS. George, Vincent, Sebastian, Christopher, and Victor, and Our Lord on the base or knop; and half-figures of the Evangelists on the arms of the cross. The ornaments consist of crockets bent and twisted, of blue enamels, filigree-work, nielli, and turquoises set in the centre of dark-blue enamels. It is, in short, a piece of metal work which might well make a modern silversmith run down swiftly into the lake and drown himself in despair at the apparent impossibility in these days of rivalling such a piece of artistic and cunning workmanship, in spite of all our boasted prog-ress!

Not much less splendid is a chalice of about the same age. It is ten and three-quarter inches high, has a plain bowl, but knop, stem, and foot all most richly wrought with figures, niches and canopies, and the flat surfaces filled in with fine blue and white Limoges enamels. The paten belonging to this chalice is very large—nearly ten inches across, and quite plain.

Half the passengers on the steamboat were, of course, Austrian soldiers and officers, the other half English or Americans, either resident at or going to Como. We, however, stopped on the way, and, leaving the steamboat in the middle of the lake, after a row of about twenty minutes found ourselves at Varenna, a village exquisitely placed just where the three arms of the lake—the Como, the Lecco, and the Colico branches—separate, affording, whether seen from here, from Bellagio, or from Cadenabbia, the most lovely lake views it has ever been my good fortune to see.

Here we had what seemed likely to be an endless discussion upon the relative merits of a four-oared boat and a carriage as a means of conveyance to Lecco. We inclined to the latter; but, leaving the matter in the hands of an active waiter, we busied ourselves with eating delicious fruit, admiring the tall cypresses growing everywhere about the shores of the lake, and watching the exquisite beauty of the reflections of Bellagio and the opposite mountains on the smooth bosom of the water.

We were soon off again, and well satisfied to find ourselves trotting rapidly along the well kept Stelvio Road, instead of dragging heavily and slowly along as one always does with a Swiss voiturier; soon, however, we were to find that our driver was an exception to the Italian rule, and that he who wishes to travel fast must not expect to do so with vetturini.

The churches which we passed were in no way remarkable; they all had campanili, with the bells hung in the Italian fashion in the belfry windows, with their wheels projecting far beyond the line of the wall; but they all seemed alike uninteresting in their architecture, so that we were in no way sorry to pass them rapidly on our way to Lecco. This eastern arm of the lake, though of course much less travelled than the rest of its course, is very beautiful, and its uninhabited and less cultivated looking shores, with bold cliffs here and there rising precipitously from the water, were seen to great advantage, with the calm unrippled surface of the lake below, and the sky just tinged with the bright light of the sun before it set above.

Lecco contains nothing to interest a traveller; we had an hour to spend there before we could get fresh horses to take us on to Bergamo, and wandered about the quaint-looking streets, which were full of people—some idly enjoying themselves, others selling luscious-looking fruit. We went into a large church not yet quite completed; it was Renaissance in style, almost of course, and on the old plan, with aisles, but very ugly notwithstanding. In the nave was a coffin covered with a pall of black and gold; six large candles stood by it, three on either side, and two larger than the others on each side of a crucifix at the west end. The whole church revelled in compo inside and out and there was external access to a wretched bone-house in a crypt.

Leaving Lecco, we had a long drive in the dark to Bergamo; the night was very dark, but the air was absolutely teeming with life and sounds of life; myriads of *cicale* seemed to surround us, each giving vent to its pleasure in its own particular note and voice with the greatest possible determination; and had I not heard them, I could scarcely have believed it possible that such sounds could be made by insects, however numerous they might be. We changed horses at a village on the road, and went on rapidly. The old town of Ponte San Pietro was passed, having been taken at first to be Bergamo, and remembered by the sound of a troop of men singing well together as they passed us in the dark in one of its narrow streets, awakening with their voices all the echoes of the place, which till then had seemed to us to be supernaturally silent. It was eleven o'clock before we reached Bergamo, and tired with our long day's work, we were soon in bed.

A prodigious noise in the streets before five o'clock the next morning gave us the first warning that the great fair of Bergamo was in full swing; sleep was impossible, and so we were soon out, enjoying the busy throng which crowded the streets of the Borgo, in a before-breakfast walk; the crowd of women selling fruit, the bright colours of their dresses, the rich tints of stuff hung out for sale, the display of hair-pins and other ornaments in the innumerable silversmiths' shops, and the noisy, laughing, talking people who animated the whole scene, made the narrow arcaded streets of the busy place most amusing.

After breakfast we started at once for the Città, as the old city of Bergamo is called. It stands on a lofty hill overlooking the Borgo San Leonardo, within whose precincts we had slept, quite distinct from it and enclosed within its own walls. The ascent was both steep and hot, but the view at the entrance gateway of the Città over the flat Lombard country was very striking, and well repaid the labour of the ascent. This vast plain of bluish-green colour, intersected in all directions by rows of mulberry-trees and poplars, diversified only by the tall white lines of the campanili which mark every village in this part of Lombardy, and stretching away in the same endless level as far as the eye could reach, was grand if only on account of its simplicity, and had for us all the charm of novelty.

Through narrow and rather dirty streets, which do little credit to the cleanly habits of the Bergamask nobility, to whom it seems that the Città is sacred, and whose palaces are, many of them, large and important buildings, we reached at last the Piazza Vecchia, around which is gathered almost all that in my eyes gives interest to Bergamo.

Across the upper end of the Piazza stretches the Broletto, or town-hall, supported on open arches, through which pleasant glimpses are obtained of the cathedral and church of Sta. Maria Maggiore, which last is the great architectural feature of the city.

But we must examine the Broletto before we go farther. And first of all, its very position teaches a lesson. Forming on one side the boundary of a spacious Piazza, on the other it faces, within a few feet only, the church of Sta. Maria Maggiore, and abuts at one end upon the west front of the Duomo. It is to this singularly close—even huddled—grouping that much of the exquisite beauty of the whole is owing. No doubt Sta. Maria and the original cathedral were built first, and then the architect of the Broletto, not fearing—as one would fear now—to damage what has been done before, boldly throws his work across in front of them, but upon lofty open arches, through which glimpses just obtained of the beauties in store beyond make the gazer even more delighted with the churches when he reaches them, than he would have been had they been all seen from the first. It is, in fact, a notable example of the difference between ancient grouping and modern, and one instance only out of hundreds that might be adduced from our own country and from the Continent of the principle upon which old architects worked; and yet people, ignorant of real principles in art, talk as though somewhat would be gained if we could pull down S. Margaret's in order to let Westminster Abbey be seen; whereas, in truth, the certain result would be, in the first place, a great loss of scale in the Abbey seen without another building to compare it with and measure it by; and in the next, the loss of that kind of intricacy and mystery which is one of the chief evidences of the Gothic spirit. Let us learn from such examples as this at Bergamo that buildings do not always require a large open space in front of them, so that they may be all seen and taken in at one view, in order to give them real dignity.

The whole design of the Broletto is so very simple as to be almost chargeable with rudeness of character. The ground on which it stands is divided by columns and piers, the spaces between them being all arched and groined. Towards the Piazza three of these arches, springing from rather wide piers, support the main building, and another supports an additional building to the west of it. Above the three main arches are three windows, of which that in the centre, though very much altered, still retains a partially old balcony in front, and was evidently the Ringhiera, from which the people standing in the Piazza were wont to be addressed by their magistrates. The windows on either side are very similar in their design and detail; their tracery is of fair middle-pointed character; and the main points in which they strike one as being different from English work are the marble shafts with square capitals in place of monials, a certain degree of squareness and flatness in the mouldings, and the very pronounced effect of the sills, which have a course of foliage and moulding, and below this of trefoiled arcaded ornament, which in one shape or another is to meet the traveller everywhere in Northern Italy; either, as here, hanging on under the sills of windows, or else running up the sides of gables, forming string-courses and cornices, but always unsatisfactory, because unmeaning and unconstructional. The origin of this sort of detail is to be found in the numerous brick buildings not far distant, where the facility of repeating the patterns of moulded bricks led (as it did in other countries also) to this rather unsatisfactory kind of enrichment. The detail of the arcades supporting the upper part of the building is throughout bold and simple, and I should say of the thirteenth century; the bases are quite northern in their section, the caps rather less deep in their cutting, but still in their general design, and in the grouping of tufts of drooping foliage regularly one above the other, reminding one much of Early French work, though they are certainly not nearly so good as that generally is. There is a flatness about the carving, too, which gives the impression of a struggle, in the hand of the carver, between the Classic and Gothic principles, in which the latter never quite asserted the mastery. The lesson to be learnt from such a building as this Broletto appears to me to be the excessive value of simplicity and regularity of parts carefully and constructionally treated; for there are no breaks or buttresses in the design, and all its elements are most simple, yet nevertheless the result is beautiful.

5.—Broletto, Bergamo.

To the west of the Broletto is a good open staircase (much like that in the Piazza dei Signori at Verona),[5] forming a portion of one side of the Piazza, and leading to the upper part of the buildings, and, I think, to the great clock-tower, which, gaunt and severe in its outline, undecorated and apparently uncared for, rears its great height of rough stone wall boldly against the sky, and groups picturesquely with the irregular buildings around it. I have omitted to notice that the whole of the Broletto, with the exception of the window-shafts, is executed in stone, and without any introduction of coloured material, so that it in no way competes with the exquisite piece of coloured construction which we have next to examine, immediately behind it.

A few steps will take us under the open-arched and cool space beneath the Broletto, to the face of the north porch and baptistery of Sta. Maria Maggiore. This is a very fine early Romanesque[6] church, but with many additions and alterations on the outside, and so much modernized inside as to be quite uninteresting to any one who thinks good forms and good details necessary to good effect. The plan is cruciform, with apses to the choir, on the east and west sides of the south transept, on the east of the north transept, and at the west end of an additional north aisle; in all no less than five apsidal ends. The nave is of three bays with aisles, and to each transept have been added, in the fourteenth century, porches, thoroughly Italian in their whole idea, and novel to a degree in their effect upon an English eye.

A domed chapel, erected as a sepulchral chapel by Bartolomeo Colleoni in the Renaissance style, on the north side of the nave, is most elaborately constructed of coloured marbles. The effect is too bizarre to be good; there is an entire absence of any true style in its design, and there is nothing which makes it necessary to criticize it with much minuteness.

The best and most striking feature in the whole church is the north porch,[7] a most elaborate structure of red, grey, and white marble, to which a drawing without colour can hardly do justice. It is supported upon detached marble shafts, whose bases rest upon the backs of rather grand-looking lions, curiously grouped with children and cubs. Above the arches which rest upon these shafts, and which, though circular, are elaborately cusped, is another stage divided by columns and trefoiled arches into three spaces, the centre of which is occupied by a noble figure of a certain Duke Lupus on horseback, with a saint on either side in the other divisions. All the shafts except those in the upper division are of red marble; the highest stage of all is entirely of grey marble; in the middle stage all the moulded parts are of red, and the trefoiled arches and their spandrels of grey marble; the space at the back of the open divisions and the wall over the main arches of the porch are built in courses of red and white marble. All the groining is divided into diamond-shaped panels, composed alternately of black, red, and white marble, all carved in the same kind of pattern. In the great arch of the porch the outer moulding is of red marble, and all the cusping of grey. The construction of the whole is obviously very weak, and depends altogether for its stability upon iron ties in

---

[5] See illustration opposite page 75.

[6] The church was built in A.D. 1134 by Maestro Fedro.

[7] For a view of this porch, see the frontispiece of this volume.

every direction.

The approach to the porch, by seven steps formed alternately of black and white marble, increases the impressiveness of the grand doorway, in front of which it is built, the whole of which is of white marble, whose carved surfaces and richly moulded and traceried work have obtained a soft yellow colour by their exposure to the changing atmosphere, and are relieved by one—the central—shaft being executed in the purest red marble. There are three shafts in each jamb, carved, twisted, or moulded very beautifully. These shafts are set in square recesses, ornamented, not with mouldings, but with elaborate flat carvings, in one place of saints, in another of animals, and with foliage very flat in its character, and mainly founded on the acanthus.

To an English eye these columns in the doorways are some of the most charming features of Italian architecture; but they must be always looked at as simply ornamental, and not as constructional features; and perhaps in all doorways the shafts, being really incapable of supporting any considerable weight, would be better if, by their twisting and moulding, it were clearly shown that their architect meant them to be simply ornamental. In the Bergamo doorway the spaces between the shafts are so strong in their effect, though carved all over their surface, that any lightness in the columns themselves is amply atoned for. Such a work as this northern porch at Bergamo is indeed a great treat to an English architect, teeming as it does with fresh and new ideas, and in a small compass showing so many of the radical points of difference between northern and southern Gothic, and at the same time offering so beautiful a study of constructional colouring, that it is impossible to tire of gazing at it.

The porch to the south transept is of a simpler but somewhat similar design. Both are placed against the western half of the gable against which they are built, with a pleasant ignorance of those new-fangled views of regularity of plan which are the curse of modern architects. This southern porch is round-arched, and fitted exactly to the doorway which it shields. Its outer arch is carried on detached shafts resting on the backs of monsters, and it is mainly constructed of black and white marble. It is of only one stage in height, and has a deep cornice enriched with a series of niches with figures. An inscription below the cornice gives the date as 1360.[8] Above the porch, but independent of it, is a lofty monumental pinnacle corbelled out from the wall, and richly sculptured with crocketed pinnacles and gablets. When the church is entered, the reason for the apparently eccentric position of the porches is seen. They were so placed to give more space for the altars to the east of the transepts, and their successful effect is good evidence that no artist need ever distress himself about a want of regularity, if it is the result of a little common sense attention to convenience in the arrangement of his plan.

The southern side of the church gives a very fair idea of what the general character of the original building of 1134 was. The windows were very plain, the walls lofty, the roof flat, and ornamented with corbel-tables up the gables and

---

[8] "✠ MCCCLX · MAGISTER · JOHANES · FILIUS · C · DNI · VGI · DE · CAMPILIO · FECIT · HOC · OPUS." This Giovanni da Campione was one of a family of architects of much celebrity. See their genealogical tree in 'Italian Sculptors' p. 106.

under the eaves, and pilasters were used at intervals instead of buttresses. There is a central octagonal lantern which may be old, but which is entirely modernized. The most interesting remains are the various apses already mentioned. They are of two divisions in height, the lower adorned with very lofty, boldly-moulded arcades, above which is an elaborate cornice, and above this again a low arcade on detached shafts, behind which the walls are considerably recessed to form galleries which produce a very deep shadow. The capitals are elaborately carved, and the upper cornice is again very rich. Altogether, little as remains unaltered of the old fabric, it is enough to give an idea of a very noble and interesting phase of art. Near a doorway into the north chancel-aisle the external walls have traces, faint and rapidly decaying, of some very exquisite frescoes or, more probably, tempera paintings.

Campanile—Bergamo.

The steeple is in a most unusual position—east, namely, of the south transept—not less, I believe, than some three hundred feet in height, of good and very simple pointed character, without any approach to buttressing, and remarkable as having an elaborately arcaded string-course a few feet below the belfry windows, which have geometrical traceries enclosed within semi-circular arches, affording, like the south transept porch, a curious illustration of the indifference of Italian architects to the use of the pointed arch where strength was not of consequence.

Italian campanili have quite a character of their own, so distinct from and utterly unlike the steeples of Northern Europe, that this, the first Gothic example I had seen, interested me exceedingly. Perhaps its detail was almost too little peculiar, if I may venture to say so; for certainly it has left no such impression of individuality on my mind as has the beautiful campanile to whose grace so much of the charm of Verona is due.

The cathedral at Bergamo, which is close to the Broletto and Sta. Maria, may be dismissed in a word. It has been rebuilt within the last two hundred years, and appeared to be in no way deserving of notice. In a courtyard on its north side is a small detached polygonal baptistery, founded in 1275, which must have been very interesting. It is all built of marble, and richly adorned with shafts; but so far as I could see every portion of it has been renewed within a few years. Beside Sta. Maria Maggiore and the Broletto we found little to see. Two churches—one in the Città, and another, desecrated, in the Borgo—have very good simple pointed doorways, with square-headed openings and carved tympana; but beyond these we saw scarcely any trace of pointed work. We had a luxuriously hot day in Bergamo, and, as we sat and sketched the Broletto, a crowd, thoroughly Italian in its composition and proceedings, gathered round us and gave us a first lesson in the penance which all sketchers must be content to undergo in Italy. Before long I found that my only plan was to start an umbrella as a defence both against the sun and the crowd, and this, though not entirely successful, still effected a great improvement.

The walk down the hill to the Borgo was more pleasant than the climb up, and we were soon at our inn again; and then, after a most delicious luncheon of exquisite fruit and coolest lemonade, concluded by a very necessary dispute with our landlord about the amount of his bill, ending, as such disputes generally do in Italy, with a considerable reduction in the charge and the strongest expressions of regard and good wishes for our welfare on our way, we mounted our carriage, and were soon on the road towards Brescia.

Not far from this road and within about eight miles of Bergamo lies one of the most interesting of the many castles of which one so frequently sees remains in the North of Italy. This is the Castle of Malpaga, which was inhabited by the famous Condottiere Bartolomeo Colleoni, of whom we have already heard at Bergamo, and of whom we shall see something again at Venice. It belongs now to a nobleman who lives in the Città of Bergamo, and leaves this old and stately pile to the keeping of his hinds, who tend his silk-worms, gather his grapes, make his wines, look after his corn and cattle, and do as much as in them lies to gather the fruits which mother earth yields in these parts with such ungrudging profusion, but trouble themselves little about the preservation of the old castle or its belongings, seeing that they seem to give scant pleasure to their lord.

The castle as originally built was a square building enclosing a courtyard built of brick externally, and adorned with a forked battlement, which is common everywhere in old buildings between this and Vicenza, and with four square corner towers, of which one larger than the others has a very bold and fine overhanging machicolated parapet. In the centre of the south front the drawbridge still remains in use, and was lowered for our exit from the castle. Outside the square castle was a space, and then a low wall again furnished with the forked battlement. This must have been a very picturesque arrangement; but unfortunately its real character is now only intelligible to the skilled eye. For the great Colleoni, finding himself in possession of a castle which gave him insufficient space for his magnificence, built up walls on the top of the old battlemented outer wall, and created his state rooms in the space between this new wall and the old external wall of the castle.[9] These rooms of his have much damaged the effect of the outside of the castle; but internally they are still interesting, owing to the sumptuous character of the painted decorations with which he had them adorned. These were executed at about the time of the visit of Christian II. of Denmark to Colleoni, and are interesting if not great works of art. The old courtyard though small is very fine in its effect. The upper walls are carried on pointed arches and are covered with fresco or distemper paintings, said to have been executed by Giovanni Cariani of Bergamo, or by Girolamo Romanino of Brescia, extremely striking and attractive in their general style of colour and drawing. The most picturesque incidents are illustrations of Colleoni's career—the Doge of Venice giving Colleoni his bâton in the presence of the Pope, and a fine battle subject.

A squalid area for rubbish, children, pigs, cats, and what not, is left all round the moat, and beyond this are all the farm buildings and labourers' residences, which go to make up the *tout ensemble* of a great Lombard farmyard. The surroundings are not clean nor very picturesque, but the castle itself has so great an interest, that no one who visits Bergamo should pass it by unseen.

---

[9] The round church of San Tommaso in Limine, described by Mr. Gally Knight as similar in plan to San Vitale, at Ravenna, is only eight miles to the north of Bergamo, and ought, equally with Malpaga Castle, to be seen. I regret that I have never yet visited it.

6.—Castle of Malpaga.

CHAPTER V.

Palazzuolo—Coccaglio—Brescia: new and old Cathedrals, Broletto—Churches—Donato—Desenzano—Lago di Garda—Riva—
Trent—Verona.

"Am I in Italy? Is this the Mincius?
Are those the distant turrets of Verona?
And shall I sup where Juliet at the masque
Saw her loved Montague, and now sleeps by him?"

Rogers.

OUR drive from Bergamo to Brescia was strikingly unlike what we had hitherto been so much enjoying. Mile after mile of straight roads, between fields so
closely planted with fruit-trees that one never sees more than the merest glimpse
of anything beyond them, are certainly not pleasant; and the hot sun above us, and
the thirsty and dry beds of rivers which we crossed on our way, made us feel glad
when evening drew on, and we found ourselves rapidly nearing Brescia.

I made notes at two or three places on the way. At Palazzuolo is a great circular
belfry, ornamented with a large figure at the top and divers others about its base,
built of brick rusticated to look like stone, and altogether about as base a piece of
architecture as could well be found, but pardoned here because of the pure blue
of the sky I saw behind it, and partly on account of the view which it commands,
reaching, it is said, as far as Milan, and including the great plain out of which,
upon a slight hill, it rises. Palazzuolo is nicely situated, and upon the first of the
many rivers which we had passed from Bergamo which had any water in its bed.
The houses, too, were almost all supported on arcades, giving pleasant shelter
from the sun.

Beyond this we came to Coccaglio, a small village with a wretchedly bad modern church, glorying in a glaringly sham front, and faced on the opposite side of
the street by the remains of a mediæval church—whose place it has taken—and
which is now shut up and rapidly going to ruin. The new church is built north
and south—the old one orientating properly; but then the west front was the great
feature of the new church, and therefore it was necessary, of course, to place it
towards the road!

Window—Coccaglio.

Coccaglio still has, however, some very valuable remains of mediæval domestic work in its houses, of which I was able to obtain some sketches. They were entirely executed in brick and terra-cotta, except, of course, the capitals and shafts of the windows, and appeared to be of the fourteenth century.

The upper portion of the house of which I give a sketch remains very fairly perfect, though its lower story has been entirely modernized. It will be seen that it is very uniform in its design, the large and small windows alternating regularly; and that semi-circular arches are used in the windows in connection with ogee trefoils. This is one of the apparent inconsistencies which occur in almost all Italian Gothic work; and might seem to give us ancient authority for any amount of licence in our combination of the elements of what we ordinarily consider to be thoroughly different styles. The windows are marked by the same elaboration of their sills which we noticed in the Broletto at Bergamo, and the detail of these, as also of the corbelling out from the wall of several chimney-breasts, is exceedingly good.

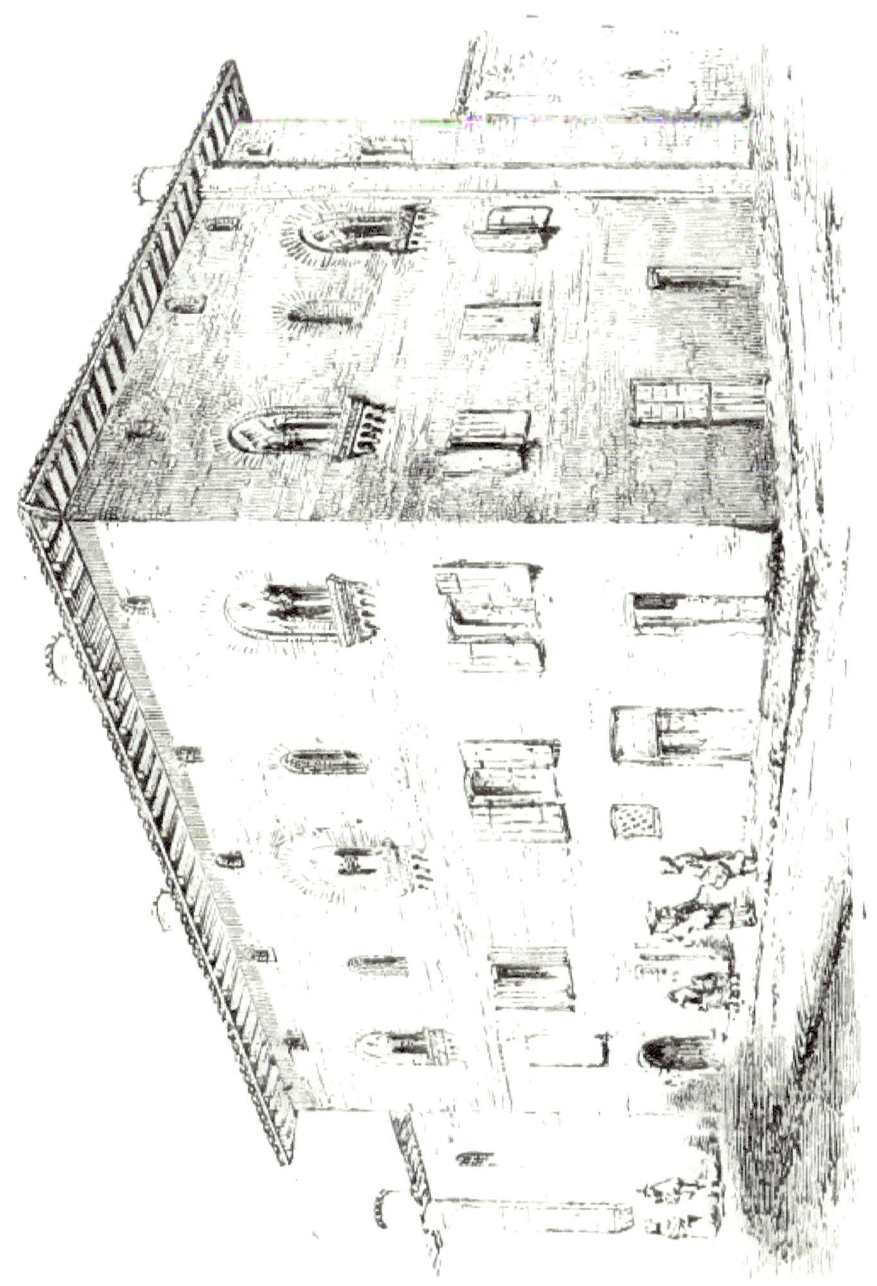

7.—House at Coccaglio.

In a back street in the village I found a house the balconies around which were corbelled forward on finely moulded beams, which, judging by the moulding, could hardly be of later date than the commencement of the fourteenth century.

Detail of windows and corbelling for chimneys—Coccaglio.

Wooden Balcony—Coccaglio.

Wooden mouldings of this kind are much rarer in Italy than they are in the North, and I particularly notice this little relic, therefore, which still remains to show how well the science of moulding was sometimes understood even there.

Such a village as Coccaglio is, as I found afterwards, a place to be made much of, for generally, except in public or important buildings in large towns, one sees very little trace of any mediæval domestic work beyond the perpetually recurring arcading under the houses which is so general a feature in all the towns in the North of Italy.

There is nothing further of any interest on the road, and just after sunset we reached Brescia, too late to see anything of the general effect of the city.

Brescia is mainly famous, I believe, first for its connection with a story of the generosity of Bayard, the "chevalier sans peur et sans reproche," and next for the large discoveries of Roman remains which have from time to time been made there. It is one of those towns, moreover, of which guide-books, with an immense list of churches and the pictures they contain, give perhaps too grand an idea before they have been seen. It is, however, undoubtedly a place of much interest, not only for the antiquary, but also for the student of mediæval art, since, though its churches are generally uninteresting, it has in the Broletto, sadly mutilated and modernized as it is, the remains of one of the most extensive and grand of these buildings, and to a considerable extent executed in very excellent brickwork.

Our first visit in the morning was to the Piazza, in which stand the two cathedrals—the old and the new—side by side, and just beyond them the front of the Broletto, stretching its great length up a slight hill and along a narrow lane beyond the Piazza, whilst at its angle, towering up between it and the cathedrals, stands a tall and rugged stone campanile, without break or window until at the top, where, just as in the corresponding tower at Bergamo, great rudely-arched openings are left, through which appear the wheels and works of the bells.

The new cathedral, approached by a flight of steps from the Piazza, has a great sham front. It has, moreover, a large dome, said to be inferior only in size to those of S. Peter's and the cathedral at Florence, but not prepossessing in its effect; nor did the church seem to contain any pictures of value. By a descent of some twenty steps from the south transept the old cathedral is reached. This is of very early date, and constructed partly in stone and partly in brick. The most remarkable feature is the nave, which is circular in plan, with an aisle round it; the central portion, divided by eight arches from the aisles, being carried up into a dome. The choir and transepts are projected on the east side of the dome, and the former is groined and has a five-sided apse. The walls retain some fair mediæval monuments, and beneath the church is a large crypt. The old stone altar in the choir is a fine example of the thirteenth century. The mensa is, as so often is the case, carried on shafts, no less than sixteen in front and six at the ends, with carved capitals. The stalls are in the apse, and a fine lectern stands behind the altar.

The whole air of the Duomo Vecchio is chill and dismal to a degree; it is neglected and dirty, and apparently shut up except for occasional services, and left no pleasant impressions on our minds of our first Lombard cathedral; and yet undoubtedly there is both here and at Aachen—where the plan of the cathedral is so very similar—much to admire in the idea of the plan, and I can quite imagine that a very noble and useful church might in any age have been founded upon this old Lombard type.[10]

8.—Broletto. Brescia.

[10] S. Gereon, at Köln, is a magnificent example of a church upon the same kind of plan; a grand choir projected from a decagonal nave, the effect of which is capital. No doubt such a nave does much more than merely suggest the possibility of adapting the dome to Gothic buildings.

Those who know anything of Spanish churches will be reminded here of the two cathedrals at Salamanca, the relative positions of which are just the same, a steep flight of steps in either case, leading down from the south aisle of the new cathedral into the old and deserted one.

From the cathedral we went at once to the Broletto, which stands in the same Piazza. The main portion of this immense building appears to have been built rather early in the thirteenth century. The arches throughout are both round and pointed, used indifferently; but this mixture does not betoken any diversity of date, as it would in England.

Cloister—Broletto, Brescia.

A large quadrangle is formed by the buildings, which has a cloister on two sides, and traces of another cloister on a third side now built up. The cloister still remaining on the cast side is ancient and on a large scale; it opens to the quadrangle with simple pointed arches resting upon heavy piers, and a row of piers running down the centre divides it into two portions, so that it may be judged that its size is very considerable. The groining has transverse and diagonal ribs, the former being very remarkable, and, as not unfrequently seen in good Italian work, slightly ogeed; not, that is to say, regular ogee arches, but ordinary arches with the slightest suggestion only of an ogee curve in the centre. Of the external portion of the building the west front is the most perfect, and must always have been the finest; it consists of a building containing in the upper story five windows, the centre being the largest, and possibly once the Ringhiera, to the south of which rises the great belfry of rough stone, and beyond that a wide building with traces—but no more—of many of the original windows; north of the building with the five windows is a very beautiful composition executed almost entirely in finely-moulded bricks; it has an exquisite door with some traces of fresco in its tympanum, executed mainly in stone, of which I give a drawing, and a magnificent brick rose window, above which is a brick cornice, which continues over the remainder of the west front and along the whole of the north side.

Detail of circular window—Broletto, Brescia.

Doorway—Broletto, Brescia.

Brick Cornice—Broletto, Brescia.

The size of the building is prodigious, and certainly the detail of all the parts (excepting perhaps the cornice, which is of the common arcaded kind) is most beautiful and valuable. The brickwork is so good and characteristic that I have given several sketches of it. All the arches have occasional voussoirs of stone, and the centre of the arch is always marked by a key-stone, and these are sometimes slightly carved to distinguish them from the other stone voussoirs. The abaci are of brick, moulded and very varied. The doorway given in the woodcut on the preceding page has stone jambs, caps and bases, lintel and outer arch, the label and cusps being of terra-cotta; above this the whole of this portion of the front is of brick, and very admirably built.

San Francesco — Brescia.

Of the churches of Brescia there seem to be but few of any interest; that of San Francesco, of whose west front I give a sketch, is the best, and, though not of uncommon design, is worth notice; the mixture of white and black marble and brick is very judicious; but I must protest once more against the arcaded eaves-cornices, which are very elaborate and heavy; nor can I bring myself to like the great flat gable, covering both nave and aisles, and divided only by pilaster strips, which characterizes so many mediæval Italian churches. In this west front of San Francesco the cornices and the mouldings of the small circular windows are all of brick, and the rest of the front of stone, the rose window having voussoirs of black and white marble. The only other part of the church which appeared to be of any interest was a campanile on the south side of the choir: this had stone belfry windows, well treated with simple plate tracery, and there is a singular and lofty lantern over one of the chapels on the north side of the church, all of rich brickwork dating from about 1480.

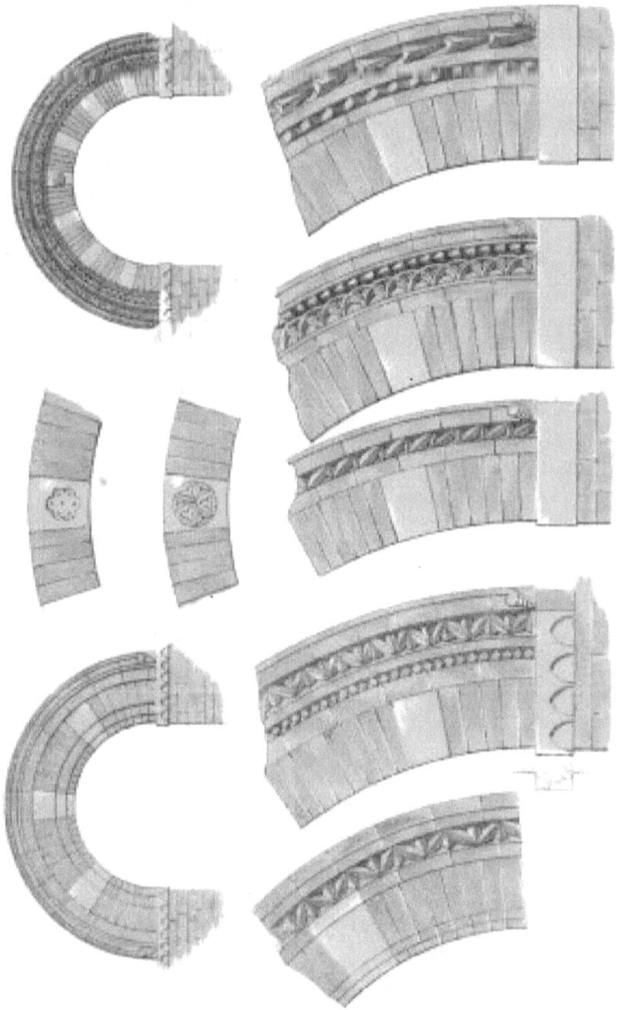

9.—Broletto—Brescia. Details of Archivolts (Details of brickwork).

The sun was at its hottest as we wandered about the streets of Brescia; but there was so much pleasure in the examination of the busy people who thronged its narrow tortuous streets, that we enjoyed it very much. In Italian towns, too, there is not much difficulty in finding the way; we ask the road to some church, and forthwith, in place of a long and not very intelligible direction, in which we are sure entirely to confuse our right hand with our left, the person we ask turns round with us, walks by our side, shews us our object, and, politely taking off his hat and bowing, takes leave of us. It was by such aid as this that we found the church of the Carmine, which is another very late Gothic church. The west front is most fantastic and unpleasing, and the pinnacles composed of round bricks, disposed alternately over each other, and common in most Italian brick buildings, are very ugly; there is, however, a good simple cloister attached to the church on the north; it is of the same design as almost all in this part of the world, having simple round shafts with carved caps and circular arches. An inner cloister which I remember of old as occupied by the ever present Austrian soldiers, is now (1872) open to all the world, and neither cared for nor used. Here the south side of the cloister is of two stories in height, the lower similar to the our just mentioned, the upper having two arches to one arch of that below, and the arches picturesquely shaped, being cinquefoils, with the central division of ogee form, and with moulded terminations to the cusps. There is a fair campanile here, with brick traceries and strings, but with a modern belfry-stage.

Cloister of the Carmine Convent—Brescia.

A little bit of cloister, or gallery, on the north side of Sta. Afra, has arcading of similar character in its upper gallery, but the arches are trefoiled.

In the Contrada della Pace there remains a very bold fragment of a castle tower. It is built of very roughly-jointed stone, and is perfectly plain till near the top, where it has a bold machicolation with tall square angle-turrets, the whole battlemented with a forked battlement. Out of the centre of the tower a tall thin tower rises to some height above the battlements.

One of the most picturesque spots in the city is the Piazza, at the end of which stands the Palazzo della Loggia; the effect on coming into it from the narrow streets in which we had been wandering was very pleasant, the large open space being surrounded with rather elaborate Renaissance work with rich coloured sun-blinds projecting from the windows over the sunny pavement, which in its turn was thronged with people in picturesque attire selling fruit and vegetables. The streets are all arcaded, and some of them have very considerable remains of frescoes on the exterior, giving much interest to the otherwise ugly walls; they have, however, suffered very greatly from exposure, and are only in places intelligible; still they give traces of brilliant external colour, and are therefore much valued in my recollections of Brescia.

Compared with Bergamo, Brescia has the air of a smart and busy place; its streets are wider and better paved, and the smells which still greeted us were not quite so bad as there. The staple manufacture of the city seems to be that of copper vessels; shop after shop, indeed street after street, is full of coppersmiths' shops; the men all sitting at work, and keeping up a ceaseless din of hammering, in open shops, so that all the world may see them. Nor is the coppersmiths' the only trade that loves publicity, for here as elsewhere the barbers' shops are very amusing, quite open in front, with perhaps a yellow curtain hanging down half way, affecting only to conceal the inviting interior, which however is always sufficiently visible, occupied in the centre by a chair, on which sits the customer gravely holding a soapdish to his chin whilst the barber operates; and this going on all day makes one think that shaving is, after all, one of the great works of an Italian's time!

When we left Brescia the heat was intense; the road, too, was deep in dust to an extent not to be understood in England. There had been a drought of some weeks' duration, and the much-travelled road from Milan to Verona, along which our way now lay, plainly told the tale which the dry, parched, cracked-looking earth on each side of our way, and the sad faces of every one as they talked about the failure of the vintage, amply confirmed. Unluckily for ourselves we had not taken the advice of our driver to have a close vehicle, but had insisted upon having an open carriage, the consequence of which piece of self-will was that we had hard work, even with the aid of umbrellas, to protect ourselves from *coups de soleil.* We now learnt that in hot weather in Italy it is not always the best plan to have as much of the sun as one can get. In England it always is, but he who acts on his English experience in Italy will surely repent his mistake.

We managed, however, to exist through the clouds of dust, relieved perhaps by the sight of a regiment of swarthy and unpleasant looking Austrian soldiers marching through the sun and dust, many of them with their knapsacks and arms, but all with great-coats on to preserve their white uniforms. When we saw them we could not help contrasting our relative lots, and then, feeling how much worse off they were than ourselves, we went on a little more contentedly than before. The road, too, became slightly more interesting; instead of miles upon miles of straight lines, we had a more winding way, and after a time occasional beautiful glimpses of the mountains which marked to us the situation of the Lago di Garda.

We drove without stopping through Donato, a place of no interest apparently save for the huge dome of its church, and then passing under a very fine viaduct resting upon a long range of pointed arches, (which carries the railway which soon after our return was opened, and now whisks only too many travellers from Milan to Venice and back without a halt on the way,) we commenced the descent towards the town of Desenzano, beyond and above whose roofs stretched the beautiful expanse of fair Lago di Garda, with its great calm surface, and fine group of distant mountains hemming in with picturesque and irregular outline, its upper end.

We soon reached the poor and desolate streets of the town, and diving into the dark court of the not over-clean looking hotel, gave ourselves up for a time to the contemplation of the quiet loveliness of the scene. The contrast between the flat shores of the lower part of the lake and the mountains which crowd around its head is very striking, and to this it is that Desenzano owes all that it has of interest. We strolled out for a short time, looked at washerwomen kneeling in small tubs on the edge of the lake, and washing their linen upon the smooth face of the stones which pave its shore, and then went on, as in duty bound, to look into the church. This we found to be neither very old nor very interesting, but curious as illustrating the extent to which, in Italy, the practice is sometimes carried of putting altars in every direction without reference to their orientation. Here the high altar and some others faced due south, whilst most of the remainder faced east, and I think scarcely one turned to the west.

The remains of an old castle rise picturesquely above the little harbour, from which steamboats sail for the tour of the lake, and bidding farewell for a time to dusty roads, let us embark on one of these for Riva at the head of the lake on our way to Trent, which is, artistically speaking, the northernmost really national city and cathedral in Italy.

Our steamboat kept to the west side of the lake, touching at a few villages and towns, and for the most part ploughing its way along beneath some of the highest and most precipitous rocks that I know. We took a band on board on the way, and discharged them into a big barge under a cliff, on the top of which was being held a village festa, at which they were to perform; and we all looked with no little compassion upon the heavily weighted performers as we saw the people who had preceded them climbing the steep mountain sides above us.

The Lago di Garda seems to me to be in its upper reach one of the most beautiful of Italian lakes. But it should always be taken in the way we went, for the contrast between the sublimity of the upper end and the tameness of the lower end is so great that nothing but disappointment would be felt by those who saw the head of the lake first.

One or two of the towns on the western shore have churches of some interest. At Salo there is a Gothic church with windows which have a wide external splay and an enriched brick moulding or label all round them. The windows are of one light, and have ogee cusped heads. Another church, at (I think) Gargnano, is of much more importance. It is cruciform, with a domical lantern at the crossing. The nave has a simple clerestory and aisles, and the west end, built in black and white courses, has one great arch which encloses the doorway, above this a lancet window, and above this again a circular window without tracery.

From Riva—one of the most pleasant resting-places on the Italian lakes—a good road through fine scenery leads to Trent, a journey of some six or eight hours. The descent upon Trent is very fine. The town standing by itself well away from the fine mountains which form the background to the view, the old walls and towers around it, and the interest of the cathedral and other buildings behind them, combine to give a sense of the importance and grandeur of the city which the facts of the case hardly justify. Perhaps, too, there is something in the historical importance of the place which, without one's knowledge, sways the judgment.

There is in fact only one building of great architectural importance—the cathedral; but, as I shall shew, it has the greatest interest, not only on account of its real merit, but also because it is a startling example of the way in which, in the thirteenth century,[11] the Lombard architects adhered to their old lessons and habits in spite of all the developments which were then universally accepted on the northern side of the Alps.

The church is a round-arched building throughout, but the mouldings and details everywhere show a knowledge of thirteenth-century work, and have none of the character of true Romanesque or Lombard art. Yet at the same time there is in many respects a most close imitation of Lombard features. There are arcades under the cornices of the aisles, arcades under the eaves of the apses, open porches supported on shafts whose bases rest on monsters, and other features which, looked at apart from the sections of mouldings and details of sculpture, might well warrant a much earlier date being fixed on for the execution of the work than I have named. An inscription which fixes the date of some works here in 1212[12] may fairly, I think, be assumed to give the date of the greater part of the fabric, though some portions, as e.g. the western wheel window and the northern porch, are probably not so early by at least a hundred years. But I am not concerned to deal with the question only from an archæological point of view, and will at once therefore go on to give some description of the building.

----

[11] I say this advisedly, though knowing very well that some German antiquaries assert this cathedral to have been built in the time of Bishop Ulrich II., A.D. 1022-1055. Those who say so must, I think, be entirely blind to all architectural detail.

[12] Anno Domini MCCXII. ultima die Februarii presidente venerabile Tridentino Episcopo Frederico de Vanga, et disponente hujus Ecclesie opus incepit et construxit magister Adam de Arognio Cumane Dioc. et circuitum ipse, sui filii, inde sui Aplatici cum appendiciis intrinsece et extrinsece istius ecclesie magisterio fabricarunt. Cujus et sue prolis hic subtus sepulcrum manet. Orate pro eis.

10.—Duomo. Trent. Eastern Doorway.

The ground-plan is in the shape of a Latin cross—with an eastern apse, two small apses to the east of the transepts, and a nave and aisles of seven bays. There is an octagonal lantern over the crossing, and the whole church is groined. The doors are, two in the east walls of the transepts, one at the west end (of marble), and one with a projecting open porch over it near the east end of the north aisle. Two western towers were intended to be built, and the staircases to them are carried up in the western and southern aisle walls in a very unusual and picturesque fashion. They commence in the third bay east of the towers, and are carried up in a continuous rise, opening to the church with a series of arches stepping up to suit the level of the staircases. The western bay to which these stairs lead is groined at a lower level, as well as at the nave level, so as to form a very lofty gallery open to the church.

The clerestory consists of very small windows, and there is no triforium; the main portion of the columns goes up to and carries the groining, and though the main arches are all semi-circular, there is nevertheless an evident attempt—and it is successful—to give an impression of height to the interior. The continuous arcades under the eaves are carried also across the front of the transepts, and give a great effect of richness to the external architecture. Of the two towers only one is complete, and this was built in the sixteenth century. The northern porch is the only place in which the pointed arch appears, and it seemed to me to be of the fourteenth century, though the doorway is of Lombard character, with very quaint but poor carving in its tympanum, of Our Lord with the four Evangelists. The whole church is built of stone, and has a Classical want of life and vigour which one notices only too often in the best Lombard work. Were it not for the building attached to its north-east angle, I suspect the general impression would be much less agreeable than it is. This is a lofty erection with two square turrets and a small apse at the east, parts of which seem to be earlier than the date I have given to the cathedral. It is connected with the north-east angle, but its axis is not parallel with that of the cathedral, and there is consequently a good deal of picturesqueness in the perspective, besides which it prevents the otherwise insipid outline of the whole building being perceived.

The porch on the east side of the south transept, of which I give an illustration, is one of the most interesting portions of detail in the building. Its front is supported on two shafts, one of which is an octagon, resting on the back of a lion, the other four shafts cut out of a single block and ingeniously knotted together in the centre, and resting on the shoulders of four sitting figures—altogether about as strong an illustration of mediæval love of change and variety as could be found. It must have been the work of a sculptor who was just a little savage with the somewhat tame uniformity of the whole of the architectural scheme of the cathedral.

I found little else to see in Trent. Sta. Maria Maggiore has a Romanesque steeple, quite plain below, but with its two upper stages arcaded, the arcades resting in the lower stage on shafts coupled one behind the other, and in the upper tripled in the same way. I do not remember before to have seen this last arrangement. A tower in the walls between this church and the cathedral is a rhomboid in plan, and was, I suppose, built of this strange shape to suit some necessity arising out of the position of streets and walls. Considerable portions of the walls remain; they are of stone, finished on the top with the forked Italian battlement, and having square projecting towers at short intervals.

Trent Cathedral and the fine church at Innichen in the Pusterthal, are quoted frequently as the two finest churches in Tyrol. That at Innichen has not the same entirely Italian character which marks that at Trent. In the latter I always feel that climate, people, and town are all in concert to make one suppose oneself in Italy, which certainly is not the case at Innichen. North of Trent the architecture of the Tyrol (as at Botzen and Meran) is entirely German, whilst in Trent itself, were it not for a steep roof here and there covered with bright glazed tiles, and a few such slight indications, no one would suspect the presence of any German influence whatever.

I have travelled so frequently from Trent to Verona by the railway that I always regard it as one of the most natural and obvious roads of approach to Italy for Englishmen. It takes its course through so fine a country that one does not easily tire of the journey, and finally, it sets travellers down in the city which, perhaps more than any other in northern Italy, charms the cultivated traveller by the beauty, interest, and grandeur of its buildings. Who that has taken this way to Verona does not remember with pleasure the last quarter of an hour of his journey, as the railway, making a circuit round two-thirds of the city, reveals first a mixed group of lofty steeples, presently the great church of San Zenone, then Sta. Anastasia, anon San Fermo, then crosses the swift-flowing Adige, and at last lands one at the station, full of anxiety to make the nearer acquaintance of the buildings of "Verona la degna," which from afar look so wondrous brave and fine?

CHAPTER VI.

Verona: Campanile of the Palazzo dei Signori—Sta. Anastasia—Monuments—Piazza dell' Erbe—The Duomo—The Baptistery—Sta. Maria l'Antica—Cemetery and Palace of the Scaligers—Domestic Architecture—Piazza di Brà—The Austrians—Ponte di Castel-Vecchio—San Zenone—San Fermo Maggiore—Chapel near the Duomo—Romeo and Juliet—Dwarfs—Wells.

"Come, go with me. Go, sirrah, trudge about
Through fair Verona."

Romeo and Juliet, act i. scene 2.

WE reached Verona in the evening, and were up early on the next morning, anxious to get a general idea of the city. But I was no sooner out of my bed than I saw from my window, over the roofs of the opposite buildings, the campanile of the Palazzo dei Signori, a lofty, simple, and almost unbroken piece of brickwork, rising, I suppose, at least three hundred feet into the air, and pierced with innumerable scaffold-holes, in and out of which, as I looked, flew countless beautiful doves, whose choice of a home in the walls of this tall Veronese tower will make me think kindly of putlog-holes for the future. Certainly, if the Italian and English principles of tower-building are to be compared with one another, the Italian need give no fairer example of its power than this simple and grand erection.

It rises, as we found afterwards, out of a large pile of buildings, and for a short distance above their roofs is built in alternate courses of brick and a very warm-coloured stone, and then entirely with brick, pierced with only one or two small openings, and terminating with a simple belfry-stage; the belfry windows, with their arches formed without mouldings, and with the sharp edges only of brick and stone used alternately, are divided into three lights by shafts of shining marble; the shafts, being coupled one behind the other, give strength with great lightness, and are very striking in their effect. These windows have, too, remarkably large balconies, but without balustrading of any kind. The upper and octangular stage of the campanile is comparatively modern, but rather improves the whole effect than otherwise.

I could hardly tear myself away from this noble work; but much more was to be seen, so I dallied not long before I set forth on a journey of discovery, giving myself up gladly to sketching and ecclesiology.

11.—Campanile, Palazzo Scaligeri, Verona.

The hotels in Verona are both of them near Sta. Anastasia, and at the eastern end of the long and at first narrow and picturesque Corso. The Adige separates the city from its eastern suburb, and from the hills crowned by the Castel San Felice and the picturesquely stepped city walls. Its yellow waves wash with an angry rush the foundations of the houses which overhang it all along its course, but the only views of it are to be obtained from the bridges, and from the open space near the Castel Vecchio. At the extreme north-western angle of the town stands the church of San Zenone. One soon finds one's self constantly on the Corso, and to the north of this lie the cathedral, Sta. Eufemia, the Castel Vecchio, and San Zenone, whilst to the south of it are the tombs of the Scaligers, San Fermo Maggiore, the Roman Amphitheatre, and the Palazzo Publico. Without further attempt to describe the map let us visit the buildings, of which the list I have given, though by no means exhaustive, includes the finest.

The Veronese architects in the Middle Ages were certainly some of the best in Italy. San Zenone is by very much the finest church of its kind that I know; Sta. Anastasia is on the whole one of the best churches of a later date; and San Fermo Maggiore affords some of the best detail of brickwork, and the tombs of the Scaligers the best examples of monuments in all Italy.

The first thing seen on turning out of the hotel is the west front of the church of Sta. Anastasia, looking so beautiful at the end of the narrow street, whose dark shade contrasts with the bright sunshine which plays upon its lofty arched marble doorway and frescoed tympanum, and lights up by some kind of magic the rough brickwork with which the unfinished church has been left so brightly, that, as you gaze, thoughts pass across your mind of portions of some lovely painting or some sweeter dream; you feel as though Fra Angelico might have painted such a door in a Paradise, and as though it were too fair to be real. There, however, it is, rich and delicate in colour, shining with all the delicate tints of the marbles of Verona, pure and simple in its softly-shadowed mouldings, beautiful in its proportions, and on a nearer approach revealing through the dark shade of its opening, and over and beyond the people who early and late throng in and out, the vague and misty forms of the solemn interior.

Sta. Anastasia is one of the most complete and representative pointed churches in the North of Italy, and deserves, therefore, a rather detailed description. Its date is about 1260 to 1290. The ground-plan is very simple—a nave of six bays, then one which is the crossing of the transepts, a very short choir of one bay finished with an apse and two chapels on the east side of each transept. The nave aisles fire narrow, and the whole design is characterized by intense simplicity of detail and arrangement. The width of the nave, and the height of the columns and arches, give, on entering, an idea of vast space and size. The columns are very simple, cylindrical in section, and support arches built of brick, and only chamfered at the edge; from the caps of the columns flat pilasters run up to the commencement of the groining, and above the nave arcades there are two small circular openings, one in the place of a triforium, opening into the roof of the aisle, the other above it and larger, filled in with plate tracery in stone, and forming the clerestory.

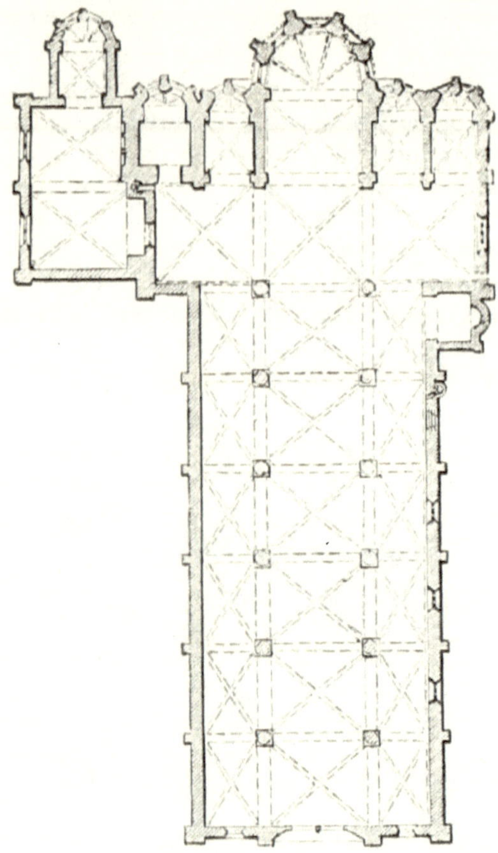

Plan of Sta. Anastasia—Verona.*

The arrangement of the plan is in several respects unlike that of northern Gothic buildings, and as most complete Gothic churches in Italy are very much of the same type, it is as well here to point out the peculiarity. The most marked features are first the shortness of the choir, and next, the fact that whereas in northern Europe it is usually the aisle vaulting bay which is square, whilst the nave bay is oblong from north to south, here the nave groining bay is square, and the bays of the aisle oblong in the direction of east and west. The difference of effect is great, simple as the statement seems. In these Italian churches there is much greater space between the columns of the nave arcades, the groining is consequently divided into much larger bays, and the whole interior has a largeness of treatment which is not common in the North. On the other hand there is much less of the complexity and intricacy which are so charming in our interiors, and you see at a glance the whole of the church.

In Sta. Anastasia the apses on each side of the choir have an even number of sides, as has also the sacristy, which is a room on a magnificent scale, to the north of the church. This is a peculiar feature, producing as it does an angle in the centre of the apse, which we shall see again at Venice and Vicenza, and which is seldom seen out of Italy.[13]

12.—Santa Anastasia. Verona. Pavements.

[13] The church of the Capuchins, at Lugo, is a Spanish example of the same arrangement.

The whole is so simple in design and construction that it depends for its rich effect on the painting which covers almost every part of it, and which harmonizes well with the architectural lines. The decorations appear to have been done, or at any rate commenced, within a short period of the completion of the church, and are therefore very valuable. The ground of the painting is white, many of the patterns of borders being very elaborate compositions of flowers and foliage. The main arches are painted to represent voussoirs of red brick and stone, but I am inclined to think that they are really entirely of brick; their soffeits, which are very broad and flat, are all painted with large scroll patterns of foliage. In the groining the diagonal ribs are painted at the intersection with stripes of colour alternating with white, and on each side of all the ribs a wide border of foliage is painted, whilst in the centre of each groining-cell some large device is painted in a medallion, some of these being merely ornamental, others having figures. The detail of much of the painting is cinquecento in its character, and not valuable as an example to be literally copied,[14] but its general effect is certainly very beautiful, and it is worthy of all praise in respect of the strictness with which it is kept subservient to the architecture, and in some respects, indeed, even serves to atone for its deficiencies, as, e.g., in the broad painted horizontal borders, which take the place, very successfully, of brick or stone string-courses, which in the construction are entirely omitted.

It surprised me, I confess, very much, to find a church painted throughout without any use of gold, and yet with good result; so it is, however; the effect is most solemn and religious, and there is a very rich effect of colour; the fact is, that the white ground answers the same purpose in a degree, though of course not to the full extent, that gold would.

But if the walls are beautiful in their colour, not less so is the pavement, which, from one end of the church to the other, remains to this day to all appearance just as it was on the day that the church was finished. The nave and transepts are all in one pattern; the spaces between the columns in a variety of beautiful designs, and divided from the nave and aisle pavements by a strip of white marble on each side; and the aisles again are on the same scheme throughout. The colours of the marble used are white, red, and bluish grey, and the patterns very simple and generally geometrical in outline, and there is a quiet richness of effect in their arrangement which is exceedingly beautiful. Such a pavement must unhappily be for ever Italian, and we in England can scarce hope ever to attain to anything so exquisite; but we do not well to forget that by the mixture of a small quantity only of marble with our encaustic tiles we should attain to much greater beauty of effect than we can by the use of tiles alone, and there are many towns—as, e.g., Plymouth—the very pavement of whose streets is of a material which might most advantageously be introduced, more often than it has yet been, inside the walls of our sanctuaries, as well as under the feet of every passer along the streets.

There are some monuments and paintings here quite worth looking at. The Pellegrini Chapel, next to the choir, has two fine trefoil-headed monuments in red marble with the background painted with subjects of about the same age (circa

---

[14] Admirable drawings of it have been published by Mr. Grüner.

1392); and in the Cavalli Chapel there is an admirably painted wall, against which has been put a monument which, though somewhat rude and coarse in its sculpture, nevertheless produces a very fine effect of colour and architecture combined.[15]

Aisle Window — Sta. Anastasia, Verona.

The window tracery of Sta. Anastasia is rather singular plate tracery, consisting of mere piercings through the stone with very little moulding; most of the windows are of two very lofty trefoiled lights with circles and trefoils pierced above, very simple and severe, and remarkable for the quaint way in which the cusping is arranged, not with some reference to vertical lines, as is ordinarily the case with us, but just as fancy or chance seems to have dictated. The clerestory windows are circular openings cusped.

[15] An extremely careful chroma-lithograph of this wall and monument has been issued by the Arundel Society, accompanied with a notice of both, written by Mr. Ruskin.

There is a curious but not very happily treated arrangement inside—a step all round the inside walls, projecting some three or four feet from them, and panelled all round against the riser with a small trefoil arcading—the whole in red marble.

Externally the church is almost entirely built in red brick with rich cornices and rather ungainly buttresses and pinnacles of brick; the windows have brick jambs with stone tracery, and on the north side of the choir is a fine lofty campanile, finished at the top with a low, very plain, and octangular capping, and unpierced with openings, except in the belfry-stage. Of the west front only the doorway has been completed; this is in courses of red, grey, and white marble, and most effective; the rest of the front is left in brick, finished exceedingly roughly, with a view to leaving a key for the marbles with which, no doubt, it was intended to veneer the entire front. The wooden framework of this door, of which I give a detail, is very curious; it is of deal, coëval with the doorway, and the framework is external, not internal.

The west front of the church stands in a small piazza, on the north side of which is the little church of San Pietro Martire, between the east end of which and Sta. Anastasia is a wall dividing a small burial-ground from the Piazzetta; on the top of this wall, and supported upon corbels, is one of those monuments peculiarly associated with Verona, because so numerous there, though they are often met with elsewhere in Italy; they are either large pyramidal canopies supported upon trefoiled arches resting on four marble shafts, with a kind of sarcophagus or an effigy beneath; or else, when attached to a wall, they have two detached shafts supporting the same kind of trefoiled arch and surmounted by a flattish pediment. Their effect is almost invariably beautiful in the extreme, and their only defect is, that they all require to be held together by rods of iron connecting the capitals of the columns. This, however, is soon forgotten when one feels that there is no pretence ever or anywhere at its concealment; and notwithstanding this slight defect, one cannot help loving and admiring them; for there is a grace and beauty about the form and proportion of the Veronese trefoiled arch, such as is never seen, I think, elsewhere, and the very flatness of the carving and the absence of deep moulding seem all adopted in order that nothing may interfere with the simple beauty of the outline of the arch. In this case the monument is supported on a large slab of stone corbelled forward and balanced upon the top of a thin wall over the archway which leads into the churchyard of San Pietro. Four shafts with sculptured capitals, resting on the angles of this slab, support four trefoiled arches, (those at the ends narrower than the others), which are almost destitute of moulding save that the outer line of the arch has a broad band of delicate sculpture all round it. The arch terminates in a small cross, and above on each side is a very flat pediment, moulded and finished on the under side with one of the favourite Italian arcaded corbel-tables; the finish is a heavy pyramidal mass of stone rising from behind the pediments. The four bearing-shafts are of white marble, all the rest of the monument of red. Within the four supporting shafts stands a sarcophagus, supported on the backs of couchant lions, very plain, but ornamented at the angles in very Classic fashion, and bearing a recumbent effigy.

Door-Frame—Sta. Anastasia.

The church of San Pietro has three or four smaller monuments enclosed within its small courtyard; two of them are on the ground and have round arches on detached shafts with an Agnus Dei carved in the centre. The third is corbelled out from the wall, and the face of the monument is covered with sculpture, that of the figures being very inferior in style to that of the foliage enrichments. This little group of monuments, varying in date from 1283 to 1392, is well worth study, and I found it more than usually interesting owing to its entire unlikeness to any English work. The church against which these monuments are built is small but deserves notice; it is of brick with a stone canopy on shafts corbelled out above the west door; the buttresses are mere pilasters, and run up without any weathering till they finish in an arcaded corbel-table at the eaves; the windows have wide brick splays outside, and trefoil heads of stone without any chamfer or moulding; on the south side, the church—in point of size a mere chapel—is divided into four bays, one of which has a monument corbelled out by the side of the window. It is built entirely of red brick, not relieved in any way, except that the window arches are in alternate voussoirs of brick and stone. The wooden framework of the west door deserves notice as being very unlike the English mode of door-framing, and very good in its effect. The accompanying sketch will best explain it: and it must be understood that, instead of being internal, as such framing would usually be in England, in this example it is external, just as in the somewhat similar door of Sta. Anastasia, of which I have already made mention.

Door-Frame—San Pietro Martire.

Turning back from the Piazzetta of Sta. Anastasia, and traversing again the narrow and gratefully shady street by which we reached it, we soon found ourselves at the end of the Piazza dell' Erbe, the most picturesque square in the city, and at an early hour in the morning quite a sight to be seen. The whole open space was as full as it could be of dealers in vegetables and fruits, all of them protecting themselves and their stores from the intense glare of the sun under the shade of prodigious umbrellas, at least five times as large as any of ordinary size, and certainly five times as bright in their colours, the prevailing colour being a very bright red. Altogether it was a thoroughly foreign scene. The houses, some ancient, but all picturesque and irregular, surrounding the irregularly-shaped Piazza, the magnificent campanile of the Scaligeri Palace rising proudly behind the houses on the left, the fountain in the centre, and the great column of red Veronese marble rising close to us, which at one time bore the winged lion—mark of the dominion of the Venetians—all combined to produce a very striking picture. An hour or two later in the day when we passed, the people, the umbrellas, and the fruit were all gone, and somewhat of the charm of the place was gone with them.

From the Piazza dell' Erbe we went to the cathedral, anxious to see and hear somewhat of a service which we found was to take place. There was a great throng of people, and we had some difficulty in finding even standing room among them; we were not at all sorry, however, to have gone, for we came in for a sermon most energetically preached, and enforcing in very powerful language the necessity of repentance. The pulpit was very large, and as the preacher delivered his sermon he walked from side to side, and often repeated again to those on his left the substance of what he had already said to those on his right. The people, who crowded every available place within hearing, were exceedingly silent and attentive; and at intervals the preacher stopped for a minute to cough and use his handkerchief, which was a signal for an immediate general blowing of noses and coughing all over the church. The *"Ebben infelici!"* with which he commenced his sermon, was a good index to its whole tone, and makes me remember with pleasure the vast crowd listening to Christian doctrine in the grand nave of the Duomo. Would that we could see any prospect of the day when in England our larger churches may be used in this way, when, with pews and all their concomitant evils swept away, we may see a vast crowd standing and sitting, leaving no passage-way and no waste room, anxious only that they may, by pressing near, join in the services at the altar, and hear every word of warning and of advice! The nave of Westminster, so thronged, would soon show how great has been our mistake in leaving our large churches so long unused.[16]

The Duomo is a really fine church, Romanesque in its shell, but altered completely internally in the fourteenth century. It has only five bays in length, but the dimensions are so large that the nave and aisles alone measure about 225 feet × 97 feet inside. There are slightly recessed Romanesque apses in the side walls, and a great tomb or shrine of S. Agatha, which is worth looking at. The columns in the interior are very lofty, of red marble, and, instead of being plain and cylindrical, as at Sta. Anastasia, are moulded with very good effect. Their capitals are, however, heavy, and the carving of the foliage on them not at all satisfactory. The whole interior is very solemn, and specially beautiful on this bright September day, with almost all the light excluded by thick curtains—here and there a stray gleam of the most intensely bright light finding its way through some chink, lighting up with sudden brilliancy the deep cool shade, and—reflected from the bright surface of some great marble shaft—suggesting the grandeur which can hardly really be seen.

The choir is divided from the nave by a screen of marble, consisting of detached columns with Ionic capitals and a continuous cornice, the whole screen semi-circular in plan, and coming forward into the nave. This, the work of Sanmichele, is certainly about the most effective work of this kind and age that I have seen.

The west front of the Duomo is still in the main in its original state. It has a rich porch supported on shafts (whose bases rest on the backs of lions), and of two stages in height, a flat pediment surmounting the upper stage. Another flat pedimental cornice is carried over the whole front at the same level; but out of this a wall rises above the central portion the width of the nave and height of the clerestory, which is again surmounted by a third flat pediment—a confused and not very graceful arrangement, which found an imitator in Palladio, when he built that ugliest of fronts, the west end of San Giorgio Maggiore at Venice.

The windows at the ends of the aisles are very Italian in their character. They are insertions in the wall of two narrow lights within an enclosing arch, which is again surrounded by a square line of moulding. The effect of this not uncommon Italian arrangement is exceedingly unsatisfactory, as it appears to make the window with its arch and tracery quite independent, constructively, of the wall

---

[16] I leave this passage as it originally stood. It is pleasant to feel how completely unnecessary it is now to use such language on the subject.

in which it is placed; it appears in fact to be merely veneered on to the face of the wall.

On the north side of the cathedral is a cloister of good detail, which was originally of two stages in height, but is now considerably altered in parts. It is exceedingly similar to the cloister of San Zenone, which we shall see presently, consisting of a long arcade of pointed arches carried on marble shafts; it is now in a very ruinous condition.

The Baptistery—San Giovanni in Fonte—is a detached church near the east end of the cathedral, which does not look as if it had been at first intended for its present use. It is a building of the twelfth century, with nave and aisles ending in three apses, lighted by a small clerestory, and with some columns which are probably Roman. The font, which stands in the centre, is of enormous size, and is sculptured with eight subjects beginning with the Annunciation and finishing with the Baptism of Our Lord. These sculptures are very rude. The bason of the font is almost seven feet in diameter, and in its centre is another smaller bason of graceful shape. I do not happen to have seen an explanation of these inner basons in the fonts in Italian baptisteries. They look as if they were meant for the priest to stand in whilst he immersed the catechumens around him.

And now that we have visited two of the great churches, we must no longer delay our visit to the church of Sta. Maria l'Antica, whose small burial-ground is fenced from the busy thoroughfares, which on two sides bound it, by an iron railing of most exquisite design, divided at intervals by piers of stone on whose summits stand gazing upward as in prayer, or downwards as in warning to those who pass below, a beautiful series of saintly figures. Within, a glorious assemblage of monuments meets the eye—one over the entrance doorway, the others either towering up in picturesque confusion above the railing which has been their guardian from all damage for so many centuries, or meekly hiding their humility behind the larger masses of their companions.

The monuments are all to the members of one family—the Scaligeri—who rose to power in the thirteenth century, and held sway in Verona until almost the end of the fourteenth. In this space of time it was, therefore, that these monuments were erected, and they are consequently of singular interest, not only for the excessive beauty of the group of marble and stone which, in the busiest highway of the city, among tall houses and crowds of people, has made this churchyard, for some five hundred years, the central point of architectural interest, but because they give us dated examples of the best pointed work during nearly the whole time of its prevalence in Verona. In the monument of the first Duke we see the elements of that beauty which, after ascending to perfection in that of another, again descends surely and certainly in the monument of Can Signorio, the largest and most elaborate of all, and, therefore, I am afraid, the most commonly admired, but the one which shows most evidence of the rise of the Renaissance spirit, and the fall of true art. Nor is it, I think, to be forgotten, as an evidence of the kind of moral turpitude which so often precedes or accompanies the fall of art, that this Can Signorio first murdered his own brother Cangrande II. that he might obtain his inheritance, and then, before he died, erected his own monument, and adorned it with effigies of

SS. Quirinus, Valentine, Martin, George, Sigismund, and Louis, together with allegorical figures of the Virtues with whom he of all men had least right to associate himself in death, when in life he had ever despised them. The inscription, which records the name of the architect on this monument, does but record the vanity of him who was content thus to pander to the wretched Can Signorio's desire to excuse the memory of his atrocious life by the sight of an immense cenotaph.[17]

The tomb of Cangrande I. forms the portal of the church as well as the monument of the first and greatest of the family. It is perhaps altogether the finest of all; the shafts which bear the pyramidal canopy are supported on corbels; between them is a simple sarcophagus sculptured with a bas-relief, and upon it lies Cangrande with his arms crossed in token of his resignation and faith. At the top of the pyramidal covering is the figure of the brave knight riding forth to war on his gaily caparisoned steed.

Next to this monument in date, as in merit, is that of Mastino II., wanting perhaps in some of the severe simplicity of the other, but even more striking, as it stands at the angle of the cemetery. It is a thoroughly grand and noble erection of two stages in height, the lower unimportant, and only serving as a means of raising the monument sufficiently high to be well seen from the exterior; upon this stand four shafts, between which, and supported upon four much smaller shafts, is the sarcophagus on which lies the recumbent effigy, at whose head stand angels with expanded wings[18] guarding the deceased. The sarcophagus is adorned with bas-reliefs—that on the west side being the Crucifixion—and has engaged angle-shafts. The four main bearing-shafts at the angles of the monument have finely carved caps with square abaci from which rise simple trefoiled arches with steep pediments on each side filled with sculpture in relief, and between these are exquisitely simple niches, each a miniature reproduction of the entire monument, and containing between their delicate detached shafts figures of saints. The whole is finished with a heavy pyramidal capping, crocketed at the angles with crockets so abominable in their shape and carving that they go far to spoil the entire work, and surmounted by the figure of the Capitano del Popolo, spear in hand, riding on his war-horse; the horse and horseman riding with their faces towards the setting sun, as all in life must ever ride; the effigy below lying so that at the last day the beams of the day-star in the East may first meet its view, and awaken him that sleepeth here in peace.

This contrary position of the figure in life and in death, observed also in others of these monuments, is an evidence of the care and thoughtfulness with which every detail of these noble works was wrought out.

The monument of Can Signorio is not worthy of so long a description; it is octagonal in its plan, and in many respects below the idea shadowed out so beautifully in the others; the reduplication of niches and gables, far from improving, only perplexes the design: and when to this is added that the carving throughout, as well as the other details, show strong signs of a leaning towards Renaissance,

---

[17] It is not a little remarkable that this should be the monument a copy of which the late Duke of Brunswick desired in his will to have erected over his grave!

[18] The wings of these angels are of metal, though the figures themselves are marble.

one may see some reason why this, the most elaborate and complicated of all the monuments, is after all far from being the most successful.

Mastino II. died in the year 1351, and we may therefore, I think, look upon his monument as a fair enough example of Italian architecture just at the period at which in England it had reached its culminating point, and a careful examination of it cannot, therefore, be thrown away. In the first place, I must notice that the sculpture, which has the air of being rather sparingly used as too sacred a thing to be idly or profusely employed, is exceedingly good. The foliage is almost always very closely copied from natural forms, is very thin and delicate in its texture, and thus really present to the gazer that idealized petrifaction of nature which it ought always to be the sculptor's effort to give, and not, as is, I fear, sometimes the case, even in good English work, so profusely scattered over the whole surface as to give one a sense of its lack of great value. The worst part of the carving is, as I have before said, that of the crockets, which are as bad as the worst modern Gothic could be. The sculpture of the human figure is throughout very good; remarkable for simple, bold, deep folds in the draperies, quite Gothic in spirit, and much more akin to our best fourteenth-century work than to any Classic examples.

As an example of the science of moulding this work is however valueless; there is absolutely no moulding upon it; and why should there be? Would it have been well that the lovely marble, whose brilliant white gloss was sure ere long to be stained with dark streaks of black by the beating of rain and the staining of age, whilst here and there the white would stand out more brilliantly than ever, — would it have been well, I say, that this should have been still further streaked with deep lines of many mouldings? Most assuredly not: the architect had to deal with a material which best takes its polish and exhibits its beauty and purity when used in flat surfaces and in shallow carving, and he did right therefore in not moulding it as he would have moulded stone.

There is a sharpness and hardness about the lines of the arches, however, which perhaps almost verges upon rudeness, and, though I can see that it may be fairly defended, I could yet wish that it might have been softened.

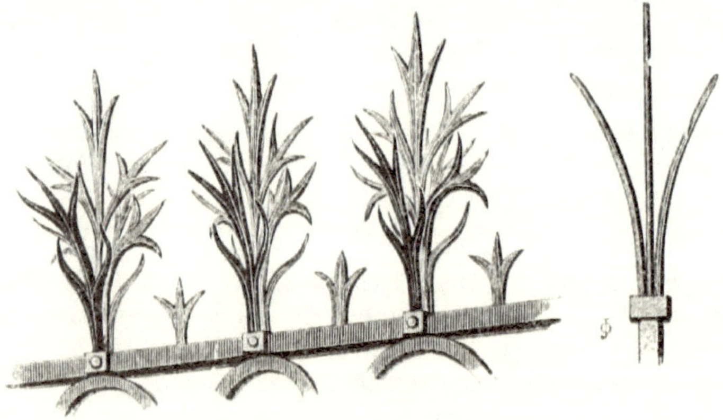

Crest of metal railing — Verona.

But the points in which such work is a grand example to us are, first, the value which it shows that we ought to place upon the simple detached circular shaft, and, next, the beauty and strength of effect which the cusping of a large arch in a proper manner gives. In these two points this monument and most of its class teach us lessons which we ought not to be unwilling to learn, and which, if we at all wish to develope beyond the point at which our own ancestors ever arrived, we must not fail to attend to in our own work.

Metal railing — Verona.

And now I must bid farewell to this lovely spot, the most attractive certainly, to me, in Verona. The situation of the monuments, rather huddled together, with the old church behind them, the archway into the Piazza dei Signori on the other side, and the beautiful iron grille[19] which surrounds them, the number of saintly and warlike figures and the confused mass of pinnacle and shaft, half obscured by the railing, do, I verily believe, make the cemetery of Sta. Maria l'Antica one of the best spots in the world for the study of Christian art in perfection. What either Köln or Regensburg Cathedral, or the Wiesen-Kirche at Söest is to Germany, the Choir of Westminster Abbey or the Chapter-House at Southwell to England, Amiens Cathedral or the Sainte Chapelle of Paris to France, such is the Cemetery of the Scaligeri in Verona to Italy—the spot where at a glance the whole essence of the system of a school of artists may be comprehended, lavished on a small but most stately effort of their genius.

Close to their burial-place stands also the Palace of the Scaligers. The old portion of this fronts towards the Piazza dei Signori, a small square used only by foot-passengers, and surrounded by elaborate Renaissance work. The buildings surround a quadrangle—the Mercato Vecchio—out of one angle of which rises the immense campanile which I have already noticed, and which is said to have been erected by Can Signorio about A.D. 1368, though I should have thought that a rather earlier date would have tallied better with its style. Besides this the most

[19] This grille is worthy of especial notice. Instead of being hard and stiff, it is all linked together, so that it is more like a piece of chain mail than of iron railing. Its intricacy adds manifold to the effect of the group of tombs which it half conceals.

striking feature is the external staircase in the courtyard, whose treatment, of a kind not uncommon in ancient Italian architecture, is very beautiful, though I fear very weak and unstable, if I may judge by the number of the iron bars by which it is held together. There are many windows here of very good detail, and an arcaded cornice all round the courtyard, and close by and also facing the Piazza dei Signori there is another fine lofty battlemented tower.

13.—Court-yard of the Palazzo Scaligeri, Verona.

In a street close to the monuments of the Scaligers, whose name I have forgotten, but in a line with the Viccolo Cavaletto, I found a most valuable example of domestic work in a very fairly perfect state. As far as I could make it out, it consisted originally of three sides of a quadrangle, the fourth side towards the street being enclosed by a wall and arched gateway. The buildings all had arcades on the ground-level, forming a kind of cloister, and the staircase to the first floor was external, and built against the wall on the road side. A great many alterations have been made in the house at various times, but in the sketch which I give I have shewn so much only of it as appeared to belong to the original foundation. In its construction pointed and round arches have been used quite indiscriminately, and in some of the arches the depth of the voussoirs increases towards the centre of the arch. This is a rather favourite Italian device, and I was always as much pleased as at the first with the effect of strength and good proportion which it produces. Most of the arches are built with alternate voussoirs of brick and stone, but beyond the outside line of the brick and stone arch there is invariably a line of very thin bricks laid all round the arch, delicately defining without pretending to strengthen the main arch, just as a label does with us. I noticed too, generally, that this thin brick was of a deeper, better colour than the other bricks, which are seldom any better than the common English bricks, and are always built with very coarse joints. This house is finished at the top with the quaint forked or swallow-tailed Ghibelline battlement, so characteristic of Verona, and which, as we found afterwards, was in use at Mantua, Cremona, and for some distance south of Verona, but which I first met with in Verona.

Doorway—Old House, Verona.

Windows—Old House, Verona.

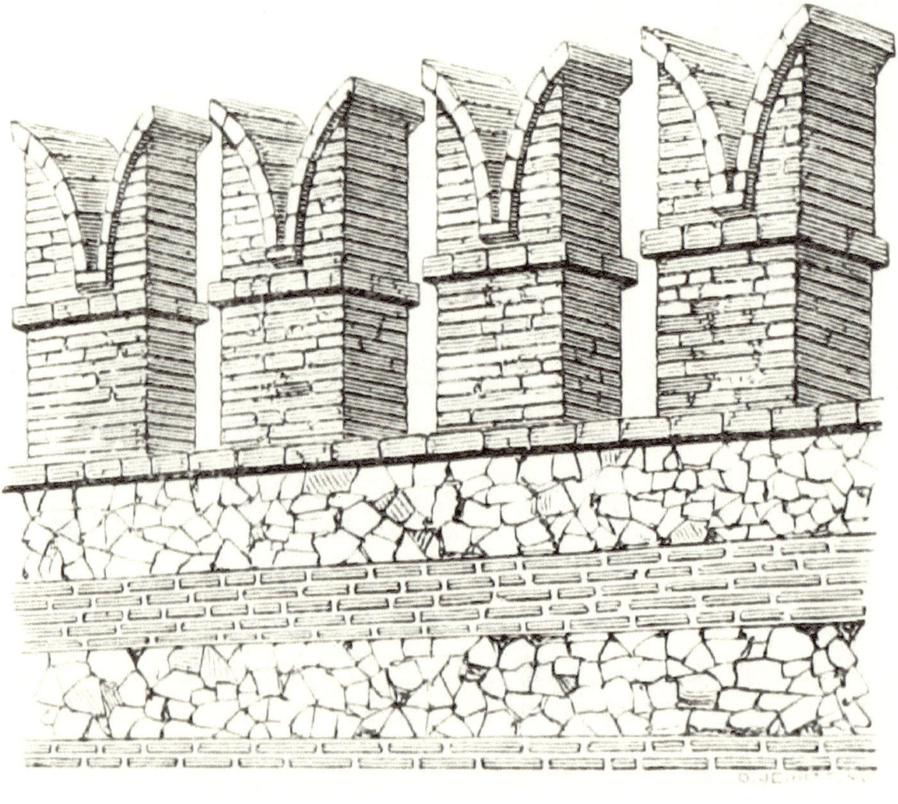

Brick Battlement—Viccolo Cavaletto, Verona.

14.—Court-yard of Old House, Verona.

I am not pretending to journalize regularly, but rather to note down the remarkable points of the various buildings as they occur to me, and, before I forget that it was Sunday when I was first looking at the Veronese churches, I must mention that in the evening we found our way to the great Piazza di Brà, surrounded by barracks and public buildings, and containing the vast Roman amphitheatre for which Verona is so celebrated. Its size is prodigious, and, except in the outer circuit of wall, it is nearly perfect; indeed, it is impossible to look upon such a vast structure without a great admiration for the men who ventured to conceive and carry it into execution.

It is difficult now to conceive how the audience could be found who would fill so vast a space; and certainly the modern efforts in this direction are mainly serviceable as shewing the immensity of the theatre. When I was last in Verona a theatre had been erected in the arena, and a performance was in progress. The audience might have been tolerably large in an enclosed theatre, but here it seemed to be the merest handful; and when we stood on the highest attainable part of the walls, we found ourselves so far from the stage as to be unable to hear a single word that was said. There is no need to describe here so well-known a building as this; suffice it to say, that though the detail of the architecture is poor, the general design and execution of the structural arrangements, and the magnificence of the whole scheme cannot fail to strike one with the same wonder that one feels in the presence of many of these great Roman works; and it is striking indeed, to see one of them so perfect as to be still capable of use, and really used.

All the Austrian portion of the inhabitants of Verona crowded the Piazza di Brà on Sunday evening to hear an Austrian military band, and we enjoyed not a little a stroll among a crowd of uniforms of all shapes, kinds, and colours. Verona more than most towns, even in Austrian Lombardy, seems to be sacrificed entirely to Austrian soldiery. It is quite melancholy to walk along a street of palaces, some of them converted into old-furniture stores, others going to ruin; and when suddenly you do come upon a flourishing and smart palace, if you look in you are sure to see an Austrian sentinel, and find that it is an officer's quarters; and equally when you meet a conveyance, if it is smart and dashing, with good horses and a stylish coachman, it is quite certain to be occupied by some dignified-looking military man. So, too, on the Monday evening, when we went to the French opera (a very pretty, tastefully got-up theatre by the way) there were absolutely none but Austrians in the house—in the boxes, officers and their wives, in the pit, subordinate officers and privates. Who can see this immense staff of foreigners in occupation of a city like Verona without feeling sadly for the people who live under such a rule, and for the ruler who is compelled to maintain such a force to keep his subjects in order?[20]

This, however, is a digression, and I must go on to describe the remaining architectural features of the old city.

On the way to San Zenone Maggiore, which is quite on the extreme western verge of the city, one passes the Castello Vecchio, a very grand pile of simple mediæval fortifications erected in the fourteenth century by Cangrande II. There are several towers and lofty walls, all topped with the forked Veronese battlement; and connected with it is the magnificent Ponte di Castel-Vecchio, a great bridge across the rushing Adige, built entirely of brick, the parapet of the regular Veronese type, and the piers between the arches rather large and angular, and finishing with battlements rather above those of the bridge. The main arch is of great size—it is said to be not less than one hundred and sixty feet—and one of the most remarkable points in its appearance is, that, instead of being in the centre, it is on the side of the river next the castle, while the other two arches, descending rapidly to the north bank of the river, give the bridge an odd, irregular, and down-hill kind of look. The architectural features of this bridge are, however, not the only objects of interest on this spot; for just after passing the castle the road bends down to the side of the river, and presents an admirable view of the campanili, steeples, and spires, with the steep hills on the opposite bank of the stream, and the mountains in the distance, with the rapid, turgid, white-looking Adige flowing strongly at one's feet.

---

[20] I need hardly say that all this is changed, and I hope changed for the better. The city looks more thriving than it did, and more of the old mansions are properly occupied than was the case in the time of the Austrians.

A longish walk through squalid suburbs leads us to the open space in front of the noble basilica of San Zenone; it is a desolate waste-looking space, and the poor, old, uncared-for church looks now as though its day was well-nigh past; as if neglect and apathy were all that men could give now where once they were wont to lavish so much of their treasure, and love, and art.

The church, as it now stands, seems to have been entirely rebuilt in the course of the eleventh or twelfth century, and its proportions are so very grand, and its detail generally so perfect, that I think it may certainly be regarded as on the whole the noblest example of its class; indeed, except the very best Gothic work of the best period, I doubt whether any work of the Middle Ages so much commands respect and admiration as this Lombard work. There is a breadth and simplicity about it, and an expression of such deep thought in the arrangement of materials and in the delicate sculpture, which with a sparing hand is introduced, that one cannot sufficiently admire the men who planned and executed it. Beyond this, the constructive science was so excellent and so careful, that with ordinary care such a church as San Zenone would seem still likely to last for ages.

The view of the west front is certainly very striking. The whole church has been singularly little modernized. By its side to the north is a fine simple red brick tower, I suppose originally belonging to the city walls; behind and near the east end of the church, but visible here, the tall and much-arcaded campanile; and on the other side the little church of San Procolo with a fourteenth-century painting of Our Lord under a gabled canopy overhanging the doorway. The west front of San Zenone is simple but dignified. The nave and aisles are finished with cornices following the flat pitch of the roofs. The walls are divided by many vertical lines of pilasters which rise from the plinth to the eaves-cornice. The main part of this front is stone, but a good deal of marble is used, e.g., the rose window has tracery of red marble enclosed within an order of white marble; the doorway and sculpture are in white marble, once much enriched with colour, and the arcaded band all across the front is of red marble. Add to this that the stone used is all of an extremely warm yellow colour, and an idea may be formed of the effort that was made here in the principal front (as often in Italian churches) to shew that God's house was the noblest that could be built.

The doorway well deserves a chapter to itself. Its lintel has illustrations of the labours of the twelve months, its jambs subjects on the right from the Old Testament, on the left from the New. In front of this door there are detached shafts standing on monsters and supporting a low canopy. An inscription on the façade "Salvet in eternum qui sculpsit ista Guglielmus," gives the name of the sculptor, the same man probably who about the middle of the twelfth century sculptured the western doorway of the cathedral at Modena. No less worthy of study are the bronze doors of this doorway. Here, as is so often the case in mediæval Italian works, we have the names of the artists employed—Guglielmo and Nicola da Figarola—with the pious expression of hope that he who sculptured the work might be saved eternally. The subjects are very rude in their detail; they illustrate subjects from the Old Testament, and are executed in thin plates of bronze nailed on to the wooden doors. A row of small windows, one in each of the many divisions of the front, extends all across near the top of the porch; whilst above is a large circular window, filled in with wheel tracery, and treated as was not uncommon as an illustration of the Wheel of Fortune. Round this window is an inscription explaining its symbolism.

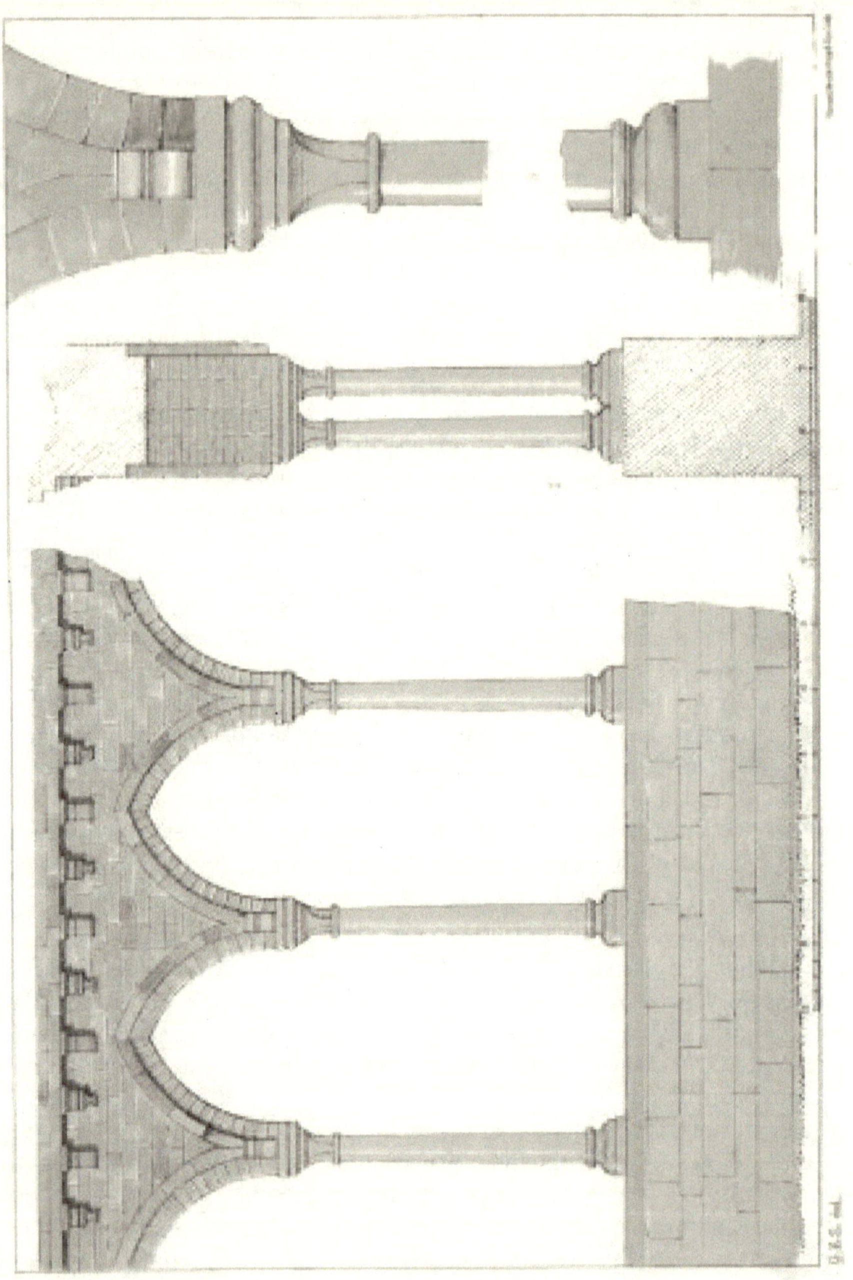

15.—Cloister of San Zenone. Verona.

We went first into the cloister on the north side of the nave. The arches are very small, and of brick, supported on coupled shafts of red Veronese marble, which have marble caps and bases, and rest on a dwarf wall of stone capped with a thin course of marble. The arch bricks are of a rich red colour, and contrast well with the brickwork of the ordinary kind above them; they are used without any kind of moulding or ornament—and yet I doubt whether I have ever seen a more lovely cloister than this. The arcades on the north and south sides have round arches; those on the east and west are pointed; and on the north is a projecting arcade of the same detail, which once formed the lavatory. The whole of this cloister is in a very sad state of filth, neglected and unused, and will, I fear, ere long become ruinous.[21]

From the cloister you enter by a side door into the north aisle of the choir; much better, however, would it always be to enter from the west, for it is there, when standing at the top of the flight of ten or twelve steps which leads down from the door to the floor of the nave, looking down the great length of the church, scanning its singular perspective of timber roofing, the great height and simplicity of its walls, and the mysterious view down into the crypt under the choir through the recently opened arches, that one feels most deeply the great and religious effect of the church. To an eye used to northern Gothic there is something very new in such a building. Its shape, its material, its arrangement, are all unlike what an English eye is used to, but I cannot say that I paused for an instant in doubt as to whether I might really admire or not; for I felt at once how very good the work was, not only in its general effect, but as much in the treatment of the details, in its colour, and in its arrangement.

The general plan is very simple—a great parallelogram, divided into a nave of vast width with northern and southern aisles; the aisles terminated with square east ends, the choir with an apse of five bays, which is, however, of later date than the rest of the church. The chief singularity in the design is the division of the piers of the main arcades into primary and secondary—the first being large heavy piers supporting great arches spanning the nave and aisles, which are finished in a line with the top of the walls; and the latter more delicate circular marble columns of very Classical character, with finely carved capitals, and looking almost too slight to support the vast height of clerestory wall which towers up above the arcade which they carry. The timber roof, or ceiling, is curious; the framing is all concealed, with the exception of the collar-beams, which connect the points of the trefoil which forms the internal line of ceiling. This trefoil outline is all boarded, divided into panels, and painted. The effect of this great length of panelled roofing, partly concealed by the great arches which cross the nave, is certainly fine. The wooden roofs of the aisles, too, are original, and their beams are painted very much like the Austrian sentry-boxes, in zigzag lines of black and buff. Much of this painting, however, did not appear to me to be old.

---

[21] This cloister is said to have been built in 1123. This is, I think, at least fifty years earlier than its real date.

16.—Interior of San Zenone. Verona.

At about two-thirds of the length of the church between the west door and the apse it is cut in two, so to speak, by that which perhaps is now the greatest charm of the interior—the crypt. When I first visited San Zenone this crypt existed, but its existence was not realized from the nave. The only access to it was from the aisles, and even here the arches were partially blocked up. A flight of steps across the whole east end of the nave led up to the choir and concealed the old entrance to it. This, it has lately been found, was originally formed by three open arches from the nave with a flight of steps descending under them to the level of the crypt, whilst two arches on either side of these gave access to it from the aisles.

This is the old scheme, and the only possible approach to the raised choir must originally have been that which has now been restored, viz., two narrow flights of steps against the side walls, so contrived as not to interfere with or conceal any part of the sculpture or other decorations on the western face of the arches to the crypt. The church as now restored yields to few with which I am acquainted in the solemn effect which is the result of mysterious light and shade, multiplied vistas of columns and arches, and picturesque originality of design. It is evidently rather a result of growth than of first intentions. The crypt—like our own remarkable example at Wimborne—seems to be an insertion. The columns and piers of the choir pass on into the crypt, whose piers and vaults are built against them. There is an obvious difference too in the style of the church and of the crypt, showing that at least a hundred years must have elapsed between the erection of the former and the insertion of the latter. The choir now occupies the three eastern arches of the old constructional nave, and beyond this has a square bay and a five sided apse, the two last divisions being groined and decorated with a good deal of colour. The apse is of the fourteenth century, but all its windows have been modernized. The crypt follows exactly the dimensions of the choir, but is divided into no less than nine bays in width, and six bays in length, exclusive of the apse. The red marble columns which support its groined roof are all monoliths, delicate in their proportions, and many of them probably antique. The vaulting is quadripartite, and there are considerable remains of wall paintings, which appear to be nearly coëval with the crypt. In the centre of this crypt is the shrine of San Zeno, half concealed by the gloomy but effective lighting, and surrounded by a metal railing made of quatrefoils, buckled or tied together, very much in the same style as the railings round the Scaligeri monuments. The altar in this crypt is worth notice on account of its sculptured front. This has in the centre a small crucifix with SS. Mary and John, and on either side, under arches, figures of the Evangelists. The face towards the nave of the seven arches which form the western part of the crypt is decorated with extreme care and finish. They are admirable examples of the really polished work of the Italian artists of the end of the twelfth century. The arches from the north aisle deserve special notice. They are carried on coupled shafts which, as well as their capital, are of red Veronese marble, the archivolt being of stone. The section of both shafts is circular, but one of them is delicately twisted to a spiral curve on its upward course. The refinement of this treatment of shafts is very characteristic of the best Italian work, and this coupled shaft, simple as its treatment is, and common as are the elements of its design, is so beautiful that it makes a real sunshine in a shady place. Not less are the arches above it worthy of admiration. The sculpture here, of a trailing branch of foliage, is very slightly relieved, but its outline is so graceful, its imitation of nature so close without being merely realistic, and its fitness for its position so complete, that I think I have never seen anything in its way more satisfactory, and certainly never anything really ornamental in the best sense, the elements of which were more severely simple.[22]

The colour of the whole interior is, to my mind, charming. It was first of all built in alternate and very irregularly divided courses of brick and stone. On this warm-coloured ground, one pious man after another came and painted what

---

[22] The sculptor of this work left his name—Adaminus—on the capital.

seemed to him best—a Madonna, a crucifixion, a saint, or a group of figures—with not much thought beyond that of making the particular work in which he was interested tell its own story well and produce its own effect. So little did he think of other men's previous work that the same subjects are not unfrequently repeated. The result is that the walls were here sober and there gorgeous, but everywhere coloured, and everywhere more or less interesting. Yet the materials of which they are built are just those which we see every day of our lives, and it was the skill of the workman, not the richness of his materials, which made his work so worthy of our admiration.

Only one portion of the church is decorated upon a regular system; this is the eastern part of the choir and the apse, which has part of its walls and its groining very elaborately painted, though with but little gold; the groining ribs are richly coloured, and on each side of them is a wide border, generally subdivided into regular geometrical figures, and the spaces between these borders are painted blue and powdered with gold stars. In the south aisle is an altar under a baldachin, supported at the angles by four clustered shafts knotted together in mid height—a capricious custom of which Italians seem to have been especially fond, and the only excuse for which, so far as I can see, is that it proves that all the shafts were cut out of one block, and therefore of more value than four plain detached shafts cut out of separate blocks could be. There is perhaps, also, a relief to the mind, after looking at a long series of similar shafts, to come at last upon some one or two marked by capricious singularity such as this. Be this, however, as it may, the eye certainly always feels inclined to admire them, though the reason is never quite satisfied; and perhaps some better excuse does exist for their use than I have as yet been able to discover. It is probable that these columns belonged originally to the baldachin over the high altar. The canopy which they now support is not old.

The vestry on the north side of the choir is worth a visit, if only for the sake of its prettily panelled and painted ceiling. Here the panels are very small, and left in the natural colour of the pine, and the ribs are decorated with white, red, and black. There is also in this room a very good fourteenth-century marble cistern and lavatory under an arch in the wall; and lastly, in the wardrobes, among many things not worth seeing, a finely embroidered bishop's mitre of the twelfth century, wrought in gold on linen. In front is a figure of Our Lord, at the back one of the Blessed Virgin, with emblems of two Evangelists on each, and a band below with figures of the Apostles, the stoles also being adorned with figures.

The arrangement of the choir shows the common Italian plan of stalls round the apse behind the altar. They are of early Renaissance character, with some relic of Gothic feeling in the traceries of the backs and elbows. There is also a good example of a square choir lectern, with a large base to contain books, and a revolving gabled desk.

Until the beginning of this century, there were only two altars in this church, one in the choir the other in the crypt. The verger told me that his father remembered the other altars being brought from a suppressed church, and erected here.

The campanile is well seen from the cloister, where it composes finely with the coursed walls of the church, and the many-shafted arcades of the cloister. It is a lofty square tower of several stages, with small pinnacles, and a low circular brick spire crowning it.

I must not leave San Zenone without mentioning the construction of the exterior, which—with the exception of the west end, which is of stone and marble—is entirely of red brick and very warm-coloured stone. The courses of stone are, as a general rule, of about the same height, whilst those of brick are very varied, some only of one course, others of four or five. The cornices at the tops of the walls, too, are very good, supported upon corbel-tables with round arches resting upon corbels, and much improved in their effect by the judicious introduction of thin deep-red bricks between the courses of carved stone, which are thus thrown out forcibly. It is in this use of red brick, and in the bold and successful way in which brick and stone are shown in the interior, that this church is so full of instruction to an English eye; and I could not see such a work without regretting bitterly the insane prejudice which some people indulge against anything but the cold, walls, chilling respectability of our English plastered walls, which to me seems to be fit only for occupation by savages.

Every time I visit this noble church, I leave it with greater regret; its exceeding grandeur appears to deserve a better fate than the spare use to which it seems now to be abandoned. To see all these painted or coloured walls, all these marble piers, and all this vast expanse of wall and roof waste and desolate, apparently not half used and never filled with a throng of worshippers, reminds me too strongly of the sad and similar fate of some of our own English churches not to awaken a sigh as I look at it. To some men it is a comfort to find that their neighbours are no better than themselves in these matters, but I confess that to my mind a great church disused is a subject only for mournful recollection, just as a noble church much used and filled with crowds of worshippers is an object for emulation and admiration. Here, in good truth, I know not where the worshippers are to come from, so decayed and forlorn is the neighbourhood.

On the way back from San Zenone into the city a small church is passed—the oratory of the same Saint—where his body is said to have rested for a time before it was taken to the Basilica. The only architectural features are of a long subsequent period, a very good circular window in the west gable, and a doorway with a pointed canopy supported on shafts above it, under which of old no doubt there was a painting.

Beside San Zenone I think the only very grand church as yet unmentioned is that of San Fermo Maggiore—a vast Romanesque basilica without aisles, but with small transepts, and a chancel and north and south chancel-aisles opening into the nave by three arches, which exactly correspond with its vast width; a not very beautiful arrangement, which we shall meet with again in the church of the Eremitani at Padua, and in others of the great churches of the preaching orders of monks.

The fabric of the east end, and the eastern half of the nave appears to be of very early date—I should be disposed to say the end of the tenth, or beginning of the eleventh century. A lofty crypt is constructed under the whole of this part, all the columns of which are square; some of them mere masses of masonry, others slender monoliths. The mouldings here are rather Roman in character than Lombard. The groining is all of brick, and very extensive remains of paintings are still to be seen throughout, the large columns having single figures painted on them, one on each face. Access to the crypt is obtained (by the clergy) from the cloister, south of the church, and by the people through a very spacious staircase entered from the outside by a door just west of the north porch. So good indeed are the means of access, that no doubt the crypt was once extensively used by the laity, for whom these stairs were specially intended. It is now not used at all—just as is the case with old crypts all over Europe—but then it is fair to say that the church is no longer served by the Regular Clergy by whom it was built, and that their conventual buildings were when first I saw them occupied by Austrian soldiers, and are now still turned, I believe, to some equally secular use. I think we may fairly assume that in 1313, when the church was restored and in part reconstructed, the old crypt was retained partly on account of its associations, and partly because of its convenience for those who might at first not quite sympathize with the novel arrangements of the church above, a great unbroken area built and contrived for the use and convenience of an order of preachers, and not for receiving a number of altars.

A monument close to the entrance of the crypt is worth notice. It represents a professor with his pupils sitting each at a desk. The books have inscriptions on them. The professor's has "Vita brevis;" a pupil, "Ars longā;" another, "judicium difficile;" and another, "tēpus fugit."

In the interior of the nave we have, as has been observed, a work which has been so much altered that it is in fact, as we now see it, a work of the fourteenth century. It is about fifty feet in width, and covered with a timber roof, constructed so as to form a ceiling of a number of cusps boarded and panelled on the under side, and tied with iron ties in place of collar-beams. Two vertical divisions of the panelling are arcaded, and filled with paintings of saints, and the whole roof is darkly stained, and richly painted. Beyond this the only very striking feature is the pulpit, which is corbelled out from the south wall about midway in its length. It is old and picturesque, and is surmounted by a delicately carved and lofty canopy—the whole in marble. It is surrounded by wall paintings of about the same age, and presents a fairly unchanged example of what such combined works of the painter and the architect were in the palmy days of the fourteenth century. These paintings are of much interest. Behind the pulpit are the four doctors and the four Evangelists seated, the ascent of Elisha in a chariot of fire, and twelve prophets with scrolls. Under the canopy is the Crucifixion.

Going to the exterior one finds on the north side two transepts, and north of the chancel a tower. East of the eastern transept and of the tower are small apsidal projections of Romanesque character, both of them in ruins and unused. The masonry here is different from that of the later work, being of alternate courses of single brick, and of stone.

The exterior of the principal apse is very remarkable, and belongs to the fourteenth century. Each side has a steep gable with elaborate cornices, mouldings, and pinnacles, partly of stone and partly of brick. The gables are built with circular bricks, and there is a cusped circular window in each gable. Seen from the bridge which crosses the Adige close to the church, this picturesque east end is one of the most picturesque things in Verona. Unfortunately the campanile does not equal in importance the church to which it belongs.

17.—San Fermo Maggiore, Verona, West Front

The west end will be best understood by the accompanying sketch. It is constructed entirely in red brick and warm-coloured stone, and I confess that it impressed me most pleasantly, as having in its four delicate lancet windows some sort of affinity to our own English work. The north porch is very fine of its kind, and the jambs of its doorway are constructed of black, white, and red marble, used alternately. The arcading against the walls is noticeable as shewing the use of thin courses of red brick for the purpose of defining the lines of the stonework.

The monuments on each side of the west door are good simple examples of a favourite Italian type. They are, as we shall see, of all dates, and even when developed to a great size, are still corbelled in the same way out of the walls. In the North of Europe, we have no analogous treatment of monumental memorials, and this rather enhances their value. The arch to the monument on the left of the west doorway is painted in a charmingly simple Giottesque style, and there is a painting also behind a modern statue in the door-arch, of Our Lord surrounded by angels. In the arcades above the monuments there were figures of saints painted, with imitations of mosaic. All these details are worth mentioning in order to give some idea to those who have not seen Verona, of the extent to which everywhere the eye is feasted with remains of early art. Indeed, one feasts uninterruptedly there on all that can delight the eye in form and in colour!

With the mention of one more church I believe I may bring my notes in Verona to an end, and this is a small chapel which stands just opposite the south side of the Duomo, and whose name I could not learn. It is much like San Pietro Martire in its general arrangement, but remarkable for the exquisite beauty of its windows, the arrangement of the bricks and stonework in which is beyond all praise. These windows are constructed with trefoiled heads of stone, enclosed within an arch of mixed stone and brick, round whose outer edge runs a band of delicate terra-cotta ornament. The spandrels of the trefoils are filled in with refined sculpture, instead of being pierced with the dark eye usually found in northern Gothic. There is, too, an entire absence of mouldings, yet, notwithstanding this, the general effect is one of combined delicacy and richness of no common kind, so much does carefully-arranged and contrasted colour do for architecture. A third window is entirely of brick, save the trefoil head of the opening. The side elevation of this little chapel is very singular in its whole arrangement; there are three bays divided by pilasters, which finish at the top in an arcaded cornice of brick; in each of the two western bays is a lancet window, and the centre bay has in addition a doorway, and a corbelled out monument above it; in the eastern bay the window looks just like one of those curious English low side windows, as to the use of which we have had so many ingenious theories; the east end has no trace of any window, and is finished with a flat-pitched roof, and a brick corbel-table running up the pediment. There is no stone used except in the window-heads and arches.

There are many other churches in Verona on both sides of the river, and into several of them we went, but without finding any of equal merit to those which I have already noticed. Santa Eufemia has a fair west front, of late pointed, and we found one or two good cloisters just like those mentioned at Brescia. Other churches have fronts built, and interiors remodelled, by Sanmichele and his successors, in a style which by no means approved itself to me; others there which I did not succeed in reaching,[23] and there is one dedicated in honour of S. Thomas of Canterbury, which is not, however, otherwise of any interest; it has a very late Gothic west front, of poor character.

---

[23] The most important of these is the interesting church of San Stefano in the suburb on the opposite side of the Adige. It has been much modernized, but has still, I believe, an early crypt and an octagonal steeple over the crossing of the same age as San Zenone.

18. — Italian Brickwork.

1. 2. Windows at Verona.
3. Cornice S. Ambrogio, Milan.
4. Cornice Broletto Brescia.
5. Windows in Broletto, Monza.
6. Wall Arcade S. Fermo Maggiore.

It is impossible to walk about Verona without meeting at every turn with windows whose design is similar to those so often seen in Venice, but the execution and arrangement are generally so inferior here to what they are there, that I shall defer saying much about them until I am describing the palaces and ancient buildings of Venice. They are almost always finished with ogeed trefoils at the top, and are arranged singly, or in couples or more together, and one above the other, the same in each story of the house; their mouldings are thin and reedy, and the carving of their finials, when they have any, is very poor. Examples of these windows will be seen by most travellers in the rooms of the Albergo delle Due Torre.

Domestic Window—Verona.

The views from the bridges across the Adige are very striking. The main part of the city is on the right bank, and the river describes nearly a semi-circle round it. The opposite bank is only partially built over, and has a largish suburb, upon rather rapidly rising ground; beyond this the walls of the city are seen with occasional towers, and marked all the way by their serrated battlements climbing the irregular outline of the hills in the boldest fashion. Then crossing over to the other side and turning round, you see the thickly-built city full of towers and churches rising far above the turmoil of the crowd below into the pure sky, and, by their number and size, making Verona one of the most striking old cities I know.

Of course no one goes to Verona without thinking of Romeo and Juliet. I fear, however, that when I was shown the Casa de' Cappelletti, a small inn in a narrow street, and asked to connect it in any way for the future with the creation of Shakespeare's brain, my fancy refused to be sufficiently lively to perform the required feat. The simple fact is that, real relics not existing, the good people of Verona have wisely met the demand which Shakespeare has created, and have discovered a tomb for Juliet, and other reminiscences of the fair Veronese, which I dare say satisfy very well the majority of travellers.

At Verona, as in the other towns through which we passed in Italy, we were quite astonished at the number of misshapen dwarfs that we saw; we could not account for this at first, but I suppose it is because children, until they can walk, are tied up in rolls of linen so stiffly as to deprive them of all power of motion. The only wonder is how any of these unfortunate children ever manage to walk at all.

In the courts of the houses at Verona there are generally wells, with ingeniously contrived arrangements for enabling the occupants of the various surrounding houses and balconies to let down their buckets for water without themselves going down to the wells. There are guide-ropes to the well from each angle of the courts round which the houses are usually built, along which the buckets run, suspended by rings and held by ropes from the balconies, until they reach the iron-work over the well, and then fall perpendicularly down to the water.

I have visited Verona many times, and each visit seems to me to give greater pleasure than the last. I fear I have given but a faint idea of the indescribable charm which it has to all who are fond of early art. There is little which one can compare with the situation and surroundings of such cities as Venice and Florence, and yet I suppose most travellers would agree with me in reckoning the interest of these three towns as not far from equal, and greater in very many ways than that of any other Italian cities.

On this first journey we were driven away by bad weather which, when it sets in, generally continues for several days, and we left, inwardly resolving that no long time should elapse before we returned—a resolution which has been abundantly and often fulfilled—and as the waiter at our hotel honestly told us that we should be very likely to find fine weather at Padua, whither we were next to journey, we took his advice, and then, getting into an omnibus contrived to hold thirty persons, and I should say at least twenty feet long, with four horses harnessed with long drawn-out traces to increase the already prodigious length, we were soon at the terminus of the Verona and Venice railway.

CHAPTER VII.

"'And whither journeying?—'To the holy shrine
Of Saint Antonio in the city of Padua.'"

Rogers.

MANY of the villages near Verona are remarkable for the remains of castles of the middle ages. I have never, however, been able to find time for the examination of any of them, and, judging from hurried views which I have had of three or four castles south of Verona, I suspect that they would scarcely repay a long détour; they seem generally to be more remarkable for their general contour, and their quaint forked battlements, than for any of that delicate detail and appliance to ordinary wants which it was especially my object to see and study.

The railroad from Verona to Vicenza and Padua is not interesting; the country is beautiful and luxuriant in detail, but rather tame, flat, and over-green in the general view. The Veronese mountains, however, are in view on the north, and as one approaches Vicenza the hills throw out their spurs into the flat country, covered with vineyards, orchards, and fruit trees; village follows close upon village, each with its white church and white campanile, contrasting strangely with the rich colour above and around, and at last the towers and roofs of Vicenza are descried on our left.

And is it possible, my readers will exclaim, that you, an architect, can have dared to pass within sight of Vicenza without making long sojourn there to drink in the lessons which the works of your great master Palladio are there to instil! Even so, reader; for in this world there are unhappily two views of art, two schools of artists—armies of men fighting against each other; the one numerous, working with the traditions and rules of their masters in the art, exclusive in their views, narrow in their practice, and conventional in all their proceedings, to the most painful forgetfulness of reality either in construction or in ornament; the other young and earnest, fighting for truth, small in numbers, disciples of nature, revivers of an art to all appearance but now all but defunct, yet already rising gloriously above the traditional rules of three centuries. The one class representing no new idea, breathing no new thought, faithful to no religious rule; the other rapidly endeavouring to strike out paths for themselves as yet untrodden, gathering thoughts from nature, life from an intense desire for reality and practical character, faithful moreover to a religious belief, whose propagation will be for ever the great touchstone of their work. The one class, the disciples of Palladio, journeying towards Vicenza with a shew of reverence to learn how he built palaces of compo with cornices of lath and plaster, already in two short centuries falling to decay, wretched and ruinous! the other stopping long at Verona, dreaming over the everlasting art of the monuments of the Scaligers, and of the nave of Sta. Anastasia, still, though five centuries have passed with all their storms about their heads, fresh and beautiful as ever, fit objects of veneration for the artist in all ages!

A disciple, therefore, of the last of these two schools, I stayed not longer at Vicenza than was necessary to satisfy myself of the truth of the charges against Palladio's work there, and to note the few, but interesting, mediæval remains. The situation of the city is beautiful. Near it to the north are mountain ranges, and where these descend into the plains there are smaller hills covered everywhere with luxurious vegetation. The first view of it is also very fine. In front is the old brick tower at the Porta di Castello, with its deep brick machicoulis sloping boldly outwards, and finished with a square battlement under a flat roof. Beyond this are seen the steeples of the city, and highest among them the Torre dell' Orologio, a tall slender brick tower in the Piazza dei Signori, in the centre of the town. The most important Gothic churches are the Cathedral, San Lorenzo, and Santa Corona. They seem all to be in very much the same style—one derived no doubt from Venice, as we shall see when we arrive there. The plans usually are of this kind. The bays of the nave are square in plan, those of the aisles oblong in the direction of the length of the church, the choirs apsidal, and the chapels on each side of them also apsidal, but with an equal number of sides so that there is an angle in the centre. The transepts are square-ended, the sacristy at the end of one of them, and the tower at the side of the chancel aisles. The Cathedral departs from the type of plan just mentioned, but is, I think, the only exception to the rule. It has a very wide nave without aisles some 55 or 60 feet in the clear, but it has been so much repaired and altered that it is now very uninteresting. Good effect is obtained by the very great elevation of the altar which is raised above a crypt, the entrance to which is by flights of steps on each side of the steps which lead up to the choir. The exterior is mainly of brick save at the west end, which has an arcade of stone with a doorway in the centre division.

This kind of west front is repeated in the more interesting church of San Lorenzo, which is finished with one vast gable in front of nave and aisles, and has for its lower stage an arcade of seven divisions, with a fine pointed doorway occupying the three central arches. This part of the front is mainly of stone, with enriched members round the arches in brick, and it is divided from the upper stage by a corbel-table. The gable is of brick with a large stone circular window in the centre, and five smaller circular windows following the line of the flat gable which crowns the whole. I was not much impressed by this design, the only virtue of which is a certain amount of simplicity and breadth.

19.—Porta di Castello. Vicenza.

The interior of San Lorenzo is lofty and spacious. The nave and aisles alone measure about 150 feet by 90, and there are spacious transepts, choir, and chapels. The columns are circular, and have capitals so badly carved that it is somewhat difficult to say whether they have shells or tufts of foliage for enrichment. Very small circular windows in the clerestory, and a groined roof, complete the design. The best portion of the exterior is, I think, the elevation of the bays of the nave aisles. Here there are two simple trefoiled lancets with a shallow buttress between them, and a circular window above in each bay. This design is refreshingly pure and simple. The steeple is on the east side of the north transept. It is of six stages in height, the stages being marked by slightly sunk panels, and corbel-tables under string-courses, which are formed by a pattern in the bricks, not by any projecting moulding, so that the straight outline of the steeple is not broken. The result is not particularly good.

Santa Corona has, like the other churches, a single gable in front of the nave and aisles, with a western doorway and a large circular window above. I have a recollection of it as of one of the most ungainly of fronts. The campanile here is much like that of San Lorenzo, but has a low octagonal belfry-stage finished with a small circular brick spire.

Santa Corona may well be more visited, for a picture by John Bellini than for its own merits. This is a picture over one of the altars in the north aisle representing the Baptism of Our Lord—one so quiet and beautiful in colour, so dignified and solemn in its design, that it is impossible to admire it too much. Behind the group of angels who hold Our Lord's garments, is a mountain landscape such as one sees from Vicenza. It is a sublime work. The marble reredos is coeval with the picture: it is furnished with two low screen walls right and left of the altar, a common and proper arrangement for its protection when, as here, the altar stands in the aisle itself and not in a chapel.

I did not find any other church worth noticing, and soon made my way to the Palazzo della Ragione. The great feature of this building is the enormous hall, no less than 72 feet wide inside, and covered with a great arched timber roof boarded on the under side, and divided into vertical panels by bold ribs painted black and white. This roof is held together by two tiers of iron ties, and being arched and boarded at the end as well as at the sides, has somewhat the look of the inverted hull of a great ship. The effect is imposing, though at the same time it is somewhat gloomy, owing to the absence of all high light.

This great hall was Gothic inside and out until Palladio cased the front with open arcades, standing out from the walls and entirely concealing from below the old windows. These were large single lights with moulded jambs, but not of very good style. The original staircase remains with good marble shafted balustrades. The old work here is said to have been done before the year 1444, the hall having been burnt in 1389. This date is of some importance, as the walls of the upper portion are faced like the upper stage of the Ducal Palace at Venice, with marble arranged in a diaper.

20.—Houses in the Contrada Porto. Vicenza.

The slender and lofty tower of brick which rises at one end of the building, the two Venetian columns (Vicenza became subject to Venice in 1404), and the Palazzo itself, in spite of its small architectural merit, combine to make a charming picture, rendered more beautiful when I saw it, by the animated crowd of peasants who filled the Piazza. The streets here are very picturesque, rather in spite of Palladio and Scamozzi than in consequence of what they did. Some of them are arcaded, and the Gothic houses are still very numerous. They are all, however, of late date—at least I saw none earlier than about 1350. They are of the same design as some of the well-known Venetian palaces, only here they rise out of narrow streets, instead of as they do there from the water. The usual arrangement is to have on the ground floor a single doorway, not necessarily central, and on the *piano nobile* a fine traceried window with balconies in the centre, single windows also with balconies near the angles, and intermediate windows of the same design but without balconies. These are always treated in the same way with small shafts, and with animals seated on their angles, and are supported on bold corbels. All the carving that I saw was weak and confused in outline, and poor in detail, and the capitals are generally too large for the arch mouldings which rest on them—a common fault in Italian Gothic work.

I give a view in the Contrada Porto which illustrates two of the best of these houses. Almost the whole of this street happens to consist of houses of the same age, and one of them has on one side of its internal courtyard open arcades on each story, the upper one having its balustrades remaining between the columns, similar in design to those in window-balconies.

In their original state most of these houses seem to have been left in red brick, the windows being of stone, with thin white marble slabs fitted into the spandrels above the arches. Projecting balls of marble are often fixed in front of this marble lining. Some houses seem, however, to have been plastered almost from the first with a view to painting, and I can hardly say a word against such a plan, with the recollection of the glowing—in spite of their being faded—tints which one still sees at Brescia, Genoa, and elsewhere in Italy. But where the house has architectural features, which are at all good of their kind, the painter is very apt to ignore them entirely in his work, so that what was meant to be a good piece of architectural work, becomes in the end a badly cut-up ground for a painting. Where there is no architectural detail to be spoilt, any amount of painting may be lavished on an external wall; and I know few examples which better show with how much good effect it may be done than the great house of the Fugger family in Augsburg, which many Italian tourists now-a-days may see and admire on their way to or from Italy. The other objection to external painting is its evanescent character; but good colour is beautiful even in its decay, and I suppose the best artist will paint what will do most good to his own generation, and trust to his successors for doing as much for their own times!

One of the most fanciful houses in Vicenza is the Casa Rigafetta, below the Palazzo Pubblico. The ornaments are not pure, and there is too much straining to make the most of an opportunity by putting everything possible into a small space, but still the whole is decidedly pretty. The balconies here are in plan half a quatrefoil. Near this house is one with carved angle-shafts, a feature which I do not remember to have seen in Venice.

Palladio's works are supposed now to be the glory of Vicenza. I cannot forgive the artist who did not care to give solidity to his work, and the power of executing a vast amount of enrichment in the cheapest way, and with the commonest materials, is about the greatest snare into which an architect can allow himself to fall. I am well aware that Palladio was not the inventor of trumpery modes of construction. His admirers might quote the architects of Pompeii fifteen hundred years before him, as offenders in the same way, and the curious preservation of their works as the justification of their offence; but Palladio followed after men of his own kind and craft who for centuries had studiously endeavoured to do their work honestly, and he deserves, therefore, all the hostile criticism of those who object to a revival of bad practices which in our own day and country have done more real damage to architecture than anything else that can be named.

One only of Palladio's works interested me, and this rather as a curious experiment than as a work of art. This is the Teatro Olimpico, a famous open-air theatre. There is first of all a semi-circular auditorium open to the sky, and only remarkable for a mean arrangement of pilasters at the back. The great object of interest is the stage, on which a permanent scene has been constructed by Palladio. In order to make this look much larger than it really is, the streets, palaces, and temples which are represented are built in perspective. To accomplish this the stage rises very rapidly, the buildings are squeezed up, and built in sharp perspective, so that in the end a triumphal arch, which is really forty feet from the front, looks as if it were four hundred. Should an actor by any chance so far forget himself as to walk into what looks like a practicable street, in a minute he would find himself able to shake hands with the statue on the top of the arch, the illusion would be entirely destroyed, and the scenery would all look like a collection of dolls' houses. As an ingenious deception from one point of view, and under certain conditions, the scheme is successful, and probably this is as much as Palladio himself would have claimed for it.

We had now seen all that we cared to see in Vicenza, and gladly found ourselves again *en route*. There was nothing to see on the road, and we were not sorry when our engine gave token by its whistle of our approach to Padua. The omnibus discharged us in a few minutes at the hospitable doors of the Stella d'Oro, and we were soon out again with the view of making the most of our time.

Padua, when I first saw it, seemed to me to be a most melancholy city; grass grew in the streets, the footways were all formed under dark and dismal arcades, and not only the externals of the half-occupied palaces, but those even of all the houses, looked squalid, dirty, and miserable; nor was there any relief when one got into the more open spaces, for the large piazze on either side of the Palazzo della Ragione, or townhall, looked as squalid and uncared-for, as dirty and unprepossessing, as they well could; nor was this universal squalor rendered at all less remarkable by the fact that Padua rejoices in a caffè, which is said to surpass any other even in Italy, for its smartness; and the array of well-dressed gentlemen who frequented it, certainly made the neighbourhood look more wretched by contrast than it otherwise would.

The Caffè Pedrocchi was however soon passed, and our first object was the Palazzo della Ragione, whose vast and singular hall, about two hundred and fifty feet long by ninety feet wide, is one of the greatest architectural curiosities in the city. Its exterior has been modernized, so that now it is only remarkable for its long expanse of roof, but the interior is still in its original state. The access to the Hall, which in this and other respects much resembles that at Vicenza, is from external arcades on the first floor, to which four staircases lead from below. The walls are low, and covered with paintings arranged in arcaded panels; some of these are said to be by Giotto, and the whole of them, I believe, were at any rate painted in his time, but have probably been repaired and retouched extensively long since. The windows are small, low down in the walls, and admit scarcely more than sufficient light for the lower part of the hall. The roof shews in section a vast pointed arch of timber, boarded and divided into panels by a succession of heavy vertical ribs scarcely at all moulded. The construction is obviously so weak as, from the very first, to have made the iron ties which hold it all together absolutely necessary. A curious feature in the design is, that instead of having gable walls the roof is hipped, and shews therefore at the end just the same section as at the sides. What little light finds its way into the dark obscurity of the roof is admitted through some small dormers high up in its framework. The effect of the hall is gloomy, and, compared to our own great halls, certainly shows some lack of knowledge of construction on the part of its architect, and its bald heaviness makes it absurd to compare it to our own noble Westminster hall, though their very similar dimensions might naturally tempt us to do so. It dates from about the beginning of the fourteenth century, and the story runs that it was designed by a certain Frate Giovanni, who, travelling in India, saw the roof of a great palace the construction of which so pleased him that he brought back drawings of it with him, and erected its fellow here in Padua. How much truth there is in this tradition I cannot say, but this much seems clear, that in some way Padua has, if not a very beautiful, at any rate a very remarkable Sala, and one which is quite unlike any other room in Europe, with the single exception of the corresponding room at Vicenza, which no doubt copied from it.

It has been burnt and damaged in one way and another repeatedly since it was first built, and in the course of the restorations the paintings on the walls have been excessively damaged, in many parts repainted, and in some obliterated altogether. The work was commenced at any rate, if not completed, just at the time that Dante and Giotto were together in this part of Italy. The walls are all divided into four panels in height by borders, with painted pilasters for vertical divisions, and the panels are generally arched and cusped. The paintings include the apostles, the signs of the zodiac, representations of the months, the planets, and the constellations. The whole scheme is far too complex to be intelligible without a key. This fortunately is accessible in the very careful and complete account of all the subjects of the paintings on the walls which was prepared in 1858 by Mr. W. Burges, and printed in the 'Annales Archéologiques.' With infinite pains he made out the meaning of the whole of the figures—no light task, as the walls being divided by painted borders and arcades into several stages in height and an almost interminable number in length, spaces are provided for some four hundred subjects.[24]

At one end of the hall was the chapel of San Prodoscimo, formed I presume by screens. The judges sat round the hall, forming so many courts in one room. At the opposite end was a cage or prison, so that here, under one roof, with walls covered with illustrations, sat all the courts of Padua, without any of those ingenious

---

[24] See also 'Pietro Brandolese, Scultura, Pittura, &c., di Padova.' Padova, 1795.

divisions and subdivisions which are now necessary for the administration of the very smallest sort of justice, and it may be hoped with as much honesty as there certainly was simplicity.

Now-a-days the hall is quite unused save as a receptacle for lumber, of which the most remarkable example is the remnant of a gigantic horse made by Donatello to travel on rollers in some old Paduan pageant.

From the Palazzo della Ragione, we found our way to what must, so long as it lasts, be the great glory, as it is the chief charm, of Padua—Giotto's Chapel, founded in 1303.

Arena Chapel—Padua, West End

This stands in private grounds and on one side of a desolate green walk which leads up to a private house to which it now forms an appendage. From the first it was a little private chapel, and in no respect remarkable for size or costliness of material or design. The plan is a simple oblong nave with an apsidal chancel, and a sacristy on the north side, and nothing can be simpler than the exterior. The walls are of brick, divided into bays by narrow pilasters. The west door is round arched, as are also the windows. The interior is even more simple; the whole nave has not a moulding, the walls are continued on into the semicircular ceiling without any cornice, and all the ornament is added in colour.

The windows all have a deep splay outside, very simple stone traceries, and glass fitted to wooden frames placed inside against the stonework. There seem also to have been shutters outside, for which the hooks still remain. A sort of pent-house, or perhaps a cloister-roof was carried along in front of the chapel, but of this nought remains but the corbels which carried it. There is no more to be said about the exterior than that it is simple and good of its kind—the kind being very humble.

Let us go inside, and we shall pass a very different verdict. Giotto is to many of us not only a person singularly gifted in a great age, but in some sort the embodiment of an idea. The idea is that of an artist, pure, simple, and direct in his work, who should excel equally in all the arts, and show—even though his work be an exception to all rules—the consummate success of such a course. The man was fortunate in his day and in his friends. Here, where we stand to admire, he painted, whilst probably Dante looked on. For merely human and artistic interest there is, therefore, no room which more rightly deserves to be the object of endless pilgrimages; and there is none in which one will find the artist more faithful to his calling, more full of recollection and self-restraint than in this.

I know, therefore, no one building, of such very small size and cost, which can claim the same degree of interest as this small Chapel of the Arena. It is, indeed, one of the glories of art that the works of its great masters cannot diminish in value, or even be competed with by subsequent masters: when once done, they are done for ever; and so the Pietà of Giotto, in this little chapel at Padua, is now—as it was when first painted in the commencement of the fourteenth century, and as it will continue to be so long as the neglect with which it is now treated allows it to exist—one of the great paintings of the world, one of those fountains from which school after school and age after age of artists may drink instruction and knowledge, and never fail to gain more, the more they study its many excellences, and its intensity of feeling and conception.

Side Window—Arena Chapel.

The architectural portion of the interior may be first of all described. The apse is simply a sanctuary, and the chancel is formed by marble screens on each side of the nave, leaving a broad entrance-way between them, and enclosing about one-third of its length. Against the west side of these screens are altars, each with a small carved marble reredos; whilst on the east of them are steps leading to the two ambons; that on the north being a book-rest, carved in marble, and fixed with its face to the east; that on the south of iron, and turning upon a pivot. Between these screens and the sanctuary arch are modern stalls on each side. The sanctuary has seats all round the apse (except in the eastern bay), each with a delicate white marble canopy. The sacristy is groined, and has a thirteenth-century press of wood of a design rather curious than beautiful, but very rich in its detail. In the nave, as I have already said, walls have neither cornices nor string-courses to break their even surfaces, and their face is continued on in semicircular waggon vault. There are six lancet windows on the south, none at all on the north, and a three-light window very high up in the gable at the west end above the doorway.

The architectural merit of the building is simply, I think, that it performs satisfactorily the office of giving ample unbroken surfaces of wall for paintings.

The arrangement of these is very regular. The vault is divided into two parts by wide coloured borders, the space between which is painted blue, powdered with gilt stars, and in each bay there are five small medallions with figures on a gold ground. The side walls are divided by borders into three divisions in height; the upper division containing subjects from the life of the Blessed Virgin; the central, those illustrative of the life of Our Blessed Lord; whilst those nearest to the ground are representations of the Virtues and Vices opposed to each other; the last division tinted only in one colour, the others richly painted in bright colours upon a field of blue.

The borders which divide the paintings are very well designed, their patterns being always very clearly defined with white leading lines, and a line of red on either side always accompanying each line of white. The paintings themselves are very wonderful; there is an earnestness of purpose and expression about them such as one rarely meets with; each subject is treated with a severe conscientiousness, not always conventionally where a departure from strict rule is for any reason necessary, but still, generally speaking, in accordance no doubt with the ancient traditional treatment. This, illuminated as it is by the thought and love and earnest intensity of feeling which Giotto lavished on all that he did, makes his work here the most perfect example of a series of religious paintings that I have ever seen. Of course in such a large series of subjects there must be great variety of excellence, and I am content to agree with the rest of the world in awarding the palm of excellence to the Pietà, in which the expression of intense feeling in the face of the mourners over the body of Our Lord is certainly beyond anything of the kind that I know.

The series is very complete, and, beginning with the history of Joachim before the birth of the Blessed Virgin (the seventh subject), is continued down through the leading acts of Our Lord's life to the descent of the Holy Ghost on the day of Pentecost;[25] whilst the west wall is occupied by a Last Judgment; and throughout

[25] Since this was written the whole of these subjects have been published by the Arundel Society, and Mr. Ruskin's notice of them has also been given to us: they are very valuable as exemplifying, as well perhaps as colourless engravings can do, the exceeding

the subjects Our Lord, the Blessed Virgin, and the apostles are always represented in vestments of the same colour.

Most of these paintings are in very perfect condition, and the *tout ensemble* is nearly as charming as it was when first painted. I was sorry, however, to notice some of the paintings lined all over by a recent copyist, and much damage has been done by damp, especially in the Last Judgment on the west wall. I do not care very much for the painting on the lower part of the walls. The figures of Virtues and Vices are very finely designed, but the imitations of marbles and mouldings painted in perspective were, I hope—being the last work to be finished—done after Giotto had completed his work.

Close to Giotto's Chapel stands the great, and to an English eye, singular church of the Eremitani. It has a very broad nave of immense length, unbroken by aisles, and roofed with one of the cusped roofs already noticed at Verona, in which the real construction is (with the exception of the tie-beams) entirely concealed by boarding on the under side; this boarding being generally arranged in a succession of large cusps or curves; the effect here is, I think, very heavy and unsatisfactory, but we must bear in mind that the span is prodigious, and the pitch of the roof very flat. The chancel and an aisle on either side of it open into the east end of the nave with three arches, and look so small as to be more like mere recesses than important integral parts of the plan. There are in this church a great many frescoes and paintings of much interest—among which are some by Mantegna in a chapel on the south side of the nave which are worthy of careful study as being, probably beyond almost any other wall paintings which exist, an evidence of the fact that interest in treatment of subject, drawing and design of consummate excellence, perspective and decorative colouring of the walls, may all be included in a fresco without interference with the wall surface, or indulgence in tricks of chiaroscuro, without which no painter now seems willing to do his work. Yet if Mantegna cheerfully accepted such rules for his wall-painting, would it be beneath modern painters to do the same for theirs, and could they ask for a better teacher or guide than this consummate artist?

Less interesting to the artist than these works of Mantegna are the paintings in the apse executed by Guarienti in the middle of the fourteenth century. Here are figures of the planets: the Sun, Moon, Venus, Mercury, Mars, Saturn, and Jupiter, each with allegorical figures, male and female, of the Seven Ages of Man influenced by the planets.[26]

At the west end of the nave is a great painted Rood, one of those curiously shaped crosses meant to receive a painting of the Crucifixion instead of a carved figure, and cut round with quaintly carved and crisped indentations, of which so

---

value and originality of this series of paintings. It is to be wished that they may produce some effect upon the minds of our modern artists, who much require to take home to themselves the lesson of sincerity and earnestness of purpose, combined with the highest kind of subject, which Giotto so eminently exhibits in all his works. An extremely good series of photographs of the whole of these paintings may now also be obtained in Venice.

[26] The order of the planets attached to the seven ages is as follows:—I. The Moon. II. Mercury. III. Venus. IV. The Sun. V. Mars. VI. Jupiter. VII. Saturn.

many examples remain, though they are generally found now in picture galleries. This no doubt stood originally on a Rood beam, where one sees such a Rood represented in one of the wall paintings in the upper church of S. Francis at Assisi.

When I was last at Padua the west front of this church was being repaired—a very dangerous and terrible operation in Italy, where, so far as I have seen, there is less feeling for, or knowledge of, Gothic architecture than in any other part of Europe. The interior, too, has been ruined by the way in which the old ceiling has been painted, in blue and shaded white. In a building whose characteristic feature is a certain grand simplicity and austerity, it is especially disgusting to see light and tawdry colouring introduced, seeing how completely out of harmony with the whole idea of the church it is.

At the west end are some fine monuments of stone and marble boldly corbelled out from the wall, adorned with good carving of foliage, and angels looking out from circles.

The east end is less altered than any part of the exterior of the building. The immense gable of the nave is divided into four parts, the outer of which have lancet windows, whilst in the centre is an insignificant apse, which is almost exactly repeated on the east side of the south transept. The large sacristy on the north side, and a campanile of not much interest on the same side redeem to some extent what would otherwise have been a most uninteresting elevation. The windows here have a wide external splay, semi-circular arches, and stone trefoil heads inserted rather clumsily under the arches.

What a grand idea it was on the part of the preaching orders to build these enormous naves for their congregations! Here, when enthusiasm for preaching was new born and general, a congregation, numbered rather by thousands than by hundreds, may have gathered round the preacher, all within sight of him, and, with the aid, probably, of an awning stretched across the church over the pulpit, all within sound of his voice.

From the Eremitani we found our way with some difficulty through miserable streets to the church of Sant' Antonio, probably the most remarkable architectural work in many respects in this part of Italy.

It seems that about A.D. 1231 it was determined to erect a great church in honour of S. Antony, the patron of Padua, and Nicola Pisano, then one of the most eminent men of his day, was sent for to undertake the work.[27] The view of the exterior which I give, will best serve to shew in how singular and original a manner he accomplished his work. S. Mark's at Venice must have been in his eye when he designed his church, and the crowd of cupolas which form its roof remind one forcibly of its most distinguishing feature.

On first sight Sant' Antonio certainly does not prepossess the beholder in favour of such a bold departure from every-day rules of art. It is built almost entirely

---

[27] This is the tradition, but it is one which is not, I think, supported either by documentary evidence or by the style of the building. Nicola left Padua four years before the church was commenced; and Fra. Carello is mentioned in the archives of the convent as one of the architects, of whom no doubt there were several before the work was finished.

of a light red brick, not much better than the common London brick in colour—a poor material wherewith to attempt the construction of a noble church. Stone is used very sparingly in the voussoirs of the arches and elsewhere. The cupolas are heavy in their effect, but relieved by that over the intersection of the nave and transepts, which rises higher than the others, and is certainly striking in its design and outline, which is, for the main portion of its height, that of a simple cone. Round and pointed arches are used indiscriminately, and the walls are divided everywhere by pilasters, and surmounted by arcaded corbel-tables, in all these respects giving the building the appearance of being much earlier than it is. The west front is very peculiar, and recalls the fronts of the churches in Vicenza which I have described, and is entirely unlike any of the churches of Pisa, which would hardly have been the case had it really been designed by Nicola Pisano. One great flat gable with an arcaded eaves-cornice finishes the whole, and out of its apex rises a tall polygonal turret, almost as high as the dome in front of which it stands. The lower part of the west front has a central entrance of mean character, and on either side two unequal arches of construction, the walls within which are pierced with windows. Above these, and just beneath the great pediment-like gable, is a long arcade of simple pointed arches, behind which are a passage and three windows opening into the church. This front is a sham front, and not excusable on account of its grandeur or its beauty. Indeed, had it followed the outline of the fabric, it would have been neither ungainly nor heavy, both of which it most assuredly is now.

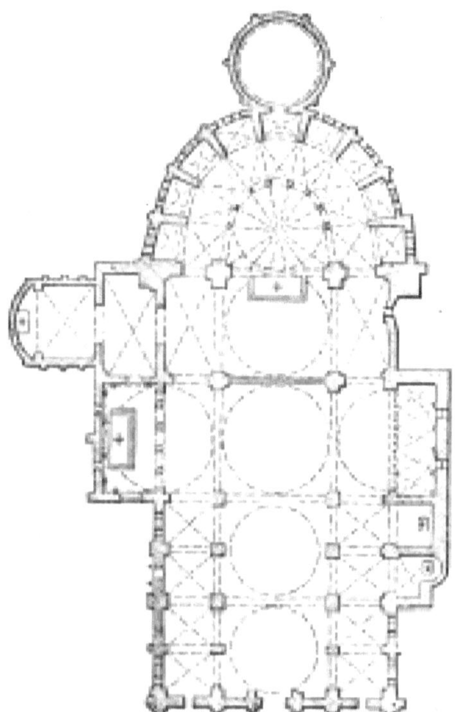

Ground Plan—Sant'Antonio, Padua.*

The interior is striking from its height, but cold in the extreme in effect; the domes are all whitewashed in the brightest and freshest manner. The plan gives three domes to the nave, one and an apse of seven bays to the choir, and one to the transept. The aisles open into the nave with pointed arches—two to each dome. The choir aisle is continued all round the choir, and a chapel is thrown out to the east of this, which is again crowned with a dome.

The north transept contains the chapel of the patron saint, full of gorgeous ornaments of all kinds, but not very ancient. Opposite it, in the south transept, is a curious groined chapel, divided from the church by five pointed and trefoiled arches of yellow marble, resting upon Classical-looking columns, and all very richly painted and inlaid. Above the arches are five statues in niches, and the intermediate wall-surface is inlaid with white and red marble in a regular pattern, such as we have seen in the pavement of Sta. Anastasia at Verona, with very good effect.

The cloister on the south side of the church is very large and good, and some fine arches occur in it, composed of black and yellow marble with bricks of varied colour introduced. On its east side three open arches, filled in with a double iron grille, open into what was, no doubt, the chapter-house. Going from this into a second cloister to the east of it, no one can fail to be struck by the extreme picturesqueness and novelty of the view. In the foreground is the simple pointed-arched and open arcade of the cloister; above this rise the gable of the south transept and the eastern apse with its surrounding aisle, and two lofty octagonal brick turrets, on each side of the apse, which look like minarets from Cairo, and combined with the collections of domes on the roof give a completely Eastern effect to the whole view. If, however, the detail of this striking building is examined, one can hardly be satisfied. There is throughout, as there so often is in Italy, a sad want of skill and neatness in the adjustment of details as compared to what is common in northern Gothic buildings. This indeed is a feature of all the works of the Pisani, and gives them the character—so common and so fatal in modern works—of being to a great extent the work of assistants and not of the master. Nothing can be much more clumsy than the provision for the steps leading to the turrets, nor weaker than the rectangular tracery inserted in the circular window of the transept. This, however, is a work of the middle of the fourteenth century, and Nicola Pisano, even if he were the first architect of the church, would not be responsible for it. I cannot say that I was at all satisfied either with the internal or external effect of the church—though it must be confessed that, when seen from a distance, there is excessive grandeur in the grouping of the multitude of domes, with the steep cone rising in the centre, and giving point and emphasis to the whole.[28] The arrangement of the windows and arches round the apse, for instance, is confused and weak to a degree; and I do not feel that Nicola Pisano has fairly settled the question of the adaptation of the dome to pointed buildings by his treatment of the domes here. The question is still, I think, an open one; and though it may be doubted whether with our present opportunities it will soon be satisfactorily answered, I still feel that it

[28] The eastern chapel and dome are comparatively modern, and the coverings of the other domes appear to be also modern; but I suppose they follow the old outline.

would not be difficult to answer it far more successfully than has been done here.

21.—Sant'Antonio, Padua, View from the East

In the evening we heard some very fine music of ancient character in Sant'An
tonio, after which there was a sermon; and though it was a week-day, there was a
large congregation, very attentive and quiet.

The Duomo is a cold, unattractive church—said, however, to have been designed by Michael Angelo—and rather bold in the treatment of the pendentives under its dome. By its side stands a Lombard baptistery, the interior of which I did not succeed in getting a sight of; and I believe that I missed some valuable examples of fresco-painting with which its walls and domed roof are covered.

We wandered about the melancholy streets of Padua, searching in vain for objects of any interest to our antiquarian eyes. It is true that the columns and arcades which support the houses are, many of them, ancient; but they are of a character very common throughout the north of Italy, and were not sufficiently novel or striking to draw off our attention from the melancholy and dilapidated look of the houses and shops which they half concealed and half supported. We saw also one or two old monuments at the corners of streets—one of them called the tomb of Antenor—similar in their idea to those which are so frequent in Verona.

The next morning, therefore, saw us making our way to the railway station for Venice, sad only in leaving Padua that we could not spend more time there for the study, more quietly and carefully, of the lovely little Arena Chapel and the paintings of Giotto.

CHAPTER VIII.

Padua and Venice Railway—Venice: Piazza and Church of S. Mark—
Torcello—The Lagoon—Murano—Sta. Maria dei Frari—SS.
Giovanni e Paolo—Sta. Maria dell' Orto—Other Churches—Do-
mestic Architecture—Fondaco de' Turchi—Other Byzantine
Palaces—The Ducal Palace—Foscari Palace—Ca' d'Oro—Other
Gothic Palaces—Balconies—Venetian Architecture—A Festival—
Paintings.

"Break, break, break,
On thy cold gray stones, O sea!
But the tender grace of a day that is dead
Will never come back to me."

Tennyson.

LITTLE is to be seen as one leaves Padua to distinguish the city at all vividly,
save the oriental-looking cupolas of Sant' Antonio, and the great roof of the Sala
della Ragione, looking like the inverted hull of some great ship, with its convex
sides towering up above the otherwise not remarkable-looking city.

And now our destination was Venice, and anxiously we looked out ever and
anon, impatient, long before the time, to see the tall outline of S. Mark's campanile
against the horizon. The view was too contracted to be really beautiful; on each
side of the railway rank and luxuriant hedges of acacia sprouted their tall branches
above the carriages, and beyond them might be seen plantations of maize, flax,
and other crops, all remarkable for their prodigious growth and size, and wa-
tered by countless small canals, and here and there with turgid, muddy-looking
streams rushing on from the mountains to discharge themselves into the Adriatic,
and gliding between great artificial banks which gave them the appearance rather
of large canals than rivers. Nothing breaks the dead monotony of the scene, for
it is misty, and the Tyrolese Alps, which ought to show their jagged peaks to the
north, are invisible. The stations follow each other in quick succession, and at each
stands some diligence or carriage whose ingrained panoply of white dust, added
to that which rises here and there white and cloud-like in the dry glare of the Italian sun which beams overhead, makes one feel grateful that   however unpoetical
such a mode of approach may be—a railroad carries us to Venice. Nor is such a
country as this along which one passes from Padua to Venice without its moral.
I suppose there is nothing more certain than that, ordinarily, the appreciation of
high art, and success in its practice, have never been so marked in countries whose

natural features are lovely as in those in which the devoutest student of nature's beauties can see nothing to admire or love. So Venice, surrounded by waters, and then by a country which would be entirely tame and uninteresting, were it not for the exquisite distant views of the Friulan Alps, fell back on her own resources, and provided herself with that substitute for the loveliness of nature which—alone of man's works—the loveliness of beautiful art can be. And perhaps, it is better for the traveller, that no interest should be felt save in the end of the journey, where the journey has so brave an end!

At last, however, the broad watery level of the Lagoon is reached; Venice rises out of the water at a distance of some two miles; and then across an almost endless bridge the railway takes us into the outskirts of the city; a confused idea of steeples and domes is all that is obtained, and one finds oneself going through that most painful of processes to an excitable man, the usual examination of luggage; at last, however, we are outside the station, the Grand Canal lies before us, and we are vehemently urged to get at once into an omnibus-gondola. But no, this is too absurd a bathos for our first act on entering Venice, and we step therefore into a private gondola, and, propelled rapidly and lightly over the still, unruffled water, sink at once into that dreamy kind of happiness which of all conveyances in the world the gondola is best calculated to encourage. A short reach of the Grand Canal is soon passed, and then, with the picturesque cry of warning, "Ah, stalì!" we turn sharply into a narrow canal to the right, and, shooting down the tortuous street of water, presently cross the Grand Canal again midway between the Rialto and the Foscari palace, dive into another canal still narrower than the former, and at last, after frequent glimpses of mediæval houses and palaces, find ourselves safely housed at our hotel close to the Grand Canal, and within two or three minutes' walk of the Piazza San Marco.

We stopped but a short time here, so impatient were we to obtain our first glimpse of the church and palace of S. Mark, to which Venice owes so much of her fame. We passed along some narrow winding alleys, lined on either side with open shops, on the counters of which lie exposed for sale not over dainty-looking edibles, and in whose dim interiors little light of day seems ever to enter to help the busy workmen who may always be seen there plying their trade; and then, going under an archway crowded with busy folk in rather noisy consultation, we found ourselves, in four or five minutes, standing under the arcade at the upper end of the great Piazza San Marco. Long lines of regular architecture, arcaded below, heavy with cornices and elaborated windows above, carry the eye not unpleasantly down to the lower end of the piazza, at the right-hand angle of which towers up into the air a vast campanile, simple and unbroken in its outline, without visible window or any buttress-like projection, until its upper stage, where it has a very simple open arcaded belfry, capped with a pyramidal roof; and then across nearly the whole width of the piazza, and partly concealed by the curiously irregular position of its campanile, stretches the low singular and Eastern-looking church of S. Mark. Before it rise the masts from which of yore hung waving in the wind the banners of the old Venetian state, and crowds of pigeons, fed here by civic liberality, cover the pavement with their pleasant fluttering presence. The charm of the west front is certainly most indescribable; and I confess to feeling a doubt, as I looked at it, whether it was not more akin to some fairy-like vision, such as one might see in dreams, than to any real and substantial erection of stone and mortar; for, indeed, to a mind educated in and accustomed to the traditions of northern Gothic, there is something so very *outré* in the whole idea, something so startling in its novelty, that it is hard at first to know whether to admire or not. It is far from imposing in size, but yet, as it is looked at more and more carefully, it grows much and rapidly on one's love, and at last imprints itself on the mind as a real work of art of a very beautiful and unusual kind, wrought out with an abundance of beautiful detail, but in such a way as to prevent its being possible that it could ever be absolutely reproduced or taken as a model.

As you pace down the broad level space of the Piazza, the feeling of the strangeness of the whole scene increases. There are of course no horses, and no vehicles of any kind; it is a large square in which all the space is footpath, and on which, in addition to the many men who pace it rapidly with busy brow, or idly lounge whilst enjoying the weather and the place, hundreds of pigeons are constantly fluttering or walking about in quiet confidence, sure that they will not be molested by any one. And then, as one draws near to the church, it is easy to understand rather better than at first in what its real charm lies; this is no doubt before anything else in its beautiful colour; the whole front is shafted to a greater extent than almost any building I know, the shafts all rather heavy, but of marble of the richest kind; the groining of the seven entrance arches is filled with mosaics, and the walls are encrusted everywhere with marble. Instead of ordinary gables masking the roof, the front is finished with great ogee gables most extravagantly crocketed, and obviously a modern alteration of the original Romanesque finish; behind these a cluster of fourteenth-century cupolas completes the view. Of the seven arches which compose the façade, four have doorways; the outer arches on either side are very narrow, and answer in width to the kind of cloister which masks the church on the south, west, and north sides; and the central arch is much wider and loftier than the others, rising indeed so high as to break through the line of balustrading which runs across the front just above the other arches.

Within this central arch is a grand doorway, the stilted semicircular arch of which is of three orders, the central plain, the others covered with carvings. The piers supporting the main arches have tiers of shafts in two heights; the lower tier corresponding in height with those of the doors pierced within the arches, and the others, which are smaller in diameter, and more numerous than those which support them, rising to the springing-line of the main arches. The side doorways have very Eastern-looking arches, the semi-circular line being carried on nearly to the centre, and then turned up into an ogee. These and some other portions as, e.g., the windows over two of the doors, and the pinnacles between the gables, belong to the fourteenth century, whilst the finish of the gables themselves—great ogee crocketed gables with figures at the apex of each—is probably of the fifteenth century. All these archways open into the cloister, or narthex already mentioned. Here, where the roofs still glow with the most precious early mosaics, and the walls with marble, either used as inlays or for shafts, one gets a first and not unworthy hint of the beauty which awaits one in the interior.

And then, on entering the nave, the deep tones of an organ are heard reverberating through the old building; many people kneel devoutly at their prayers around us; the hot glare of the sun has gone, and in its place a cool, quiet, dim light reveals the whole magnificence of the design. It is quite in vain to describe this in formal architectural terms. The colour is so magnificent that one troubles oneself but little about the architecture, and thinks only of gazing upon the expanse of gold and deep richly-tinted mosaic all harmonized together into one glorious whole. The mosaics commence throughout the church at the level of the crown of the main arches dividing the nave from the aisles, and are continued up the remainder of the wall and into the domes; even the angles or arrises of the walls and arches are covered with gold mosaic; so that all architectural lines of moulding are entirely lost, and nothing but a soft swelling and undulating sea of colour is perceived. There is nothing violent or garish in all this profuse decoration. The gold mosaic, used as it always is in early works, set irregularly in, and surrounded by a white line or joint of plaster, is never conspicuously bright; the drawing of the figures and subjects may be criticized, but at any rate it is always direct, simple, and intelligible, and the colours of the draperies bright and harmonious, whilst the arcading and wall-lining which fills the lower part of the walls is all of marble, which has now a rich, warm, but quiet tint, singularly suitable as a base to the more gorgeous colouring of the upper part of the walls and domes.

Altogether this is a church beyond most others suggestive of worship. Other churches sometimes suggest the same feeling either by enormous size or vast height. At Köln or Milan man feels so small and so contemptible in comparison with the vastness of his own work that he is subdued in spite of himself. In countless other great Gothic minsters the same feeling is produced. But at S. Mark's it is produced in an intensified degree, and by a building the scale of which is in every way small, if not almost insignificant. There is no long vista of arches, no complicated perspective, and no vast height to awe the beholder, yet the mystery of colour does for it even more than the mystery of size does for Köln or Beauvais, Milan, Toledo, or Bourges. It is, therefore, emphatically a church for worship, one in which even the most careless treads with hushed footstep and bated breath, and where, in spite of crowds, an aweful silence seems always to reign supreme save when it is broken by the religious sound of the services of the church.

The ground plan is no doubt known to most of my readers. It is a typical example of the Greek or Eastern church as distinguished from the Romanesque, a cross whose arms are not far from equal, covered by a series of cupolas, one in the centre, one to each of the three eastern arms, and two to the western—with aisles to the nave and choir, and a cloister round the north, west, and south sides of the nave, of which the two former are the porches, and the latter the baptistery of the church.[29]

Under the eastern limb of the cross is a crypt, which has in recent years been

---

[29] The dimensions are worth giving to show how little this church owes to mere size. It is 245 feet long, 201 feet across the transept, and 170 feet across the west front. The height of the central cupola is 90 feet, and that of the west front 72 feet.

opened and drained, and is now always open to inspection. This is divided under the choir into five aisles in width by a multitude of small shafts carrying quadri-partite vaults, and in the centre of which just under the choir altar, is the shrine of S. Mark. Another apse is formed under the south aisle of the choir, and under the north aisle is a corresponding crypt save that there is no apse to it. Much modernized as this has been in the course of repair, and entirely devoid of all colour or decoration as it is, it is still full of character, and adds largely to the interest of the church.

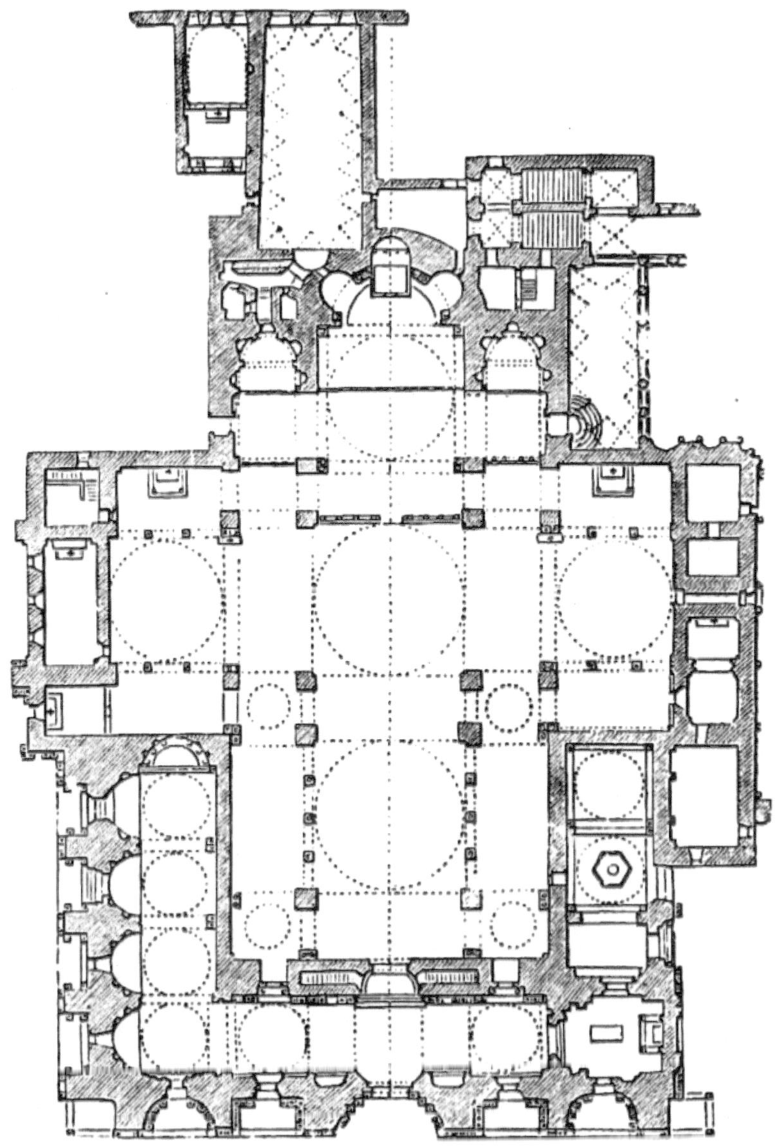

Ground Plan—S. Mark, Venice.*

If we return to the nave, we shall find that it is not only in general effect it is so very worthy of admiration; it still retains much of its old furniture, and in spite of a few modern mosaics, and one or two more modern altars, is less altered in its general effect since the fourteenth century than any great church that I have ever seen. The screen between the nave and choir with the ambons on either side of it first deserve notice. The screen is mainly a work of A. D. 1394.[30] It consists of a series of columns carrying a flat lintel or cornice on the top of which is a row of extremely good statues of the apostles. They have that grand sweep of the figure which one knows so well in early fourteenth century work in France, and are free from the somewhat heavy and clumsy treatment which marks so much of the work of the Pisani. The screen has been raised on the base of the older Byzantine screen, which consisted of a simple continuous arcade now nearly hidden by the more modern steps to the choir. The ambons are probably of the same age as this older screen; the gospel ambon being of two stages in height, with a good staircase to it from the choir aisle, that for the epistle being comparatively low and simple, but still large enough to contain two or three modern pulpits. The screens to the choir aisles are of the same sort as the main screen, but are placed one bay to the east of it. They are all three interesting as showing that a Gothic architect could use with good effect a common Classic arrangement, and indeed lend fresh grace to it by the detail of the sculpture and inlaying with which he adorned it.

Dimly seen from the nave through the Rood-screen, but far more interesting than even it, is the great baldacchin or canopy over the altar in the choir. Here we have the simplest form—four columns carrying round arches and the wall above them finished with a plain horizontal capping. The arches may be modern; though if they are so, they are copied from the old, as is evidenced by the painting at the back of the Pala d'Oro, which shows the placing of the shrine of S. Mark under a similar baldacchin; but the groining is old, and the alabaster columns are of extreme interest, being covered all over with most elaborate sculptures of Scripture subjects. The subjects in the north-east column give the history of Joachim and Anna, and the birth of the Blessed Virgin Mary; the north-west has the nativity of Our Lord, the marriage in Cana, &c.; the south-west subjects from the Passion; and the south-east the miracles of Our Lord. Few modes of decorating an altar are altogether so fitting and beautiful as this, and I hope the day is not far distant when we shall see many of our English altars standing under canopies of the same sort. St. Paul's cathedral may well prepare the way for us in this, by reviving what was usually accepted as the best kind of reredos by our English church-builders in the eighteenth century.

Here, too, is a brass eagle so like one of our own, that one might almost give it credit for coming from an English smith or founder.

Returning to the nave, one finds nothing more worthy of admiration than another smaller baldachin over an altar between it and the north aisle. This is hexagonal, carried on shafts with stilted arches and roofed with a steep roof. Its dimensions render a small altar a necessity—a matter of common occurrence in

---

[30] The inscription on the screen, which gives the date and the name of the Doge Antonio Venerio, gives also the names of the sculptors.

old examples. Another reredos and altar in a chapel at the north end of the north transept, dating from 1430, may also be noticed. Here the altar is panelled in front and carved with two angels censing a cross, and low open screens with arcades carried on shafts are placed a few inches from the ends of the altar. The footpace is not carried round the altar, so that it can only be approached from the front.

Of another sort of furniture—monuments of the dead—S. Mark's has, as might be expected, a good many examples. The earliest are the probably Roman sarcophagi,[31] which lie in the outer aisle or cloister right and left of the entrance; the next, near them,[32] where the sarcophagus is still retained, but adorned with Christian emblems and sculpture; and of considerably later date, and much more artistic interest, are the tombs of the Doge Andrea Dandolo, and of Sant'Isidoro. Here the sarcophagus is surmounted by a canopy, reverent angels stand on either side drawing back partially the curtains from the front of the effigy, and in the centre of the tomb is a bas-relief of the Madonna, and at the ends the Annunciation, S. Gabriel on one side, the B. V. Mary at the other. This is the type of monumental memorial on which so much of the time of Venetian sculptors seems to have been spent. Here, indeed, and on the very similar figures of the Virgin on so many of the tympana of doorways throughout the city, we have to study the sculptor's art from the time of the Byzantine carvers who wrought the still numerous early capitals, until the artist of the Ducal Palace came to revive the art with his original and splendid series of capitals.

But of all the features of this grand church, that which next to the gorgeous colour of the walls most attracted me was the wild beauty of the pavement. I know not what other word to use which quite describes the effect it produces. It is throughout arranged in the patterns common in most Opus Alexandrinum, but instead of being laid level and even, it swells up and down as though its surface were the petrified waves of the sea, on which those who embark in the ship of the church may kneel in prayer with safety, the undulating surface serving only to remind them of the stormy sea of life, and of the sea actually washing the walls of the streets and houses throughout their city. It cannot be supposed that this undulation is accidental, for had it been the consequence of a settlement of the ground we should see some marks of it in the crypt and in the walls, and some tokens of disruption in the pavement itself. And the corresponding example of Sta. Sofia, Constantinople, where we have it on record that there was an intentional symbolism in just such a floor, is conclusive as to the intention of its imitators here.

Of the mosaics with which the church is richly adorned I cannot pretend to give a complete account. They deserve a volume to themselves. As regards choice of subjects, it is noticeable that the most prominent figure is that of Our Lord, who is seated and surrounded by prophets. Below are the emblems of the four Evangelists, and the four rivers of Paradise. Whilst again in the west dome He is surrounded by the apostles and the Evangelists, and everywhere the general scheme is a lesson to those who now-a-days too often forget the relative importance or the proper order and arrangement of the divine story in the schemes they adopt

[31] The tomb of Vitale Faliero and another.
[32] The tomb of the Doge Marino Morosini.

for stained glass and mural decoration. As regards colour, I need not repeat what I have already said; but it may be observed that wherever modern mosaics have taken the place of old ones there at once we see a complete collapse, and a loss of all good effect. This is mainly owing, beyond doubt, to the attempt which their designers made to produce the effect of pictures, instead of thinking first and mainly of the decorative effect of their work on the building. But at the same time it is obvious that their eyes had lost all feeling for good colour, and that in attempting to draw with a certain amount of academical accuracy, they had equally lost all sense of the prime necessity in such works of simplicity of arrangement, and directness in the telling of their story. There is no part of the church in which some of the best of this sort of decoration can be studied with more ease and advantage than in the cloister on the north side of the nave. Here the mosaics are so near the eye, and the details of design and colour so fine that one is never tired of admiring them.

I never leave S. Mark's without taking one look at least at the four bronze horses, which, placed as they are on columns high above the ground, add so much to the strange character of the west front, and are in themselves such exquisite examples of their kind. Strange ornaments these for the façade of the chief church of a city where horses' feet have hardly ever trod! Equally strange, if you are to have horses in such a position at all, is the way in which these are supported. They stand balancing themselves nicely on the caps of small columns. Extremes meet; and I am not so sure but that this extraordinary arrangement is not better than that which is usually adopted. If horses are to be supported above the ground, they may almost as well be so in this way as on the ordinary pedestal, which looks equally unsafe if the bronze is instinct with life. These horses were brought from Constantinople after the fourth Crusade, circa 1203. They are of admirable character, and are probably of Greek workmanship. With every other moveable thing worth moving, they were taken to Paris, and returned after the Peace in 1815.

There is a picture in the Accademia by Gentile Bellini, which ought to be looked at after a visit to S. Mark's. In it we see the church much as it is at present; but an enormous procession which winds its tortuous way about the piazza, defiles before houses every one of which seems to be ancient, and I never look at the now uninteresting lines of houses which surround it without wishing for the resuscitation of the buildings which G. Bellini saw and drew.

We went into the treasury to see the treasures and plate belonging to the church, but I was much disappointed to find that, in an artistic point of view, there was really very little to admire, or else what was admirable was not shewn. The treasury is a dark room lighted up by a few wax candles, but so badly that it was difficult to see at all satisfactorily.

I was unable to obtain a sight of the Pala d'Oro, as the altar-piece behind the high altar is called; it is only uncovered on feast days, and I have never happened to be in Venice when it was visible. I was very anxious to have seen it, as it is a most magnificent piece of workmanship in gold and enamel. It was executed in Constantinople, and brought to Venice in 1102. Some Italian writers have claimed it for their forefathers as an Italian work; but the documentary evidence of its Eastern origin is supported by the details of the design and execution of the earliest portions of the work. M. Durand has published a very careful description of it in the 'Annales Archéologiques,' vol. xx. He gives a list of no less than one hundred and sixty-nine panels or figures, in a considerable number of which the accompanying inscriptions are in Greek characters. The Pala was "restored" in the thirteenth century and again in the fourteenth, when no doubt considerable additions were made to it. The painting at the back has fourteen subjects on a gold ground, and is dated 1345.

Over and over again when at Venice must one go into S. Mark's, not to criticize but to admire; and if ever in any building in which the main object is the study of art, assuredly here one must go for worship also. I think I never saw an interior so thoroughly religious and religion-inspiring as this, and it is well, therefore, not lightly to pass it by as useless for our general purposes. It seems to shew, as strongly as any one example can, how much awefulness and grandeur of character even a small building may attain to by the lavish expenditure of art and precious materials throughout its fabric; for it is to this that S. Mark's owes its grandeur, and to this only. There is nothing imposing either in its size or in its architecture; on the contrary, they appear to me to be both moderate, and the former rather mean; and yet this grand display of mosaics upon a gold ground makes the building appear to be both larger and better than it is, and fully atones for all other defects. Could we but place one of our cold, bare places of worship by the side of S. Mark's, and let the development of Christian art in the construction of the fabric be ten times as great in our Northern church as in the Venetian, we may yet rest assured that every religious mind would turn at once to the latter, and scarce deign to think of the former as a place of worship at all. If this is so, does it not point most forcibly to the absolute necessity for the introduction of more colour in the interior of our buildings, either in their construction, or afterwards by the hand of the painter? And architects must remember that this ought all to be within their province as directors or designers, and therefore that they must not, as now, venture to design cold shells which may or may not afterwards receive these necessary and indispensable decorations, but from the very first must view them as part and parcel of the work in which they are personally concerned; and then, but not till then, shall we see a satisfactory school of architects in England.

The interest of S. Mark's is not, however, only religious and artistic; on other grounds it is certainly one of the buildings most worthy of study in all Europe. Its architecture is purely Byzantine; and whether its design was derived from Constantinople or from Alexandria, it presents us with an almost unique example of the architecture of the Eastern church transplanted almost without alteration to the domains of the Western. Nor is this all. It played no small part in modifying the distinctly Roman influence by which otherwise the whole of Northern Europe would have been affected. When we see a church so far from S. Mark's as that of S. Front at Périgueux modelled after it, and in its turn influencing a vast number of churches in that and the neighbouring districts, we may realize what S. Mark's did towards the development of Romanesque into new forms and combinations, and may then value properly every portion of its fabric. Byzantine architecture was the development of Greek art in the hands of the then vigorous and active Eastern

Church. It is not a direct reproduction therefore of Classic art which is to be seen in S. Mark's, but one stage of a development the influence of which—partly owing to the effect of commerce, partly to her isolation—was largely felt, down to the very last days of active Venetian artistic life. This has been well condensed in a short sentence by Mr. Ruskin. "All European architecture," he says, "good and bad, old and new, is derived from Greece through Rome, and coloured and perfected from the East. The Doric and Corinthian orders are the roots, the one of all Romanesque buildings—Norman, Lombard, Byzantine; the other of all Gothic—Early English, French, German, and Tuscan. The old Greeks gave the shaft, Rome gave the arch. The Arabs pointed and foliated the arch." But in the colouring and perfecting the church of S. Mark had the lion's share, just as in the ground-plan it is to Venice and the East that we owe the cruciform arrangement of so many of our buildings, instead of the basilican form to which we might otherwise have been condemned.

There is another respect in which S. Mark's is extremely Eastern. This is in the almost entire absence of figure-sculpture in its original construction. The subjects and figures on the columns of the baldachin are too delicate to be noticed from a distance, and it was not until A.D. 1394 that the choir-screen was introduced, with figures of the Apostles on either side of the rood, erected no doubt to supply a want which had been long felt before it was gratified. At the same time figures were added in niches between the gables of the exterior, but even now they form a small and inconsiderable part of the decoration of the church.

I have lingered on paper as I did in reality about S. Mark's; but if we wish to see Venice we must tear ourselves away from it. We will go out by the baptistery, and here we are at once on the Piazzetta, the noble façade of the Ducal Palace on one side, and a great work of Sansovino's—the library of S. Mark—on the other; at the end of the Piazzetta are two monolithic granite columns, one of which bears the lion of S. Mark, the other the figure of the ancient patron saint of Venice, S. Theodore; between them is seen the dark-blue line of the sea rippled into a thousand twinkling waves, and beyond this the Isola San Giorgio, remarkable for one of Palladio's churches—a building, as I think, irredeemably ugly, but, nevertheless, much admired by many. If you walk down to the strand, where a hundred gondolas wait for hire—some black and funereal-like, others dressed up with gay awnings, and all of them proud and swan-like with their bright steel prows rising lightly and high out of the water—and then, turning round, look first down the Riva dei Schiavoni, towards the sea, taking in the long sea-front of the Ducal Palace, then the narrow gap bridged by the famous Bridge of Sighs, and on again, noting bridge after bridge, and the Gothic palace now turned into the Hôtel Danieli, and then on to the promontory running out towards the Adriatic, occupied by the Public Gardens and planted with the only trees that Venice boasts—how lovely is the scene! or if, looking back up the Piazzetta to S. Mark's, noting the tall campanile and the quaint clock and clock-tower beyond, and the domes and turrets, niches and figures, which crown the church, how much more vividly does it not impress the mind!

Venice is full to excess of striking pictures, and it would be endless to say in how very many respects it has a character of its own which can never be forgotten.

The strange silence of its watery streets, broken only by the cry of the gondolier or the delicate plash of his oar in the water, is not the least impressive thing to the stranger; and when, after trying in vain to thread on foot the labyrinth of passages which confuse him irrecoverably in a few minutes, he commits himself to the dark recesses of a gondola, how delightful is the quiet, smooth, and yet rapid way in which, without more labour than is necessary in looking about, he finds himself now following the narrow winding of some small canal, awakening the echoes between the high walls of palaces or warehouses on either side of the way, or anon, upon turning with a graceful sweep into the smooth broad reach of the Grand Canal, making his gondolier move gently and slowly, as one by one the great palaces which grace its banks and form its retaining walls are carefully scanned, whilst the various and ever-changing perspective of the whole is dwelt upon, to be remembered afterwards with such intense pleasure!

From S. Mark's I remember trying to find my way to San Stefano; and, taking a map of Venice, and calculating upon the orientation of the churches being fairly correct, I flattered myself that I might without difficulty make my way: the result was simply that for half an hour I was threading the mazes of all the passages around the church, and at last reached it only by chance; and I found afterwards that it would not at all do to take the churches as marking the cardinal points of the compass, for, as may be seen from the campanile of S. Mark, there are scarcely two churches in the city exactly alike in their orientation.

But pleasant as it is to recall one's recollections of highways and byways in Venice, I think, if we wish to understand her architecture thoroughly, we shall do well first of all to make a pilgrimage to Torcello, that sad and weird cathedral, standing forlorn and deserted on a wretched island in the lagoon, wherein we see the handiwork of the earliest Venetians, and the prototype of much of the later work in Venice itself. The story of Torcello has been told often—by no one with more feeling or more pathos than by Mr. Ruskin, and I need not attempt to repeat it. Suffice it to say that about A.D. 641 the church was first built, whilst in 864 it was restored, and being nearly decayed by age, was again most studiously repaired in 1008;[33] whilst in 1361, according to the testimony of Cornaro,[34] there were still standing on the same island divers churches (forty-two in number) adorned with columns of pietra dura, and with mosaics. Strange indeed is the difference here between then and now!

My first visit to Torcello was sad and sombre enough to begin with. We started early from Venice in a thick mist, making our way first to the cemetery, where there is a good tall campanile, then to Murano, and through its shabby water streets, passing the end of San Donato (which shall be described later), and then on through long canals edged on either side by miles of green mud, and thronged with market boats and noisy boatmen. Here and there across the lagoon we saw a tall campanile marking the position of each settlement or island in this waste of sea and mud, and, last of all, that of the cathedral of Torcello, some five minutes' walk among decaying walls and unmown grass from the half-ruined land-

---

[33] 'Sagornino Chronicon,' p. 119.
[34] 'Il Palazzo Ducale di Venezia,' per Francesco Zanotto, i. p. 9.

ing-place to which our gondolier tied his boat. All that remains of the city is before us in small compass. On the left a fourteenth-century building, said to have been the Palazzo Publico; in front a stone seat or throne in the centre of what was once the market-place; on the right, the Byzantine church of Sta. Fosca; and beyond, and connected with Sta. Fosca by a cloister, the modernized-looking cathedral, plain, bare, and uninteresting on the outside, with a detached campanile near the east end. This is all Torcello has to shew; but, forlorn and decayed as everything in the place is, it is precious in the highest degree to the architect who cares about the growth of his art. The cathedral is full of interest, though much damaged by extensive repairs, carried on in a reckless mood by the Austrians, not long before they lost Venetia, when new roofs were put on, and the mosaics were so much damaged that I remember collecting a handful of fragments from a barrow of rubbish before it was shot into the canal; at the same time a scaffold was erected for a proposed restoration of the great western mosaic which, though threatened and indeed commenced in 1857, had not in 1872 been proceeded with. The exterior has been completely modernized. In plan the cathedral consists of three parallel naves of ten bays, all finished with apses. The columns dividing the nave from the aisles are of veined marble, with capitals of exquisite workmanship, founded, indeed, on Corinthian examples, but modified by Byzantine influence and by study of nature. The arches are stilted and high; above them is a small clerestory of very simple windows. The central apse retains its raised rows of seats, though their brickwork alone is left; the throne for the bishop is placed in the centre, and retains some of its marble inlay. Under this raised east end a descending passage is formed, connecting the two smaller apses, and with a small apse formed in the thickness of the east wall opening into it. Three bays of the church are given to the choir, which is fenced round with richly sculptured marble screens. On the west the screen has marble columns carrying a flat entablature, and below them is a solid portion some four feet high covered with panels of flat sculpture, one having two peacocks drinking out of the same vase, another two lions at the foot of a branching tree, and another a complicated interlacing pattern of foliage. Such a screen is the obvious prototype of that in S. Mark's, and the sculptures with which it is adorned are evidently the work of some early Byzantine workman—whether brought from Aquileja from the ruins created by Attila's invasion, or wrought on the spot, I cannot say, but of a character which we still see in some of the nearly corresponding screens in the existing cathedral of Aquileja. North-west of this rood-screen stands the marble ambon—a pulpit of two divisions, one (circular) facing south, the other (square) facing west. This and the staircase leading to it are full of delicate and good carved work. The arrangement has an absurd likeness to many a modern English scheme of pulpit and reading pew, and there is certainly force in an observation which Mr. Webb makes,[35] that such an arrangement would never have been thought of, unless the Gospel was to be understood by the people. Now they do not understand it, it is no longer said from an ambon, and ambons seem to be much less useful to Romans than rood-screens are to us!

---

[35] 'Continental Ecclesiology,' p. 306.

22.—Duomo. Torcello. Ambon and Screen.

The screens north and south of the choir do not seem to be so old as the other, and are simple low screens.

In the mosaics of the apse and western wall we have, perhaps, the finest examples of Venetian mosaics. The apse is lined with slabs of veined marble below, and has above a mosaic of the Blessed Virgin Mary with Our Lord and the twelve Apostles, and the patron of the church, S. Heliodorus. The whole west wall is covered with a grand mosaic of the Crucifixion at the top, the Descent into Hell under it, and a Last Judgment at the base, which is carried down on each side of the west door, in the tympanum of which is a half figure of Our Lady. A mosaic at the end of the south aisle has Our Lord with SS. Michael and Gabriel, and below them S. Gregory, S. Martin, S. Ambrose, and S. Austin.[36] Save where these mosaics occur, the walls have been persistently whitewashed, so that the appearance of the church is now far from attractive. It is not the less of great interest, as an example of a very early church founded on a Roman basilica, but with Byzantine influence most conspicuous in the sculpture of its ornaments. Here, as in S. Mark's, the floor is paved with Opus Alexandrinum, of which, in spite of damage done during the late repairs, it is a fine example. There is nothing to admire on the exterior, though the large stone shutters to the windows—single slabs of stone about four inches thick, working on stone pivots—have a most primitive air. The campanile has not much to distinguish it from others, but the top affords an interesting view of the lagoon and the sea with Venice in the distance, and the Alps of Friuli far away to the north.

A few yards through the cloister bring us to the church of Sta. Fosca. Here by the side of the Romanesque we have a capital example of a Byzantine plan, which seems to me to be of the greatest value in connection with the whole of the round-arched palaces of Venice of which so many remains still exist. Sta. Fosca is a square church with small projections on the north, south, and west sides, and a deeper projection for the altar on the east. There are three eastern apses, and the western side is screened by an open cloister, which is octagonal in plan. The square centre is domed on very simple pendentives, and the capitals are similar in character to those in the cathedral. The best detail is to be seen outside the east end, where there is some good arcading and an enriched band of chevron ornament, formed by recessing the brickwork, and a mixture of red and buff brickwork, which is very effective.

The last time I was here, I found myself, in the middle of making a sketch of the west front of Sta. Fosca, suddenly struck by the strange likeness of its octagonal cloister to the most typical elevations of the Byzantine palaces in Venice. These always have a centre and wings divided by piers; and whilst the arches in the centre are of ordinary proportions, those in the wings are narrow and considerably stilted. In Sta. Fosca precisely the same effect is produced by the elevation of the three sides of the octagonal cloister, two of them being reduced in width and seeming to have narrow stilted arches, owing to their being canted and not seen in true elevation. I confess I could hardly help thinking that here I saw the accidental germ of an arrangement which, commenced in Romanesque or Byzantine buildings, was imitated in many of the finest of the Gothic palaces, and was revived with invariable persistency in the Renaissance.

---

[36] The mosaics here, as in Venice, are wholly of glass. The gold is covered with a thin film of glass, and the other colours used are dead white, black, dark and light blue, green and red. The very smallness of the palette was here, just as it was with the old painters on glass, a distinct advantage, saving them from the bizarre and confused effect produced in such works by the use of too many colours or shades of colours.

East End—Sta. Fosca, Torcello.

The return to Venice was more pleasant than the journey out had been. The water had risen enough to cover the mud everywhere, and now a vast expanse of apparent sea was lighted up by the hot sun, and in the far-off distance the horizon was lined with the long picturesque range of the Alps, tender and transparent in hue, and sweet reminders to the dwellers on this monotonous lagoon of the world which lay outside their boundaries in the far north. On the road we stopped at Mazzorbo, where there is a dated example of a Gothic doorway. This has a square-headed opening, and above this an ogee canopy or label over a figure of Our Lord, and some kneeling figures. The date inscribed on it is A.D. 1368.

Farther on Murano is passed, and a halt made for a visit to the church of San Donato—once a building of the highest interest and well known to all readers of Mr. Ruskin's books. Unfortunately my first visit to this church was after it had been in part "restored," in the largest and worst sense of the word. The old brick-work was being renewed, plastered, and painted up, till most of its interest had vanished; and now, I fear, only those who saw San Donato some ten years ago can have any idea of its architectural value and interest. This was chiefly centred in the east front, where there is a central apse with a lean-to end to the aisle on either side. The wall is divided into two stages, by a bold string-course and double line of chevrons formed by recessing the brickwork and inserting panels of coloured and carved white marble. The lower stage is arcaded mainly in red brick, whilst the upper has a wall deeply recessed behind arcades under the eaves, with delicate balustrades between the columns which carry the arcades. This upper part of the building is mainly of buff-coloured bricks, with thin lines of red to mark the pattern of arches, and it is curious that the light bricks are much larger than the red.[37] The pavements here are very fine examples of Opus Alexandrinum, with a more than usual proportion of black marble, and there is a grand mosaic in the apse, of the B. V. Mary and Our Lord on a gold ground.

One or two Gothic houses in semi-ruinous condition, and a very fine fragment of late Byzantine work quite in ruins—the Palazzo da Mula—remain in Murano, but of these there is such good store in Venice itself that we may pass them by.

Most visitors, I suppose, go to Murano in order to visit Dr. Salviati's glass and mosaic manufactory. He has succeeded in reproducing a material quite equal to that used in the old mosaics. Still more difficult feat—he has succeeded also in making glass so like the old Venetian glass in colour, texture, and design, as to puzzle all ordinary judges. I cannot sufficiently admire or praise the singular power which Dr. Salviati has shewn in the education of his men. A party of six or eight made for me before my eyes, in a few minutes, a tall, delicate, and richly adorned goblet, in which every part was done by eye and fancy; no modern accuracy was attempted, and the result was a thoroughly beautiful and artistic work. All artists know how difficult it is to get a workman nowadays out of the hard mechanical groove of dull uniformity, and Dr. Salviati's success is an encouragement to all of us when we are tempted to despair of making the attempt.

From Murano a few minutes take us again into the watery streets of Venice. We have now seen the two buildings which ought first of all to be studied—Torcello and S. Mark's, and in them we have the key to everything that follows. The Venetians commenced in their earliest buildings with works which shewed but little original invention or power. It was their fortune to have, by reason of their situation and their commerce, a great connection with the East. They received, therefore, a great impetus at the first from Byzantine art. Nowhere in Europe was so great an influence of the kind exerted; and to us, whose early architecture was almost entirely Romanesque in its origin, it has a special interest and novelty. But if the early Venetians copied Byzantine models, employed Byzantine workmen, and thought rather more of the beautiful colours for which their Eastern acquaintances gave them a taste than did their neighbours on the mainland, it must be frankly conceded that in later times they developed a very original form of Gothic out of these very materials, and owed comparatively little to any external aid in their great works of the fourteenth and fifteenth centuries.

The first business of a tourist in Venice is to secure a gondolier with intelligence enough to understand his proclivities, and patience enough to humour them. I have more than once or twice had to thank my gondolier for shewing me old work which otherwise I should never have seen, and I am grateful according-

---

[37] The red bricks are 2¼ thick × 9½ in. long, whilst the yellow bricks are 3¼ thick × 12 in. long.

ly. I am grateful, too, whenever I think of a gondola, for the most luxurious machine for sketching from which has ever been constructed; and the more so, when I recollect how for an hour at a time I have been persecuted in most Italian towns by all the idlest, dirtiest, and worst-behaved people of the place whilst I have made my sketches of their buildings. In a gondola in Venice one knows no such troubles, and the sketcher's life, as long as he can work in it, is as happy and undisturbedly serene as is possible. But no artist must suppose that everything worth seeing can be seen from the water: a few walks will convince him that, in the narrow *calli* as well as on the water-side, much that is interesting is to be found; and when he has studied Venice both by boat and by pavement, he will find, as I do, that the subject is too large for a chapter, and requires rather a volume for its thorough elucidation.

The buildings of Venice divide themselves into two great classes—the churches and the civil buildings; of these the former is the smaller and the less interesting class. But as we have already seen at S. Mark's and Torcello the earliest examples of the churches, it will be best to say all that has to be said about them here, and to take the palaces and houses by themselves afterwards.

We have seen that S. Mark's was built in the eleventh and twelfth, and largely altered in the fourteenth century. Between these two periods little if anything was done in church-building in Venice; or if it was, it has disappeared. Just as in Germany, the thirteenth century seems hardly to have existed for Venice, and we go at a bound from the simple nervous round-arched work of S. Mark's to the here somewhat poor and tasteless churches of the fourteenth century. One or two small campanili—San Polo, San Samuele, and San Barnaba are the best—remain to show what the size and character of the earlier work were. They have plain arcades in the walls, rising from the ground to the belfry, and this has generally windows of two or three lights carried on shafts. At San Barnaba[38] a spire with parapets and pinnacles was added to such a steeple in the fourteenth century, the spire being circular in plan and built of round-ended bricks. San Paterniano has an hexagonal brick tower with two light belfry windows, also of Romanesque character. The whole of these works are of brick, and usually the walls batter outward towards the base. In this respect, as in the general design, the great tower of S. Mark's follows those early examples, as also in its means of access to the top, which is a continuous slope in the thickness of the wall in place of the newel staircase in use all over the North of Europe. Finally, all these older works are very small and modest in scale and design.

Let us now give up all thought of early works, and see what the fourteenth and fifteenth centuries did for Venice in the way of churches. Taking them in their order of merit, we will go first to the Frari, the church of the Franciscans, thence to SS. Giovanni e Paolo, that of the Dominicans, to the Madonna dell' Orto, San Stefano, the desecrated church of the Convent of La Carità, now forming part of the Accademia, San Gregorio, Santa Zaccaria, San Giacomo del Rialto, and some smaller fragments.

---

[38] The twelfth-century bricks here measure seven inches by two inches, and are built with a half inch mortar joint; they are of red and yellow colour, used indiscriminately, and, though good and lasting, extremely rough in their make.

23.—Interior of Sta. Maria Gloriosa dei Frari. Venice.

I must confess that on the whole, in spite of the grand size of some of them, I was rather disappointed on first seeing these buildings. One cannot but be impressed with the magnificent size of such a church as the Frari, with its many interesting details, and its monuments and woodwork. But in spite of all this, there is something wanting. I had not expected larger churches, but I had imagined that their style would be more pure, and at the same time more unlike what I was accustomed to elsewhere. The impression they left on my mind was decidedly that they were very inferior in almost every respect to churches of the same size and degree of ornament in the North of Europe, whilst in scarcely any point did they seem to me to have features which could with any advantage be imitated by us. I had allowed myself to expect a very different result, and was proportionately disappointed. There is no church in Venice—(in what I am now saying I mean always to except S. Mark's)—comparable either to Sta. Anastasia or to the cathedral at Verona in the interior; and the exteriors, though fine as examples of the bold use of brick, are nevertheless not first-rate, nor at all superior to what one sees elsewhere.

Sta. Maria Gloriosa dei Frari ought first to be described, as being certainly the finest of its class. The first stone is said to have been laid on April 3rd, 1250, Nicola Pisano being the architect. The campanile was begun in 1361 under Jacopo Collega, and completed in 1396 by Pietro Paolo his son.

The first impression of the church on landing from the gondola on the desolate-looking piece of pavement which here, as in many of the Venetian churches, forms a court between the canal and the west front, is not pleasing. The design of the west front is nothing short of being positively ugly; it is finished with a great sham gable, with a curved outline, somewhat akin to the degraded taste of our worst Jacobæan art, and entirely without any beauty or even picturesqueness of appearance; the doorways, too, are particularly poor, consisting of a succession of twisted and reedy mouldings, thin and shadowless, like so many cords stretched from cap to base and round the arch, without any proper distinction of jamb and archivolt.

The internal effect of the church is much finer than its west front would lead one to expect. The plan is simple; a nave and aisles of six bays, transepts with three eastern chapels to each, and a choir of one bay with an apse of four bays projecting beyond the others. The tower is in the angle between the north transept and the nave, and a large sacristy with an eastern apse is built against the south transept. The nave and aisles measure about 230 feet by 104, and the transept 160 feet by 48,—magnificent dimensions undoubtedly. The columns are simple, cylindrical, and very lofty, their capitals carved with foliage, which looks late and poor in its execution, though grouped in the old way in regular tufts or balls of foliage. The arrangement of the wall above the main arcade is very similar to that of the Veronese, and, indeed, to that of most Italian Gothic churches; a plain wall being carried up to the groining, relieved only by a small clerestory window at the high est point. One is apt to compare this arrangement with the artistic arrangement of clerestory and triforium in our own churches; but herein we do not act quite fairly to Nicola Pisano, who is said to have designed the Frari, and his brethren. They had to work in a country where light must be admitted very sparingly, and where therefore it is impossible for architects to revel in the rich traceries which fill the bays of the churches of the North; they lived among a nation of painters, and deemed, perhaps, that these plain surfaces of wall would one day glow with colour and with Scripture story. For these reasons, then, I defend them for the bareness and over-great plainness which are certainly at first felt to be so remarkable in their work. The real beauty of these interiors is owing, more than to anything else, I believe, to the simplicity and purity of the quadripartite groining which covers them in, and which, even where other features would seem to tell of debasement and absence of pure feeling, invariably recalls us to a proper recollection of the infinite value of simplicity in this important feature—a point lost sight of in England after the thirteenth century, to the incalculable detriment of the beauty of some of our greatest churches. It is not difficult to prove that this must be the case, for I take it for granted that we all feel that ornament for its own sake is valueless; and equally, that doing in a troublesome, and therefore costly way, that which may be done as well and as strongly in a simpler manner, is unpleasant and distasteful as an exhibition of the wasteful expenditure of human skill and energy; and therefore, as simple quadripartite groining with diagonal and transverse ribs, and no lierne or intermediate ribs, is quite sufficient for the construction, and as the vaults are in no degree whatever strengthened by the multiplication and ramification of perplexing ribs, such as we see in later days in fan tracery and other contemporary modes of vaulting, that it is the truest and most agreeable system of roofing in stone.

The simple groining of the Frari is entirely executed in brick, and springs in the aisles from pilasters corbelled out of the walls midway in height, just as in Sta. Anastasia at Verona, and in the nave and choir from clusters of shafts rising from the caps of the columns.

The apse is the noblest feature of the whole church; its windows, with their singular and not quite pleasing transome of tracery, are refreshing because they have tracery, though indeed it is of a rude and heavy kind.

There is something impressive about the arrangement of the church. The choir is prolonged by the length of about one bay and a half into the nave, and fenced off to the west by a great screen, surmounted by figures of the Apostles, with a crucifix rising in the centre. The nave is, of course, quite free from any fixed seats; and this, with the great area of the transept and the fine perspective of the long range of seven apsidal chapels on its east side, gives a grand air of spaciousness to the whole interior. There are some fine monuments here, quite worth notice as very characteristic of Italian art. They are generally high tombs corbelled out from the walls, with arched canopies over them, inclosing paintings. Here the south transept wall over the door to the vestry contains a group of such monuments, which is extremely picturesque. The monument of "Beatus Pacificus" (A.D. 1437) has a graceful painting of the Annunciation over its arch, and sculptures under it of the Baptism, and, on the tomb, of the Resurrection and the Descent into Hell.[39] Another monument has a life-size figure on horseback, and all have so much freshness to an English eye, and yet so much identity in principle with our own old mon-

---

[39] The crockets on the monument of A.D. 1437 are exactly similar to those on the western gables of S. Mark's, and prove that these are of about the same date.

uments, that they are well worthy of study. Last, but not least, are two immense monuments facing each other, near the west end of the nave, to Canova and Titian, preposterous in size, heavy, ugly, and cold in character, quite unsuitable to a church, and, so far at least as I could judge, entirely devoid of merit as works of religious art. There is, too, a painting by Giovanni Bellini of the Madonna and Saints, which ought to be visited, in the grand and well-used sacristy—a room such as one never seems to see save in Italy. It is still in its old frame over the sacristy altar. Both in artistic interest and in religious effect it is perfectly fine; the subject—a Madonna and Child, such as Gian Bellini alone could paint. Angels playing instruments, sweet and pretty in character, and saints full of reverence and awe for Our Lord, all treated with a colour of exquisite depth and richness throughout, make this as worshipful a picture as I know. There is also in the north transept a most elaborately framed Gothic triptych, with figures well drawn and rich in colour.

The stalls in the Frari are all placed in the nave west of the transept, as in Westminster Abbey. They are of very rich Renaissance character, but with some late Gothic features. In the north transept is some elaborate Gothic panelling— very German in character—which looks as if it had come from the back of the old choir stalls. Here, too, is a crucifix, probably the original rood. Some fragments of stained glass are still visible; they are coarse and rude in detail, but extremely fine in colour; and one must picture the church full of rich glass in order to do justice to the scheme of the mediæval architect.

To the south of the nave are large uninteresting cloisters, and it is only at the east end that the exterior at all repays the ecclesiologist for the pains he must take to get all round it. The view which I give will best illustrate its general character. The windows are all transomed, the tracery and portions of the arches being executed in stone, the rest of the wall being entirely of brick or terra-cotta with some red marble in the eaves-arcading; the bricks are not particularly good, and the terra-cotta borders, cornices, and ornaments are poor and meagre in their design. The most observable point about the detail is the great and ugly splay on the exterior of the windows, and the facts that the window mouldings are returned round the sills and that all the apsidal terminations in the church finish with an angle in the centre—a peculiarity which is very seldom met with, but very much to be commended as a variety.

There is a degree of clumsiness about the way in which the arches of the windows are set upon the jambs which is very characteristic of Italian Gothic; but this, and other points open to criticism, do not prevent the east end of this church from being a very noble conception, broad and grand, unbroken with the lines of buttresses which generally too much confuse apsidal terminations, and yet very vertical in its effect. There is no petty attempt at relieving or ornamenting plain wall where it occurs, but it is left in the native rudeness of the rather rough-looking red brick, which is in no respect better than the bricks one may get anywhere in England. The cornices are very marked, and those in the clerestory have the common and ungraceful corbelled arcading in brick, to which I have a special antipathy. The clerestory windows of the transepts and choir are, I need hardly say, quite modern, and of a kind, unfortunately, most popular throughout the north of

Italy. North of the choir is a tall brick campanile, leaning rather dangerously to the North, finished with an octagonal upper stage, and, though not very remarkable, making a conspicuous feature in most of the views of this part of Venice, and at any rate to be admired for its simplicity and the absence of effort in its design.

24.—Exterior of Sta. Maria Gloriosa dei Frari. Venice.

Next in order of merit to this church are those of SS. Giovanni e Paolo and of the Madonna dell' Orto, both of them savouring most strongly of the influence of the Pisani, and in very many points remarkably like the church of the Frari.

We will take SS. Giovanni e Paolo first. The plan is of the same sort as that of the Frari—nave with aisles, and transepts with two chapels opening on each side of them. These are all apsidal, but planned in the usual way and not as at the Frari. The east end is a fine composition, having an apse of seven sides, and is the only part of the exterior to which much praise can be given. It is divided into two stages by an elaborate brick cornice and a good balustraded passage in front of the upper windows. The traceries are all unskilfully designed, and set back from the face of the wall with a bald plain splay of brickwork round them; the lower windows here have two transoms, and the upper a single band of heavy tracery which performs the part of a transom in an ungainly fashion, though not so badly as in the great south-transept window in the same church. Here, just as at the Frari, it is obvious that the absence of buttresses to these many-sided apses is the secret of the largeness and breadth which mark them; and, to say the truth, not only are large buttresses to an apse often detrimental to its effect, but at the same time they are very often not wanted for strength. The interior is remarkable on account of the fine scale on which it is built, and for the large number of interesting monuments corbelled out from its walls. Many of them are mediæval and rich in sculpture of figures, not only on the tombs themselves, but again in the face of the wall, around their canopies. The effigy of the deceased is almost always placed on the top of the high tomb or sarcophagus, which, in order that it may be visible from below, is made with a slope towards the spectator, the effect of which is most distressing. Much more beautiful generally is the curtained tester often put above the figure, on either side of which guardian angels, holding back the folds of the draperies, allow us to join them in looking at the figure on the tomb. There is here a very fine lectern—a double-headed eagle standing on a scorpion—with a rich mediæval stand and base.

There are small two-light windows just over the arches in the nave which take the place of a triforium, and which look almost as if they were the clerestory windows of an earlier church whose arches were much less lofty than those which now exist.

In the small piazza in front of the church stands one of the glories of Venice—the monument of Bartolomeo Colleoni. As is the case with too many equestrian statues the base seems dangerously small for the steed, slow and stately as his movement is. What a grand air of valiant determination this old warrior wears! what a serious purpose the artist had in his work, and how carefully he has rendered every detail of trapping and armour on both man and horse! We have already heard of this famous condottiere in his chapel at Bergamo and in his castle of Malpaga. His statue was the work of Andrea Verocchio, but was completed by Alessandro Leopardi, between 1479 and 1488. Colleoni had left his whole fortune to the republic of Venice on condition that his statue should be placed in the Piazza of S. Mark. This being contrary to the laws, an ingenious loophole for escape was discovered; the bequest was secured by the erection of the statue in front of the

Scuola di San Marco, whose strange Renaissance front (built with coloured marble in a horrible sort of perspective, which is the lowest depth to which architecture ever reached) stands at right angles to the front of SS. Giovanni e Paolo. For any one who wished to be remembered near S. Mark's church, the catastrophe would be as great, if he cared about art, to find himself connected, instead, with such an abortion as the Scuola of that ilk, as it would be to Bartolomeo Colleoni to find himself here in the suburbs when he stipulated so carefully for a place in the very centre of the city!

Next in order of merit to SS. Giovanni e Paolo I should place the church of Sta. Maria dell' Orto. This church is in a very bad state, and so far ruinous as to require to be supported in its interior by a forest of shores and scaffold-poles, which makes it quite impossible to get a good idea of the general effect. It has fair pointed arcades resting upon very Classic-looking columns, with capitals of poorly grouped and executed foliage. It is decidedly inferior to the two churches just described, in every respect save the treatment of its west front, which, poor as it is, sins less against all acknowledged rules than do theirs; its character is of a kind of pseudo-pointed, very flat, hard, and awkward. The cornice, with the open Italian pinnacles above it, over the central portion, is better in its effect than the singular row of niches which stands in lieu of cornice for the ends of the aisles; but it is worth while, nevertheless, to observe how simple is the design of these niches, taken separately, and how far this simplicity and the genuine beauty of their cusping and arching go towards redeeming the want of taste which is shown in the choice of their location. The doorway and rose window in the west front are of red and white marble, and in the side windows the tracery and monials are of white marble, and the jambs alternately red and white. The rest of the wall is brick, but has been plastered and washed with pink. The windows at the end of the aisles are remarkable for transoms of tracery supported upon two heights of delicate marble shafts, and entirely independent of the glazing which is fixed in frames within them. This kind of arrangement, incongruous and unsatisfactory as it is here, is worth recollecting, as being suggestive of an obvious opening for the use of traceried windows in domestic work; and it is a plan of most frequent occurrence in the best Italian ecclesiastical architecture. Many of the windows of Sta. Anastasia at Verona are constructed in this way, showing on the outside elaborately cusped and pierced plates of stone, against which on the inside the glazing is fixed, surrounded only with a plain circle of stone.

San Stefano is another really striking Gothic church. Its interior, notwithstanding the gaudy red damask with which the Venetians here and elsewhere delight to clothe the columns of their churches, is very fine and unlike what is common in the North of Europe. The dimensions are very large. The nave is about forty-eight feet wide, and the whole length about one hundred and seventy feet. There are a cloister and a chapter-house north of the nave, and a campanile detached at some distance to the east. The arcades of six pointed arches dividing the nave from either aisle are very light, and supported on delicate marble columns, whose capitals, with square abaci and foliage of Classical character, hardly look like Gothic work. The masonry and mouldings of the arches are not arranged in a succession of orders, as is the case in almost all good pointed work, but have a broad, plain soffeit, with a small and shallow moulding at the edge, finished with a dentil or billet ornament, which, originally used by the architect of S. Mark's in order to form the lines of constructional stonework within which his encrusted marbles were held, was afterwards, down to the very decline of pointed architecture, used everywhere in Venice—not only in its original position, but, as at San Stefano, in place of a label round the arch. Its effect is much like that of the English dog-tooth ornament—a succession of sharp hard lights and shades, useful as giving value and force to a very small piece of stonework, and therefore exceedingly valuable when used as it is at S. Mark's, and equally contemptible, I am bound to say, when used, as it is in later work at Venice, simply as an ornament; for this it is not and cannot be, as it is the result of no skill or taste on the part of the workman, but just such an enrichment as might be rather better done by machine than by hand. The roof of the nave is a painted timber roof, boarded in a series of cusped lines on the under side of the constructional framework, so as to hide it. I must not forget to add that the interior of San Stefano requires to be held together by iron ties in every direction—a sin to which, in Italy, the eye soon has to become accustomed.

The whole of the exterior is very carefully executed in brick, the moulded work being well done, though very late in date and not good in effect. The western doorway is of a favourite Venetian type. It is square-headed, enriched with mouldings and carving, and above it is an arched canopy with pinnacles on each side and with an ogee arched label carrying enormous crockets. The finial is a three-quarter figure, and an angel occupies the spandrel between the arch and the label. Above the door is a large circular window, unadorned with tracery or filling-in of any kind. The window from the east end of the church, of which I give an engraving, is a very characteristic example, of great width, and utterly unlike any example out of Venice.

Window—San Stefano, Venice.

25.—Campanile, San Giacomo del Rialto. Venice.

Perhaps the very worst traceries in Venice—which is saying a good deal—are in the windows of the apse here, where the traceried arches of the head are repeated over the transom, but inverted and standing on their points. More worthy of admiration is a fine tomb corbelled out from the cloister wall to Andreas Contarina, "MCCCLVII. Dux creatus MCCCLXXXII. in cœlumn sublatus," the arched bridge under the choir (which is carried over a canal) should also be noted, as well as the very fine campanile, which, though not boasting of any Gothic detail, is full of the spirit which made the earlier campanili so effective. But if we wish to see the best campanile in Venice, I think we must go back to the Rialto, and there, not far from the Grand Canal, we shall see in that of San Giacomo a perfectly fine example.[40] It is almost entirely of brick, and the fine long lines of its arcades give a great effect of height, whilst the details are all good and quite Gothic in their character.

The other churches in Venice are of less importance than those which I have described, but the number of remains, of which only too many are desecrated, is very large. The Accademia has attached to it the desecrated church of the convent of La Carità. This has three parallel aisles ended with apses, the usual traceries and cornices, and the unusual (I am glad to say) feature of three western gables with arched outlines[41] filled in with much small tracery in brick and terra-cotta. Another desecrated church near this—that of San Gregorio—is more interesting. It is of the same general design as La Carità and, like it, is built of yellowish bricks. The window traceries are of white marble. The most interesting feature here is the cloister, entered by a remarkable doorway from the Grand Canal. The doorway is square-headed, with an ogee trefoiled archway or window on either side, and a sitting figure of a bishop under a slight canopy over the doorway. The cloister has five bays on each side, divided by columns which rest on a marble and brick base, and carry a wooden framework enriched with very good mouldings.

Another desecrated church is that "dei Servi," which has a fine lofty brick front with a large rose window.

In the Campo Sta. Zaccaria is a portal much like that of San Stefano, save that it has in the tympanum a good figure of the Blessed Virgin with Our Lord with a saint on each side—the two Saints John, I think. The Virgin is seated on a Gothic throne carved in very low relief, and the whole composition is decidedly fine; comparing it with the doorway at Mazzorbo, I should say this must be a work of A.D. 1380. The church of Sta. Zaccaria is an early Renaissance building, with many of its arches pointed. It has an aisle and chapels round the choir, an unusual plan in Venice, but otherwise it has no interest.

The church of l'Abbazia has some fair detail in its cornices, with pinnacles at its west end of the same type as those in the Madonna dell' Orto, and has poor ogee-headed pointed windows; near it is another of the canopied doorways—the gate of the Corte Vecchia—with an outer arched canopy, within which under an ogee-shaped label stands the Blessed Virgin with Our Lord in an aureole on her

---

[40] I refer here to San Giacomo del Rialto. Its neighbour, San Giacomo del Olio, has also a brick campanile, but of inferior merit.

[41] A view in the 'Nuremberg Chronicle' shews these three gables just as they now are.

breast. Two saints stand at her side, and groups of little figures kneel at her feet, whilst from the upper finial Our Lord gives His blessing. This bears the date of 1505.

I think I have now said enough about these late Gothic churches. I have never been able to interest myself much about them. The work of which they are specimens is so exceedingly poor, cold, and distasteful to me, that I feel much inclined when I attempt to sketch them to give up ecclesiology in despair. The truth is that, S. Mark's excepted—and of course it is a very wonderful exception—the churches in Venice do not come up to the expectations of any one who has ever experienced the delight of visiting the churches of much smaller cities in France, Germany, and England. True, indeed, there are much interest and a great breadth and dignity about the general effect of such a church as that of the Frari; but for all those lovely points of detail which in every direction amaze us by the art they display and the rich array of beauty with which they clothe the walls of Northern cathedrals, there is here no kind of equivalent.

When I had thoroughly come to this conclusion, and settled in my own mind by repeated inspection that my judgment was not harsh or unfair, I confess I felt a weight off my mind. I was now free to indulge myself to the full in the search for what Venice really has in greater abundance, perhaps, than any other city in Christendom—remains, namely, of mediæval domestic work. Nothing can be conceived more delightful than such a search. You seldom go a hundred yards—often it is much less—without coming upon some remains, or perhaps some nearly perfect example, of an old Venetian palace; and then, with the gondola fastened to one of the great posts which line all the canals, the well-satisfied gondolier lying stretched on his back behind the awning, your friends laughing and talking within its dark recess, you sit most luxuriously, and make your notes and sketches with a degree of quiet comfort which is not a little conducive to accurate and careful sketching, and to diligence in its pursuit.

Venetian palaces divide themselves naturally into two great classes—the Byzantine and the Gothic; and it surprized me very much to find remains so perfect and so extensive of the former class even on the banks of the Grand Canal itself, where change has been ever so frequent and so rife. Indeed, it is singular that nearly all the Byzantine palaces are situated on its banks.

Of these palaces, certainly the most striking by far are the Ca' Loredan, the Ca' Farsetti, and the Fondaco de' Turchi. They all agree singularly in the general idea of their design, and consist of a grand scheme of arcading over the entire front. Divided generally into two stories in height, they are again divided in a marked manner in width into a centre and wings. This division is effected solely by a great difference in the spans of the arches forming the arcades, which in the wings are much narrower than in the central division. In the upper arcade the spaces between the columns, and indeed the whole arrangement, are often studiously unlike those in the lower range; but, at the same time, there is so very much similarity in the detail of the whole, that this variety, far from being perceived as an irregularity or a fault, does in truth just suffice to give force and vitality to what might otherwise appear to be monotonous and too often repeated, and recalls to mind not a little the very similar kind of difference between the upper and lower order of shafts already described in the west front of S. Mark's.

We cannot do better than take, as an example of the finest type of a Byzantine palace, the magnificent, though now desolate, decaying, and ruined façade of the Fondaco de' Turchi, once the palace of the Dukes of Ferrara. The whole front of this was originally cased with a thin facing of marble, like the coeval works at S. Mark's—a kind of decoration which, neglected as this fine relic has been for years, we cannot be surprized to find almost altogether destroyed; small fragments do, however, still here and there remain to tell of the original magnificence of the work. The lower stage of the Fondaco consists of a continuous arcade of ten open arches, with three narrower arches at either end, forming the wings, so to speak; the upper stage has eighteen arches in the centre, and four in each wing. In the wings the piers supporting the arches are, I think, all moulded pilasters; in the centre all the arches rest upon columns; and throughout the whole building the arches, which are all semicircular, are considerably stilted. The entire building is constructed in brick, which was originally, as I have before said, covered all over with a thin veneer of marble; in the spandrels of all the arches this is relieved by small circular medallions delicately carved, and over the upper stage is a string-course, above which there would seem to have been a long series of slightly sunk panels with round-arched heads, filled in with delicately arranged and beautifully sculptured patterns in marble. These panels are immediately below the eaves of the roof. Many of the abaci and string-courses, and all the thin pieces of marble which form the soffeits of the arches, have their projections finished either with a nail-head or dentil moulding, and between the shafts of the upper stage there are traces of balconies.[42]

A very noticeable point in the general effect of the façade of the Fondaco de' Turchi is that, from the peculiar shape and great projection of the capitals of the shafts and the narrow span of the arches, the whole of the arcading has, at a small distance, almost the effect of a series of trefoils, and so seems to pave the way for the continuous traceries of the Ducal Palace and other later buildings.

There is a ruined fragment of a house of the same age as the Fondaco de' Turchi in a canal behind the Foscari Palace. Here the centre arch is very wide, has four stilted arches on the sides, the archivolts are all delicately carved, and small sculptured medallions are introduced in the spandrels. Here, I think, the red brick of the walls was always intended to be seen. Of very similar character is a much larger fragment on the right of the Grand Canal after passing under the Rialto. Here there are two stories still remaining. The round-arched doorway has two open and stilted arches on each side, and then a space of blank wall; and the upper stage has a group of seven arches in the centre, and a single arch at each end over the blank wall below. The labels of these upper arches are turned up at the point into an ogee shape, which, strange as it may seem, must be original, as the detail is early, and they are surmounted by a collection of carved medallions and a carved

---

[42] I leave this description as it stood in 1855. Since then the whole of this interesting building has been so elaborately restored, that I doubt whether an old stone remains. It has lost all its charm, and this was once intense.

string-course of early style.[43]

26. — Byzantine well. Venice.

The Ca' Loredan has two stages in height, above which all is modern—but <u>all the Byzantine</u> arrangements of these two stages are perfect. There are five

[43] This house is in the Sestiere di Cannaregio, Parrochia San Canciano.

open arches in the centre, and an arcaded pier on each side; and in the next stage, though the division of centre and wings is preserved, the arches are increased in number, and consequently the columns of this stage do not come above those of the lower stage. The string-courses are formed with a billet mould; the capitals are some of them genuine Byzantine, and some copies of Corinthian. The wall-faces were all inlaid, but they were in part altered in the fourteenth century, when some coats-of-arms and figures were added. Those at the extreme angles are of David and Goliath, and on each side of the centre sitting figures of Justice and Force.

Next to the Ca' Loredan is the Ca' Farsetti (now the Municipio), which is, I think, slightly the older building of the two. Here there are three arches resting on shafts in the centre, and an equal number resting on piers on each side, and a continuous arcade of fifteen arches on the upper stage resting on coupled shafts.

The Palazzo Businetto on the Grand Canal opposite the Ca' Grimani, has remains of Byzantine work in its two lower stages. Here the caps are Byzantine in character, the archivolts flat inlays, with a billet mould on each side, and a carved string-course of running foliage inclosed between two lines of notched or billet mould.

This short notice of some of the more important Romanesque and Byzantine remains enables me to make a few general deductions: (1.) These buildings were always of two stages in height. (2.) They had the entrance in the centre, and had generally a distinction between the centre and the wings. (3.) The capitals were generally Byzantine in character, but often copied from Corinthian. (4.) They were of brick, but generally veneered with thin slabs of marble. (5.) They were enriched with circular, square, and arched medallions inclosing carving of foliage and animals, and frequently of coupled birds or animals regarding each other,—a device always indicative of an early date and an Eastern origin; and (6.) The string-courses were generally carved either with continuous running foliage, or with leaves arranged in threes; the centre turning over, the side leaves extended flatwise, and upward. This last string-course is exactly copied from Sta. Fosca, Torcello, and is carved all round S. Mark's inside; whilst the former, though it is Byzantine in origin, is carried round the wall of the Ducal Palace between the south-east angle and the Bridge of Sighs. The illustration of a Byzantine cistern from the centre of a courtyard which I give, is useful as shewing very clearly the character of the carved foliage which adorns the string-courses and panels of these Byzantine buildings. This is always effectively carved with deep cuttings, which produce bright and sparkling effects of light and shade.

One especial fault of the Venetians seems to have been their proneness to repeat the same architectural idea an infinite number of times; and there is something in this so characteristic of the place and the people, that the reason for it is worthy of some consideration. Venice, surrounded by water, and cut off from that kind of emulation which in other places always has the effect of producing life and change very rapidly in the phases of art, seems to have contented herself, when once she had well done, with the conviction that improvement was either impossible or unnecessary, and so, whilst changes were going on in the mainland, to have rested satisfied with a slight alteration only, and that one of detail always, for centuries; and it is thus that I account for the singular sameness which characterized all the efforts of her Gothic artists. The façade of the Ducal Palace is really precisely the same in its idea as that of the Fondaco de' Turchi or the Ca' Loredan, altered only in detail—its very beautiful traceries taking the place of, but doing the same work as, the simple encrusted arcades of its predecessors. And again, in the fronts of other and much smaller palaces—indeed, in all the fronts of the Gothic period—it is singular how exactly the same idea in the general arrangement is always preserved. Let me describe an ordinary palace. It is divided into three or four stories in height, the several stages being generally separated by string-courses. The lower story opens, by an arched doorway in the centre, to the water; and on either side of this doorway a few small windows serve to light the basement. The second stage has a grand window of some five or six lights, divided by shafts of marble, and rich with tracery, in the centre; and on either side, one or two single lights, with tracery corresponding with—and often, as it were, cut out in a slice from—the traceries of the central window. The third stage is nearly a reproduction of the second, though sometimes slightly less important; and the upper stage is either again a repetition of the others, or else consists of a few small windows placed over the others, and very unimportant and unpretending. The whole is crowned by a slightly projecting eaves-cornice, generally very meagre in its character, and with a line of genuine dog-tooth ornament on its lower edge. Above this, probably—for only one or two examples remain at all in their original state—was a parapet like those which still in part remain on the Ca' d'Oro, at the back of the Ca' Foscari, and on the Ducal Palace, light and fantastic to a degree, and almost masking the flat roof behind.

Such, as will be seen by the views with which, I doubt not, almost all my readers must be familiar, is the general idea of the Gothic palaces in Venice, and it admits of very slight modification. Occasionally, as in the Ca' d'Oro, the windows are inclosed within a square line of delicate moulding, the space within which is encrusted with marble, and entirely distinct from the string-courses, so as to give very much the impression of a plain wall veneered here and there with a window; or, again, sometimes the whole central division of the first and second stories is veneered on to a façade in which the other windows are treated constructionally but in all cases from first to last (except, as we shall see, in the Ducal Palace, and for this exception there is some explanation in its vast size and other reasons), the distinction between the centre and the wings was never lost sight of, and never forgotten. This was the great idea of all these buildings, and most perseveringly was it reproduced down to the last, when, gradually losing even the life which beautiful detail had once lent, it sank through successive stages, until at last, easily and well-nigh imperceptibly, it succumbed, without a struggle, to the rise of the Renaissance feeling, giving only in revenge to its successor, the curse of an obligation still to go on building to the last, for whatever want or on whatever occasion, with the conviction that a centre and two wings must ever be necessary to a grand façade. It so happens that, in addition to the large and purely Byzantine palaces in which this arrangement is preserved,—in a delicate manner, it is true,—there still remains one remarkable example of the period of transition from Byzantine to Gothic, in a house which forms one side of the Corte del Remer (facing the Grand

Canal just above the spot where it is spanned by the Rialto), which serves to shew clearly the first attempt at translation of this Byzantine idea into Gothic.

In the principal story of this house the central feature is the entrance doorway, whose finely ornamented arch of markedly horseshoe outline is very conspicuous. On either side of this, and connected with it in one group, are two windows divided by shafts and with arches of very singular shape; it is as though a stilted semi-circular arch had been suddenly turned up in the centre, not with the graceful ogee curve of later days, but with simple, hard, straight lines. Beyond these windows, one of later date, but probably inserted in the place of the original window, completes the similarity which the arrangement of the openings in this house bears to that common in all the later Gothic palaces. The arches which support the staircase in front of this house are entirely executed in brick, and are probably later in date than the house itself, though it is noticeable that they are of a very early and pure type, and that here, as generally throughout the North of Italy, the pointed arch was first used in construction, and then, some time after its first introduction, and very generally in some modified form, for ornamentation also.

27.—Corte del Remer, Venice.

And now, having so far cleared the way, let me ask my readers to go with me to the Ducal Palace, and there undertake a somewhat careful examination of its very famous design.

I shall not enter into a general description of the entire building, because, as this has undergone prodigious alterations since its first erection, it is unnecessary to do much more than refer to the two fronts, which still retain, nearly without alteration, their mediæval design, and to those portions only of the interior and courtyard which have not been altered.

The whole building forms three sides of a hollow square: one side rises out of the deep recesses of the Rio del Palazzo, spanned near its outlet by the famous Bridge of Sighs, and is entirely of Renaissance work; the next side, rising from the Riva dei Schiavoni, faces the Giudecca, and is of the purest Venetian Gothic; and the third, facing the Piazzetta di San Marco—the small square which connects S. Mark's with the water—is also Gothic, and of the same type. The back or north side of the palace abuts upon S. Mark's.

I cannot pretend to decide at all absolutely upon the vexed question of the dates of the mediæval portions, because, as the reader will find in an interesting discussion on the subject in the second volume of Mr. Ruskin's 'Stones of Venice,' it is a source of hot disputes. But the following appear to me to be the main points.

The Ducal Palace was burnt in 1105, restored in 1116, and rebuilt in 1173-1177. The two columns on the Piazzetta were brought to Venice in 1172, about which time the two Piazze were formed. Between this date and 1301, nothing is recorded to have been done to the palace. But even at this date it was a grand building, and is described in 1275 by Maestro Martino da Canale as "Grande e bellissimo a maraviglia."[44] He was equally enthusiastic about the church of "Monsignore San Marco," and of his campanile, "so great and so high that one cannot find its equal." Sivos in his chronicle (A.D. 1621) says that the Sala Grande was commenced in 1301, and completed in 1310, at which date the Grand Council consisted of nine hundred members; and one Pietro Baseggio is said to have been the architect between 1309 and 1361; he was succeeded or assisted by Filippo Calandario, and both of them, according to Zanotto, were described as being architects, sculptors, and navigators![45] Calandario had raised himself from the humble post of shipbuilder at Murano, to that of Capo Maestro of the Ducal Palace, a man of great weight in the city, but finally finished his career only too much in accordance with custom, being convicted as one of Marino Falieri's fellow-conspirators, and hung from the balcony of the Ducal Palace in A.D. 1355.

On the 28th of December, 1340, a decree was issued ordering the construction of a staircase on the east side of the palace to lead to the new rooms, which seems to establish the fact that at this date a considerable portion at any rate of the second stage was built. The plague visited Venice in 1359 and 1361, and stopped all work. In 1362, because the unfinished work was going to ruin, the Council determined to complete the new hall; and in 1365, this being done, Guariento of Padua began

---

[44] Zanotto, 'Il Palazzo Ducale di Venezia,' i. 39.
[45] Ibid., i. 52-60.

to paint it, in the time of the Doge Mario Cornaro.[46]

The capital next the south-west angle of the lower stage bears a date which appears to some[47] to be 1344 (as to which I have never been able to satisfy myself), and long afterwards we find the date, 1404, on the large window of the highest story of the sea-front. Finally, in 1419, there was a great fire which damaged the old portion of the building, so much that a decree was passed to rebuild it in conformity with the rest, and this work was completed in 1423, when the council sat in their great council chamber for the first time; and in 1439-41 the last Gothic work was added to the palace by the Doge Foscari, viz. the Porta della Carta, built (as appears by their contract) by Giovanni and Bartolomeo Bons, between the years 1438 and 1443, in the small space which intervenes between the north-west angle of the Ducal Palace and the south side of S. Mark's. All these dates are important, and I believe undisputed, the only question being as to which parts of the building they refer to.

And now, before I say more about dates, let me describe these two Gothic fronts—the sea-front and the Piazzetta-front—and then we may perhaps see our way to some sort of comprehension of the relative ages of the various portions of the fabric.

The whole design is divided into three stages in height, the upper nearly equal to the united height of the two lower stages, and faced entirely with a delicate diaper of marble cut in small oblong pieces, which look, save in their texture and colour, only too much like bricks. In this marble-faced wall are pierced a number of windows with pointed arches—the tracery of which has been taken out—and in or near the centre of each façade a much larger window and balcony, which look as though they had been subsequently inserted. The lowest stage consists of a long and uniform arcade of very simple pointed arches resting upon circular columns with elaborately carved caps; these have been shortened by some twenty inches of their old height, by the rise of the water, and the consequent elevation of the pavement of the Riva, to the great damage of their effect. The intermediate stage is a magnificent arcade, supporting very vigorous tracery, too well known to everybody to require much description, and divided from the stages above and below it by large and pronounced lines of carved and moulded string-courses.

It is important to observe that up to the top of the second string-course the whole of the architecture is of the very best kind of Venetian pointed; the arches of the lowest stage are well proportioned, and, though very simply, still well moulded; and the detail of the whole of the second stage is, to say the least, not at all inferior. They form together, without exception, I believe, from all I have either seen myself or heard, the very best and truest specimen of Gothic architecture south of

---

[46] "1362, die iv. Dec. Quia est magnus honor civitatis providere quod sala magna majoris consilii nova non vadat in tantam desolationem in quantam vadit cum notabili damno nostri communis: et sicut clare comprehendi potest, leviter potest compleri, et reduci ad terminum, quod satis bene stabit cum non magna quantitate pecuniæ; vadit pars quod dicta sala nova compleri debeat," &c. &c.—Decree in Zanotto, i. 72.

[47] Mr. Burges, in his account of the capitals, 'Annales Archéologiques,' vol. xvii. pp. 74-88.

the Alps.

Above this noble work the third stage comes, and I confess, to my eye, with patent marks in every stone of which it is composed, that it was designed by some other hand than that which had been so successful below. There is something quite chilling in the great waste of plain unbroken wall coming above the extreme richness of the arcades which support it; and moreover, this placing of the richer work below and the plainer above is so contrary not only to all ordinary canons of architecture, but just as much to the ordinary practice of the Venetians, that I feel sure that the impression which I have had from my first acquaintance with drawings of it is substantially correct, viz. that the line at which alterations and additions have been made is to be looked for rather in a horizontal than in a vertical direction; that in all probability, consequently, the builder of A.D. 1301 commenced with some portion of the sea-façade and gradually carried on the greater part of the building to the height of the two stages as we now see them, leaving his building finished in precisely the same way as the corresponding halls at Padua and Vicenza—two stories in height, with arcades covering the outer walls of the upper as well as of the lower stage; and that when the Council Chamber was found to be too small, and larger rooms were required, another architect suggested the advantage of obtaining them by raising an immense story above the others, and, without destroying much of his predecessor's work, providing rooms on the most magnificent scale for the Doge and his Council.

The assumption that the Piazzetta-front has been copied from the sea-front involves a belief in a veneration for and exact imitation of older work which is (to say the least) extraordinarily rare, if not unique, in mediæval works. It involves a belief also in the possibility of a spirited and successful copy being made of an old capital by a mediæval sculptor without fresh thought or any fresh invention of any kind. This will be seen if we examine the capitals of the lower stage of the palace. Here at first sight one is struck by what appears to be the astonishing variety of the capitals. They are nearly all adorned with figures or subjects as well as with foliage, and are certainly in both fronts of various degrees of merit; but on closer acquaintance it is perceived that the variety of capitals is not so great as it seems, for that several of those in each front are merely replicas of those in the other. If any portion of the two lower stages had been built before the rest, it would have been the whole of the sea-front and six arches of the Piazzetta-front, for at the end of these there is a column equal in size to those at the angles, and which might therefore by possibility itself have been an angle column for a time. But its larger size may also fairly be accounted for by the fact that it comes under the side wall of the large building above, and was in any case therefore a convenient arrangement if not quite a necessity; but the real difficulty seems to me to be, that if there were any considerable difference in the date of these works, all experience would lead one to expect that the earlier works would be the most uniform and the best, whereas in point of fact this is far from being the case. For instance, in the sea-front there are various capitals which are of poor execution. These are, counting from the south-east angle, the third (large and coarse heads), the eighth (also coarse heads), the thirteenth (lions' heads), the fourteenth (beasts), and the fifteenth, which is certainly not so fine as the replica in the Piazzetta-front (the twenty-sixth capital, counting as before).[48]

The case for the contemporaneous erection of these two fronts becomes even stronger if we ascend to the open gallery on the first floor and examine the capitals there. They are all similar in general character; and though they become gradually better as one goes from the south-east to the north-west, they give the impression of all being of nearly one date, and moreover they all appear to be later in date than the whole of those in the lower stage.

On the other hand, there seem to be at least two points which make strongly in favour of the later date which has been given to the twelve northern arches of the Piazzetta-front. These are, first, that all the eight capitals which are replicas are in this northern part of the front, and none of them in the first six arches from the south-west angle; and, secondly, that the plate armour in the sculpture above the capital of the north-east angle (Judgment of Solomon) is later in date than the period which I assume for this work, and later than the chain mail shown in the third and eighth capitals of the sea-front. To the first objection a sufficient answer is that some of the best of the capitals to these twelve arches are of original design—not replicas; and in reply to the last objection (which is of much force) the only, but at the same time obvious reply is, that the Trajan capital, just under this late armour, is one of the most beautiful of the entire series, and that on the whole it is much more likely that some of the sculpture was left in block and finished later, than that no difference should be made in any of the mouldings or details of the work of two periods. There is indeed some, though not very strong, evidence that the sculpture of this capital is not earlier than about 1423. There is, according to Zanotto, an inscription on it, "✚ Duo Soci Florentini incise," and he argues from the use of this last word, that the two men were the same who made the monument to the Doge Tommaso Mocenigo in 1423, in which, according to Sansovino, they used the same unusual term "inciserunt;" this interpretation of the inscription is the more allowable in that, as I have said, the details of armour in themselves suggest a date not much earlier than this for the sculpture connected with it on the angle just above the cap. This date of course brings this work to very nearly the same period as that of the execution of the Porta della Carta, and it has been assumed by some that these capitals were the work of the Bons who built it. Such an assertion is as wild as that of M. Didron, who says something as to their belonging to the thirteenth century, for the very shortest inspection of the Porta della Carta would convince the most sceptical that no part of the capitals could have been executed by any of the men who wrought at it. In comparing the merits of the carvers of the earliest and the latest capitals, it is due to the latter to say that one of the finest of the whole series is this Trajan capital at the north-west angle, and there is no internal evidence in it which could lead one to suppose it to be the work of a man who would ever condescend to copy another's work.

---

[48] The capitals which are replicas of each other are the 4th and 35th, the 7th and 28th, the 8th and 31st, the 9th and 29th, the 10th and 30th, the 11th and 34th, the 12th and 33rd, the 15th and 26th. The 25th, 27th, 32nd, and 36th (north-east angle) are original, though they are in the northern portion of the Piazzetta-front. See Appendix, with key-plan.

No one can examine the building without seeing that there is not only in the detail, but equally in the general design, a marked difference between the two lower stages and the upper stage. In place of the extreme boldness which marks every part of the former, we see mouldings reduced in the latter to the smallest and meanest section possible; the windows of the upper stage are badly designed, whilst the traceries of the second stage are as fine as they can possibly be; the angle-shafts of the upper stage are of the latest type, elaborately twisted and violently defined, instead of being merely delicate roundings off of the hard line of wall, as all the early Venetian angle-shafts are; the parapet, too, is not equal in its design to any of the lower work, and crowns with an insignificant grotesqueness the noble symmetry of the two lower arcades; and finally, the chequer-work of marble which forms the whole of the upper wall is a mode of construction which I have not seen in any early work, though it is seen in the Porta della Carta (A.D. 1429), and in one other late work, the Palazzo in the Campo Sta. Maria Mater Domini.[49]

Looking at all the circumstances of the case, I think the fairest explanation of them is, that the whole sea-front and the six arches of the Piazzetta (columns 1 to 24 on the plan) were first built, that the extension to the north (columns 25 to 36 on plan) was then immediately undertaken by the same artists, and finally that the whole upper story was built and the sculpture of its capitals completed before 1423. The capitals of the lower arcade were probably sculptured by degrees, and certainly not by one hand, between the years 1310 and 1361.

There is a confirmation to some extent of this view in a MS. in the Bodleian Library of the fourteenth century (the Romance of Alexander), which contains a curious contemporary view of Venice. This drawing has been engraved at p. 26 of the second volume of the 'Domestic Architecture of the Middle Ages;'[50] here it will be seen, with the usual amount of licence which characterizes most mediæval representations of places or towns, that it has nevertheless been intended as an absolute representation of what its draughtsman had seen. The columns with S. Theodore and the lion of S. Mark on their capitals, the bronze horses and the domes of S. Mark's, the position by the waterside, and the representation of the Ponte di Paglia, are all proofs of this; but the important point for my present purpose is, that he drew the Ducal Palace as a building of two stories in height—the first a simple arcade, the second an arcade with tracery. In the distance behind this, his drawing shews a picturesque assemblage of buildings, whilst figures are represented behind the upper arcade as though it were only a kind of immense balcony. There can be no doubt whatever that this old drawing tells in favour of the view that the upper stage was not built until after a considerable interval; for it is almost impossible—looking at the way in which the rest of the drawing is made—to believe that all reference to it would have been omitted, had it been in existence at the time the artist saw it.

---

[49] The similar marble facing at Vicenza was executed between 1400 and 1444. See p. 97.

[50] Published by Mr. Parker, of Oxford, to whose courtesy I owe the use of this illustration.

28.—View of Venice, from the Romance of Alexander, Bodleian Library (Venice in the fourteenth century).

From the Romance of Alexander.

It will be seen that my supposition that the original design of the Ducal Palace was of considerably less elevation than the present building, would tend to make it very much more like the Byzantine type than it is; but even now no one can dispute the family likeness. The amount of constructive art is as nearly as possible the same. The weight is supported by a succession of shafts placed at very short intervals from each other, and in neither is there any approach to the system of pier, arch, and buttress, so distinctive of Gothic art in the North of Europe. The pointed arch is used, it is true, in the palace; but, after all, the mere use of the pointed arch does not make thorough pointed architecture, and therefore, interesting as it is as a variety of the style, the Ducal Palace is, I think, not properly to be placed in the first class of Gothic buildings. Indeed, the second stage, whose exquisite beauty is the charm of the whole building, does not exhibit the pointed arch at all in a properly developed form, and is strong enough to support the great weight of wall above, only by reason of the massy character of its tracery, and not by the proper application of constructional arches. I have already said that there is no approach to buttressing; but the angles require some help, and this is given partly by increasing considerably the size of the shafts, and partly by iron ties at the springing of the arches running for some distance in each direction from the angles.

All the mouldings are very simple; they are generally composed of three-quarter beads, small fillets, and large flat hollows, constantly arranged in the same order. The label of the main arcade is a plain bead. In the string-courses boldly-carved flowers are repeated with a slight interval between each, and the upper string-course has a row of nail-heads in one of its members. The cusping of the tracery is quite square in its section, and the cusps finish with a square end, to which is attached—and with good effect—a small circular ball of red marble. The parapet is of the somewhat peculiar kind I have already mentioned, and I confess I have never been long enough in Venice to accustom myself to, or to admire, its extreme peculiarity of both outline and design.

And now before we leave this subject let me offer a remark, as every one who writes on it must, on the admirable story of these sculptures. I have never sat in front of one of them for any space of time without seeing some wayfarer stop to study the story of some one of the capitals. They are a book at which more thousands have looked with pleasure for some five hundred years than at any other single book in the world, with the one exception of the Bible. And the lesson to architects is obvious. Concentrate your labour and your story on some one part of your building where all men may read it; tell some simple story and you will interest your readers, if you will but tell it so simply that by good chance they may be able to read it. Lay out a scheme so well that if you die your successor may carry it on. Here, as I believe, the architect completed his two stages of arcades, whilst the sculptor was changed, but kept generally to the scheme of subjects first of all laid down. At the three exposed angles are the three archangels, below them the moral lesson—as much wanted now as then—of the Drunkenness of Noah, and the Story of Tobit (with S. Raphael); at another angle The Fall (under S. Michael); and at the last the Judgment of Solomon (under S. Gabriel). In the lower range of capitals the stories and catalogues of virtues and vices; the illustrations of fruits, animals, every-day life; the labours of the months, trades, sciences, and arts—are all illustrated, and complete a cycle of subjects which, ill-treated, would always have a certain value, and which, well treated as most of them are here, have the very highest charm.

For a building which owes its general impressiveness entirely to the uniform character of its architecture, it is especially fortunate that there should be so much also in the detail to attract and reward constant and minute examination. It is for this reason that the range of great capitals to the columns of the lower arcade is of so much importance. They are so large, so close to the eye, so interesting in their story, and on the whole so carefully and artistically executed, as to afford the greater pleasure the more the building is known. The key-plan to these capitals which I give[51] will be useful to shew what the general arrangement of the subjects is. I have already shewn that there are repetitions of many of the subjects, but it is equally worth notice that the foliage which forms the framework for the subjects is also repeated. There are, I think, only four varieties in its arrangement. In the first the capitals are arranged very simply—in some cases rudely—with tufts of foliage or heads. The capitals numbered 2, 3, 6, 13, 16, 20, 23, 27, and 34, are examples of this. In the next the foliage of the lower part grows up vertically, bending slightly out to support the sculptured subjects. These are generally the most graceful of all, and infinitely richer in effect than the first class. The capitals numbered 1, 7, 9, 12, 18, 24, 26, 28, 33, and 36, are examples of these. In the third class the foliage is generally marked by the same feeling, but it rises vertically to the angles, and curls over under the subject; the 19th and 25th capitals are examples of this class. In the fourth class the foliage curves over downwards, both at the angles and under the subject. The neckings below the capitals are wrought on the shaft itself. They are sometimes moulded, sometimes corded, and sometimes delicately carved with foliage; these last are by very much the more beautiful, and generally accompany the best wrought of the capitals, whilst the inferior capitals have, in all cases, the plainer necking.

The capitals in the upper arcade have not so much story as those below. They have generally a head on each side in the midst of foliage, and are square in plan, though the lower caps are octagonal—a few only have their names written over them; but on the ground-story most of the capitals have, or have had, explanatory inscriptions. Some of the upper capitals close to the north-west angle are among the best. The curves of the foliage in the angles of the capitals are admirably wrought, and may be compared, to the damage of the latter, with some of the lower capitals in the sea-front. The upper range of capitals gradually deteriorates from the north-west angle as you go to the south-east. These last are really very bad, having rude gross carving of the human figure, and foliage feebly massed and treated; but the upper capital of the south-west angle with the figures of the four winds, and the two or three capitals near it, must be excepted from this remark, being superb in design and execution.

The remains of original work in the quadrangle are much less important. The arcade on the first floor remains, but none of its details are good, and on the east side it is a poor Renaissance copy of the other sides. The whole of the lower arcade has been destroyed or altered. But in the upper walls, which are faced with brick,

---

[51] See Appendix at the end of the volume.

some of the original windows remain; they are small, but of the same sort of detail and character as the larger windows in the outer walls.

The building has lost much by the gradual raising of the pavement. This is now about twenty inches above the old base of the columns, and their proportions are so far altered for the worse. And it has lost immensely also by the destruction of the inlaid marble which once filled all the spandrels of the main arcade. Two panels only of these remain, and both in the sea-front. They are charmingly designed, inclosing circles which exactly touch the labels and strings.

Of the modern additions to this grand building I shall not say anything. They are not beautiful in themselves nor interesting by reason of their decorations, if I except those walls on which Tintoretto has lavished so much of his skill. The architects of the fourteenth and fifteenth centuries were artists in very deed, and it is with their work only that I can feel any real sympathy.

Such, then, is the Ducal Palace: a building certainly in some respects of almost unequalled beauty, but at the same time of unequal merit; its first and second stages quite perfect in their bold nervous character, and in the almost interminable succession of the same beautiful features in shaft and arch and tracery, forming perhaps one of the grandest proofs in the world of the exceeding value of perfect regularity and of a repetition of good features in architecture, when it is possible to obtain it on a very large scale.

Leaving the Piazzetta, and stepping into the gondola which has been waiting for us hard by, let us now go in search of other palaces; but let us not imagine that we are to see anything equal to the Ducal Palace. There is, it appears to me, a great gap between it and all other Venetian buildings; and yet all others seem to have been founded on it, or on the buildings out of which it grew. Their traceries, seldom absolutely alike, have still so much general similarity that at first one may well fancy that there is no variety at all; and, as I have before said, the general arrangement of their windows and doors is so nearly identical, that this impression is the more likely to grow upon the mind.

We will not attempt to take the buildings as they come; but rather as we think of them, and to some extent in the order of their merit, let us note down a few of the glories of the domestic work of Venice. And first let us stop in this narrow canal, for we have by our side one of the most exquisite little pieces of detail in the whole city. It is an archway, simple and delicate in its proportions, lovely as it is simple, and appropriately placed hard by the bridge called "del Paradiso." I trust that my sketch is clear enough to shew how pure and good the work is. The main points to be noted are the characteristic flatness of the details, and the line of dentil-moulding, which defines all the leading architectural features, originally invented for borders of incrustations at S. Mark's, and here, as everywhere in Venice, used for decoration afterwards. The incrusted circles of marble on each side of the figure give great life to the spandrel beneath the arch, and the windows seen behind shew us a late example of the not unfrequent use of the semicircular and ogee arches together in the same window.

29.—Archway, Ponte del Paradiso, Venice.

Another precious fragment—the Palazzo San Giorgio, I believe—is reached from the land side by passing under an arch somewhat similar to that on the Ponte del Paradiso. This arch is turned between the upper stories of two houses at the end of a *calle* properly yclept "dell' arco detto bon," and is finished with a steep gable. Beyond it is seen a fragment of wall veneered with marble, with the upper part of an early two-light window, and two circular medallions; and above this a piece of wall veneered in diamonds of red and white marble—so far as I know, a unique example of such a treatment. The window-head is of that earliest form of ogee, a circle just turned up to a point in the centre, which has so manifestly an Eastern origin, and which must not be confounded in date with our English ogee arches.

In another, and rather desolate, canal in the outskirts of the city, wider than usual, and with a footpath at the side of the water, instead of having the walls of the houses running down into it, and forming its boundary, is the Palazzo Cicogna, which I remember gratefully because it is one of the few exceptions to the general rule of regularity. The whole design of this building is very irregular: a detached shaft at one angle supports a portion of the house which overhangs and forms a sort of open passage-way; to the right of this opening is a four-light shafted window, and then a plain wall pierced with two windows, each of a single ogee trefoiled light. The upper story has two single windows over the others, whilst over the larger windows and the passage-way is a large window conspicuous from its size and the peculiarity of its tracery. It is of six lights divided by very good shafts, and properly arched with pure and good trefoiled arches; above these, and inclosed within the perpetual indented or billeted string-course, is a complicated system of intersecting circles pierced at regular intervals with quatrefoils. The section of this upper part is very much thinner than that of the arches beneath. This window is in a most shaken and decayed state, and not likely, I fear, to be long preserved. The whole elevation is finished with a shallow cornice supported on corbels.

A doorway on the Ponte San Tomà is quite worthy of a visit. It has the usual square opening of reddish marble, and above this is a pointed arch of moulded brick; the tympanum is filled in with a square carved centre panel, and the ground beyond this with quatrefoils of brick or tile very prettily disposed, and quite deserving of illustration.

And now let us go back to the Grand Canal; we shall enter it by the side of the Palazzo Foscari, which, with two other contiguous palaces, occupies quite the post of honour at the bottom of the principal reach of the canal, and commands the whole view of its noble and ever-busy way to where the arch of the Rialto and another bend in the canal close in the view. We will go a few strokes only towards the Rialto, and then turn round to look at the palaces we have just passed. They certainly form a most magnificent group, and are in every way worthy of their conspicuous position. The palace at the junction of the two waters is that of the Foscari; the others belonged, I believe, to two of the Giustiniani family; and but a few yards up the canal, which runs by the side of the former, is one of the smaller remnants of Byzantine work already referred to. This group is so well known as scarcely to need any description—suffice it to say, therefore, that throughout these palaces the windows are shafted, and the glass is fixed in wooden frames behind the stonework. This is beyond all doubt what we ought to do; it is the only sensible and rational mode of adapting the system of traceried and shafted windows for domestic purposes, and has here, as elsewhere, the prestige of ancient authority to recommend it to the consideration of those amongst us who will do nothing without it. I have enlarged on this point elsewhere, and will, therefore, say no more upon it now, save that in Venice such a thing as an English monial ordinarily is, was never known. Windows were invariably shafted from the earliest period to the latest, and so far invariably of the highest order, inasmuch as they admitted of the definite expression of the point at which the monial terminated and the arch commenced, and inasmuch, too, as the coloured surface of the detached marble shaft must ever be far more lovely than the lines of tracery mouldings carried down even to the sill.

30.—Doorway on the Ponte San Tomà. Venice.

The angle-shafts of the Palazzo Foscari have caps and bases in each stage of the building; those of the other palaces continue up without interruption.

The date of the smaller palaces, and probably of the large one also, is very early in the fifteenth century; and the latter had, in 1574, the honour of being the grandest palace that the Venetians could find in which to lodge Henry III. of

France. They are all three very similar in their design. Their water-gates are pointed, and the windows in the water-stage small and unimportant. The second stage is more important, and has cusped ogee window-heads and balconies. The third stage is, however, the *piano nobile*, all the windows having deep traceried heads and large balconies. The fourth stage is very nearly like the first, save that instead of balconies there is a delicate balustrading between the shafts of the windows, which is very frequent in good Venetian work, and always very pretty in its effect. All the windows in these three palaces have ogee-heads generally finished with carved finials, and inclosed within a square outline formed by the small dentilled moulding, and giving what I have before had to refer to—to some extent the effect of a panel with a window pierced in it, veneered on the front. The Foscari Palace is the only one of these three that has any string-courses. The arrangement of the windows—large in the centre and smaller at the sides—is so nearly regular and of a sort of two-and-two kind of uniformity, that one scarcely notices that nevertheless, when internal arrangements make it necessary, a departure from this strict rule is allowed.

The back entrance to the Foscari Palace is on the side canal. It is of some interest as retaining, in a very perfect state, an example of a very picturesque treatment in brick of the Venetian battlement. This consists of a series of piers finished with a steep gabled outline, and pierced with trefoiled openings. A good example of this sort of battlement remained near the Fondaco de' Turchi, and deserves illustration. It is quite a Venetian invention, and errs on the side of quaintness.

Brick Battlement—Venice.

In a small courtyard, desolate and dreary, reached after crossing the Ponte di Paglia and one or two other bridges on the Riva dei Schiavoni, is the Palazzo Badoer, a fourteenth-century palace, the ogeed arches of the windows in which are more than usually good; whilst the beauty of the central window, inclosed within a square line of moulding, within which the wall is incrusted with marble relieved by medallions, is very great. The structure of this, as of most Venetian palaces, is brick which has been frescoed; but it is now in a very lamentable state of decay.

The balconies of the lower windows are clearly modern, but there is a trace of the original balustrade between the shafts of the windows in the second stage; and in front of the side-lights to the upper window is a grille of iron-work taking the place of a balcony, and composed of a combination of quatrefoils. The arrangement of the windows in this front is not absolutely regular, but still the centre is very marked; and though it is of early date, the true use of the arch nowhere appears. The usual[52] dog-tooth cornice finishes the walls under the eaves. In the courtyard of this house are two of the wells which give so much character to all the courts in Venice. They appear generally to be of early date, and look, frequently, like the capitals of large columns, taken down and placed upon the ground. Those in front of the Palazzo Badoer are perhaps more like fonts.

Another palace, also said to belong to one of the Badoer family, placed at the junction of two canals very near the Scuola di San Giorgio and the Greek Church, is remarkable as being now one of the very few houses in which the red brick walls are still in their original state, and not defiled by compo, paint, or whitewash. This house has three fronts, with one old doorway on the canal, and two on the land. The back facing the Campo San Severo has an unusually fine and lofty entrance, a square doorway with a pointed arch above (which I suppose once held tracery), and a group of five windows with circles or disks of marble in their spandrels above. Amongst other things it is remarkable as an instance of the way in which windows were sometimes placed absolutely at the very angles of the building. Judging by the similarity of its tracery to that above the Porta della Carta in the Ducal Palace, this angle window must date from about 1400 to 1430. It has a very bold shaft at the angle, whilst the jambs have pilasters ornamented at their angles by a twisted cord-like moulding, which is frequently met with in the later work. There is a small angle-shaft elaborately twisted just above this window, and very much like the angle-shafts of the Ducal Palace.

The composition of the main window in the front of this house is, I think, very striking. The lower window of four lights (one of which is larger and loftier than the others—a curious instance of the junction of regularity with irregularity), and whose arches are ogee trefoils, is surmounted by another window of four lights, with delicate balustrading between the shafts; and on each side of this upper window, and forming part of the composition, is a single light, with projecting balcony. The effect of the whole arrangement is pleasing, and is frequently repeated in other palaces. The marble incrustation over this window is very much like that in the other Palazzo Badoer; and from the centre of the medallions of marble small balls of marble project, fixed with metal, and giving great life and beauty to the medallions, and I think without any sacrifice of truth. The main fabric of this building must be of the latter part of the fourteenth century—the arches of the principal window being of a very excellent though simple type. Venetian balconies, of which this palace affords such good examples, are very beautiful and very characteristic. Nowhere else are they seen in such perfection; nowhere else,

---

[52] I say "usual," because it is really quite curious to see how repeatedly either the dog-tooth or the nail-head is used in this position. The commonest eaves-cornice consists of a simple chamfered stone—the chamfer covered with dog-tooth—supported on moulded corbels at short interval.

perhaps, were they ever so absolutely necessary. The palaces rose out of the dark water which washed against their foundations, and no ground could be given up for shady arcades as in other Italian cities, nor were there any paths to be strolled along; the only resource was, therefore, to gain from the air that which the land could not afford, and by projections in front of the windows to obtain that power of enjoying the delicious evening atmosphere, so cool and pleasant after the fatigues of the too sultry day. These balconies are almost always very similar, consisting of a number of delicate shafts with carved capitals, supporting a piece of stone whose under side is notched up in a series of trefoils (generally ogee), resting upon the capitals of the shafts. These are divided occasionally by pilasters, under which are corbels jutting out boldly to support their weight; and above which sit, generally, quietly and placidly eyeing the gondolas as they shoot silently by, small lions, dogs, or other animals—a quaint finish which one soon learns to like; their angles are often marked by corded mouldings, and the edges of their floors and copings are almost always moulded and specked with the perpetual notchings of the nail-head, and their under sides or soffeits are frequently carved or panelled.

31.—Angle Window, Venice.

Balcony — Venice.

There was great variety in the planning of these balconies. In the Palazzo Persico, for instance, in which the central windows of the second and third stages form one great panel, the lower balcony is continuous across all four lights of the window, whilst the outer lights only of the upper window have balconies, the two middle lights having instead a balustrade between their shafts. In other cases the balconies extend to four lights only of a six-light window, whilst in most they are confined to the central windows, to which they give much additional dignity. The Ca' Fasan affords an almost solitary example[53] of tracery in a balcony; and the effect of this is so vastly inferior to the usual shafted balconies, that it seems scarcely necessary to pause to consider why it should be so. Obviously, however, it is not very convenient to have the fretful points of cusps and traceries set, as it were, to catch every projection or point of your dress whenever you lean over the edge of the balcony to inhale the fresh air or scan the busy scene below.

In the Casa Persico, to which reference has already been made, the central window is an elaborate composition of the same kind; but the lower one is of more importance, and has a continuous balcony; and here I may notice the finials with which the ogee arches of Venetian windows are so often finished. They appeared to me to be invariably tasteless and poor in execution, and very mean in their outline. I did not see one finial in Venice which was satisfying, even when found in conjunction with otherwise fine work; and I used to wish heartily, when I reached

[53] There is another traceried balcony in the canal near the Bridge of Sighs. It is the only other example I know in Venice.

some palace not before seen, that I might find its arches finished without them. There was some reason for the wish, too, in the fact that it is in the later work that these tasteless ornaments are commonest. I saw them first at Verona, and lamented over them there, but at Venice I was positively annoyed by the persevering and endless thrusting of their poverty and badness upon my wearied eyes.

And now let us go again into the Grand Canal, and we shall not have gone very far up the broad water above the Rialto before we shall find, on our right hand, one of the most striking groups of mediæval palaces and houses which can be seen anywhere, even in Venice; this is where the famous Ca' d'Oro unites with some three or four other houses, of rather earlier date, and gives a very fair idea of what the water-scenery of the ancient city once was. There is some difficulty in criticizing the Ca' d'Oro, because, in the first place, it has been restored to render it fit for the occupation of Mdlle. Taglioni; and, in the next place, much of the elaborate decoration from which it derived its name, has perished or been destroyed. As it is, however, it is still a very sumptuous example of the later fourteenth-century Gothic. Its whole face is inlaid with squares of red and white marble, and a great amount of carving is spread over the entire surface, round and between the windows. This is very flat, but good in its effect. The arcade on the water-story, and the traceried arcades above, all open into recessed courts—an arrangement peculiar, I think, among Gothic houses, and similar in its purpose to the arcades in the Byzantine palaces. Some of the balconies are good, and the carving of the capitals and moulding of the window-traceries are very characteristic of Venetian pointed. The whole design is one-sided, and gives the impression of a house to which an additional wing has been added. The water-stage consists of an open arcade of five arches, the central arch round, the remainder pointed, and on one side of these are two windows with a continuous balcony. The second and third stages have, above the five open arches, elaborately traceried windows, of no less than eight lights in width, filling almost the entire front, the outside lights having balconies, whilst the others have balustrading. Over the two windows of the water-stage are single-light windows in each stage. There are throughout this front many medallions of dark marble, which, let into a field of light marble, are most brilliant in their effect.

The most remarkable features in the Ca' d'Oro are, however, the triple and elaborately carved and chevroned angle-shafts, which I have nowhere else seen,[54] and the very singular parapet. The height of this is greater about the centre and at the two ends than elsewhere; but this appears to have been done rather with the intention of carrying up to the very top the noticeable division in the building itself than for any other reason. A very small portion only of the parapet is perfect, and this it is rather difficult to get at. The small balls of marble affixed to the outer edge of the trefoils are like those in the tracery of the Ducal Palace, and in the centre of the medallions of marble everywhere throughout the city. Their effect is certainly very piquant.

---

[54] They may be compared with the chevroned and spiral columns in the archway, leading from the north aisle into the baptistery of the Frari, erected between 1361 and 1396, which is probably about the date of the Ca' d'Oro.

Capital of window-shaft—Venice.

By the side of the Ca' d'Oro there are three ancient houses of considerable interest, and the second from the Ca' d'Oro, the Palazzo Segredo, was a very good example indeed; it has unhappily, I believe, all been restored and painted, so that now few would believe that it could ever have been (as it was) one of the very best works in Venice of its age. It quite deserves illustration, on account of the extreme vigour and beauty of its great window, which has more of the flavour of the arcade in the Doge's Palace, than anything else in Venice. These three houses are all more than usually irregular in the arrangement of their windows.

Lower down the Grand Canal, and nearly opposite the Post-office, is the Palazzo Pisani-Moretta—a very late building, in which all the balconies are Renaissance, with ordinary balustrading; but this occurs so often in connection with the latest examples of Gothic work, that I am disposed to believe that they were possibly, after all, contemporary in their erection. This palace, too, is remarkable for its double entrance-doors, with ogee arches, and for the manner in which the central window is carried up in an uninterrupted way to the very cornice; the lower traceries being very fair, those in the upper story very weak and bad.

The Palazzo Falcanon (alla Riva Tonda) is another fine house. It has two water-gates; is four stories in height, the third being the principal floor; the angle shafts are all spiral, and the string-courses all ornamented with cable mouldings, which, as is usual, are twisted in reverse ways from the centre of the front.

The Palazzo Celsi, near the Frari, is, like the Badoer Palace, an example of a fine regularly designed house with its brickwork left in its natural state; and the Palazzo Orfei is an instance of the finest (and a very fine) front being turned towards a *campo* and not towards a canal. The long group of mediæval houses which formed one side of the Campo Sta. Maria Formosa was equally worthy of admiration, but has lately been modernized—a fate which is only too rapidly overtaking most of what one used to admire in this once fortunately neglected city!

32.—Palazzzo Segredo. Venice.

The window of which I give an illustration, on the Ponte del Fornaro, is a rare but extremely good example of the combination of sculpture and tracery. Here the carvings are good examples of the emblems of the four Evangelists very ingeniously treated, and the whole window has more force than most of the traceried windows.

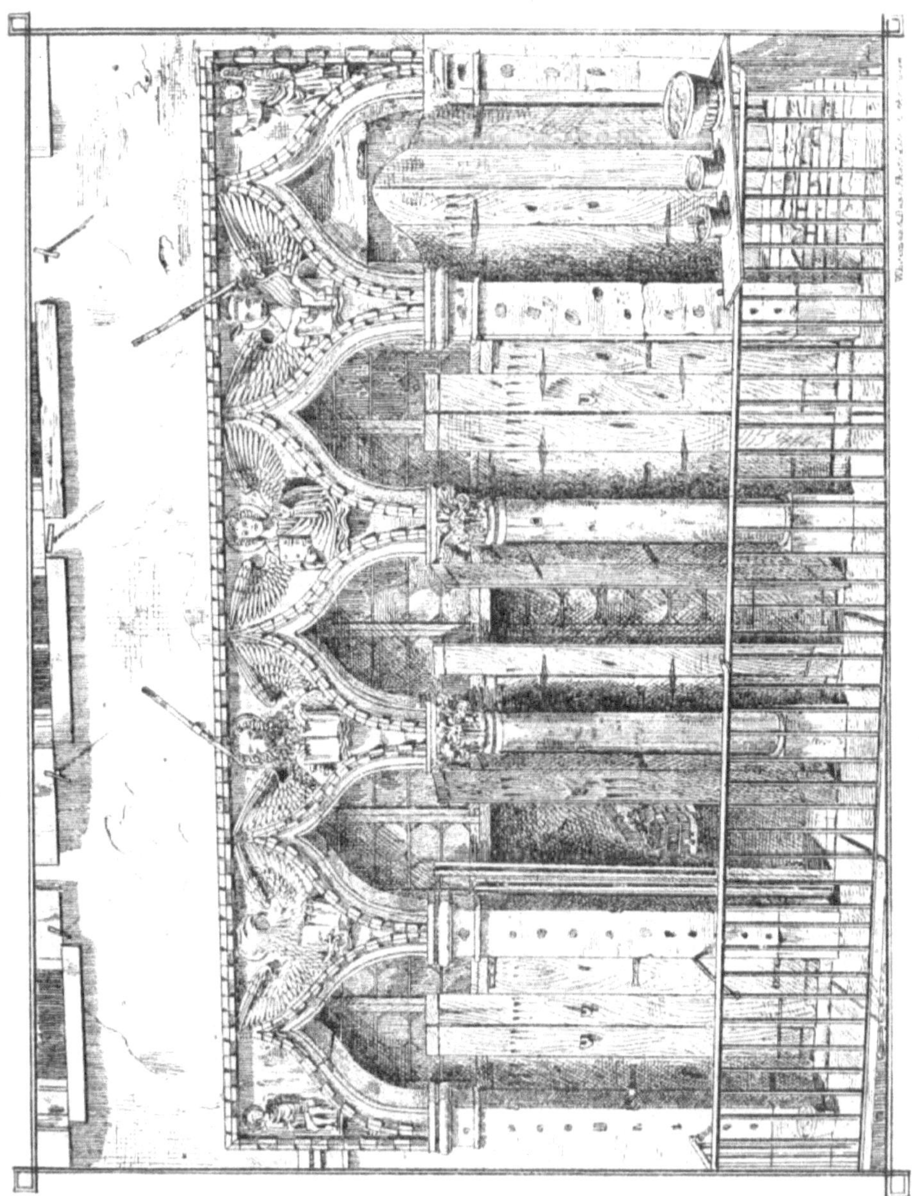

33.—Window. Ponte del Fornaro. Venice.

With notices of two more buildings, the Palazzi Cavalli and Barbaro, I shall conclude my remarks upon the existing examples of Venetian domestic work. Neither of them calls for much remark. The traceries of the Cavalli Palace are heavy and unsatisfactory, and contrast unfavourably with the greater simplicity of the windows in the Palazzo Barbaro. The two palaces stand, however, in a very fine position on the Grand Canal, commanding the view from the Foscari Palace in one direction to the church of the Salute and the mouth of the canal in the other. Nearly opposite them is a very striking house, the Ca' Dario, built, I imagine, about the commencement of the sixteenth century, before the revived Classic feeling had fully possessed the Venetians, and displaying some effective and beautiful arrangements of constructional decoration with coloured marbles. It is, in fact, an attempt to revive, to some extent, the art of incrustation, as practised at S. Mark's; and so successful is it, that I wonder much that more examples are not met with.

34.—Staircase, Casa Goldoni. Venice.

In the Grand Canal, and near this spot, are many other buildings, all worthy of illustration, but adding, I think, nothing to what we already know. The Ca' Fasan is the most unlike the other mediæval houses of any; but it pleased me so little that I could not bring myself to waste time by sketching it. It is only fair to say that in its traceried balconies it approaches more nearly to the latest northern pointed than any other building in Venice, and that it has perhaps at the same time less breadth and dignity than any.

Two fine palaces[55] are now turned into hotels, and that at which I stopped was full of remains of pointed windows; indeed traces of pointed work are singularly plentiful, and I might go on to an interminable length were I to attempt to describe them all. The Arsenal is old, I believe, but has been modernized. It may be visited now for the sake of the grand and quaint old lions which sit before its entrance.

Of the interiors of these houses I cannot say very much. They usually have a great hall in the centre of each floor, into which the various rooms open; and the windows of these halls are generally the most important in the elevation. The frames of the windows were of wood, placed behind the traceries, and the original ceilings were the moulded beams of the floors. I have only seen one good Gothic staircase in Venice. This is in the Casa Goldoni, and has for its balustrade a series of shafts with piers at intervals. Its detail in short is that of the balcony, but sloped up to suit the rise of the steps. Pointed arches of brick carry the steps. This house may well be visited by other than architectural pilgrims, and will be found near the Ponte San Tomà. A fine early Renaissance staircase remains in the Palazzo Minelli, near San Paterniano. This is circular, with continuous open arcades following the rise of the steps, the usual shafted balustrade filling the lower part of the openings between the columns. The chimneys of these palaces are very singular. Not many old examples remain, but they are still copied, and that some of them are really old is proved by the extent to which they are shown in early Venetian paintings, as e.g. in the works of Gentile Bellini and Carpaccio. In my illustration the examples Figs. 2 and 3 are copied from paintings, and Fig. 1 is from a palace near the Ponte Bernardo.

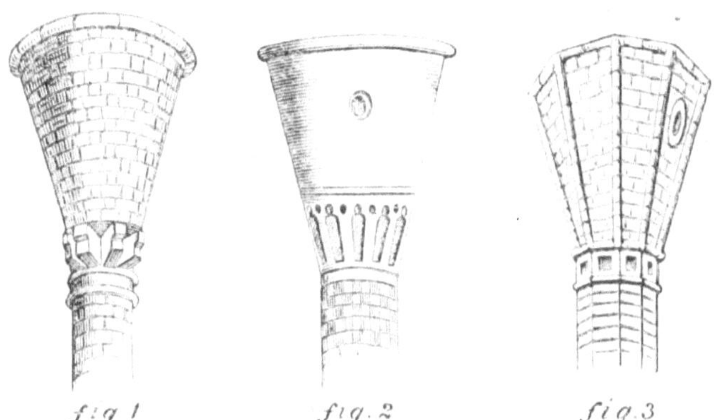

Venetian Chimneys — Venice.

[55] The Europa and Danieli's.

And now that we have so far passed in review a series of the finest remains of mediæval architecture in Venice, it is time to inquire how much is to be learnt by what we have seen, and in what degree it differs from the developments of pointed architecture with which we are familiar in Northern Europe.

I think the very first point to be observed is that in Venice architecture was never essentially constructional in the sense in which it was in our own land. The pointed arch is rarely used except in churches, and in its place traceries, increased in size and scale to do their work, are made to carry the entire weight of walling above them, as is the case, to take the foremost example, in the second stage of the Ducal Palace. And it is remarkable that, when the arch was used, from a very early date it was the ogee arch, and not the arch formed by two simple curves; indeed it may almost be said that the pure pointed arch was never used, save where it would have been quite impossible with any other contrivance to bridge the necessary gap, or provide sufficiently for the weight to be supported. How striking a contrast this is to the way in which in England men worked with and exhibited the pointed arch, evidently as if, and because, they loved it!—using it not only as a sturdy servant to do heavy work, but as the friend of whose friendship they were ever the most anxious to boast. I do not complain of the flatness and lack of breaks or recesses in the masses of the great Venetian buildings, because this no doubt arose in part from the value of every foot of ground so hardly gathered from the sea, and the difficulty of throwing out buttresses into the narrow depths of the canals out of which they rise. And the same conditions which enforced this flatness are grateful because they involved the charming balconies which are so peculiarly Venetian, and gave a breadth and simplicity to the outline which has its own artistic charm.

In the science of moulding I cannot but think that it is quite useless to compare works executed for the sunny skies of Venice with those fitted for the gloomy sunlessness of a northern climate. The one kind are as properly soft, gentle in their alternations of light and shade, and delicate, as the other are piquant and sharp, rejoicing in the dark shade of deep hollows and endless intricacy of outline and arrangement. But I feel no doubt whatever that, unfair as it may be to compare one school with the other, seeing that each worked for its own wants, it is yet most clear that the Northern architects were developing a much deeper art, and working with much more consummate skill, than were the Venetian. The endless variety of the arrangement of; capitals, and the necessary grouping of mouldings to fit, their varying outlines, was carried to the extreme point of perfection by the one school, whilst in the other not only was there much less depth and relief, but also very much less variety. The abacus of the Italian capital was almost always square in plan, and, as an almost necessary consequence of this, mouldings retained very much the same arrangement and shape for the whole period of the prevalence of the pointed style, and generally rather leaned to the side of heaviness than of delicacy. Venetian mouldings are composed of the constant combination of a three-quarter bead and a shallow hollow, divided by small fillets, and so invariably arranged in almost exactly the same order, that it requires very great care to decide upon the date of buildings by their mouldings with any sort of approach to certainty.

In addition to simple mouldings, there are also the ever-recurring ornamented mouldings which are so peculiarly characteristic of Venetian works of all dates. These consist generally of sections which in England we should consider Romanesque, but which in Venice appear to be much more common in the latest works than in the earliest; chevrons, cable-mouldings, billets, and the like, are seen everywhere, and suggest the question whether this class of ornamented mouldings, so largely used in the early days of architecture in England and so little afterwards, might not with some advantage be rescued from the contempt into which it has fallen with modern builders. They have the advantage of being within the power of any ordinary workman to execute, and do not, therefore, require the handiwork, which is so rare and so precious, of thoroughly good carvers. Add to this, that some features originally invented for use in the way of holding together marble incrustations, were afterwards used universally for their own sakes as ornamental mouldings, for which office they were in no way fitted, and I think nearly as much has been said as can be of Venetian mouldings in stone. Those in brick are even less satisfactory; but they occur mainly about the churches, and, as I do not recognize anything at all distinctively Venetian in their design or arrangement, it will be better to say more about them after we have seen the brickwork in other cities in the North of Italy, compared with which that at Venice is not of the first order.

In the practice of carving, as in that of moulding, I see no reason for yielding the palm to the Venetian. It is true indeed, that the Byzantine capitals—of which such magnificent examples exist at S. Mark's—are some of the most exquisite I have ever seen, true and precise in their sculpture, revelling in the utmost delicacy of intricate work, and always refined and elaborated with great evidence of care and thoughtfulness; but after the earliest school, and those later examples in which they were copied and regarded as models, there appears to me to be much less to admire. There is a confusion and want of fixed purpose about many of those which are commonly referred to as the best types of Gothic sculpture, which is at best not satisfactory; and I confess that I came away much more pleased with some of the Byzantine capitals than with any others. They have some notable points of difference from those to which we are used. They are generally much larger in proportion to the shaft than ours; and instead of having a regular neck-moulding, they rise out of the shaft with a kind of swell, which, as being less definite, is to me less satisfactory than our neck-moulding. The capitals of all dates are very generally similar in their outlines—this in part arising from the constant occurrence of circular columns with capitals whose abaci are square, and in part from the imitation, more or less closely, of Byzantine models. Indeed, it is impossible not to see how great an influence the earliest remaining work—that of the eleventh century—had in Venice until the end of the fourteenth and far into the fifteenth century; the most beautiful and striking arrangements of the former age are reproduced and only slightly modified in the finest work of the latter to a very remarkable extent: and so much more decidedly and frequently than are the traces, in northern pointed, of any hankering after the features of Romanesque buildings, that I think but one conclusion can fairly be drawn from the sculpture of Venice as well as from its architecture, viz. that pointed architecture was never developed as purely and thoroughly in Venice as in the North of Europe; and that, though it retained its sway there nearly as long as it did elsewhere, it never thoroughly understood or felt its own strength, and worked and toiled tied down and encumbered by Byzantine fetters and Classic sympathies. There is much, notwithstanding this, to admire—and, above all else, the greatest beauty of the style, wherein it so far left us behind, the thorough appreciation and unsparing use of the shaft. It is quite astonishing how very little this was ever used in England. Occasionally, indeed, it was freely used in grand buildings, and in some individual features it was frequently seen in thirteenth-century buildings; but at the very period when, if ever, architecture was in its perfection—in the early part of the fourteenth century—it was almost entirely forgotten and thrown aside. All honour, therefore, to the men who so perseveringly and determinedly used it as did the builders at Venice for three centuries! And all shame to us if we do not attempt for the future so far at any rate to follow in their steps! So rare are any but shafted windows in Venice, that at present I hardly remember a single instance of a window with monials formed by the continuous mouldings of the tracery; and it is obvious that this gave occasion, not only to the use of beautiful marbles—never so well used as in shafts—but also to the constant use of carved capitals. In domestic buildings, as I have before remarked, this arrangement of shafted windows is very valuable, because it suggests one obvious way in which we may unite traceried windows with the very newest arrangement of window-frames or sashes in the most comfortable nineteenth-century houses; for in these Venetian palaces the glass was always contained in a separate wooden frame set within the marble shafts and tracery.[56]

Besides the use of the shaft in the ordinary way, I must not forget to say that parapets frequently (or perhaps it were better to say balustrades)—as, e.g., at S. Mark's—and balconies everywhere, are composed of a vast number of very delicate shafts, set very close to each other, and surmounted by long pieces of stone cut out in imitation of arching, and not really to be regarded as a succession of arch-stones, but rather as coping-stones to hold the shafts together. And, again, they are used very beautifully for the support of open pinnacles, one at each angle, inclosing a figure, just as in the monuments of the Scaligers at Verona. Examples of this are to be seen in the pinnacles which have been added between the gables of S. Mark's, which are exceedingly good in their effect; and again in the pinnacles which terminate the church of the Madonna dell' Orto.

One more point is worthy of remark—the treatment, namely, of the angles of buildings. These were almost always marked either by a roll-moulding or by a succession of nook-shafts, sometimes extravagantly chevroned or otherwise ornamented. This, when done simply, was always satisfactory, but, in its later and more elaborate form, was, I think, as unsatisfactory. The delicate rounding off of

[56] This arrangement is not by any means unknown in Northern Europe, though certainly uncommon as compared with Italy, where it was almost universal. There is an example of the thirteenth century at Easby Abbey, Yorkshire, and another at Oakham Castle; whilst in France the ancient houses at Cluny all have it; and at Ratisbon, one of the most interesting cities in Germany, a great number of houses of the twelfth and thirteenth centuries, of prodigious architectural interest, have it.

the angles of walls was a point not unthought of in England. In the thirteenth century a nook-shaft was the common contrivance; in the fourteenth, a chamfer; and in the fifteenth men reverted entirely to the square form. Here, however, there is a great and very interesting variety in this apparently simple feature. The most satisfactory plan of all is where a quarter circle forms the angle, and is finished with a small incision in the form of a V on either side, as it unites simplicity with strength of construction and softness of contour, and does not force itself too prominently upon our observation; and, next to this, the most satisfactory form is where, instead of the moulding being round, it is pointed at the angle. The twisted shafts of the upper stage of the Ducal Palace, and the triple and chevroned shafts of the Ca' d'Oro, are not improvements upon the refinement of the earlier mode.

I have already spoken of the exquisite beauty of the inlaid marbles in S. Mark's; nothing can be better than their effect, and nothing seems more wonderful than that they should not have been used more frequently in later buildings. I was, perhaps, a little disappointed in not finding, as I had expected, the marble arranged generally in geometrical patterns; but this is quite the exception; and one sees only, in a medallion here and there, the exquisite beauty which their arrangement in this way may produce. As a rule the walls are faced with thin slabs of marble, each of the size in which it came to hand, sawn into as many slices as its substance would allow, and then riveted to the walls and held in place securely by projecting thin lines of stonework built into the wall, and cut with indented or billet ornaments along their edges. There is, however, a degree of real as well as apparent weakness which is not at all satisfactory in this system of incrustation, and I thought how much more noble such work might well become, were it to be inlaid only where no strong work was required to be done—as, e.g., in spandrels of arches,[57] or within arches—and not as here to the concealment of every one of the necessary constructional features. It is to be observed, however, that the slabs of marble are generally higher than they are wide, so as at once to destroy any thought of their being really constructional.

The south side of S. Mark's is, perhaps, the place above all others in Venice where this inlaid work may be seen to the greatest advantage. Some of the great arches which stand in place of gables are divided into four or five square-headed lights by shafts supporting semicircular arches, the tympana of which are filled in with delicate and perpetually varied filigree-work in marble, whilst above them a succession of panels or medallions shews all the resources of the rich materials which were to be exhibited. In another case, just over the entrance from the Piazzetta to the church, the tympanum of the arch is filled in with large medallions, one exquisitely carved, the others plain; whilst the arch of the window below the tympanum has its beautiful marble spandrels adorned on either side with medallions which, for exquisite arrangement of vari-coloured marbles in geometrical patterns, are perfectly admirable. There is enough, therefore, in the Venetian system of incrustation, though much unhappily be lost, to give ample food for our study and admiration; and its only weak point is, as I have said, its too frequent neglect or concealment of the constructional features of the buildings it adorns.

---

[57] It was only so used in the Ducal Palace.

It is easy, however, to cavil at particular details, and scan with a critical eye the architectural beauties of Venice; but let it not be thought for an instant that all the wonderful pictures which every new turn or new point of view brings before the eyes are unappreciated. A few days spent there suffice almost to fill a lifetime with reminiscences of all that is novel, beautiful, and strange; and days such as I have spent, year after year, rejoicing in the daytime in the full brilliancy of a September sun, and at night in the calm loveliness of a Venetian night, have been just the most delightful in every way that could be passed.

We were at Venice on the festival of the Nativity of the Blessed Virgin—a great feast-day, which it had been my fortune to spend some two or three times before in Roman Catholic countries. I confess that here we were not edified. We came in, as we went from church to church, for rather more than the usual number of the *désagrémens* which always seem to attend the decoration of the churches, and especially the altars, for such festivities abroad. The strongest impression left on my mind was one of wonder at the paltry character of the long array of what by courtesy are called, I suppose, wreaths of flowers, manufactured of pink gauze, or some equally unnatural material. These, with vulgar draperies hung outside the church doors, and in additional quantity about the altars, with the most noisy and gladsome ringing of bells, completed the external demonstrations; all the shops were most studiously closed, and the churches and open places were thronged with people. At S. Mark's we heard[58] some abominably light opera-music, which sounded, as may be imagined, very discordant within its solemn walls.

One morning we devoted partly to the ascent of the campanile in the Piazza. The ascent is entirely by inclined planes; the outer walls of the tower are in fact double, and in the space between them these inclined planes are formed; and it is worth notice that to this day, in all buildings which we have seen in progress in this part of the world, inclined boards are used instead of ladders for obtaining access to scaffolding; and in one of the mosaics in the entrance-porch of S. Mark's, where the building of the Tower of Babel is depicted, precisely the same kind of arrangement is shewn. This is interesting, as shewing the tenacity with which old customs are adhered to. The view, when the top is reached, quite repays the labour of the ascent, as it gives the best possible idea of what Venice really is. We get an impression of a very densely populated town, hemmed in on all sides by water, and looking very flat and low; in the distance small islands pave the way to the mainland, or shelter us from the sea; these, where they are more distant, look like mere black spots on the smooth, unrippled expanse of water: and in the far horizon we see to the west the purple outline of the mountains about Vicenza; and to the north of these, and rising grandly into the sky, the snowy peaks of the southern range of the Friulan Alps. Below and around are countless churches, all placed confusedly without respect to orientation—a neglect, if anywhere excusable, surely so here, where land is the exception and water the rule.

The last day we spent in Venice was most enjoyable. We had been all day in our gondola, now stopping to sketch some Gothic palace, anon shooting into some narrow canal to escape the bright heat of the sun, winding our way now here, now

---

[58] I *have* heard a polka played by the organist in S. Mark's!

there, just as the fancy of the moment seized us, and realizing more than ever that "the longest summer's day was all too short" for a last day in so fair a place. In the evening, just before sunset, we went out into the Lagoon, and, rowing round the small island of Giudecca, watched the gradually waning light reflected on the smooth, calm water, which seemed too silent and too soft to be disturbed by a word from any of us; and then at last, turning back and coming suddenly through a short canal into the main stream just opposite the Dogana, we moved on gently till we came abreast of the Ducal Palace. It was just dark; the moon was rising behind us in all her beauty, and in front, lamp after lamp was suddenly lit along the Piazzetta, then along the palace-front, all along the Riva dei Schiavoni, until at last, before we landed, as far as we could see, the bright lights, reflected in a hundred gleaming, flashing lines, were fitfully dancing in long streams of light upon the bosom of the waters.

We stepped on shore to find ourselves led on by the sound of military music, and to be tempted by the luxury of ices eaten *al fresco* in the Piazza; and then, when the crowd gradually dispersed, we too, among the last, found our way to our hotel, charmed so much with our last night in Venice that it is impossible not to recollect that evening with the deepest pleasure.

It is not without purpose that I have held silence with regard to the churches and buildings generally of the Renaissance school in Venice. These have had in their time many more admirers than have the examples of architecture which it was alike my business and my delight particularly to examine; and to the present day I doubt not that nine people out of ten, led by their valets-de-place, go to see what is worst in point of taste, and so reap the reward of allowing themselves to be made to see with another's eyes, instead of enjoying the intense pleasure of working out and exploring for themselves all the treasures of this mine and storehouse of ancient art. It is partly because I feel the greatest repugnance to the buildings themselves, and partly because I fear to make my notes, already lengthy, far too long for the patience of my readers, that I do not venture upon this additional field of study; but not in the least degree because I doubt the result, for I believe firmly that, tried by the fair rules which must regulate merit in a constructive art, the Renaissance buildings of Venice would be no nearer perfection than those of any other city. Something perhaps there is in the gloomy grandeur of their vast masses rearing their rusticated walls and deeply recessed windows darkly above the comparatively cheerful and bright-looking walls of the neighbouring Gothic palaces, which may impress the minds of some, but they must be of a sombre temperament who really love them. Still more must they be of a tasteless temperament who can endure with patience the succession of eccentricities with which Palladio and his disciples have loaded their churches. I pretend not, however, to discuss the point. I had not time for everything, and preferred giving up the attempt to like what from my heart I have ever disliked, and what nothing that I saw in Venice would make me dislike at all less heartily.

Neither do I pretend to say anything about Venetian pictures; guides without number may be found of more service and more knowledge, and to their hands I leave their proper charge. A word only upon one point—their adaptation, namely, to the sacred edifices of which they are the most notable ornaments.

Now I must at once say that there is no church, so far as I saw, in Venice, with the single exception of S. Mark's, which is to be compared in this respect (in its effect, that is, as heightened by colour) with such buildings as the Arena Chapel at Padua or the church of Sta. Anastasia at Verona—the one an example of the very noblest art working under strict architectural limitations; the other, of simple decorative painting. The fact is, that the Venetian pictures give the impression that they might do elsewhere as well as in a church, and therefore entirely fail in identifying themselves with the walls on which they hang; whilst no one can ever think of the noble works of Giotto at Padua, without recalling to mind the religious order of his works and their identification with the building which contains them; and at Verona the result of the system adopted in the painting is marvellously to enhance the effect of the architecture without in any way concealing or damaging it. In Venice the case is quite different. The church of San Sebastiano, in which Paul Veronese is buried, and which internally is almost entirely covered with his paintings, is an example of what I suppose I must call the best Venetian treatment. This consists, however, of immense oil-paintings covering entire walls, and absolutely requiring, in order that they may be at all properly appreciated, that the spectator should stand in a particular spot—in some cases by the side of the altar—and that the windows should first have blinds drawn down, and then, when he goes to look at another painting, have them drawn up again. This is all very unpleasant. But besides this, there is no very sensible advantage to the colour of the buildings from these decorations; certainly they are far behind mere decorative paintings as vehicles for bringing out the architectural features; and so they are visited very much as pictures in a gallery, and without in any case being identified with the churches in which they are preserved. The mosaics at S. Mark's are, on the other hand, some of the very grandest examples of the proper mode of decorating interiors with representations of religious subjects, all conceived and arranged with some order and relation to each other. But of the other Venetian churches there does not seem to me to be any one whose artists at all succeeded in equalling the example so early set them.

I do not pretend in these pages to speak at all of paintings irrespective of architecture, or I might find much to say upon the store of works, of a very noble school, in which this great city is so rich. The immense rooms of the Ducal Palace, covered as their walls and ceilings are with the works of Tintoretto, Titian, and Paul Veronese, cannot be forgotten; still less can the many works of Giovanni Bellini, and of other painters in the churches, and in the collection in the Accademia—rich among others in the works of that great and interesting painter Carpaccio—be passed over; whilst the decorated walls of the various Scuole are in many cases of hardly inferior interest. I am sorry that I was obliged to take the great merits of some of the grandest works somewhat on faith; it was in vain to think of actually studying them in a short time, and, educated as I have been to love the works of an earlier date and another school more heartily than these, I must confess, barbarous as the confession may appear to be, that I was not thoroughly pleased with what I saw. The magnificence of the chiaroscuro and colouring of these great pictures scarcely atoned to me for the degree to which—owing generally to the immense array of figures and confusion of subject—I failed to carry away distinct conceptions of the story intended to be told. It may be said that this is the result of want of taste or education, but still the feeling is so different when for the first time pictures by Fra Angelico, Ciotto, Raffaelle, Perugino, or Francia are looked at, that it is hard to avoid believing that, though their power over colour may have been somewhat less, their power of attaining to the highest point of the true painter's art—that of leaving indelible impressions on the minds of all beholders—was immeasurably higher. Thus much only by way of excuse for not saying more about what the world in general rightly conceives to be one of the great glories of Venice.

And now I must say farewell, and, doubtful though I may be as to the claims of Venetian art in the Middle Ages to be considered as at all equal to that of the same period in Northern Europe, I am very grateful for many new ideas gathered and much intense pleasure enjoyed in the examination of its treasures; and so, rather sadly laying myself down to sleep for the last time in Venice, I began to deem that my journey henceforward must be rather less interesting than it had been; with Venice a thing of the past, instead of, as it was on my outward course, full of all the beauties with which the liveliest fancy could crowd its walls and palaces by anticipation.

CHAPTER IX.

New Roads to Venice—The Pusterthal—Innichen—Dolomite Mountains—Heiligenblut Kötschach—Kirchbach—Gail Thal—Hermagor—Ober Tarvis—Predil Pass—Gorizia—Aquileja—Grado—
Udine—Pordenone.

"A sea
Of glory streams along the Alpine height
Of blue Friuli's mountains."

Childe Harold.

TO those who wish to find new roads to old haunts let me recommend the
road to Venice described in this chapter. A more interesting way for any one who
has already travelled through Lombardy to Venice cannot be desired. It affords a
sight not only of charming scenery, primitive people, and churches of some interest, but gives an opportunity for a visit to Aquileja, Grado, and Udine, all of them
places well worthy to be known by all lovers of architecture. Leaving the Brenner
railway at Franzensfeste, we made our way first of all to Innichen. Here I found a
very fine Romanesque church which, placed as it is not very far to the north of the
distant mountains which one sees from Venice, and full as it is of Italian influence
in its general design, may well be included in my notes. It is a cruciform church
with a central raised lantern, three eastern apses, a lofty south-western tower, and
a fifteenth-century narthex in front of the rest of the west end. The nave is divided
from the aisles by columns which are, (1) ten-sided, (2) four half columns attached
to a square, and (3) octagonal. The first and third are massive columns decreasing
rapidly in size from the base to the capital. The central lantern has an octagonal
vault upon very simple pendentives, and the apses have semi-dome roofs. A fine
south doorway has the emblems of the four Evangelists, sculptured around Our
Lord in the tympanum. Innichen is a small and unimportant village, but boasts,
I think, of no less than five churches; and fine as is the mother-church, I suppose
most travellers would agree with me in thinking the background of mountains to
the south of it, the most delightful feature of the place. Truly I know few things
more lovely than the evening view of the church and village, with the tall fantastic
peaks of the Dolomite Drei Schuster behind, lighted up with the glowing brilliancy which is so characteristic a result of the Dolomite formation, by the last rays of
the setting sun. Below all was gloomy, dark, and shaded; above the whole series of
towering peaks seemed to be on fire, and most unearthly did they look. The attraction of such sights as I had seen before compelled me to give a day to an excursion

southwards to the Kreuzberg pass, to have a glimpse, at any rate, of the Auronzo Dolomites, and I had no reason to repent the day so spent.

Leaving Innichen and going eastward, we went first to Lienz; then, after a *détour* to Heiligenblut, we crossed from the Pusterthal to the Gail Thal, and from thence across the Predil pass to the Adriatic at Gorizia. From Innichen till we reached the Italian sea-board, we saw and were much interested in a series of churches, generally of the fifteenth century, and all built apparently by the same school of German architects. They are small mountain churches, and are mainly remarkable for the complicated and ingenious character of their groined roofs. They have usually aisles, columns without capitals, and no distinct arches between them, but only vaulting-ribs. The panels between the ribs are often ornamented with slightly sunk quatrefoils, or in some cases regularly filled with tracery.

One of the best of these churches is that at Heiligenblut, in Carinthia. Here, where the main object of every one is the exploration of the mountains grouped around the beautiful snow-peak of the Gross-Glockner, it is not a little pleasant to find again, as at Innichen, a remarkable church just opposite the inn-door. This was built as a pilgrimage church to contain a phial of the sacred blood, and is extremely interesting architecturally as a church, built with a regular system of stone constructional galleries round the north, south, and west sides of the nave. The aisles are narrow and divided into two stages in height—both groined—and the upper no doubt intended for a throng of people to stand in, and see the functions below. Now, however, just as in most modern galleries, raised tiers of seats are formed in them, and their effect is destroyed. A pretty Retable at the end of the north gallery suggests that originally perhaps they were built in part to make room for side altars, but this was clearly not the primary object. The fronts of the galleries are covered with paintings of no merit, which illustrate the beautiful legend of S. Briccius, who is said to have brought the phial of blood from the East, and to have perished with it in the snow just above Heiligenblut. There is a crypt under the choir, entered by a flight of steps descending from the nave; a grand Sakramentshaus north of the chancel where the holy blood is kept (not over the altar); and there is a lofty gabled tower and spire on the north side of the chancel, whose pretty outline adds not a little to the picturesqueness of the village.

From Heiligenblut, looking at churches by the same hands on the way at S. Martin Pockhorn and Winklern, we made our way back to Lienz, and thence, crossing the mountains, descended on Kötschach in the Gail Thal, passing a good church on the road at S. Daniel.

Kötschach is in one of the most charming situations for any one who can enjoy mountains of extreme beauty of outline, even though they are not covered with snow to their base, nor are more than some nine thousand feet in height. To me this pastoral Gail Thal, with its green fields, green mountain sides, wholesome air, and occasional grand views of Dolomite crags, among which the Polinik and Kollin Kofel are the finest peaks, is one of the most delightful bits of country I have ever seen. At Kötschach the architectural feature is a fine lofty gabled steeple with an octagonal spire. It is very remarkable how German these Germans are! Here, close to the Italian Alps, we have a design identical with those of the fine steeples of Lübeck, and as vigorously Teutonic and unlike Italian work as anything can possibly be.

From Kötschach a pleasant road runs down the valley to Hermagor, another charming little town beautifully placed, and with—no small attraction—a capital hostelry. On the road, at Kirchbach, the drivers of the country waggons in which we were travelling pulled up their horses, to my no small delight, in front of a most interesting mediæval churchyard-gate; this is a simple archway overshadowed by a shingled pent-house roof, to whose kindly guardianship we owe it that a fifteenth-century painting of S. Martin dividing his cloak with the beggar, and several saints under craftily-painted canopies, are still in fair preservation on the wayside gate, making one of the most lovely pictures possible on the road.

At Hermagor, where the grand and massive mountain range of the Dobratsch to the east, and the Gartner Kogel to the west, give never-failing pleasure to the eyes whichever way they turn, there is another fine church, very much of the same character as that at Heiligenblut, but without galleries.

Between Hermagor and Ober Tarvis the churches are not important, but one in the village of S. Paul has the unusual feature of a cornice under the external eaves effectively painted in the fifteenth century, with elaborate and very German traceries in red and buff, which are still fairly perfect.

At Ober Tarvis the Predil Pass is reached; and starting from thence in the morning, passing on the ascent the pretty Raibl See, and on the descent some of the most stupendous and aweful rocky precipices I have ever seen, we reached Flitsch to sleep, and on the following afternoon emerged from the mountains at Gorizia, not far from the head of the Adriatic, after a long and beautiful drive down the valley of the Isonzo.

I found absolutely nothing old to see here. It is a smart town, in which the hand of the improver has been particularly busy in the work of destruction; but it is the most convenient starting-place for a visit to Aquileja and Grado, and provides good horses and vehicles.

It is a drive of about a couple of hours from Gorizia to Aquileja. The country is perfectly flat, but teeming with vegetation, and it is not until the end of the journey is reached that one realizes under what baleful conditions life or existence is endured here. A Roman capital and a fragment or two of Roman columns or mouldings are all that one sees at first to show that one is driving into one of the greatest of the old Roman seaports. Here, where before its destruction by Attila in A.D. 452 the population is said to have been about a hundred thousand in number, there are now only a few poor houses, and a sparse population, pauperized and invalided by fever and swamps on every side, whilst the sea has retreated some three miles, and left the place to its misery without any of the compensating gains of commerce. Certainly Torcello is a degree more wretched and deserted, but these two old cities have few compeers in misery, and I advise no one but an antiquary to make the pilgrimage to Aquileja, who is not quite prepared to tolerate dirt, misery, and wretchedness with nothing to redeem them.

Patriarch's Throne. — Aquileja.

The one great interest in the city now is the cathedral. This is a great cruciform basilica, with a central and two small apses east of the transept, and eleven arches between the nave and aisles. The arrangements of the apse are interesting; two flights of steps lead up to it from the nave, and in the centre of the east wall is the patriarch's throne of white marble, well raised on a platform above the seat which goes round the apse. The whole arrangement is singularly well preserved, and looks very well in spite of the destruction of most of the mosaic pavement with which originally no doubt the floor was laid, of which only a few tesseræ now remain, and in spite also of the modernization of the rest of the apse. This throne appeared to me to be not earlier than circa 1150, though the church is said to have been built between 1019 and 1042. These dates must, I think, be taken with large allowance for alterations. With the exception of the apse and the crypt under it, I believe the greater part of the church was rebuilt in the fourteenth century; for though the Roman capitals (which were everywhere ready to the hand) were used on the ancient columns, the arches carried by them are pointed, and the clerestory is evidently of the same age. This combination of Classic columns and sculpture with pointed arches is so very unusual, that it is quite worth while to give an illustration of the interior. The columns, capitals, and bases are of varied shapes and sizes, and evidently a mere collection of old materials which happened to be handy for the builder's use; the arches are rudely moulded, and the clerestory of cinquefoiled windows, each of a single light, is as insignificant as possible, and yet withal there is so grand an area inclosed that the effect is good and impressive. The nave is divided from its aisles by eleven arches on each side, and measures about one hundred and fifty feet in length, by one hundred and five in width. The aisle roofs are modern, but the nave still retains its old roof, a fine example of a cusped ceiling, boarded and panelled in small square panels. The whole of this ceiling is painted, and with extremely good effect, though the only colours used are black, white, and brownish yellow. Each panel is filled with a small painted hexagon filled with tracery painted in black and white, and all the ribs and leading lines are yellow and black. The purlines, which are arranged so as to form the points of the cusps, are very decidedly marked with black. Simple as the treatment is, the effect is admirable, and it appeared to me to be owing to the large amount of white in the panels. Near the west end of the north aisle is a singular circular erection, which is said by the cicerone to be the receptacle for the holy oil, but which without this information I should have taken for the baptistery. It is a perfectly plain circular mass of stonework about fifteen feet across, with a doorway on the west side, a moulded base and cornice, and above the latter a series of detached shafts carrying a second cornice of marble. A square projection on the north side abuts against the aisle wall, and seems to have been the special receptacle for the vessel which held the oil. At present it seems to be as little used and understood by the people of Aquileja as it would probably be if it were in some country beyond the Roman pale; a remark by the way on old church arrangements which one finds oneself making almost everywhere, when one contrasts the intentions of the old builders with the uses to which more modern ideas—reformed or deformed, whichever they may be—are in the habit of applying them.

At Aquileja the appropriation of pagan fragments was carried so far that we found Classic capitals doing service as holy-water stoups.

The interior of the eastern part of the church is more interesting than that of the nave. It is all probably of the original foundation, and retains most of the old arrangements. The floor of the choir is raised some ten or twelve steps, with two flights of steps on each side of the centre. At the top of these steps, projecting sideways into the transepts, are tribunes with open balustrades which seem to have served as ambons. The apse has two rows of seats, with the patriarch's seat raised in the centre, and the altar stands in front of this on the chord of the apse. It is curious that this, which is an apse internally, is a square projection from the transept externally.

35.—Interior of Duomo. Aquileja.

A descent on each side under the tribunes leads to the crypt under the raised choir. This is very small, but is divided into three aisles in width, and four bays in length. The central space is screened round jealously with close grilles reaching from floor to vault, so as to protect the shrine of S. Hermacora, which occupies the centre. But little light steals into this crypt, and that little has to find its way between rank weeds which grow up round the windows; but there is quite enough to reveal vaults covered with paintings of subjects, and to show as picturesque and beautiful an *ensemble* as one need wish to see. Kneeling desks were placed round the shrine, but the cultus of S. Hermacora seems to be no longer popular, and the only pilgrims are curious visitors like ourselves. The paintings on the groining appeared to me to be of not earlier date than the fourteenth century, and are very cleverly contrived to suit the early vaults.

The transepts remain to be mentioned. Each has a small eastern apse near the extreme end, and a tomb or shrine between this apse and the choir-tribune. These are of the thirteenth century, and are enormous blocks of stone, panelled and carved in front, and supported on four detached shafts. In the south transept there are fragments of a Byzantine screen round the altar in the small apse, which are of rare beauty and intricacy. The screen consisted of a solid base, breast-high, covered with carving, and upon which columns stood originally at intervals of six feet, just as in the screen at Torcello, of which I have given a view.

There is an early painting of Our Lord, seated on a throne in the semi dome of this apse, and there are remains of an early wall-painting in the choir-apse, partly covered by a fifteenth-century picture in a good frame. The choir stalls are of elaborate intarsiatura work, and date from the end of the sixteenth century.

A little way to the north of the church stands its campanile, a tall plain mass of masonry, with the date MDXLVIIII. on the upper stage, and the inscription "*Tadeus Luranus hoc o. fecit.*" It is worth the climb to the top to get the view over the flat surrounding country, which reveals what one fails to see from the dead level of the road, that the Adriatic is not far off—far enough, it is true, to have ruined the port of Aquileja—but so near as to be a very important element in the fine prospect. From here we saw through the haze the island of Grado, on which I cast longing eyes in vain. My information as to the distance had been all at fault, and I thought that in a long day from Gorizia, I might see both Aquileja and Grado. This is, however, quite impossible, as the boatmen required, they said, three hours for the *trajet* each way. It was a misfortune to miss the church at Grado, which contains much that is worth seeing, and has considerable historical interest, as the seat of a patriarch, whose jurisdiction included Malamocco, Venice, Torcello, and Chioggia—and whose importance is vouched for by its old titles, "Venetæ oræ Istriæque Ecclesiarum caput et mater," and "Aquileja nova."

The patriarch's throne and the ambon or pulpit, which still remain in the church at Grado, are evidently extremely fine examples of Byzantine furniture. The former corresponds with that of Aquileja, but has the rare addition of a flat canopy or tester supported in front by two columns, which rest on the side walls of the steps leading up to the seat. Probably there was a similar canopy at Aquileja. The dignity of the patriarchal throne is not a little increased by the addition, simple as it is in its decorative features. The pulpit is even more striking; it is six-sided, all the sides being arranged in a series of bold circular projections, with sculptures of the Evangelistic emblems on their face. The pulpit is supported by a central shaft, and six smaller columns alternately plain and spiral, and above the pulpit a series of octagonal shafts are provided to support a canopy or dome over the head of the preacher. These columns carry arches which are of the common Venetian ogee trefoil outline, and, there can be little doubt, are later than the pulpit. The combination is, however, very picturesque, and not the less interesting in that it has a most strangely Eastern look.[59]

The rest of my party went, whilst I was sketching in the cathedral at Aquileja, to look at the baptistery. They reported it to be as completely modernized inside as it certainly is outside, and so I failed to enter it. I believe I lost nothing, though at one time it was well worthy of a visit.

A rapid drive back to Gorizia was made with the advantage of a view of the mountains before us all the way; and we arrived in time to avail ourselves of the last train to Udine, which we did not reach until after dark.

I arrived here in entire ignorance of what might be in store for me in the way of my art. I had seen no drawings of any of its buildings, and I suspect that most of my readers are in the same state of ignorance. It was with no little pleasure, there-fore, that my earliest stroll in the morning brought me to a Palazzo Publico, which if not exactly magnificent in scale is at least very important, and has the special merit in my eyes of being all Gothic, and almost unaltered on the outside since its erection. It stands in a piazza which some sixteenth or seventeenth century scenic architect has treated with considerable skill. One or two public buildings and a steep hill behind them have been dealt with in such a way as to call to mind such a disposition of buildings as one sees, e.g., on the Capitol at Rome, and no doubt so as to increase very much the apparent importance of this little city. The Palazzo Publico is a building of two stages in height, the lower entirely open with pointed arches resting on columns, and the upper presenting on its principal front a large balconied window, or Ringhiera, in the centre, and smaller windows on each side of it, and at the ends. The cornice and roof are modern, otherwise the whole design is intact, and exactly in the state in which its architect left it. The character of the design is clearly Venetian, and the date about the beginning of the fifteenth cen-tury, but still it is not slavishly Venetian as the houses of Vicenza are, but on the face of it the work of a local architect who knew enough of what was being done in Venice to profit by it without absolutely copying.

The lower or ground story is open on three sides, and has ten arches in front, and five at each end. The space inclosed is irregularly divided by a longitudi-nal line of columns, carrying semicircular arches, which support the walls of the rooms above, the access to which is by a modernized staircase in the rear. The ma-terials of the walls are generally red and white marble. The balustrades between the columns and the staircases leading to them are so good and complete as well to deserve illustration. The upper part of these, including the cusped heads to the openings, is of white marble, whilst the shafts are alternately of the same material and of serpentine. The upper story is modernized within; but one learns to be grateful for small mercies, and it was certainly with every feeling of gratitude to later architects that I sketched this really beautiful building, which they have been good enough to leave so nearly unaltered on the outside.

[59] I take these notes of Grado from 'Mittelalterliche Kunstdenkmale des Oesterre-ichischen Kaiserstaates.' Stuttgart. 1858.

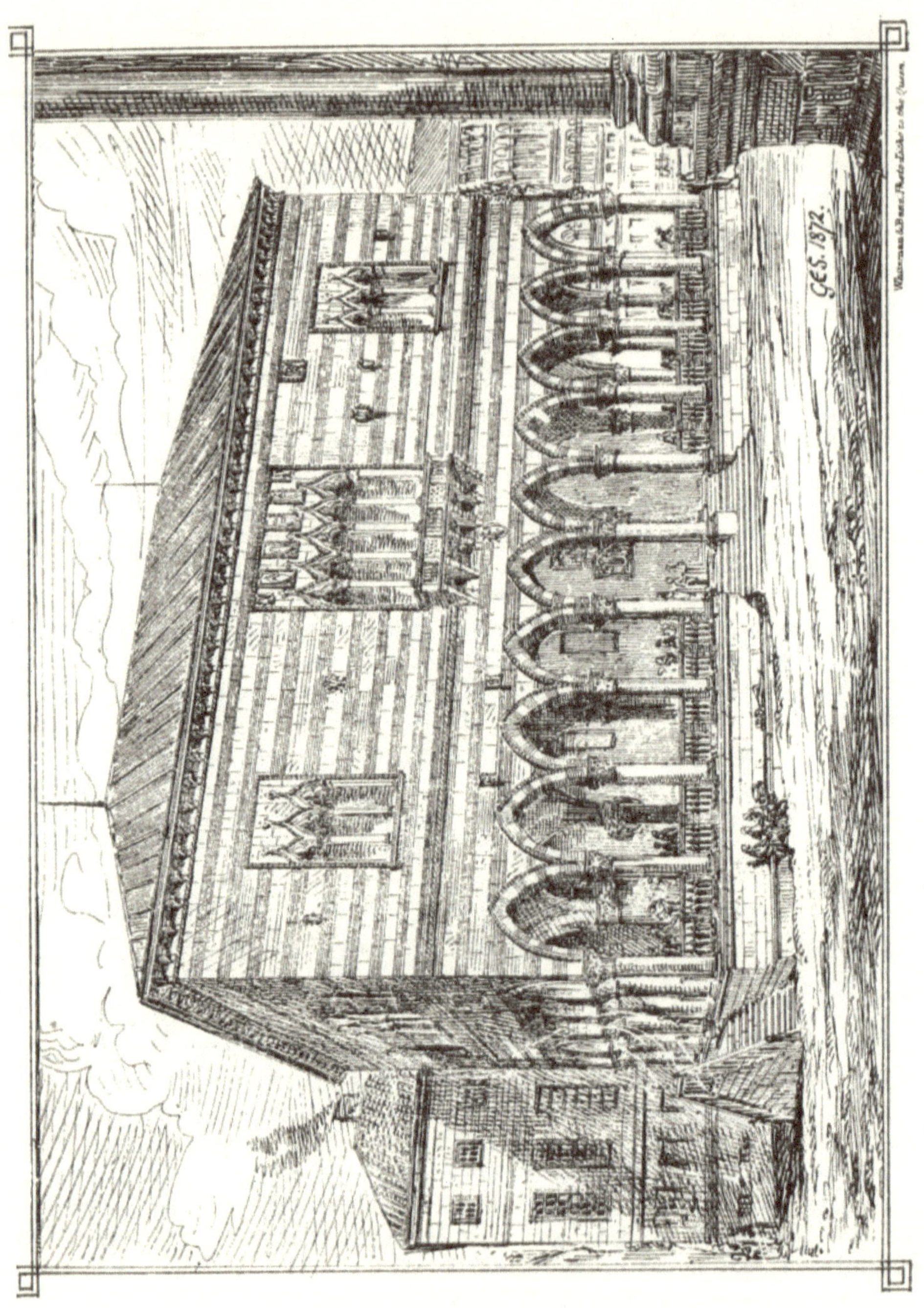

36.—Palazzo Publico. Udine.

37.—Steps to Palazzo Publico. Udine.

The state of the cathedral is less a subject for thankfulness! The whole building has been completely modernized within and without, with the exception of the west front and the lower. The former was the façade to a nave with two aisles on either side, or perhaps with one aisle and chapels beyond. All the roofs are of the same flat pitch, and stepped regularly so as to give a broken and bad outline to the mass. The work is mainly of brick, with some good detail in the windows of the outer aisles, of which I give an illustration. The west doorway is of the fourteenth century, with a very steep crocketed gable between pinnacles, and a badly sculptured tympanum with a curious assortment of subjects; in the centre the Crucifixion, right and left of this the Resurrection and an Agnus Dei, and above it the Nativity. Three circular windows light the three centre divisions of the front, and the two lower are connected by a broad band of brick arches which crosses the entire front just below the central circular window. There is not a word to be said in favour of such a design. It *is* old, and that is its only virtue!

Aisle Windows—Duomo, Udine.

The tower is more interesting, though it is only an incomplete fragment. The lower stage is of stone built in dark and light courses, with a large sunk recess on each side. On the west side is a fine doorway built of alternate courses of white marble and serpentine, and there are small circular windows in the cardinal sides just above the lowest stage. Above these the whole is a plain mass of brickwork, of which a very small portion only seems to be original. This tower is no less than fifty-two feet in outside diameter, and its lowest stage is finely groined, with no provision for the passage of bells. It might almost as well have been intended for a baptistery as for a tower! It stands close to the north side of the choir, and by its side is a rather fine doorway leading into the transept, with a good deal of late Gothic sculpture and architectural detail. There are niches and figures in the jambs and round the arch, the Coronation of the Virgin under the latter, and figures of the Annunciation stuck against the wall on either side in a very haphazard fashion. The strange contrast in style between these two doorways will be seen in the illustration which I give. Here we have, side by side, examples of the most pronounced kind of two national styles of Gothic; the door into the tower being as clearly Italian in its beautiful colour and refined simplicity, as that into the church is German in its cleverness, want of repose, and hard angularity of detail.

38.—Duomo. Udine, Tower and Cathedral Doorways.

The only other old churches I could find in Udine were San Giacomo and that of the Ospidale. The former is modernized, but retains an early square brick belfry, arcaded below, and with simple pointed windows of two lights above. The church of the Ospidale is also modernized. The façade has a gable with an old brick eaves-arcade, and the only too common feature of a large circular window inclosed within a square border.

A picturesque Renaissance well-canopy (dated 1487) over the Fonte di San Giovanni was the only other feature I could find worth sketching or making a note of; and having seen everything, I took the railway on again to Venice.

The views of the Friulan Alps, under which one travels for some distance, are very exquisite. We passed Conegliano, where I once left the railway for a journey through the heart of the Dolomite country to Cortina d'Ampezzo, and, to my regret, hurried past Pordenone, having forgotten that at any rate a tall brick campanile was there, which seemed to promise some reward to the visitor. It is of plain arcaded brickwork below, and the upper stage is slightly battered out with very tall machicoulis, from within the parapet of which a smaller octagonal stage rises, covered with a low spire. The whole composition as one sees it from the railway is unusual and very good, and recalls just a little the campanile of the Palazzo Publico at Siena.

CHAPTER X.

Venice to Verona—Verona to Mantua—Villa Franca—Mantua: its
Churches and Palaces—The Theatre—Montenara—Campitello—
Casalmaggiore—Longadore—Cremona: the Cathedral—Churches and Public Buildings—Lodi—Pavia: its Churches—Castle of
the Visconti—The Certosa—Drive to Milan.

"With all its sinful doings, I must say
That Italy's a pleasant place to me,
Who love to see the sun shine every day,
And vines (not nail'd to walls) from tree to tree
Festoon'd."

Beppo.

OUR gondolier, anxious not to be too late for us in the morning, slept in his
gondola beneath our windows, and did his best, when the sun rose, to rouse the
sleepy porter of our hotel, but in vain; and at last, when I awoke, I found we should
have a very narrow escape, if indeed we did not absolutely lose our train. The
thing was, however, to be done, and was done. We shot rapidly—only too rapidly
for the last time—along the smooth waters on which we had been so pleasantly
loitering before, and soon found ourselves at the railway station. Our journey was
much like what such journeys usually are: as far as Verona we were only retracing
our steps, but now the hot sun had quite cleared away the clouds which, when we
passed before, hid the Tyrolese Alps from our sight, and these, whenever the high
acacia hedges which line the railway allowed us a sight of them, made the journey
so far beautiful.

The names of the engines on this railway are very unlike the kind of nomen-
clature indulged in at home; we were drawn to Verona, I believe, by the Titian, and
saw, as we rushed along, engines named after Dante, Sansovino, and other artistic
and literary celebrities.

We reached Verona at ten o'clock; the station, however, is so much out of the
town, and the day was so intensely hot, that we gave up the idea of again going
into it, and, contenting ourselves with the general view of its quaint and picturesque walls rising over the rugged hills which girt the city on its northern side,
we sat down to a breakfast of iced lemonade and some of those deliciously light
cakes which are never had in such perfection as in Italy, and amused ourselves by
watching the way in which the guards and drivers of the train by which we had
travelled proceeded to solace themselves with a game at billiards, upon a table
provided, I suppose, by the very considerate directors of the railway company.

39.—Ducal Palace, Mantua.

The railway from Verona to Mantua crosses a country which is thoroughly uninteresting in point of scenery; it carried us on well into the great plain of Lombardy, rich, teemingly rich, in its produce, but flat, arid, and sultry to a degree. This was altogether one of our hottest days, and took us fairly into a kind of district in which the heat is most oppressively felt.

On the road we passed Villa Franca, a small town which has a rather striking castle, with battlemented walls and a good many square towers, still very fairly perfect; the whole built in brick, and with battlements finished square at the top, and not forked like those at Verona.

We reached the station at Mantua by twelve o'clock, but, as this was very far from the city, it was nearly an hour later before we were fairly landed at one—I forget which—of the abominably dirty and bad inns to which sojourners within its walls have to submit with the best grace that they can.

Mantua is nearly surrounded by water; two large shallow and unwholesome-looking lakes giving it this far from pleasant kind of isolation. Over a long mediæval bridge between these waters the way into the city from the terminus lies. One of the lakes is higher than the other, and accordingly twelve mills, each adorned with a statue of an apostle, are formed upon the bridge, and give it its name of Ponte Mulina.

The general aspect of Mantua is very dreary and unpleasing, not less forlorn in its appearance than Padua, and possessing but little attraction for an architect. The chief architectural feature of the city is the Ducal Palace, which contains, in the midst of a mass of Renaissance work of the poorest and most unsatisfactory kind, some very good remains of pointed architecture.

The finest portion is a long building of vast height, and retaining more or less of Gothic work throughout, but especially remarkable for the range of windows in its upper stage. Its front faces on one side towards the Piazza di San Pietro, and on the other with a very nearly similar elevation towards the Piazza del Pallone, one of the courts in the vast palace of the Gonzagas, of which it forms a part. This building is said to have been commenced about A.D. 1302 by Guido Buonacolsi, surnamed Bottigella, third sovereign of Mantua, and this date quite agrees with the character of all the detail. The interior has been completely modernized, mainly by Ginlio Romano, who carried out very extensive works in other parts of the palace. The windows in the upper stage of this portion of the palace deserve notice as being about the most exquisite examples of their class that I anywhere met with, though those in the campanile of Sant'Andrea, hard by, are only second to them. The main arch is of pure pointed form, and executed in brick with occasional voussoirs of stone—one of which forms a key-stone—and over it there is a label of brick effectively notched into a kind of nail-head. The same kind of label is carried round the arches of the window-openings, and down the jamb as a portion of the jamb-mould, and again round a pierced and cusped circle of brick in the tympanum. In the sub-arches the key stones and cusps are formed of stone. The whole of the jambs are of brick, but instead of a mortal there is a circular stone shaft, with square capital and band and base. The whole is so exceedingly simple as to be constructed with ease of ordinary materials, and it is quite equal in effect to any stone window of the same size that I have ever seen.

40.—Mantua (Windows in Ducal Palace).

Window in Ducal Palace.

The accompanying drawings will, I trust, sufficiently explain the merit of this magnificent piece of brickwork. The arcading upon which it rests, and the perfectly unbroken face of the whole, are very characteristic of Italian work.

On the opposite side of the Piazza di San Pietro is the cathedral, the only ancient portion of which is a small part of the south aisle. It is of very elaborate character, entirely built in brick, and so far as it remains appears to have been part of an aisle finished with a succession of gables, one to each bay, a common arrangement in German and French churches, where additional aisles are so frequently met with, but uncommon in Italy, where, as in England, churches have seldom more than one aisle on either side of the nave.[60] The brickwork in this small fragment of the cathedral, though elaborate, was not pleasing, being of rather late date.

On the same side of the Piazza as the cathedral is the Vescovato, a large pile of ancient building, but very much modernized. There still remain, however, some good three-light windows in the upper stage, inclosed within a circular arch, without tracery, and divided by marble shafts. Some old arches remain also in the lowest stage, which, though now built up, are still valuable as examples of the best mode of treating brickwork. They consist of three orders—the two inner formed of alternate voussoirs of brick and stone, carefully and regularly counterchanged, and the outer of a moulded terra-cotta ornament. Between each of these lines a brick of deep red colour is set edgeways, shewing a dark line of little more than an inch and a half in width, and valuable as very clearly defining the lines of the arch. All these courses are on the same plane; and probably another rim of the arch is concealed by the walling which has been filled in underneath.[61]

Going on from the Piazza San Pietro, and passing under an archway, we came upon the Castello di Corte, also a part of the ancient palace of the Gonzaga family, who were for a long time lords of Mantua. It is certainly a very remarkable piece of mediæval fortification, but its effect is much damaged by the erection of walls between the battlements, which in my view I have thought it much better to shew in their original state, which is evident enough upon careful inspection. The heavy machicolations which run round the main building have a peculiar and rather grand effect, particularly in the flanking towers. This portion of the palace is said to have been erected just at the close of the fourteenth century.

Close to the Castello di Corte is the Ponte di San Giorgio, one of the entrances to the city, and built between the Lago di Mezzo and the Lago Inferiore.

Retracing our steps, we soon found ourselves at the great Palazzo della Ragione, or town-hall. It has been very much altered, but one gateway remains in a very perfect state, and is quite worthy of illustration. The marble shafts in the upper stage of the building are coupled one behind the other with very beautiful effect. Brick and stone are used alternately in the main arch of this gateway, with thin dividing lines of brick, as in the Vescovato. In a wall close to the gate is a sitting figure, intended, it is said, to represent Virgil, of whom the Mantuans are still, as in duty bound, very proud. I cannot say much for the figure or its canopy, both of which are, however, mediæval.

[60] It is to be seen, however, in the church of San Petronio, Bologna.

[61] See for an engraving of this archivolt, Chapter XIV. p. 298.

41.—Castello di Corte, Mantua.

We found nothing else worthy of notice in this building; but close to it stands the church of Sant'Andrea, a hideous Renaissance edifice tacked on to a most beautiful brick campanile.

The detail of this is throughout very fine. The tracery is all of a kind of plate-tracery, consisting, that is to say, of cusped circles pierced in a tympanum within an inclosing arch; the shafts between the lights are of polished marble, and coupled one behind the other. The relative proportion of the cusps in this and in most other Italian buildings is very good. In trefoils, for instance, the upper cusp is usually smaller than the lower; and in all good cusping it must be so. Modern men generally reverse the order, and, at the present day, so little is the subject really understood that at least ninety-nine out of every hundred cusped window-openings are designed without feeling, and quite unlike the best old examples; and this, though apparently a point of very small importance, is really of great consequence to the perfection of any pointed work.

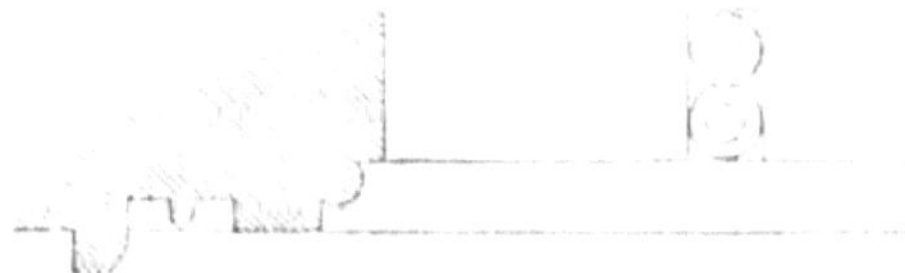

Brick Window—Sant'Andrea, Mantua.

42.—Gateway, Palazzo della Ragione, Mantua.

43.—Campanile, Sant'Andrea, Mantua.

The faulty portions of this campanile are the elaborate arcadings in brick beneath the string-courses, and the awkward and abrupt manner in which the octagonal stage and the round tile spire are set upon the square tower. The present appreciation of the building by the good people of Mantua is shewn by the opening pierced in its lower stage, in front of which the modestly withdrawn folds of a green curtain disclose the interior devoted to a barber's shop, and in which the patient, seated in the middle of the shop, and looking into the Piazza, submits to the painful operation of shaving—a common picture in almost every street of an Italian town, but not pleasant when the place is a portion of a church.

Brick Window—Sant'Andrea, Mantua.

The guide-books speak of the church of Sant'Andrea as "among the finest existing specimens of an interior in the revived Roman style." If it really is so, I advise all architects interested in the failure of the said style to venture, notwithstanding the forbidding west front, into the nave, when they will perhaps find comfort in seeing how miserable a building "one of the finest" of its class may nevertheless be!

The people at Mantua seemed to be excessively disturbed by my attempts at sketching, and at Sant'Andrea they mobbed me so thoroughly that I was really beginning to think of giving up the attempt in despair, when a kindly-disposed hatmaker, seeing my distress, came down to the rescue, and gave me and my party seats in a balcony on the first floor of his house, in which, sitting at my ease above my persecutors and listening to the good man's wife and daughters, I finished my sketch with great comfort.

In Mantua there are two or three other churches with brick campanili, but they are very inferior in their character to that of Sant'Andrea, and hardly worth special notice. We owe it to the French that there are not more interesting churches, for, having succeeded in capturing the city after a very prolonged siege, they sacked it, and are said to have destroyed no less than about fifty of them.

Here, as elsewhere in this part of Italy, most of the streets are arcaded on either side, affording pleasant shelter from the hot sun, but every twenty yards we come upon one of an unpleasant class of shops, in which cheese, oil, and the like comestibles are sold, with most objectionable effects on all people blessed with noses.

In the evening we found an Italian performance going on at the theatre, and so thither we went, anxious to see how far Italian comedy might be amusing. I fear our inquiry was not much to our edification, for the favourite performers were mainly remarkable for the prodigious rapidity with which they uttered their facetious sayings, and so we lost more than half the dialogue. The theatre was almost entirely filled with Austrians, but still there was a sprinkling of Italians among them, which did away with the absurdly martial appearance of the only other theatre we had been into—that at Verona.

The next day was Sunday, but we were obliged to push on; and so, resigning ourselves to the diligence which left Mantua at about nine, we booked ourselves for Cremona, under the promise that we should be delivered there punctually by five o'clock.

We lost sight of Mantua almost immediately, for, travelling along a dead flat and by roads whose sides are lined with high hedges of acacia or orchards thickly planted, you never see any place or building until you have absolutely arrived at it. There was not much to interest me on the road, and the weather, at first cloudy only and sultry, gradually became worse, and, before we had gone far, settled into a steady pouring rain; so we read, wrote, and occupied the many hours in the rumbling diligence as best we might.

At Montenara, which we passed on our road, the church has a brick campanile, with pilasters at the angles, and in the belfry two-light windows, with marble central shafts and round arches. It has one of the usual brick conical spires, with small angle-pinnacles—a finish to these campanili which certainly does not improve upon acquaintance. They are constructed of bricks with semicircular ends laid side by side, the joints being broken in each course, and so making a very jagged kind of cone.

The only noticeable point about the church at Montenara is that it has been lately rebuilt in the very worst taste, and at an angle of forty-five degrees with the old steeple!

At Campitello there are several remains of interest.

There is a small domestic building, with four pointed windows of two lights at the side; the windows have central shafts of stone, but are otherwise entirely of rough brickwork. The church has a kind of double belfry-stage, arcaded similarly in each stage with round arches. There are also here the remains of a castle by the river, with a fine tower of the same type as the angle-towers of the Castello di Corte at Mantua, and covered with a very flat-pitched roof.

| Brick Window—Campitello. | Brick Window—near Casalmaggiore. |

At Casalmaggiore, a town of some importance on the Po, we stopped for dinner; but it was too wet to attempt to look at the river, and the only note I made was of a large new church now in course of erection, Renaissance in style, and with a large dome, and a choir and transepts, all terminated with circular ends. The redeeming feature about it was that it was entirely constructed in brick with considerable care, though probably ere long this will be covered with a coat of plaster, of which modern Italians are not one whit less enamoured than are modern Englishmen.

At a village, the name of which I did not learn, between Casalmaggiore and Cremona, the church had a remarkably good simple brick campanile. The belfry windows were pointed, of two lights, with a small pierced circle in the head, the shafts being of stone of course. Beneath the string-courses there was arcading, and the tower was finished with three forked battlements of the Veronese type on each face, and behind these rose a circular brick spire. This tower was to the south-east of the church.

At Longadore we saw another church with a good early campanile, of which I made a sketch. This was Romanesque, with angle pilasters, and a central pilaster carried up as high as the belfry-stage. The belfry windows were of three lights and shafted. The battlement was most peculiar—a quarter circle at each angle and a half circle in the centre of each side, with a narrow space between them; the whole executed in brick and covered in with a flat modern roof. The angle pilasters finished under arcaded string-courses. Generally speaking, in these churches the only ancient features seem to be the campanili, and these are always of brick and nearly similar in their general design, with pilasters at the angles, a succession of string-courses—generally arcaded underneath—and windows in the belfry-stage only.

It was quite six by the time we reached Cremona, and, depositing our passports at the gate, we trotted on along the smooth granite (which in these towns is always laid in strips between the rough ordinary paving for the wheels to travel on), and after traversing a long tortuous street, and getting a glimpse only of the cathedral as we passed near its east end, we were soon deposited at the Albergo del Capello. a comfortable hostelry, which we enjoyed the more by contrast with the miserable quarters with which we had to put up at Mantua.

Cremona is a city full of interest. The piazza in front of the cathedral is equal in effect to almost any small piazza I know of. On one side is the great marble west front of the Duomo, backed by its immense brick campanile, whose wide fame is proved by the old rhyme, of which the Cremonese are still so proud—

> "Unus Petrus est in Roma,
> Una turris in Cremona."

On another side is the Lombard baptistery, a grand polygonal building; on the third, a most interesting domestic building—the palace of the Jurisconsults—and the Gothic Palazzo Publico; whilst on the fourth, a narrow, busy street makes up, by the diversity of colour and costume of the crowd which is always passing along it, for what it wants in architectural beauty.

The cathedral must be first described, and it is rather difficult to do this clearly; but so far as can now be made out it seems much as though it had at first been built upon a simple plan, with nave, north and south aisles, and three semicircular eastern apses; and that then to this, in the fourteenth century, had been added, with hardly any disturbance of the original fabric, immense transepts, loftier even than the nave, and so long and large as to give the impression now that two naves have been placed by some mistake across each other. The groining of the nave is original in its outline, but barbarously painted in sham panelling so as entirely to spoil its effect, but otherwise there is little to notice in the interior, the whole of the church having been converted with the plasterers' help into Renaissance in the most approved manner. The walls are covered with painting, and round the columns, when we were there, were hung great tapestries, all of which gave the building a rich though rather gloomy colour.

The west front (if you can forget that it is a great mask only to the real structure) is rather grand from its large plain surface of arcaded wall; it has been grievously damaged by alterations, but the old design is still not difficult to trace. The doorway is very noble, and the open porch in front of it is carried up with a second stage, in which, under open arches, stand a very fine figure of the Blessed Virgin, and figures of other saints of more modern character on either side of her; above this is a great circular window, whilst the wall on either side of the porch and window is nearly covered with small arcading. The marbles in the wall, where the arcading does not occur, are arranged very regularly in horizontal lines alternately of red and white, each course being about ten inches or a foot high, and divided from the next by a strip of white marble about two or three inches in height. The great rose window is all of red marble, with the exception of one line of moulding which looks like green serpentine. There are some round windows in the lower stage on each side of the entrance, but they are quite modern.

On the north side of the nave rises the Torrazzo, as the campanile is called here—the "una turris in Cremona"—rising about four hundred feet from the pavement of the piazza. Its design is much like that of all the other brick campanili in this district—a succession of stages of nearly equal height, divided by arcaded string-courses, and marked with perpendicular lines by small pilasters, and almost without windows until near the summit. The dark red outline of this magnificent tower tells well against the deep blue Italian sky, which shone brightly behind it when we saw it; and the effect of its immense and almost unbroken outline, rising to such an extraordinary height, is so utterly unlike that of any of our Northern steeples that we need not trouble ourselves to compare them. Both are fine in their way; but the Italian campanili are made up of the reiteration of features so simple and so generally similar that we cannot fairly class their builders with the men who raised in England such a multitude of steeples, all varying one from another, and yet all so lovely.

A door in the east wall of the north transept leads into a small courtyard, sacred now to the cathedral clergy, from which the original scheme of the eastern part of the church may be fairly well seen. It appears to have been a stone building treated in the common fashion of Lombard churches, but with buttresses and a passage through them round the apse in front of the windows. There is a modernized crypt under the choir. The side walls of the north transept are seen very well from the same courtyard; they are well arcaded in brick, and entirely concealed from sight elsewhere by the enormous false transept-fronts, the backs of which as seen from here are certainly among the most ungainly works ever erected for the mere sake of being beautiful.

The rest of the exterior of the Duomo is almost all of brick. The most remarkable features are the two transept fronts, which are certainly magnificent in their detail, though most unreal and preposterous as wholes; they are, both of them, vast sham fronts, like the west front, in that they entirely conceal the structure of the church behind them, and pierced with numbers of windows which from the very first must have been built but to be blocked up. They have in fact absolutely nothing to do with the building against which they are placed, and in themselves, irrespective of this very grave fault, are, I think, positively ugly in their outline and mass. And yet there is a breadth and grandeur of scale about them which does somewhat to redeem their faults, and a beauty about much of their detail which I cannot but admire extremely. Both transepts are almost entirely built of brick and very similar in their general idea; but, whilst only the round arch is used in the south transept, nothing but the pointed arch is used in the northern, and it is quite curious to notice how very much more beautiful the latter looks than does the former. The filling-in of stilted round-arched windows with ogee pointed tracery and much delicate cusping gives the south transept a singularly Eastern look, and it is impossible not to feel that some such influence has been exercized throughout its design. It would indeed be most interesting to find out what this was, but I am not aware that there is likely to be any clue to it. The date of the work is in all probability somewhere about the latter part of the fourteenth century. The detail and management of the whole of the brickwork are exceedingly delicate and effective, surpassing in their way anything I have yet seen.

44.—North Transept, Cathedral, Cremona.

Brick Window—Cremona Cathedral.

The putlog-holes are left unfilled, as they almost always are in Italy. The only stone used is in the doorway and the window-shafts, and these last are almost always coupled in depth. The windows are elaborately moulded, and courses of chevrons, quatrefoils, and other ornaments are introduced occasionally as a relief to what might otherwise be the tedious succession of mouldings which are necessarily rather similar. The cusping of brick arches is always managed in the same way; the bricks all radiate with the arch (not from the centre of the cusp), and look as though they might have been built, allowing plenty of length of brick for the cusps, and then cut to the proper outline, the edges of the cusps being almost invariably left square. Some of the terra-cotta arch ornaments and diapers are exceedingly good of their kind. The most remarkable feature, however, about these transepts is the prodigiously heavy open arcade which runs up the gables under the eaves-cornice—so heavy and so rude-looking, that, taken by itself, it would probably be put down as being of much earlier date than it really is. The façade finishes with three heavy pinnacles arcaded all round, and finished with conical caps.

To the north transept very nearly the same description would apply, save that the doorway is much finer, and entirely of marble.[62] It is part of the original Lombard church, and has no doubt been taken down and rebuilt where we now see it. The tracery of the rose windows is all finished in brick, and the detail generally is better and more delicate in its character than that of the south transept. In both the bricks are all of a pale red colour, and no dark bricks are anywhere used.

Rose Window—Cremona Cathedral.

The baptistery—which, as has been said, stands south-west of the Duomo—is entered by a doorway with a projecting porch, whose shafts rest on the backs of animals. It is octagonal in its plan, built of brick with the exception of the side in which the door is placed, this being of marble, and is very simple in all its detail. There are three altars in it, and an immense erection of masonry in the centre, which, though not open, is evidently a font, amply large for immersion. Each side has three recessed arches on marble columns, above which the whole is of red brick with stone string-courses between the stages. These have corbel-tables under them, which are the only enrichments in the building. All the brickwork is left to view inside, and the light is admitted by a pierced arcade very high up in the walls. The whole is domed over with an octagonal vault of brick, in the centre of which is a small lantern, and the effect is exceedingly fine and solemn, and enhanced very much by the grave sombre colour of the bricks.

---

[62] The two transepts are so very similar, that it seemed unnecessary to engrave my sketches of both.

45.—Palace of the Jurisconsults, Cremona.

Close to the baptistery is a building, called in Murray's Handbook the Palace of the Jurisconsults, turned when I first saw it into a school for a not very polite set of children and teachers, who all apparently felt the most lively interest in my architectural pursuits. It was originally open below, but the arches on which it stood are now filled up. This upper stage is very simple and beautiful, and the whole is finished at the top with a cornice and parapet, with battlements pointed at the top like those in the Torrazzo, and not forked as we have been lately so accustomed to see them. At one end of this parapet a chimney rises above the battlement, which is, so far as I have seen, a unique example of the ancient Italian contrivance for this very necessary appendage.[63] It is exceedingly good in its detail, and coeval with the rest of the work. There is a simplicity and truthfulness of construction about this little building which make it especially pleasing after the unreal treatment of the great transept-fronts of the Duomo.[64] By its side stands the Palazzo Publico, out of one side of which rises one of those singular and very tall brick towers, without any openings whatever in its walls, which give such peculiar character to some Italian cities, and of which we afterwards saw good store at Pavia. The whole of the building shews either traces of arcades or perfect arcades upon which the upper walls are supported; they are, however, so much modernized as to be comparatively uninteresting, though enough remains to shew that their detail was once very good. The building incloses a quadrangle, which is rather small, but arcaded on three sides, and opens from the piazza by open arches under the principal façade, and probably dates from the middle of the thirteenth century, the date 1245 being given in an inscription in the courtyard.

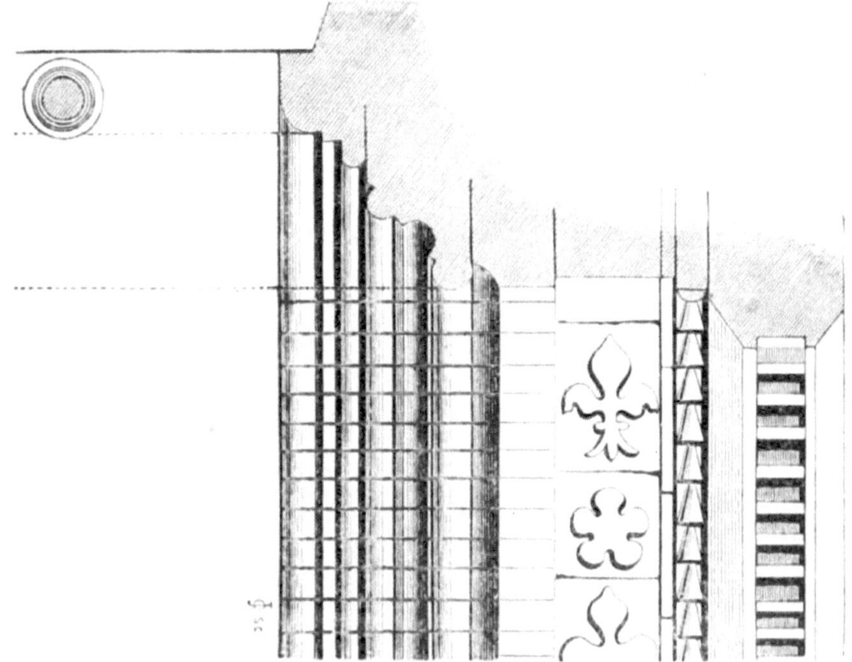

Window-jamb—Palace of Jurisconsults, Cremona.

There are many churches in Cremona, all more or less appearing to be founded upon the work in the transepts of the cathedral, but generally very inferior to them in merit.

---

[63] The chimneys so common in Venice are ancient, but yet hardly redeemed from ugliness. They are cylindrical, with heads sloping out in a strange fashion, and in the form of inverted truncated cones. See p. 165.

[64] This building has recently (1872) been restored, and with not much gain, though the barber's shop which used to occupy the ground-floor has been removed.

Chimney and Battlement—Cremona.

San Domenico has a west front singularly like theirs, but debased in its detail. It has, however, a very fine campanile, lofty, very simple, and pierced with pointed windows in each stage, one above the other. The interior is completely modernized, and not worth notice.

SS. Agostino and Giacomo in Breda is another church of the same class, with a west front which is again a very bad second edition of the cathedral, and which has been horribly mutilated and modernized inside. It is, however, to be remembered gratefully for a most lovely picture by Perugino, representing the Blessed Virgin with Our Lord seated, with SS. Augustine and James on either side. The Virgin is very calm, dignified, unearthly, and very simple and stately. Our Blessed Lord, in her arms, has perhaps rather too much the character of an ordinary infant; and the two saints have more than is quite pleasant of the bend in their figures of which he was so fond; the heads stooping forward, and the knees considerably bent, are a little too evidently straining towards a reverential posture. Such a criticism is a bold one to venture upon with the recollection of so glorious a picture fresh in my mind—one from which I really derived intense pleasure. The date of this very fine work is A.D. 1494.

Sta. Agata is another church which still has its old campanile intact, with round-arched windows, very simple and not large. The church which has been built against it tells its story so well, that at first we all mistook it for a theatre! So much for Classic symbolism.

Another church, dedicated in honour of Sta. Margherita, is a very poor erection of brick, with a simple campanile. One or two other churches we saw with fair brick campanili, which were not otherwise remarkable; and one there was, San Luca, close to the Milan gate, which seemed to be very singular in its arrangements. It had a projecting western porch, with its columns supported on beasts; and at the north-west angle an octagonal building of brick, of exceedingly late date, which appeared to be a baptistery.

I enjoyed the architectural remains in Cremona very much indeed: its rich array of buildings in elaborate brick-work is very striking; and the campanile of the cathedral, towering up high above the many other steeples, combines well with them in the general views, and helps to convert into a fine-looking city what is, perhaps, in its streets and houses generally, very far from being anything of the kind. The way in which the old walls and towers of the Palazzo Publico combine with the steeple of the cathedral is extremely fine, a large piazza a short distance to the west of the palazzo affording perhaps the best point of view.

From Cremona we went to Lodi, on our way to Pavia, and had a very pleasant drive. The heat was intense when we started, and the drivers of all the carts we passed were prudently ensconcing themselves in the baskets swung beneath their carts, to escape its effects. Throughout the Lombardo-Venetian territory there is a great traffic always going on, and there is a much nearer approach to English arrangements, in the way of harness and tackle, than it is at all usual to see on the Continent; though, indeed, it ought in fairness to be said, that their carts are much more scientific than ours generally are. Any vehicle with more than two wheels is rarely if ever seen; and these two wheels are sometimes of prodigious size—I should say quite ten feet in diameter—whilst the length of the cart from end to end is immense. The extent to which they are loaded is almost incredible, and of course it requires great care in order to make the trim exact; but when loaded, the draught must be light for the weight. It is impossible to talk about horses and carts without thinking of the magnificent cream-coloured oxen which are everywhere doing hard work on the roads and in the fields. They have most magnificent, large, calm eyes; and this, with their great size and slow and rather dignified motion, makes them look very grand. They are always yoked to a pole, which rises up above their heads at the end, and has a carved crosspiece attached to it, against which they press their foreheads.

At Pizzighettone we crossed the Adda, here a very fine and full stream, and then, changing horses, went on rapidly towards Lodi. Leaving the main road, we travelled along a less frequented byroad, infinitely more pleasant, and in many places very pretty indeed. We followed the course of a small river, which was turned to good account for irrigation; its stream being at times divided into no less than three channels, in order to water the pasture-land on which are fed the cows whose milk is to produce the far-famed Parmesan cheese. Some part of the road reminded us pleasantly of English lanes and English scenery, but here and there a distant glimpse of the Apennines far behind us, and of the Alps beyond Milan before us, made us aware that we were indeed in Italy.

There is little to be seen in Lodi. It has a large and rather shabby-looking piazza, at one corner of which is the cathedral, whose only good feature is its doorway, which is, however, very inferior to the western doorway of the cathedral at Cremona, to which it bears some little resemblance.

Another church has a Gothic brick front. The real roof is one of flat pitch, spanning nave and aisles; but in the façade the central portion is considerably higher than the sides, so as to give the idea of a clerestory. This is a foolish sham, and unhappily only too common in late Gothic work in Italy. The centre division of the front is divided into three by pilasters, which are semicircular in plan. In the central division are a door and a circular window, in each side division is a pointed window, and a brick cornice finishes the gable, crowned with five circular brick pinnacles.

Another church in Lodi has a very beautifully painted ceiling; this has been engraved by Mr. Grüner, but unluckily I did not know of its existence until I returned home; it seems to be an admirable piece of colour, and to be well worth careful study.

There seemed to be nothing else worthy of notice in Lodi; but, as in duty-bound we walked down to the bridge, — a rough, unstable-looking wooden erection over the broad rapid Adda, with nothing about it to recall to mind the great event in its history, its passage by Napoleon in 1796.

We left very early in the morning for Pavia: our way led us through a country most elaborately cultivated, and irrigated with a great display of science and labour; every field seemed to have some two or three streams running rapidly in different directions, and the grass everywhere was most luxuriant. No view, however, was to be had on either side, as the road found its way through a very flat line of country, and all the hedges were lined with interminable rows of Lombardy poplars. It was a country which would have done more good to the heart of a Lincolnshire farmer than to that of an architect!

The only remarkable building passed on the road was a castle at Sant' Angelo; a great brick building, with square towers set diagonally at the angles. The walls were finished with a battlement of the Veronese kind, and there were several very good early pointed brick windows with brick monials in place of shafts. A campanile, detached near one angle, has fine machicolations in stone, now, however, partly destroyed. The effect of the whole building was very grand.

We soon reached Pavia, and were, as we expected to be, well rewarded by its churches. The general aspect of the city is singular, owing to the number of tall slender brick towers which seem to have formed a necessary appendage to almost every house in the Middle Ages. They are entirely without openings or ornaments of any kind beyond the scaffold-holes, and one can compare them to nothing that I know so well as to the great shot-tower at Waterloo Bridge, save that they are always square and not circular.

We did our best to see the cathedral, but were unsuccessful; it was being repaired, and was so full of scaffolding that we could see nothing. It contains a shrine said to contain the body of S. Augustine, which I much wanted to see, but seemed in most respects to be an unprepossessing church.

From the cathedral we found our way to San Michele, a very celebrated church, and as interesting to an antiquary in search of curiosities as to an architect in search of the beautiful. The west end is very curious, and has a succession of sculptures, introduced in the most eccentric manner, and with but little method in their arrangement. There are three western doorways, and all of them are elaborately ornamented with carvings, the central door having above it a very singular figure of S. Michael.

San Michele, together with San Teodoro and San Pietro, seem all to be of about the same date, and are of the same character; the most remarkable feature being in each case the octagonal cupola, which rises above the crossing of the nave, choir, and transepts: externally these cupolas are arcaded all round under the eaves, and roofed with flat-pitched roofs, and are far from being graceful; open arcades are introduced under the eaves and up the gables, and everywhere there is a profusion of carving. It is likely enough that this Lombard-Romanesque style, as we see it at Pavia and elsewhere, did, as has been supposed, set the example which was very soon after followed in the great churches at Köln and elsewhere along the borders of the Rhine. In size, however, the children far exceeded their parents, for San Michele is not remarkable for its dimensions, except in the width of the transept.

The church consists of a nave and aisles of four bays, a transept of great length, a central lantern, and a short choir with circular eastern apse; small apses are also built in the east walls of the transepts. A fine crypt is formed under the whole of the eastern arm of the cross, and is entered by steps on each side of the thirteen steps which lead up to the choir. The nave aisles have a second stage or triforium, groined throughout; and the whole of the church is vaulted, the transepts having barrel vaults and the three apses semi-domes. The internal effect of the lantern is extremely good; the pendentives under the angles are very simple, and low windows are introduced in a stage between them and the octagonal cupola or vault. The whole church is still left in its original state with red brick walls and stone piers and arches, save where, as in the eastern apse, the vault is painted with a Coronation of the Blessed Virgin, executed in the fifteenth century. It is very seldom, consequently, that a church of this age is seen to so much advantage; and undoubtedly the fine, simple, but well-ordered arrangement of the plan, and the dignified character of the raised choir and the central lantern, would, even if the colour were not as picturesque and agreeable as it is, make this interior one of extreme interest. One of the best portions of the exterior is the east end. Its extreme loftiness is enhanced by the groups of shafts which divide it into bays, and rise from the plinth to the cornice. This part of the building is mainly of stone, except in the fine gallery below the eaves-cornice, where brick and stone are used together. In addition to the west door already mentioned, there are two very elaborate doorways north and south of the nave in the bay next to the transepts.

46.—San Michele, Pavia Interior.

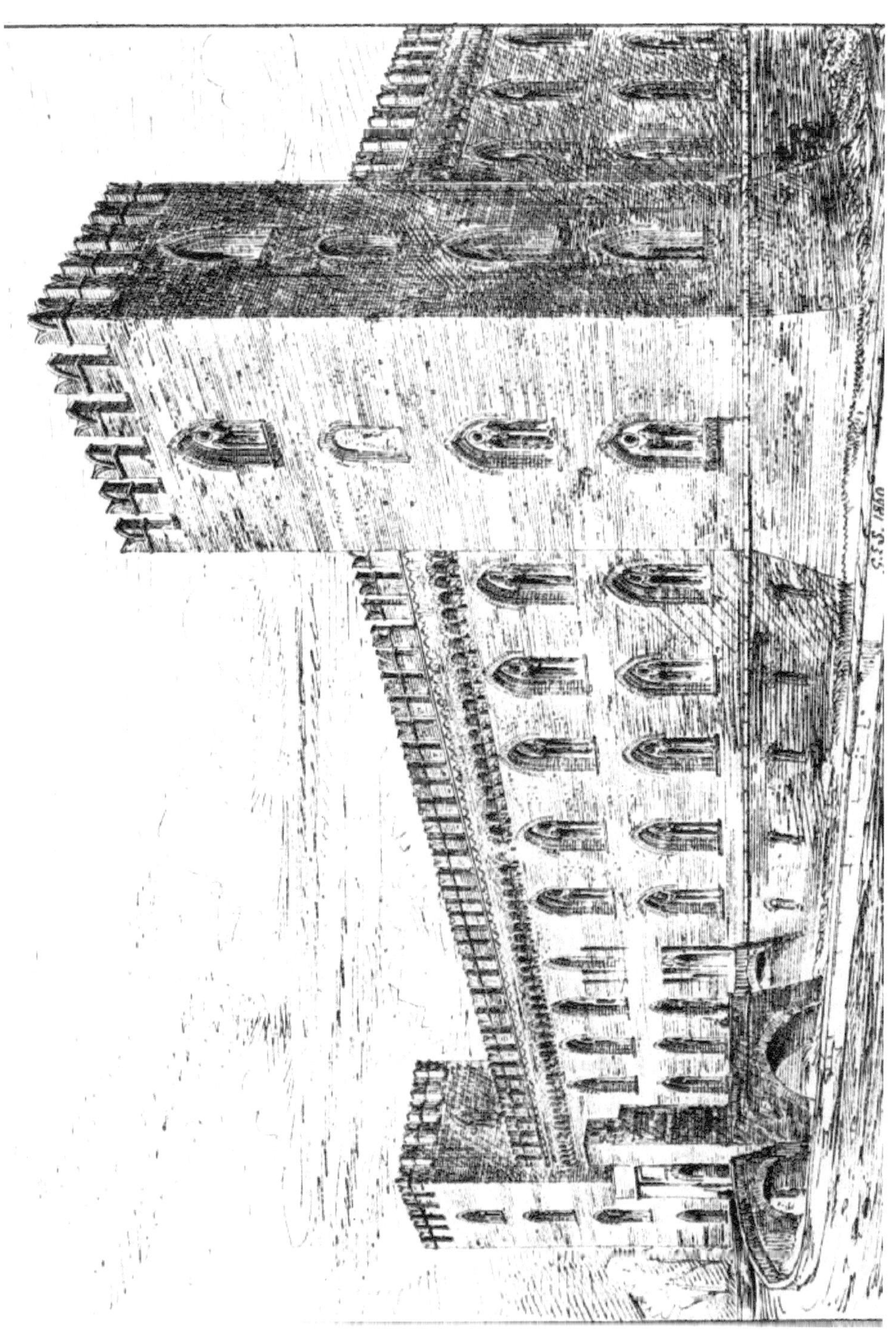

47.—Castle of the Visconti, Pavia.

San Michele is, on the whole, the most interesting building in the town, but is hardly superior to the grand remains of the old fortified castle of the Visconti, which stands just on the outskirts of the city, close to the Milan gate. This is only a portion of the original erection, only three sides of a great quadrangle which is inclosed by the building now remaining. The plan originally was a vast square with lofty square towers projecting at the angles, and of these only two remain. The whole front is still very nearly perfect, and is not far from five hundred feet in length, the main building of two stories in height and the towers of four, and all the old windows more or less intact. The whole is crowned with a forked battlement, and the old bridge still remains opposite the entrance with its outer gate, though the drawbridge has given way to a fixture. This grand pile is now used as a barrack; its most valuable architectural features are all towards the internal quadrangle, which is of grand dimensions, more than three hundred feet in the clear. Towards this court there is the same sort of arrangement throughout (though many modifications of detail)—an open arcade of pointed arches below, and a series of fine windows lighting a corridor above. The lower arches are of stone, everything else of brick, and the details everywhere are refined and delicate almost beyond those of any brickwork that I know elsewhere. The original scheme is best seen on the south side of the quadrangle, of which I give an illustration. This work dates, I suppose, from about A.D. 1300, but it was soon found to be inconvenient to have open traceries for the upper corridor, and the arches on the other two sides were filled in before the middle of the fourteenth century with very good two-light windows. Fortunately the whole of this work is still in very excellent preservation, and deserves much more notice and study than it has ever, I believe, received.[65] The ordinary bricks used here measure 10½ in. × 5 in. and are 3 in. high, whilst in San Pantaleone they are 3½ in. high and as much as 15 in. long. Here (as generally in the centre of Italy) the bricks have all been dressed with a chisel, with which diagonal lines have been marked all over the face. I can only assume that this has been done to improve the texture of the bricks in appearance, and, perhaps where two bricks are side by side on the same plane, to make a little distinction between them by tooling the bricks in opposite directions. Two other features of Pavian brickwork may also here be mentioned: one, that the depth of the arch-bricks is almost always increased from the springing line to the centre—the intrados and extrados not being concentric; the other, that the arch-bricks do not radiate from a centre, but are arranged so as to obtain a vertical joint in the centre. The first is a very defensible practice, the second seems to me to be the contrary.

---

[65] Mr. Grüner has published some very careful drawings of these details, in which he has restored the painted decorations with which the coloured construction of the walls was enriched. The style of decoration was much like that of Sta. Anastasia, Verona.

48.—Castle. Pavia. (Bay of Courtyard of Castle, Pavia.)

49.—West Front, San Pantaleone, Pavia.

There are several other churches to be noticed here. The most interesting to me after San Michele is that of Sta. Maria del Carmine, or San Pantaleone (for it seems to rejoice in a double dedication), which, in some respects, is more akin to our northern Gothic work than any other Italian church I have as yet described. The plan and all the details of the interior are exceedingly simple. The nave is divided into four groining bays, each of which has two arches into the aisles; the transept takes one bay and the choir one, and there are an aisle and a row of chapels on either side of the nave, and chapels on the east side of the transept. The only openings between the arches and the groining are small circles by way of clerestory, ludicrously small as compared with the immense space of blank wall below them, which seems to call loudly for decorative painting. The whole of the interior is executed in red brick, which has, however, been much daubed with a coloured wash; its effect is, notwithstanding, very fine and well worthy of imitation. As in Italian churches generally, the choir is very short as compared to the length of the nave. The exterior is even better worth examination than the interior; the design of the west end is an exaggerated example of the mode of finishing west fronts not uncommon in Italian Gothic; it is to some extent a sham, and therefore bad, but there is much which is of value in its detail, as it is even more than usually elaborate; and apart from the general outline of the mass, which pinnacles and pilasters cannot redeem from ugliness, there is considerable beauty in the group of windows and doors arranged so as to rise gradually to the centre. The cornices are very heavy and elaborate, and the whole front may be looked at as a masterpiece of terra-cotta and brick architecture. It is purely Italian in its great breadth and general arrangement, and, I confess, very far from being to my taste, though I could wish that we had more often some of the same breadth and simplicity in our own elevations.

It is very curious that this west end is the only elevation in this church which is at all distinctly Italian in its design; for those of the transepts and choir might much more reasonably be put down as imitations of Northern work; they are very similar, and a description of the latter will therefore suffice. It is flanked by massive buttresses, and has two large and lofty trefoiled lancets, surmounted by a circular window of great size; the whole is very richly moulded and executed entirely in brick. The buttresses and roof finish at the top in a rude temporary-looking manner, and it is therefore impossible to solve the interesting question of their original terminations, which must, I imagine, have been pinnacles. The ordinary bricks used here are about 10 in. × 3 in. in size, and laid with very wide joints of mortar; those used for window-jambs and arches are of much deeper colour and finer clay than the others. There is something quite refreshing in coming suddenly and unexpectedly upon such a simple and English-looking elevation, after the multitude of thoroughly Italian fronts it has been our fate to see lately.

On the north side of the nave there seems to have been a fine row of pointed windows, but they have been all destroyed to make way for Renaissance improvements. There are very large buttresses dividing the bays in this aisle—a feature which is unusual in Italy, and which, in addition to the design of the choir and transepts, would seem to show that this church was not entirely the work of an Italian. In the plan, too, it is remarkable that, though the general arrangement is quite that of the large Italian churches, such as the Frari at Venice and Sta. Anastasia at Verona, in one particular it is unlike them. The groining bays of the aisles are square, and not oblong; and as two of the aisle arches make one bay of the nave, the groining compartments in both are as nearly as possible square. This is an arrangement which occurs often in German Romanesque, but is not seen so often in Italy.

50.—West End, San Francesco, Pavia.

There is a fine campanile between the south transept and the choir; it has four stages above the roof of the church, and scarcely any opening below the belfry windows: these are exceedingly good, of three trefoiled lights under an inclosing arch, with two plain circles pierced in the tympanum, the monials being shafts of white marble. A low spire of circular bricks finishes, but does not improve, this very beautiful belfry.

There is another brick pointed church at Pavia—San Francesco—which has a fine west front redeemed from the common Italian character by the grand window-arch in its central division; and though this has been filled in with later and barbarous work, to the entire concealment of the tracery, its effect upon the whole front is astonishingly good. The detail is very elaborate, and in the arch a great number of terra-cotta ornaments are introduced. The front is divided by large pilasters into a centre and wings corresponding with the nave and aisles, but these are again subdivided by smaller pilasters, each of which is composed of three circles on plan, and finished rather nicely with a kind of finial at the top.

San Francesco is lighted by a succession of small clerestory windows, and the aisles have large buttresses, the greater part of the upper portion of the west front being a mere mask to make out the desired outline. I begin really to wonder whether I shall see a west front before I leave Italy which is not a purely unnecessary and unprepossessing sham!

Pavia is a busy and a pleasant city, and one that improves on acquaintance; it is true that it was very hot and sultry, but to this I have been fairly acclimatized, and so rather enjoyed it, except when a piazza had to be crossed in the sun, or a walk to be taken along a street unprotected by arcading, which by the way is much rarer here than in Padua, Mantua, and other cities which I have been describing. The main street of the city is very picturesque, with somewhat of a fall towards the south, so that just a glimpse is obtained between the houses of the distant Apennines.

From Pavia we went, on our road to Milan, to pay a visit to the renowned Certosa. The road thither, which is also that to Milan, pursues a monotonously straight course by the side of a canal, or canalized river, and between rows of stiff trees, until, about four miles from Pavia, a turning at right angles out of the main road soon leads to the gateway of the monastery, and through this—which stands open apparently rather through carelessness than out of hospitality—we drove into the courtyard in front of the church. This, grown all over with weeds, looked certainly very desolate and wretched, and but a poor preface to the polished marbles of the west front, and the riches and paintings of the interior of the church.

The west front is of great magnificence of material, though a kind of design which seems to have proceeded upon the principle of setting all established architectural styles and customs entirely at defiance. This indeed may be said of the whole church, which is a kind of mixture of Lombard-Romanesque features with some Gothic, and no slight dash of the Renaissance spirit; altogether a most magnificent hybrid, but certainly a hybrid. The doors stand wide open, and from the decaying and desolate court in front of the church we enter into the nave, full of everything that is magnificent in material, and all preserved with jealous care and in admirable order; we look up to the lofty vault which spans the grand width of the nave, and find the groining ribs arched overhead in pure pointed form, and cannot help marvelling how far this one pointed feature harmonizes—I had almost said sanctifies—the whole interior, though in fact, save this one point, there is scarcely a single detail throughout the church which would ever pass muster as really being of Gothic character.

I think it is hardly possible to scan or criticize the architecture of such a building; it is better to follow the guidance of the cicerone, and look at the pictures behind the many altars set around with precious stones, and inclosed within reredoses made of such an infinite variety of marbles, that, with some degree of envy, one thinks how precious such an array would be on this side of the Alps, even if spread through fifty churches.

The nave and aisles are divided from the side chapels and from the transepts by high metal grilles, and the transept is again divided by another screen from the choir: this produces a very singular and unusual effect, and makes the transept appear somewhat like a nave placed at right angles to the choir. All the chapels on either side of the nave communicate with one another, so that the monks are able, without entering the nave, to obtain access to all of them, whilst females are carefully excluded both from the chapels and from the transepts and choir. Except a Perugino in one of the chapels on the north side of the nave, and one picture in the sacristy, there seemed to be no pictures of any very great value; in fact, travellers are asked rather to admire the value of the stones which are used in the altars, and the marbles in the reredoses behind them, than the paintings which they inclose. The groining of the church, enhanced as it is in effect by the way in which it is painted—with a blue ground, powdered very richly with gold stars—conduces more than anything else to the very fine effect of colour which the nave produces; and the beautiful pavements, composed mainly of red and white marbles, laid in elaborate geometrical patterns, increase not a little the general effect. This is an instance of the superiority of decorative painting over pictures as far as improvement of architectural effect is concerned.

South of the church are two cloisters; that nearest to the church of ordinary size, but the other, to which it leads, prodigious in its dimensions, and very singular in its effect, being surrounded at regular intervals by the houses of the monks rising out of and above the regular line of the cloister roof. I went into one of these houses, and found its accommodation exceedingly ample; three rooms, closets, and a garden being provided for each monk. The arches of the cloisters are exceedingly rich in terra-cotta ornaments, and throughout the exterior of the church and other buildings it is remarkable how very elaborate these ornamental mouldings are; they are left in the natural reddish colour, and, as the walls are whitewashed, they have a very singular effect. We found here, as at other places, men busily engaged in making casts for the Crystal Palace at Sydenham, whose managers certainly seemed to have ordered casts of everything that could be modelled throughout Europe!

51.—Certosa of Pavia.*

There are now[66] twenty-five monks at the Certosa, and the number appears to have been gradually on the increase since the reconstitution of the monastery in 1844; it was certainly very gratifying to see that, whilst all the rest of the buildings looked forlorn and dilapidated the church itself was most scrupulously well preserved, presenting in this respect a great contrast to the fate of monastic churches generally in the North of Italy.

A tedious drive by the side of a long straight canal, passing on our way large well-managed farms and other signs of uncommon agricultural activity, took us from the Certosa to Milan; and long before we arrived there the white pinnacles of the Duomo, with the Alps in the far distance, came in sight; certainly, seen thus, the Duomo is one of the least satisfactory or imposing great churches I have ever seen, and does but little in the way of imparting character—as most cathedrals do—to the city which lies at its foot. At last we reached Milan, and entering through a triumphal arch—the Ticinese Gate—and passing the front of Sant'Eustorgio, we threaded our way down a very long narrow street, by the side in one place of a row of Roman columns, still standing tolerably perfect in the midst of the crowded highway, until at last we found ourselves housed in a more luxurious hotel than it has been our fortune to meet with for some days.

---

[66] This was written in 1855.

CHAPTER XI.

"In the elder days of art,
Builders wrought with greatest care
Each minute and unseen part,
For the gods are everywhere."

Longfellow.

ANY one who has followed the route from Venice to Milan described in the last chapter will do well, instead of following it on a subsequent visit, to make a détour from Padua to Ferrara and Bologna and thence by Parma, Modena, and Piacenza to Milan. I shall give some notes of such a journey in this chapter, the towns visited on the road completing the subject which I have set before me in this volume, and leaving no important city north of the Apennines, save Ravenna, undescribed. This exception is serious; but the omission will be remedied naturally when, as I hope I soon shall, I ask my readers to go with me to the towns on the east coast of Italy.

The journey from Padua to Bologna is now, and I suppose always was, extremely uninteresting. The only objects on the road which possess much attraction for the artist are the towns I have mentioned, and these certainly much more repay a visit than do those on the parallel line of road which we have just travelled. Scenery there is none to speak of, and fortunately a railway makes the journey a quick one now; but when I first travelled it I retained no recollection at the end of the route save of long straight and dusty roads lined on either side with tall poplars, and wearisome to the last degree. At Monselice we found a picturesque town domineered over by the ruins of a large castle, whose walls climb the steep sides of the hill on which it stands. Here I saw a good and little altered Romanesque church, with pilasters in place of buttresses, and walls crowned with the usual eaves-arcade. At Rovigo, further on, there is one of the tall brick towers so common here, with its Ghibelline battlement perfect. Just before reaching Ferrara we crossed the Po—here a large, unbridged, and dreary-looking river, flowing rapidly between high artificial banks to the sea. Its bed is, I suppose, now quite above the level of the plain, and year by year the question becomes more urgent and yet more difficult of answer, what is to be done with it? Certainly there are rivers and rivers; and this great stream left none but painful and disagreeable impressions on my mind. At length, after ten hours and a half of the slowest of drivers and worst of vehicles, we reached Ferrara—a *trajet* now performed by railway in about an hour and a half, with advantage to every one's time and temper, and no counter-balancing loss.

52.—Duomo. Ferrara.

The entrance to the city through a dirty suburb of tumble-down houses was not prepossessing. I knew nothing of what I had to see, and my delight was therefore all the greater when we drove into the piazza in front of the Duomo, and I found myself gazing at a building which at first sight looked as though it had been brought straight from the North of Europe, and planted here in the thirteenth century as a warning against Italian fashions! Further examination proved that I was not far wrong in my first estimate of the west front; but it revealed also, I am sorry to say, that this and part of the south side were the only parts of the old cathedral which had been spared, when in the seventeenth century the whole of the church was gutted and converted into about as bad a Renaissance building as one could wish not to see.

The west front is a great screen, and does not and never did follow the line of the roofs. It has three gables of about equal height covered with arcading, which increases in depth and richness of moulding and shadow to the top, where there are very fine open arched galleries, stepped up to suit the raking lines of the gables. I know no Italian work which imitates so closely as this does the extreme richness which some of the Norman and English churches of the same period exhibit. The arches of the arcades are carried upon clusters of columns which are set with extraordinary profusion one behind the other. The centre of the three divisions of the west front is almost wholly filled with a very fine porch of three stages in height, and finished with gables on its front and sides. The lower stage of this porch, as indeed of the whole church, is round-arched, and belongs probably to the church consecrated here in 1135. The knotted shafts which carry the front wall rest on figures sitting on lions. The doorway is deeply recessed, and has figures of saints with scrolls.[67] The tympanum of the arch has a sculpture of S. George and the Dragon, and the lintel below it eight subjects, beginning with the Salutation, and ending with the Baptism, of Our Lord. At the top of this stage is an inscription which contains the date given above.

The next stage is later, and has three arches with traceries carried upon chevroned and twisted shafts, with a statue of the Virgin and Child in the centre. This stage forms a sort of balcony. The upper stages are covered with sculpture. In the gable is Our Lord as Judge in a vesica-shaped aureole; around and above Him are saints and angels, and below a group of angels dividing the good from the bad. The subject is continued on to the wall on each side of the porch, where on one side are represented the souls of the just in the lap of God, and on the other the descent of the wicked into the jaws of Hell. The whole scheme is a picturesque and unusually disposed treatment of the Last Judgment. There is, however, not much merit in the sculpture as a work of art, though as an enrichment of the buildings it is most effective. The statue in the centre is said to be by Nicola Pisano. The south front of the cathedral has a long range of arcading carried on engaged columns, each arch inclosing a small arcade of three divisions. Above this, below the eaves, is a very fine arcade of later date all carried on groups of shafts, and treated in the Venetian manner with ogee-arched labels above round arches. This stage is built

[67] Said to have been carved by Nicolò, who is supposed to be the same man who wrought on the west door of San Zenone, Verona. This does not appear to me to be likely; the work at Verona being, I think, earlier than that at Ferrara.

of red marble; the lower part of the wall, of brick and stone.

A large font of white marble is the only relic of the original church which is still to be seen inside.

There is not much more to see here. The castle is remarkable as standing surrounded by its moat in the very midst of the city. The old portions of it are much like the castle at Mantua, and present the same boldly battered base, and the same heavy machicoulis and battlements. I saw also two or three old churches here, but of no interest; they were of the latest phase of Gothic—bordering on Renaissance—and very poor in their detail.

The picture-gallery is in a rather magnificent palace of the D'Este family. Garofalo—the best of Ferrarese painters—is represented by a fine Adoration of the Magi, and other works. But the collection generally is not interesting. There are also in the churches a great number of works of other Ferrarese painters, and most travellers go also to see the house of Ariosto and the prison of Tasso. But on the whole the attractions of the city are not great. The streets are grass-grown and deserted, lined with palaces of coarse and bold but uninteresting design, and I was in no way sorry to leave it for Bologna, expecting to find there much more to interest and occupy me.

The drive from one city to the other was very wearisome. The land was rich with vines, mulberry-trees, and rice-fields. The grapes were being gathered, and everywhere along the road we met vast casks borne in grand waggons drawn by white oxen, carrying home the grapes to the wine-press. These waggons have an elaborately carved tree from back to front, and the wheels and casks are also similarly adorned. They are really very handsome, and quite carry one back to those old times when even in utilitarian England the adornment of a carriage was not thought beneath the notice of an artist.

On the road we changed horses at Altedo, where I sketched the good brick campanile of the church, which has windows much like the example figured at page 198.

Bologna is, I fear, only known to many Englishmen at the present day as the one station in Italy at which you may always depend on getting some food, and not less as a station which seems to be on the road to and from every part of the peninsula. There is no excuse, therefore, for not visiting it; and if the general feeling is not one of enthusiasm for what one sees, there is still very much that is worth seeing, and in San Petronio a fragment of a church which, had it been completed on the scale intended, would have been one of the finest and, I suppose, almost the largest in Italy.

The streets are not of the best. They are very narrow, and often arcaded with pointed arches supported on circular columns, but contain few houses of any interest, whilst the churches have been a good deal altered and damaged in modern times.

53.—San Petronio. Bologna, South Aisle.

The cathedral is a recent building of no beauty. Two lions which once supported the columns of a Lombard doorway now carry the holy-water stoups; and in a

passage near the sacristy is a carved, painted, and gilded rood of the twelfth century—a piece of furniture which is rarely found remaining in Italian churches. The grandest church in Bologna is undoubtedly San Petronio, which is well placed on one side of the Piazza Maggiore. It was not commenced until 1390, so that we must not be surprized to find the faults in detail which mark the period. But the general scheme of the church is so magnificent that these faults do not strike the eye at all offensively. As it stands even now, with only its nave and aisles finished, it gives a vast idea of size and space, though this is hardly appreciated at first, owing to the enormous dimensions, the fewness of the parts, and the extreme simplicity of all the details. The west front is of immense size and width, but its only finished parts are the plinth and doorways, the whole of the rest being left in rough brick. The detail of this finished part is of poor character, and later than the fabric. It is rather richly carved with figures, which are sometimes much praised, but which seemed to me (with the exception of a Pietà over the south-west doorway) to be of poor style and character. Going round to the side of the building, the design is of earlier date and much more interesting. The aisle-windows are noble designs of four-lights in each bay, separated by buttresses and surmounted by steep-pitched gables. The detail is an extremely good combination of brick and stone, whilst a magnificent plinth of stone and marble gives great force to the work. The transept was never built; but at the point where it was intended to be connected with the aisle, there is a curious conceit—a window at a projecting corner with half its arch and tracery facing south, and the other half facing west. It is, so far as I remember, a unique example in a church, but is just a little like the angle-windows in some of the Venetian palaces, though these never indulge in such an absurdity as is the construction of two halves of pointed arches over such an opening.

The interior is very magnificent. The columns, arches, and walls generally are of brick, now coloured and whitewashed (but originally intended to be seen, as is evident from parts of the incomplete work where the internal brickwork is still exposed and is executed with the greatest care), the capitals and bases being all of stone. The columns of the nave are bold clusters; they are about sixty feet from centre to centre, rather short in proportion to the height of their capitals, which are carved with stiff foliage. Above these is a large pier running up to carry the groining, and there are pointed arches opening to the aisles of very lofty pitch, but which, owing to their great size, certainly look very attenuated. Two chapels open into each bay of the aisles: these are lighted by the large four-light windows already mentioned, whilst both nave and aisles have no windows except cusped circular ones of no great size, placed as near as possible to the groining, which is very simple throughout the church. There is scarcely a horizontal string-course or a label to be seen, and the mouldings are few and simple; yet, nevertheless, the effect is grand. Such a church may well trouble the mind of the English student who thinks that no building is complete which has not its arcade, its triforium, and its clerestory. One of our puny churches would stand—nave, aisles, chancel, tower, and spire and all—within one of the bays of the nave and aisles here; and there is a grand sense of restraint and simplicity about this work which impresses me more each time I see it. At the same time the interest is of this grand kind—there is a sense of the immense and infinite, but no condescension to the love of detail and delight in dainty variety which undoubtedly strikes us in most good Gothic works, and makes them so enjoyable.

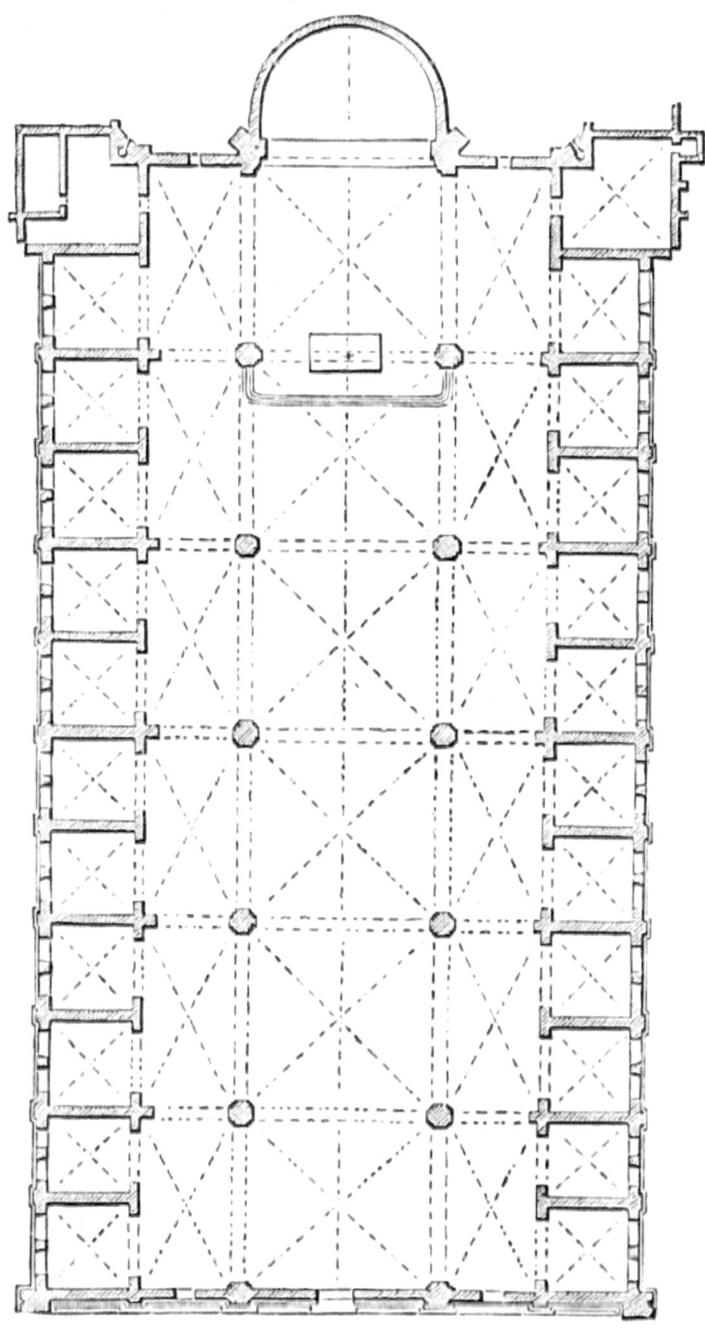

Plan—San Petronio, Bologna.*

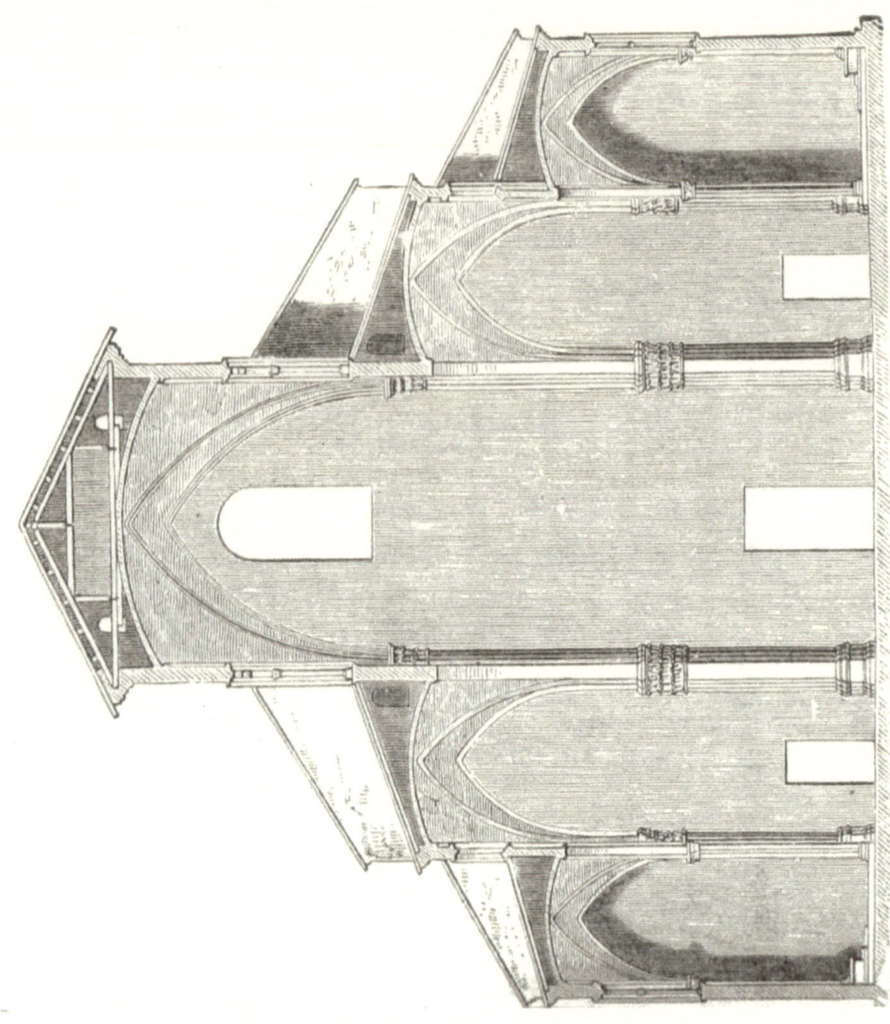

Section—San Petronio, Bologna.*

The church which inspired the design of this was, no doubt, the cathedral at Florence. But of the two the design of San Petronio seems to me to be the more beautiful. The addition of chapels beyond the aisles and the traceries in their windows make the design a little less bald and insipid, and also give a somewhat truer impression of the real scale than one has at Florence. But at the best such work does not create enthusiasm. The principal effort of the architect was to build something very big, and he succeeded; unfortunately he so contrived as very nearly to prevent one from quite realizing how vast his work is, and I hardly know a more serious charge that can be made against an architect than this.[68]

---

[68] The complete church was to have been 800 feet long, and 525 feet across the transepts, with a central dome 130 feet in diameter.—Fergusson's 'History of Architecture,' ii. 210.

54.— San Petronio. Bologna, Interior.

From this church I went to San Domenico, famous for a very elaborate tomb or shrine of the saint by Nicola Pisano. This is not a work that entirely pleases me. It is a high coped tomb covered with sculpture on the sides, erected behind the altar. The history of its erection by Nicola Pisano in 1265 gives it value as a dated work by a great artist. He seems to have been a good deal assisted by his scholar, Fra Guglielmo Agnelli, whose work is by no means equal to his master's. The tomb alone is the work of these artists, the rest of the work about the altar having been frequently added to and altered in later days, and each sculptor employed having done his best to glorify his own skill and dexterity instead of thinking, as Nicola Pisano evidently did, simply of telling his story in the most straightforward way.

The stories represented in the bas-reliefs had more than common value for a sculptor of original power. In the centre is the Madonna; on one side the resuscitation by S. Dominic of a youth who had been thrown from his horse, and on the other the saint disputing with heretics and burning their books. At the angles are the four Doctors, and at the back two more subjects from the Life of S. Dominic, probably designed but certainly not executed by Nicola Pisano.

The church which contains this tomb has been ruthlessly modernized; but in the open piazza on the north side of it are two monuments of much interest. One of these has a square basement of brick, supporting detached shafts, above which are round arches, the whole being finished with a brick pyramid. Under the canopy thus formed is placed the sarcophagus, marked with a cross at the end, and finished at the top with a steep gabled covering. The detail of this is all of late Romanesque style. The other monument is of later date and much finer design, though keeping to the same general outline. In place of the brick basement of the first this has three rows of three shafts, which support a large slab. On this are arcades of pointed arches, three at the sides and two at the ends, carried on coupled shafts, and within this upper arcade is seen the stone coffin carved at the top, and with a stiff effigy of the deceased carved as if lying on one of the perpendicular sides. This monument is also finished with a brick pyramid. The whole design is certainly striking; it has none of the exquisite skill that marks the best Veronese monuments, but it is a very good example of the considerable success which may be achieved by an architectural design without any help from the sculptor, without the use of any costly materials, and with only moderate dimensions. The upper tier of arches is kept in position by an iron tie, and, in spite of its slender look, still stands after five hundred years' exposure, in perfect condition.

San Giacomo is another example of a modernized church, which has, however, some interesting features. On the exterior there is a rather good treatment of the polygonal apse, with steep gables and pinnacles over the windows on each side. This is somewhat like the apse of San Fermo, at Verona. The campanile on the south-east of the nave is a very lofty late Gothic erection, finished with an incomplete Renaissance belfry-stage. The old portion is divided into a succession of stages of equal height, and is mainly striking on account of its good colour—being all of red brick—and simple outline. The west front is, as is usual here, a great gable divided into three parts by pilasters and half columns; the doorway is of the thirteenth century, and its columns rest on lions' backs. The detail of the windows at the ends of the aisles is extremely good, and seemed to me to be of the same date. The windows are of two-lights, with shafts for monials, and a broad transome of plate tracery; the tympanum of the arch at the top is similarly filled: here, though the jambs are of brick, the whole of the rest of the design is executed in stone, and the likeness to some of the later Venetian church windows in the Madonna dell'Orto and SS. Giovanni e Paolo is too great not to be observed. The cornices here are very good. I noticed not only bricks of unusual shapes, very well arranged for effect, but also disks of earthenware, set with the convex side in view, and of brilliant glazed colour, generally blue or green. Their effect is extremely good.

55.—Monument near San Domenico, Bologna.

The church of Sta. Maria Maggiore is less altered internally than the rest. It is of great length, groined throughout, and in general effect and proportions seemed to me to have a somewhat less Italian air than the other churches. The apse has an aisle and chapels round it of which the brick detail externally is effective. Here there are large tiles cut to a trefoil shape placed flat against the wall-face as an ornament. They are good-looking, but have not stood well.

In front of this church there is a court or atrium, surrounded with a perfectly open arcade, which is continued all along the north side of the church next the road and over the public footpath. The columns are very slender and of marble; and though the arches which they carry are segments of circles (not an agreeable form), the whole effect is extremely light and graceful.

Cloister—San Stefano, Bologna.

San Francesco *was* one of the finest churches in the city. It is now so shabby and decayed outside, and so covered with painters' and decorators' work inside, that all its good effect is ruined. Its interior was the victim of what was, I daresay, a very well-meant restoration some years ago, and little of it has been left in its original condition. It has a chevet with aisles and chapels, and externally the rare feature (in Italy) of flying buttresses to support the choir vault. They were built by men who had never seen one before, I suppose, and are as crude and misshapen as they well could be.

Two campanili close to each other, south of the choir, group strangely with it in the perspective view. They are unlike in size and design, and illustrate the perfect indifference with which all mediæval architects viewed the gravest departures from laws of symmetry. The larger of the two has rather rich Gothic details, the belfry-stage having traceried windows of three lights with spiral shafts for monials. The gables in this church have large white marble crosses let into them; these are rounded at the ends, and each end has a bright green tile disk inserted. The west front is of the usual description—a great sham front of hideous outline. Most of its windows are lancets, new, but probably copied from old examples, and the doorway under a canopy is of good character.

I have left to the last what, I suppose, is in fact the oldest of the Bolognese churches—San Stefano. It is a collection of seven churches, rather than one church, and, in spite of modernization without end, it is still a most curious and interesting jumble of old buildings. The churches are dedicated to—1, San Stefano; 2, San Lorenzo; 3, San Sepolcro (a circular church); 4, The Corte di Pilato (a cloister); 5, Sta. Trinità; 6, SS. Pietro e Paolo (with three Romanesque apses); and 7, San Giovanni. No. 3 has an aisle round the circular portion, and was probably a baptistery, and there is still an old ambon in it. One gets fairly puzzled in this nest of queer little churches or parts of churches, and I found but little of architectural—as distinguished from antiquarian—interest in them. The brickwork in the cloister and in some of the external walls is extremely good. Some of the latter are diapered or reticulated on the face with square yellow tiles with dividing lines of red brick, and the cornices are of the same two colours also. In the cloister the columns and inner order of the arches are of stone, the rest of the walls and cornices being of red and yellow bricks, and in one part there is a course of red, green, and yellow tiles alternated. The effect of this work is extremely pretty.

Probably travellers remember Bologna more by its two leaning towers than by any other feature. One comes here however, from either side, after rather a surfeit of this sort of thing. On the one side is Pisa, with its leaning tower, and on the other we may see them at Rovigo, Ferrara, and elsewhere. The soil here is generally bad for foundations, I suppose, and these plain brick towers without any projection at the base are the most ill-contrived constructions for such foundations that one can conceive. In this case it is possible to get views of the two towers which shew an apparently impossible amount of overhanging on the part of the smaller one, and I confess to a strong preference for walking to what one may call the windward side of such an erection! There is no beauty in these towers, their only features being the vast array of putlog holes in their walls, and the machicolated battlement of the higher of the two.

Of domestic buildings of the Middle Ages there are not many remains. The Casa dei Mercanti, though it dates from the end of the fourteenth century, is not pleasing. The front has two lofty pointed arches on the ground story, and a canopied Ringhiera of very poor design above. But as the whole front has been restored, the bricks painted bright red, and the stonework cleaned and repaired, I am disposed to believe very little in the antiquity of any of the details. Certainly

I found it not worth sketching, which was the more disappointing as I had heard of it always as a fine building. The Pepoli Palace has some old brickwork and a Ghibelline battlement of unusually picturesque outline. The Piazza Maggiore in front of San Petronio is certainly the best feature in this not very striking city. As always in Italian towns, it must be visited early in the day if it is to be seen to advantage. In the morning it is crowded with fruit and vegetable dealers, sitting under bright-coloured umbrellas; in the afternoon it is *triste* and deserted, save by the cabmen, who pursue the stranger with their importunities. One side of this piazza is occupied by the Palazzo Publico—a large pile of building altogether Gothic in its inclosing walls, I fancy, but they have been so much altered from time to time that not much detail remains. It seems, however, to have been much like the Castle at Mantua in its character, with bold machicoulis at the top of the walls, and a well battered-out base to the whole building. In a tower here there is a window which I engrave, because it shews well how good an effect may be produced by the skilful use of the very simplest materials. The combination of stone with brick adds much to the effect; and though this is in itself a very small and unimportant work, it appears to me to be exceedingly suggestive.

Brick Window—Palazzo Publico, Bologna.

The Academy of the Fine Arts will be visited by every one who cares for Francia, and by many who fancy they care for the Caracci. As one of the former class, I recommend it very heartily. It contains a large collection, gathered in papal times from convents and churches, and mainly by painters of the Bolognese school. This school has the redeeming virtue of counting Francia on its list of painters, which may atone for much. He is seen here to advantage; and one trio, consisting of two of his pictures on either side of one of Perugino's, forms the noblest group in the gallery. Here one sees how much in common the two men had in spite of Francia's more forcible character. The same love of pure and rich colour, the same well-defined grouping, the same religious feeling mark them both. And never, I think, has the Madonna—pensive, lowly, and simple—been more beautifully represented than here by Francia. It is a face that one hopes to remember. Here, too, is Raffaelle's S. Cecilia, no doubt a very great work, but not great quite in the sense one wishes to understand the word at his hand. S. Cecilia and S. John are very fine, but S. Paul is a sort of burly ruffian. The heavenly choir is very mundane, and the whole work somewhat academical in its design and treatment. The earlier pictures here are very disappointing. The early Bolognese painters seem to have painted coarsely and heavily, and to have drawn badly, and there is no comparison for a moment between their work and that of the early Sienese and Florentine painters on the one hand, and those of Padua and Verona on the other. One has indeed in their works a sort of foretaste of what one has from their followers—the Caracci, Domenichino, Bagna-Cavallo, and to some extent Guido. Dismal colour, great striving after chiaroscuro, violent and distorted attitudes, and a purely conventional and academical style, are not great recommendations of any school, but they are things which must be accepted if one is to enjoy these works at all heartily.

A very short railway journey takes one from Bologna to Modena. The one object of interest here is the cathedral, but this is a building of extreme historical and architectural value, and has fortunately been left with so few alterations that we can make out its history with fair certainty. At Bologna everything was built of brick—here at a short distance we find our eyes rejoicing again in the sight of stone and marble.

The ground-plan of the cathedral consists of a nave with aisles terminated at the east end by three semicircular apses. There are a sacristy on the north of the choir-aisle, and a tower to the north of this. There are two doorways on the south side, three at the west end, and one on the north side. A grand crypt with arches on slender shafts occupies the whole space under the eastern part of the church. The access to the choir from the nave is by stairs against the aisle walls in the same position as at San Zenone, Verona. Here the stairs and their handrails are not later than the thirteenth century, and the choir is divided from the aisles by screens of the same age; solid below, and with a continuous cornice carried on coupled shafts above. The cathedral is said to have been founded in 1099, but an inscription on the south wall gives the date of the consecration of the building by Pope Lucius III. in July 1184. I believe that the former date represents the age of the plan, and of most of the interior columns and arches still remaining, but that before the later date the whole exterior of the cathedral had been modified, and the groining added inside. The work of both periods is extremely good and characteristic. The columns of the nave are alternately great piers and smaller circular columns of red marble. The great piers carry cross arches between the groining bays, and each of these in the nave is equal to two of those in the aisles. The capitals here are very close imitations of Classical work, with the abaci frequently concave on plan. The main arches and the triforium openings of three lights above them are seen both in the nave and aisle, the vaulting of the latter being unusually raised. There is also a plain clerestory, and the vaults are now everywhere quadripartite. The outside elevation of the side walls is very interesting. Here we seem to have the old aisle wall with its eaves-arcade added to and raised in the twelfth century, and adorned with a fine deep arcade in each bay, inclosed under round arches, which are carried on half columns in front of the buttresses or pilasters. These arches shew exactly what the original intention was at Ferrara, where it will be recollected they still in part remain. Certainly they would have made the side walls very rich in their effect, even if there had not also been two porches, a projecting pulpit, and various bas-reliefs inserted in them.

All the doorways deserve special mention. The eastern of the two on the south side, with the porch of two stages in front of it, is remarkable for the extreme skill and delicacy of its enrichment. The shafts are of white marble, and the mouldings which separate them of red, while the former are all carved in the most delicate manner. The porch is mainly built of red marble, and is carried on detached shafts, cut out of one block knotted together and resting on lions. The whole of this work is evidently an addition to the aisle, and dates from about A.D. 1180. The other doorway on the same side may probably be a work of the original foundation in 1099. It has the twelve Apostles on the jambs, and rude shafts carrying a canopy in front of it. The west doorway has also a porch, and sculptures of the twelve months on its jambs. It is covered with carving of foliage and figures executed by the same Wiligelmus who was employed on the western doorway of San Zenone, Verona. Among other figures are those of King Arthur and his knights, inscribed with his name,[69] "Artus de Bretania," above his head. The west front is very remarkable. The ends of the aisles have two arches inclosing small arcades similar to those in the bays of the side walls, and the end of the nave has the same arcade on each side of a porch of two stages in height, the lower of which is carried on detached shafts resting on lions' backs. The upper part of the porch was altered in order that a great wheel window might be inserted, sometime in the fourteenth century.

This rose window fills the whole upper part of the western gable, and is, like many Italian examples, very unskilful in its design. The vast number of divisions or spokes, and the very slight prominence of the arcuated part of the filling-in, make it look in very truth a wheel window and nothing better. Above it are an insignificant figure of Our Lord and the Emblems of the four Evangelists sculptured in low relief. The lower portion of the walls is covered in the most promiscuous manner with bas-reliefs, and a medley of mural tablets, the number of which would delight the eyes of an English parish clerk; but nevertheless the rich character given to the work by the fine shadows of the arcades in the lower half of the front, is worthy of special notice and recollection. The tower and spire are very lofty. The former has six stages of nearly equal height, all round-arched, and on the top of this two octagonal stages crowned with a modern spire. The lower stage of the octagon is old, and was finished in 1317 by Enrico da Campione, one of the family of architects of whom I have before spoken. The tower has pilasters at the

[69] Mr. Perkins, 'Italian Sculptors,' p. 251, says that the nationality of Wiligelmus has been much disputed. Kreuser says that he came from Nürnberg; and the representation of King Arthur's victories over the Visigoths is adduced as a proof that he was not an Italian.

angles, and two intermediate on each face, so that there is a triple division in elevation, and all the horizontal string-courses are marked by arched corbel-tables. The repetition of these very simple features, and the absence of all openings in the lower part of the steeple, shew how simple the elements of a good work may be.

56.—South Front of Duomo. Modena.

I found nothing else of any interest in Modena, and made my way from thence to Parma, impatient to see not only the cathedral and the baptistery, but also Correggio's treatment of the decoration of the former. In spite of the great fame of these works, I fear I must at once confess that they took away most of the pleasure which I had anticipated from my visit to the cathedral at Parma. This is a grand Lombard church, fairly perfect in its architectural details and arrangements, but entirely ruined in its architectural effect by the frescoes with which most of its walls and roof have been covered. These have been painted without the slightest thought of the requirements of the building, and as a matter of course they have entirely ruined its effect. The frescoes in the dome are by Correggio, and are amongst his most celebrated works. Like all the rest of the paintings here, they present, when regarded from below without the assistance of a glass, a confused mass of distorted figures and limbs, not at all relieved by the dark and dismal colouring in which they are executed, and which doubtless is not what it once was. It is true that when examined in detail, and still more when examined in Toschi's careful engravings, they are full of beautiful drawing and skilful chiaroscuro, but the impression they have left on my mind is mainly one of the extreme risk of attempting to decorate a building without previous training in and knowledge of the requirements of architecture. As an example of Lombard architecture the cathedral at Parma is almost ruined, whilst it would be difficult to conceive a worse-fitted building for the display of Correggio's fancy and skill. The ill-assorted union, in itself ruinous to both, has been aggravated by the bad state of repair which has damaged and no doubt altered the colour of the frescoes; and the impression now produced is that of simply the gloomiest interior in Italy.

The church is cruciform, with a central cupola and apses to the three eastern arms of the cross. The nave and aisles of seven bays are vaulted, and there is a large and striking crypt under the whole eastern part of the church which goes far to redeem its otherwise barren character. The effect here is remarkable, owing to the complex perspective and great number of single slender marble shafts carrying the vaulted roofs, and in part also to its unusual height. The capitals are all carved—frequently with coarse volutes; the church was founded in 1058, and no doubt this crypt is of about that age.

Very near to the cathedral on the south-west is the now much more interesting baptistery. This is on the exterior a large and lofty octangular building, adorned in a succession of stages by small detached shafts carrying the cornices and strings which divide the elevation. Internally the scheme is very different. The eight-sided interior is subdivided, so that sixteen shallow apses are set around the inside face of the walls. These are separated by columns, and above them on each side are two stages in height, each subdivided into three divisions, which are again subdivided by smaller columns. A great vault or cupola covers the whole, and from its height gives an air of solemnity to the interior. It seems never to have been treated as a real dome, being covered with a flat roof, resting on the external walls, which are carried up far above the vault. The paintings with which the walls are covered are arranged without any order or general scheme of design. They seem to have been given by various donors, and each gave what best pleased his fancy; but owing to the early date of most of the work, there is in parts—especially in the vault—a fine effect of colour.

Plan of Baptistery, Parma.*

Section of Baptistery, Parma.*

57. — View of Palazzo Publico. Piacenza.

This baptistery is said to have been commenced by the architect Benedetto di Antelamo in A.D. 1196,[70] who is also credited with many other works here, and specially with much of the early sculpture in the Duomo and baptistery; it was not completed until 1260.

There are three great doors to the baptistery. On the northern is sculptured the Tree of Life, and over this twelve prophets carrying medallions with half figures of the Apostles. Below are subjects from the lives of Our Lord and S. John Baptist. The western door has a sculpture of the Last Judgment, and the southern a not very intelligible, though no doubt symbolical, figure of a man seated in a tree and gathering honey. Inside there are various sculptures, and among them a series of illustrations of the labours of the months.

My day in Parma was pleasantly concluded with a visit to the Gallery, and then, finding no more mediæval remains, I pushed on to Piacenza.

This is a city of no small interest, and remarkable above everything else in the possession of a Palazzo Publico of unusual and striking design—a building of special value and interest to me, since it is a capital example of the use of brick and marble together. Before looking at any of the churches I devoted myself to this building with the more satisfaction when I found that it was really, in some respects, one of the very best works of the sort that I had ever seen.

An inscription carved under a banner on a square stone, in the front, records the commencement of the work in 1281, and I think we may assume that no part of it is of much later date than this. It consists, as do most of these buildings, of a lofty open ground story, and a principal story above this. The façade is very dignified in effect. On the ground level are five lofty arches, very slightly moulded, and resting on square piers just rounded at the corners. The material of this stage is marble, mainly white, but with just a line of red and another of grey near the string-course which divides this from the next stage. From this point up almost the whole work is executed in brickwork of very elaborate and delicate detail. The two stages have no kind of uniformity or connection with each other, six windows being arranged above the five arches. In the centre of the first floor is the old doorway to the Ringhiera (which was altered in the seventeenth century); the windows on each side are of three lights, inclosed under a round arch with a deep archivolt very slightly recessed—all the enrichments being on very nearly the same face as the wall. These windows agree in size, but vary very much in all their details. Some of the subordinate arches are pointed, some round, and the tympana are everywhere filled with fine brick diapers. Above this stage the walls finish with a good marble cornice of intersecting arches, and then with a forked battlement. At the four angles of this are raised turrets, and the ends are finished with battlemented gables, very quaint and picturesque, as will be seen by the illustration which I give. The niches between the two arches in the principal story seem to have been intended for paintings. The marbles used here are red and white. Red is used for the arcades under the cornices, for the middle order of the rose window, and the

[70] The inscription on the north door is as follows:—

> "Bis binis demptis. Annis de mille ducentis
> Incepit dictus, opus hoc sculptor Benedictus."

inner order of the main arches. Elsewhere the marble is white, except the one grey course below the principal string. The whole of the lower stage is open below on all sides and groined—in brick, I think—though it is now plastered; indeed, save the parts already described as being of marble in the principal fronts, the whole of this building is built of red brick. Behind the open ground story there remains a portion of an internal quadrangle, which, incomplete as it is, shews, nevertheless, the same delicate attention to detail which is conspicuous on the façades. I know hardly any detail of Italian brickwork which is so refined and good as that in the arches and some cusped circles between them in this quadrangle.

Brickwork—Palazzo Publico, Piacenza.

I have seen this building, full as it is of eccentric departures from ordinary rules and customs—piers being placed over openings, and round and pointed arches used indifferently—quoted for our benefit as a remarkable example of a public building erected in the Middle Ages in the most regular and formal fashion! It is, on the contrary, if the plain truth is to be spoken, an example of a very bold disregard of such fashions indulged in without any detrimental effect.

Piacenza cannot boast of any very fine churches. They have been much ruined internally by modern alterations, and externally they do not seem ever to have been very attractive. The cathedral is a Lombard church of fine size, and with some good points. There are three western porches of two stages in height, according to the usual Lombard fashion. The doors are rudely sculptured; that in the centre with the signs of the Zodiac, and the northern door with the Annunciation, Salutation, and other subjects on its lintel. The columns rest on monsters, griffins, and men. The whole front is now finished with one large low-pitched gable, which has an arcade stepped up to suit its cornice. This is, however, a fourteenth-century alteration of the older church, as is also a rose window in the centre. A brick tower of late date rises at the north-west angle of the church, and is finished with a circular spire built of round-ended bricks. The external walls of the Lombard church were all built of stone or marble with shallow buttresses; the windows were very simple, and the effect was mainly due to the fine open arcade below the eaves, carried now on shafts, now on figures. The north-east view is very picturesque, owing to the number of angles and apsidal terminations which are seen together. These are produced by a plan of most unusual character, the transepts as well as the choir being finished with three apses, and an octagonal brick lantern rising out of the centre. Internally the cathedral, in spite of alterations, is still very interesting. The nave opens with eight arches to the aisles and transepts; but the three arches which open to the latter are much loftier than the five western arches, so as to allow of the transepts opening to the nave to nearly its full height. The groining of the nave is divided into three bays of sexpartite vaults—each bay being equal to two bays of the aisles, and there is a lantern over the two eastern bays. The transepts and aisles have quadripartite vaulting.

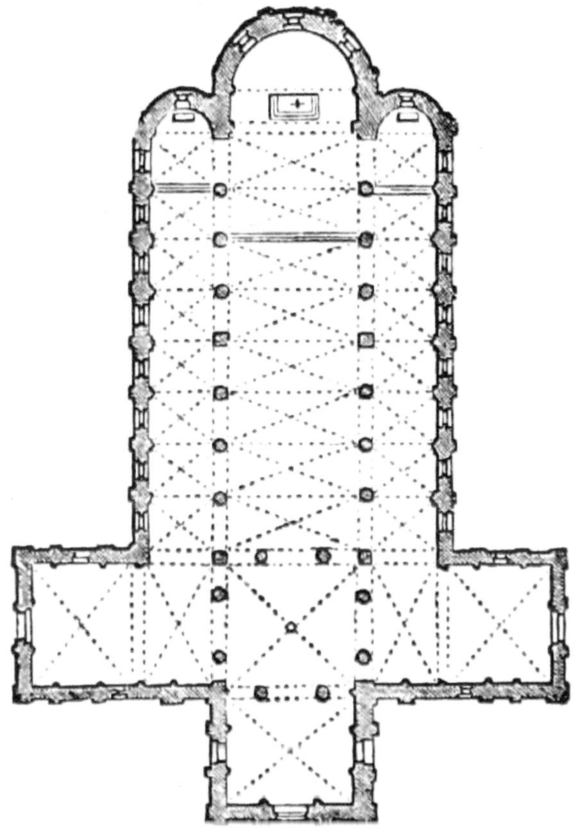

Plan—Sant'Antonino, Piacenza.*

Under the choir is a crypt of great interest and beauty, owing to the vast number of delicate columns which carry the vault. It is planned on a cruciform arrangement, with the principal altar in an octagonal central compartment. Here the priest celebrates on the eastern side with his back to the choir stalls in the apse, and his face toward the west. The access to this crypt is by two staircases at its south-west and north-west angles.

The large brick church of San Francesco is of the fourteenth century; it is very simple, but not striking in effect. The east end has been planned irregularly—to suit the site, no doubt—with an apse and aisle round it, and irregularly shaped chapels beyond the apse. The effect is bad, owing to the unskilful way in which the work has been done. The west front has the favourite sham gable adorned with circular windows, some of which are absolutely above the roofs of the aisles! San Giovanni in Canale is another church which has nothing of interest, save a few remnants of old brickwork.

Sant'Antonino is a remarkable church, hopelessly modernized with plaster enrichments. Like the cathedral, it has a lantern in the centre crossing, carried on eight columns from the ground, which produce internally a very new and really striking effect. The lantern is finished above the roof with three stages, each of which is lighted with a two-light window in each face. There is a fine early marble doorway to the north transept, with men and monsters supporting the shafts, and some delicate carving. In front of this, at the end of the fourteenth century, was built a lofty porch with a great open archway to the north. It is finished with brick pinnacles and cornices, and is higher than the transept. The hinges on the west door here are very good, and the windows in the aisles—lancets with seven cusps in the head—are quite worth notice. Piacenza struck me, both in its churches and Palazzo Publico, as a town which had possessed a very distinctly developed school of architecture of its own. The churches are peculiar, not to say eccentric, in their planning, and the Palazzo Publico is quite unique in its design and general treatment.

The only other old work I noticed here was a house in the Strada San Marco. This is all of brick, and has arches of slightly horse-shoe shape. The bricks are all axed on the face, and are of large size—11¼ inches long by about 2¾ inches high.

Not very far to the east of Piacenza is Asti, a dull city, distinguished, however, by some remarkable features in its churches. The most important of these are the Cathedral and San Secondo. They are extremely similar in general design: they have naves with short choirs, transepts, low octagonal vaulted lanterns over the crossing, and apsidal chapels in front of the transept gables, and at San Secondo to the several bays of the aisle. Their towers are on the east side of the transepts. The peculiar feature of their detail is the very elaborate way in which brick and stone are counterchanged in the jambs and arches of windows and doorways. The moulded members of a jamb are alternately of brick and stone, and in each course stone comes above the brick of the courses below. San Secondo cannot, I think, be earlier than circa 1400, but at first sight looks like a building of 1200. The cathedral is probably somewhat though not very much earlier. Its plan was evidently derived from that of the cathedral at Piacenza. Its proportions are bad, and it is only redeemed by the picturesqueness of some of its details. Another church has an octagonal campanile; and another, one of sixteen sides. This is of brick, except the upper stage, which is coursed in brick and stone. Its sixteen sides have alternately a window and a shaft running up to the cornice, and in the stage below it there are eight windows below the shafted sides of the belfry. The composition of this tower is certainly very good. Another fine lofty tower with bold cornice and Ghibelline parapet recalls the Veronese towers to mind, and there are besides not a few remains of mediæval domestic work, so that a day may be well spent at Asti by an architect.

Section—Sant'Antonino, Piacenza.*

CHAPTER XII.

Milan: the Cathedral—Sant'Ambrogio—Sant'Eustorgio—Sta. Maria delle Grazie—Certosa of Chiaravalle—Novara—Vercelli—Monza: the Cathedral—The Broletto—Sta. Maria in Strada—Como: the Broletto—The Cathedral.

"Launce! by mine honesty, welcome to Milan."

Two Gentlemen of Verona, act ii. sc. 5.

MILAN is better known to the generality of English travellers than, perhaps, any other city south of the Alps; and its older portions afford a fair idea of some of the most salient points of Italian manners and customs, whilst its new and much-vaunted arcades and streets seem to be not only so cosmopolitan as to be un-Italian, but so bald and poor in design as to be repulsive wherever they are! Its narrow busy streets, though they are wanting indeed in the arcading so character-istic of very many other towns we had passed through, have that peculiar charm which life and bustle always give to strange places; the crowds of foot-passen-gers threading the narrow ways, with no protection from the omnibuses and carts which jostle against them, are full of animation, and lively and picturesque in their costumes. Elbowing our way between them, we soon found ourselves in a piazza, with the Duomo rising before us in all the magnificence of its white marble walls. If it be indeed true that it was designed by a German,[71] there is on the outside even more cause for astonishment at his work than if it had been the work of an Italian. The west front is quite modern, but the rest of the exterior, all in its original state, is as little German in its character as any building I have ever seen, and—shall I add it?—as little really grand as a work of art. I had just caught a glimpse of its general outline and effect by the bright moonlight, on the evening of my arrival, with the

---

[71] It is commonly said to have been designed by Heinrich von Gmünden in 1387; but in a most interesting note at p. 116 of 'Italian Sculptors,' Mr. Perkins gives the evidence for and against the claim of a German to be the architect of this cathedral. He believes that there is no longer any reasonable doubt that the first architect was Marco Frisone da Campione. Heinrich Adler von Gmünden, who has commonly been stated to be the architect, did not come to Milan until five years after the foundation of the church. Marco da Campione died in 1390; and the church was ready for divine service in 1395. The criticisms I have made in the text appear to me to be equally applicable to an Italian architect trained in Germany, or to a German working in Italy; and if Marco da Campione was the architect, one is com-pelled, by the logic of the building itself, to say that either he had studied north of the Alps with a view to perfecting his design, or that he depended very largely on the help given him by such men as Henry of Gmünden, whom he had called in to his assistance.

music of an Austrian band sounding pleasantly in my ears, and, thus seen, there was certainly something wild and striking in its effect. I saw the brilliantly light colour of the white marble in the full brightness of the moon, and little of the poverty of moulding, or the heaviness of traceries, or the preposterous tenuity of pinnacles, which daylight revealed, to the destruction of any belief I might still have in its beauty; and the more I examined it in detail the less satisfactory did it appear; for neither in its general mass, nor in its detail, does it bear examination. Its walls are panelled all over, the panelling having a peculiarly painful kind of pendulous, unsupported, and unconstructional character, and the string-courses are marked by a continuous trefoil arcading on their under side, which recalls the frequent Italian string-courses in brick. The buttresses are bold in their formation and scale, but poor and weak-looking in their design, and finish at the top with pinnacles, whose thin outline, seen against the deep blue sky, is painfully bad and unsatisfying. The panelling of the walls is continued up to their whole height without any decided line of parapet or cornice, and finishes in a rough serrated line of small gables, which is particularly restless and wanting in repose. Great flying buttresses span the aisles, and then in the clerestory is repeated exactly what we have already seen below, the same panelling, the same parapet, and the same light pinnacles; the windows, however, are here very small and insignificant, whilst those in the aisles are remarkable for their large size and for the singular traceries with which they are filled. All the lower windows are transomed with a line of tracery, surmounted in each light by a crocketed canopy running up into the light above. In the apse this tracery fills the four outer lights only on each side of the two centre lights, the others being continued without interruption to the sill; and in these windows it is remarkable that each light is subdivided with a small monial below this band of tracery.

Altogether, an effect of a prodigious number and repetition of vertical lines is produced, and yet, notwithstanding this, the effect of the entire building is decidedly rather horizontal and depressing than the contrary; this is not more owing to the absence of all visible roofing than to the way in which the parapets, with their irregular gabled outline, attract the eye to a markedly horizontal feature.

Upon the whole, therefore, the exterior is in no respect more Italian than it is German in its style; it belongs to no school, and has no fellows: from the beginning it has been an exotic, and to the end of time will probably remain so, without a follower or an imitator in the singular development of which it is the only example; and there does appear, if we consider the matter, to be some intrinsic probability that such a building must have been designed by a foreigner rather than by a native. It has, in fact, all the appearance of having been the work of a stranger who was but imperfectly acquainted with the wants or customs of Italian architecture, working to some extent with the traditions of his national school before him, but, at the same time, impressed with a strong sense of the necessity under which he lay, of doing something quite unlike what he had been taught to consider necessary for buildings in his native land. It will be found upon examination that there is absolutely hardly one point in which this vast building follows the traditions of Italian pointed work. Its plan has not any Italian characteristics in its arrangement or proportions. Its windows have moulded monials instead of shafts; its walls are buttressed instead of being marked with pilasters here and there; its pinnacles are Northern in their idea, for strength rather than (as Italian pinnacles were) only for ornament; its walls have no cornices, and there are no sham fronts or attempts at concealing the necessary features of construction; the walls are panelled instead of being arcaded, and there is a constant endeavour to break up plain surfaces of wall, unlike the predilection for smooth broad surfaces so usual in thoroughly Italian work, and destructive of the kind of breadth and dignity which this last generally has; finally, if rest and life may be taken—as by some they are—to be respectively the distinguishing features of Italian and Northern pointed work, then, assuredly, the lack of repose in Milan Cathedral—caused mainly by the degree to which the system of panelling is carried over the whole building, and the extent to which the use of the simple horizontal line is carefully excluded—goes far to consign its exterior to some school of life and restlessness of the most unsatisfactory character. The one point in which an Italian model has been at all followed is the section, where the proportions of the aisles to the nave and the pitch of their roofs certainly shew a knowledge of San Petronio, Bologna. But its architect appears to me to have been shocked at the necessity under which he lay of sacrificing the steep lines of roof so dear to him in his native land, and to have striven with all his might to provide a substitute for their effect by the vertical lines of his panelled buttresses and walls, by the gabled outline of his parapets, and by the removal even of such a slight horizontal mark as the commencement of the traceries of his windows on one line. And his work is a most remarkable standing proof of the failure of such an attempt; for, despite all these precautions, and I incline to believe in consequence of them, the general effect is, after all, entirely horizontal. Extremes meet, and so the attempt to avoid absolute horizontal lines has completely failed, because in their place we have a succession of vertical members placed side by side in such endless numbers that we really think more of the horizontal arrangement of these members, slight though they are, than we should of the simplest defined horizontal line.

And the same consequence followed the same kind of work in England. I know no building in which the horizontal line is more painfully predominant than in Henry the Seventh's Chapel at Westminster, where, nevertheless, it is broken endlessly by vertical lines of pinnacles, and where the walls are covered in all parts with perpendicular lines of panelling.

Indeed, I should have but little respect for such a building as this exterior of Milan were it not for its rare material (used though it is in a prodigal manner, and without particular reference to its nature) and its immense size—though this is far less in appearance than in reality. But my detraction and harsh criticisms must end here; for if, having first made the circuit of the entire church, the flight of steps which leads up to the west door is last of all mounted, the first feeling must be one of perfect amazement and delight—amazement that the same mind which conceived the exterior should have been able also to achieve anything so diverse from it as is the interior, and delight that anything so magnificent and so perfect should ever have been reared on the southern slope of the Alps, to exhibit, to the eyes as it were of enemies, the full majesty and power of the pointed architecture of the North. And mark, upon consideration, how very natural this was. Its architect had been tied down in his exterior by the wants, or supposed wants, of a climate unlike his own, and a material to which he was unused; his genius had thus been fettered and kept under; but here all shackles were undone, and he was free to carry out to its very greatest perfection what he had learnt or dreamt of in his Northern home. And what a result has he not achieved!—absolutely and without doubt one of the grandest interiors in the world is, I do believe, this noble work of his; its grandeur amazes one at first, and delights all the more afterwards as one becomes on more intimate terms with it, and can look at it with less emotion than at first. And how shall I describe it?—for to say that it has so many bays in length or in width is not sufficient; all this, and even the detail of its design, were familiar enough to me before I saw it, but still the reality was so very far beyond any description, that I felt, and feel still, averse from attempting it.

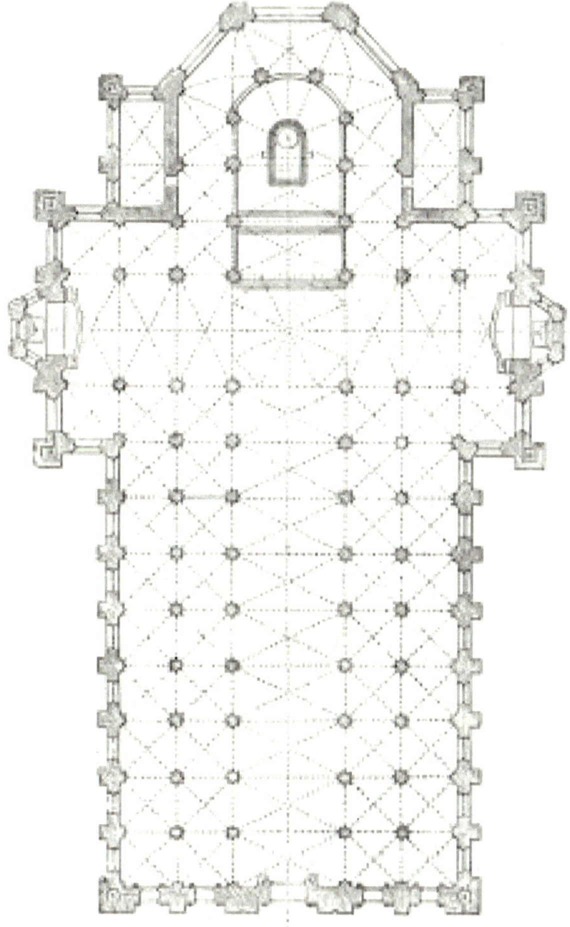

Ground-Plan—Milan Cathedral (Duomo, Milan).*

A few only of the most noticeable points, therefore, shall be touched; and, as it seems to me to teach less of Italian art or architecture than of Northern, I shall feel myself acquitted of neglect, inasmuch as the main, if not the sole, object of my Italian notes is as to the development of really Italian work. I was struck at first by the prodigious width and height of the building. The nave is enormously wide, and has two aisles on either side, those next to it being also of great size and height, and having clerestories in their outer walls. The outer aisles are lighted with large traceried windows, filled with stained glass, which gives the church a character very unlike that of the generality of Italian Gothic churches, in which coloured glass is so rarely seen in large masses.

There is, therefore, a regular gradation in the heights of the five main divisions of the church, which are well proportioned to their respective widths; and, resting as these divisions do upon four rows of clustered columns of immense size and height, a more magnificent internal effect is produced than I can recollect even any approach to in any other church; for not even in Köln or in Amiens is there any effect so magnificent as that of this forest of prodigious piers. They are finished at the top with capitals peculiar to this building, and quite unlike anything I have before seen—I suppose at least twelve feet deep, with a kind of arcade of tracery surmounted by a crocketed gable on each side, and finished above and below with courses of foliage, and with figures standing in the niche-like panels of the arcade.

Such a contrivance would be clumsy and absurd if attempted on a small scale, but here, at the summit of these immense columns, it is thoroughly successful, and, I believe, the only contrivance which could have been successfully adopted. The capitals vary very much in detail and in merit; but one of the finest is seen close to the west entrance, and recalls forcibly the best Northern pointed work, having indeed, neither in detail nor in design, one single trace of an Italian influence.

So grand are the columns that the excessive poverty and lightness of the arches which divide the nave from the aisles, which is perhaps the greatest defect of the interior of the church, is not for a long time noticed; they have, however, but little apparent work to do, and so their lightness may perhaps be a virtue.

Throughout the interior there is a very remarkable love shewn everywhere for a moulding which was never used by Italians, but was so much used among ourselves—the wave-mould. Then, again, all the shafts are filleted, and the fillet turning off gradually into the round line of the shaft, produces the same moulding; a fulness and richness are consequently very noticeable in all the interior, very different indeed from anything else that I saw in Italy. The solitary blot upon this otherwise noble work is one for which its architect is in no way responsible—the cells of the groining are all filled in with painted imitations of elaborate traceries in brown colour, an abominable device, which never ceases to offend and annoy the eye more and more every time it is observed.[72] The window tracery throughout is meagre, confused, and unmeaning, and the traceries introduced at mid-height

[72] When I first saw this I thought it was an entirely modern device. In 1871, however, in passing through France, I found at La Fère a church of flamboyant character, with all the cells of its groining covered with sunk traceries; and at Chambéry the painting on the roof of the Sainte Chapelle is said to be old.

most unsatisfactory; but the glass with which it is filled, though poor and late in its character, contains much rich colour, and gives the entire building a very grand and warm tone.

Compared with other foreign churches, there is in this—the largest of them all—a singular absence of side altars. There are indeed some three or four; but so great is the prominence given to the high altar in the choir, that one scarcely thinks of the possibility of the existence of any others, and has to look about a good deal before discovering where they are to be found.

In common with so many of the Italian churches the pavements here are very fine, and impart no small degree of additional magnificence to the interior.

Many are the works which might be catalogued in this great church, but I must content myself with noticing one only—the great bronze candelabrum. This is, I suppose, the most precious work of its kind in Europe. It was placed in the cathedral in 1557, a date too late for its execution by some three hundred years. The supports are four winged dragons, heads downwards, and with tails intertwined. The shaft has bosses in the centre, and branches out above into a profusion of branches full of exquisite leafage. This is all conventional in character, and entirely like thirteenth-century work. In spaces formed for the purpose and on the bosses are various figures and subjects all wrought with singular skill, and a lavish profusion of ingenuity which cannot be too much admired. Among these are the Temptation and the Expulsion from Paradise, the signs of the zodiac, figures illustrating architecture and music, and a variety of others.

After I had seen the cathedral I had, by way of enjoying the pleasures of a contrast, to devote myself patiently to all the troubles attendant upon personally procuring my passport. At Milan personal application was absolutely enforced; and there, in a small room crowded by vetturini and other Italians of the lower order, relieved by one or two unfortunate travellers like myself, I had for nearly two hours to endure heat, noise, and all the other annoyances of such a work, before I succeeded in getting my passport *visé*, with permission to abide three days only within the walls. This system is certainly most vexatious to an Englishman; but at the same time, if people will make a point of keeping the rulers of a city constantly on the *qui vive* with plots, or rumours of plots, I do not see what other resource their rulers can have. Some idea of the state of the population may be drawn from the way in which the soldiers patrol the streets, in companies of three or four, during the whole day, giving an impression of a place where men keeping guard singly would be in danger; and then again the great number of the troops at the gates and elsewhere throughout the city certainly presents very much the impression of a place whose normal condition is one perpetual state of siege.[73]

Next to the cathedral the great architectural attraction of Milan is the famous church of Sant'Ambrogio, which has equally as great claims upon the antiquary and upon the ecclesiologist as upon the architect.

---

[73] I leave this passage as it was written in 1855. Such troubles are now all passed and gone; but we run some risk of forgetting how much we have gained in this way by the political changes that have occurred since then.

Entering from the west, it presented a most striking and, to me, most novel effect. In advance of the church is an open atrium, surrounded by a cloister of Lombard-Romanesque character, the columns having quaintly and stiffly carved capitals of stone, and the wall and arches being built of mixed bricks and stone.[74] Three arches, open from the atrium to the west end of the church, and above them three other arches of similar plan, and arranged in triplet fashion, that in the centre being the highest and widest, nearly fill up the great flat pediment of the church, on either side of which rise towers—that on the north divided into stages by means of arcaded strings, like most Lombard belfries; that on the south perfectly plain and rude, and perhaps therefore of the very early date at which some antiquaries appear to place the building of the main structure of this portion of the existing church.[75]

This arrangement, borrowed though it may be from heathen days and civil buildings, is nevertheless uncommonly satisfactory; it serves to prepare the mind for the entrance to the church itself, and, instead of the abrupt transition commonly made from the world to the holy places, here the intermediate atrium gives time and space to throw off all worldly thoughts, and to enter entirely into the religious feelings proper in such a place.

The entrance by the west doorway is of great interest, for in its very ancient doors are inserted some still more ancient fragments, said by tradition—and there is every reason to believe it to be true—to be portions of the gates which S. Ambrose shut against the Emperor Theodosius.

The interior has suffered much at various times, either by repairs or alterations; and as most of the groining is of pointed character, the first impression is that of a very low, simple, and solemn-looking pointed church of early date. Upon more close examination, however, it is found that the main walls throughout are Romanesque, and that this groining was subsequently inserted, and again in later times strengthened and supported by great piers and arches of Classic character.

The plan, after passing the atrium, is a nave of three bays, each subdivided into two by arches into the aisles, a lantern over the altar, and three eastern apses. There are no transepts. The most striking object in the interior is the magnificent Romanesque baldachin above the high altar. This is supported on four marble shafts, and has a semicircular arch on each face, with figures and foliage in the four flat pediments or gables which finish it above. Three flights of five steps lead up to the altar from the north, south, and west, and the whole is protected both on the east and the west by high metal screens. Here is a splendid shrine for the relics of the tutelar saint, of the same age as the early church, which is however so jealously concealed that I have never seen it.[76] The front of the altar itself is very magnificent, executed entirely in metal, and containing subjects from the life of Our Blessed Lord and from that of S. Ambrose. A modernized dome rises above the baldachin; and behind this an apse decorated in mosaic upon a gold ground very grandly finishes the interior of this interesting church.

[74] See plate 18, p. 91, for an illustration of the cornice of this atrium.
[75] The atrium was added, it is said, in the ninth century.
[76] See, for description of it, Hemans' 'Mediæval Christianity,' &c., p. 305.

58.—Baldachin. Sant'Ambrogio. Milan.

On the north side of the nave is a very curious pulpit, coeval with the church and remarkable for its carvings, and for a Roman sarcophagus which occupies the space between the columns which support it.

From Sant'Ambrogio I made my way under a burning sun to what I expected to find a very interesting church, that of Sant'Eustorgio. I was, however, very much disappointed; the interior is abominably modernized, though still retaining enough of its old Romanesque features to be intelligible if carefully studied, and remarkable for many ancient monuments on its walls. It has nave, aisles, and chapels beyond the aisles, the whole groined, and there is a prodigious ascent to the choir, which is raised upon a crypt.

That for which it ought to be visited is the exquisite monument to S. Peter Martyr, executed by G. Balduccio da Pisa, in 1339. It consists of a sarcophagus supported on pilasters, in front of which are statues representing virtues. Few works of the kind have ever been executed, in which the skill of the sculptor has been more happily united with that of the architect than in this. It deserves all praise.

Sta. Maria delle Grazie, which I next visited, is a church known generally as that in the refectory attached to which is to be seen all that remains of L. da Vinci's painting of the Last Supper. I know not how much this may have suffered within the last few years, but really, when I read the kind of remarks which I so frequently see about it, I cannot help fancying, rather strongly, that they have perhaps been written before instead of after seeing the veritable picture. It is in fact in the last stage of decay, with scarcely any of its colouring or drawing intelligible; and has probably been entirely repainted since Leonardo's death. Visitors who go to admire and do admire the Leonardo, might do worse than in examining and admiring the extremely fine and fairly well-preserved earlier fresco or distemper painting by Montorfano which covers the opposite wall of the refectory, and contains a good and busy painting of the Crucifixion, painted in 1495. The church is of very late pointed date, entirely of brick, with a large and ugly dome added by Bramante. The nave arcades are pretty good—pointed arches springing from the square Classical-looking capitals of equally Classical-looking columns; very much as in the church of San Francesco at Venice. Elaborate brick cornices and the usual sham front leave the same kind of impression on my mind in respect to this church that it has of all late Italian pointed work in brick—one of a tasteless, unreal, and unsatisfactory school of art.

South of the cathedral there is a fine late brick campanile attached to the church of San Gottardo, which rises from behind some of the great public buildings in which the city abounds. This is a very elaborate work, octagonal in plan and covered with arcades one above the other, and finished with a low spire. It is a fourteenth-century building at the earliest, but in spite of this most of its arches are semicircular. It is certainly a rich and picturesque tower, and well deserves inspection.

The remaining churches in Milan seemed to be all Classical, of different grades of merit and size. There were indeed some very late examples of brickwork of some value, but really, save the cathedral, there is not much architectural art to be studied or dwelt upon in Milan. The cathedral, too, teaches little; its main office is, rather, to prove the consummate beauty and magnificence attainable by the pointed style, carried out severely and simply on the very grandest scale, and this its interior does triumphantly beyond all cavil.

59.—Piazza dei Mercanti. Milan.

A visit to Milan had always been looked forward to by me with great interest: first, from curiosity as to the real effect and merits of the Duomo; and, secondly, from a longing to see the magnificent Sposalizio of Raffaelle, which is the gem of the collection in the Brera; and this famous gallery was therefore one of the first objects of my curiosity. The careful examination of the pictures which adorn its walls was, however, when we were there, much hindered by an exhibition of modern Italian pictures, hung in the same rooms as, and in most cases in front of, the old works. We were able, fortunately, to get a fair view of what I believe to be not far from the greatest work of one of the greatest painters in the world—the Sposalizio being in a room unoccupied by other pictures and unmolested by the modern exhibitors. The man who could so paint at the age of twenty-one must, assuredly, have been almost matchless, for never have I seen a painting more thoroughly noble and delightful, in every way recalling to mind, it is true, in every figure the manner of his master, the great Perugino, but not the less enjoyable on that account.

The modern pictures were almost invariably worthless, and shewed no sign of any revival parallel to that which I trust I am not too sanguine in believing that one sees at the present day in England.

In the Piazza dei Mercanti is a much-altered building of the thirteenth century (its date is said to be 1228), which looks in its arrangements like a Palazzo Publico, and which in its original state must have been very charming. On the lower stage are five open arches, which have been modernized, I believe; above this a line of square panels, inclosing shields, forms a bold string-course, the central portion being brought forward on corbels for a Ringhiera. The *piano nobile* consists of five pointed arches carried on delicate shafts, and above was a deeply sunk line of arcading, each division garnished with a statue. There was once evidently a canopy over the Ringhiera. The materials of this front are black and white stone, but they are used with such moderation that there is nothing at all bizarre in the general effect of the façade.

In addition to these buildings there is still to be described another very grand brick domestic building of late date—the Ospidale Maggiore—which contains a great deal of very rich detail, half Renaissance and half Gothic in its character, though the general scheme of the building is wholly Renaissance. This building has been much extolled, but I think those who have praised it so much have mistaken clever manipulation of detail for good architectural design. The terra-cotta enrichments with which it is so richly set are hardly surpassed in their way by any of the same period in Italy, but I cannot admire the building as a whole.

With this building my architectural notes in Milan must end, but I should advise all students of architecture to include in their visits one of about half an hour's drive to the Certosa of Chiaravalle just outside Milan. The church here has been much modernized, but over the centre of the crossing still rises a brick lantern and steeple of singular interest. My engraving will explain what the character of this work is, better than any words. The construction is singular. Behind the base of the second stage of the great octagon a spire is constructed which carries the upper steeple, and the whole of the walls pierced with the second, third, and fourth series of windows are really only screen-walls or parapets in front of the spire. The height of the whole lantern from the ridge to the base of the spire is about ninety feet, and the effect of the complicated brickwork is not bad. It is somewhat difficult to say exactly when it was built. The Certosa itself was founded in 1135, and consecrated in 1228, but my impression is decidedly that though the whole steeple is built with round arches, it is not really a work of earlier date than about A.D. 1370 to 1400. The steeple of San Gottardo in Milan, which also has round arches everywhere, and is in some other respects somewhat similar in detail to this, dates from 1339, and it would be a great mistake to argue for an earlier date in either case from the mere use of the round arch. If I recollect right, the low third stage in height at Chiaravalle is modern.

60.—Certosa of Chiaravalle.

Milan was on the whole rather disappointing to me in my architectural capacity, though pleasant enough in every other; and after I had lounged and driven about, first in one direction and then in another, and had really enjoyed my last great Italian city very much, finding that little more was to be done but to eat ices, look at smart carriages on the Corso, and long for more chance of a clear view of the Alps than the hazy sultry weather afforded, I made up my mind to leave earlier than I had originally intended.

No architectural student should turn his feet homeward from Milan without having first of all visited Vercelli. It is easily reached by railway, passing on the road Novara, where there was only a few years back a fine Lombard cathedral, which has unfortunately been lately supplanted by a modern Italian fabric, even more than usually vapid and uninteresting, and where there is still an old baptistery so plastered and painted as to have lost almost all its old interest. The traveller has therefore to content himself with the views—which become better as he proceeds—of the snow-capped Alps (including their noblest peak, Monte Rosa) to the north of the railway, which, in clear weather, are most glorious in their effect.

The cathedral at Vercelli is modernized, and I believe not worth visiting; I confined myself to the remarkable church of Sant'Andrea, which is fortunately close to the railway station, and of unusual beauty and interest. The interest is historical as well as architectural. The church was built by Cardinal Guala de' Bicchieri, who had been in England as legate from the Pope at the very beginning of the thirteenth century, and is said to have brought back with him to Vercelli a French or English architect. The evidence of the building itself is in favour of a French rather than an English influence, but neither is felt anywhere save in the interior, and the outside views shew to my eyes no trace of any but an Italian hand. It is the square-ended choir probably which has made some writers say that it was designed by an English architect. This choir is short, and on the east side of each transept are two chapels, which are apsidal. The whole church is groined; the columns between the nave and aisles are well clustered, and all the mouldings and details are well and skilfully drawn. The church is well designed to suit the climate, all the windows being small except at the east end, where there is a fine triplet, with a circular window filled with well-designed tracery above. Over the crossing of nave and transepts is a raised lantern, groined, and lighted by very small windows high up. The angles under it have extremely well-designed pendentives with carvings of the Evangelistic emblems in the centre. Brick is used for the main portion of the work, counterchanged in many parts with stone, and the proportions and details of the interior are so good that I found myself in the rare state of mind (in an Italian church) of admiring without grumbling! The dimensions are good without being imposing, the total length being a little over two hundred feet, and the width across the transepts about a hundred and twenty feet.

The exterior has a great bald west front with three round arched doorways, and a false gable between two small but lofty flanking towers. The walls are arcaded under the eaves, and over the crossing rises an octagonal lantern, which is gathered in after a rather ungainly manner above the lowest stage. This steeple is finished with a low circular brick spire adorned in the most curious fashion with small circular brick pinnacles—one over each side of the tower—which look extremely like a collection of chimneys.

61.—Sant'Andrea. Vercelli, Interior.

Detached from the church, and standing at an angle to it, is a simple campanile of later date (1399), and of four stages in height. The combination of this eccentrically placed tower with the rest of the church is very remarkable, and appears to have been simply a caprice. Its effect certainly does not warrant the sort of admiration which should lead any modern architect engaged in studying the church to recommend the copying of the relative positions of it and its bell-tower. I ought not to forget one feature—the buttress—which is treated here in quite the French or English fashion, with bold projection and good steep sloped weatherings instead of in the usual Italian fashion as a mere pilaster.

North of the nave of the church is a good cloister, on the east side of which is a fine square chapter-house, divided by groining piers into nine bays. The original triple entrance to the chapter-house—a door with window on each side—still remains, and there is a communication also through a groined sacristy with the north transept. I know few churches which shew more just sense of the best treatment of a good Gothic interior than this does. In its original state, when the brickwork was exposed in its natural colour, the effect was of course much better than it is now; but the effect is still so good that I may safely assert that, were the exterior equal to the interior, there would be few more beautiful churches in Northern Italy.[77]

There is an interesting monument in the south-east chapel, corbelled out from the wall and decorated with sculpture and painting. In the gable is the Coronation of the Blessed Virgin, below a figure kneeling before her, and said to represent the architect of the church, who died in 1246, being Abbat as well as architect. Immediately opposite the church is a hospital founded by the same cardinal. It has been much altered, but there are still some ancient portions, which I could not get leave to see.

From Vercelli we retraced our steps to Milan, and halted no longer than was necessary before going on to Monza on our way to Como. Here we were well rewarded and most agreeably surprized. We found a very curious and good Broletto, a cathedral of fine and elaborate brickwork with a great west front of marble, and another brick church of most elaborate detail. The west front of the Duomo is a very fine example of Italian Gothic in marble; it is divided into five divisions in width, those in the centre and at the sides being the widest, and is constructed in yellow and dark grey marbles in alternate courses, the former very deep, the latter generally shallow, but varying without much rule.

All the roofs are flat, but finish at the west at different levels, and not in one continuous slope. The eaves have heavy cornices, and under these, all the way up, is an arcade resting upon shafts supported on corbels. The windows are all filled with traceries which are certainly not at all equal to English tracery, as they are very flat in their effect, and have no proper subordination of parts. There is a large rose window in the centre division treated in a better manner than is usual, and set within a square line of moulding, with small circles in the spandrels, and a line

---

[77] It is worth notice that the regular-looking bays of the nave are of very various widths. The two eastern are 21 feet; the next two, four feet less; and the fifth still narrower. The bricks here measure 1 ft. ½ in. × 5 in., and are 3¼ in. high, and have all been chiselled on the face.

of square panels on each side continued in the most unpleasing way above; five other smaller circular windows are similarly treated. In some parts of the wall the courses of black marble are continuations of the black arch-stones of the windows, which, though not uncommon in Italian pointed work, is never satisfactory in its effect. In the upper part of the front this is not the case.

Window in Duomo, Monza (Cathedral—Monza).

The central division has a porch resting upon detached shafts, and with a semicircular arch, which is, however, richly cusped; and throughout the front semicircular and pointed arches seem to have been used quite indiscriminately. The buttresses which divide the front were originally finished with pinnacles, of which one only now remains; this is certainly very beautiful, of precisely the same type as the pinnacles on some of the tombs of the Scaligers at Verona, standing on detached shafts, with gables on either side, supported on trefoiled arches, and with small pinnacles between the gables, all of which are crocketed; the mouldings are very flat, but in the pure white marble seen against the deep blue sky of Italy this flatness is as much a virtue and a beauty as its counterpart executed in stone in chilly England would be poverty-stricken and tame. All the remainder of the exterior of the Duomo is of red brick, with some particularly good detail. I give one window from the south side of the choir as an example.

62. — Broletto, Monza.

There is a large low cloister on the north side, and from this the central tower is best seen; it is an octagon of two stages in brick and stone, a good deal arcaded, and has a pyramidal tiled roof, with a square turret in the centre. This forms a dome internally, which is however (as is the whole of the church) miserably modernized.

The cornices under the eaves here are of brick of good detail, but of the common arcaded character. I noticed an inscription on the east end, referring to the erection of the church in 1390, a date which tallies very well with the character of most of the external detail. Internally there is a rather remarkable pulpit or ambon on the north side of the nave. It is a gallery measuring some twenty feet east and west, supported on detached shafts with a projection in the centre, and of combined Gothic and Renaissance detail; so large a pulpit certainly suggests rambling discourses.

On the whole, such a church as this is very interesting, and to some extent striking; but, much as I admired the conjunction of the two marbles, and the more than usually Gothic character of some of the details, there was yet enough in the ungainly outline of the sham front, and in the capricious use of round and pointed arches indifferently, to damp my pleasure, and make me cease to admire the work very decidedly. There is a difference in construction which ought to be noted between this marble front and the marble work at Venice; for, whilst the latter is not at all constructional, this is entirely so, the marbles not being veneered on to the wall, but forming a portion of its substance. I need not say that in this respect, when we wish to use marble in England, the paucity of our supplies will probably always compel us to imitate the Venetians rather than the architects of Monza, Como, or Milan.

The sacristy here is worth visiting. Among other relics are two fifteenth-century chalices of unusually good workmanship. They appeared to me to be by a German rather than an Italian hand.

The Broletto, which stands near the cathedral in the centre of the city, is very interesting. It is raised upon open arches of stone, two at either end and five at the sides. In my sketch of it the southern end is shewn with the projecting Ringhiera in the second stage; the northern end is very singular, the tower rising out of one side, with the steep-pitched roof of the other half abutting against it. The detail of the windows is very good, the arch-stones in some of them increasing in depth towards the centre, with an effect of very great strength. All the windows are shafted. The dimensions of this building are forty-two feet from east to west, and sixty-four feet from north to south.

The only other ancient building which I could find was the church of Sta. Maria in Strada; the most elaborate example of late work in brick and terra-cotta that I have anywhere seen. The effect is not satisfactory; for when, as here, carvings are imitated and repeated in terra-cotta, and traceries entirely executed in it, one begins, I confess, to long much for a little of the fire and spirit which some mark of the individual artist might have given such an amount of elaborate decoration in stone. The west front is the only part of the church of any interest, the interior having been thoroughly modernized, and retaining no traces of its original character.

Window in Broletto—Monza.

The door and windows in the lower stage have been interpolated, and besides this there is a strangely ugly window above them, about which—as this is the last of its class we shall see—I wish to say a word. In starting on a continental journey, between London and Croydon on the South-Eastern Railway you used to pass under several great semi-circular arched bridges. When first built, the engineer chose, in order to gratify some odd fancy, to prop these up by two piers of brickwork, dividing the arch into three, and putting the whole in great jeopardy. It is curious that this singularly supported and divided arch finds a counterpart in almost every large church in the North of Italy. It was the one great idea of the Renaissance builders, and, until they had taken out one of the old windows and inserted in its place one of these hideous contrivances, they were never satisfied. In Venice every church, even the noble church of the Frari, has them, and I believe scarcely a large church in the North of Italy is without at least this one evidence of the delicacy of taste which characterizes the Renaissance age!

The skill which is shewn in making and fitting together brickwork such as that in the front of this church is very great indeed, but, after all, I fear, rather mistaken, for the effect is most unsatisfactory, and every one must see that throughout the façade there is an evident attempt to satisfy the eye by the exceedingly elaborate character of the detail, rather than by the fitness of the thing itself, or by the beauty of the proportions. The insufficiency of the windows for the extent of wall is an obvious fault, and not less so is the fact which I am almost tired of referring to, that the whole front is sham and designed without any reference whatever to the wants of the building, to which it forms the street-front.

In the evening we left Monza for Camerlata, a village within about a mile of Como, availing ourselves again of the Milan and Como railway.

The Camerlata station was soon reached, and after some little delay we found ourselves ensconced in one of those long omnibuses so fashionable in Italy, and driving down a long hill, planted on either side with trees, towards Como. Above us, to the right and to the left, we could see, by the bright moonlight, the shapes of the mountains which hem in this arm of the fairest of lakes; whilst just above us, proudly perched upon a crag, were the ruins of a castle, which lent, when we saw it by daylight, an additional charm to the otherwise beautiful view.

Soon we were in the outskirts of the town; but it was long before we reached the borders of the lake, after following the windings of an almost interminable street, passing the guardhouse, and, to our sorrow, parting again for the last time with our passports, then crossing the piazza in which stand the Duomo and the Broletto side by side — for me the main attraction of the place — until at last we were fairly discharged at an hotel on the very edge of the water.

We had heard an Austrian band as we rolled across the piazza, and so without delay thither we returned in time to hear the last of Austrian music, and to revel by moonlight in the beauty of the many-coloured marble front of the fair Broletto. We stood listening to the music for about a quarter of an hour, when suddenly a word of command was given, the men who held the lanterns marched to the front, the band formed behind them four abreast, the lights were extinguished, and, suddenly breaking into a lively march, the band disappeared, and the crowd soon left us in quiet possession of the piazza, whose old houses still rang with the wild and clamorous echoes of the beautiful music.

We returned to our inn, and had infinite trouble in the attempt to find a voiturier to take us to the Lago Maggiore in time for the steamer on the morrow. The route by which I had fully intended to return was to go by the lake to Menaggio, thence to cross to Porlezza and by the Lake of Lugano, and then from Lugano across the Monte Cenere to Bellinzona; to my great annoyance I found, however, at Milan that, owing to the long-standing quarrel between the Emperor and the Confederation, no travellers were allowed to pass immediately from the Austrian into the Ticinese territory, or *vice versâ*, and we were obliged, therefore, to defer seeing the beautiful Lake of Lugano, to go instead to Laveno, and thence to Bellinzona, by the Lago Maggiore; and our difficulty at Como was to find any true account of the time that it would take us to reach Laveno, or of the time at which we were likely to find the steamer to Magadino. In the end it was decided that we should start at seven the next morning, and accordingly soon after five I was out in the piazza taking notes and sketches of my last Italian building, the Broletto of Como.

In general character this is somewhat similar to the Broletto at Bergamo, but in real beauty it is scarcely inferior to any one building I have seen in Italy. Towards the piazza it has four arches on the ground story, which is divided from the next stage by an arcaded string-course. This second stage has three windows only over the four arches below; and another very noticeable irregularity is, that one of these windows, and that not the central, has a pedimental canopy above its arch, and has more shafts than the others. The central window has been modernized to some extent, but this was the Ringhiera, and the balcony still remains, though looking more modern than the rest of the front. Some of the arches of these windows are very noticeable; for though they are semicircular, the back of the stones which form them is cut with a different sweep, so as to produce an outer pointed line, and thus to leave an impression on the eye of absolutely pointed windows. Another arcaded corbel-table finishes the façade, or rather ought to finish it, for above this some barbarian has added another stage, nearly to the destruction of the effect of the building.[78] North of this façade a great plain tower of rough stone recalls to recollection those of Bergamo and Brescia; it boasts of an immense clock and some faint traces of painting, and is left unfinished at the top. The whole of this façade (with the exception of the campanile) is built of red, white, and dark grey marbles, which are very carefully and effectively contrasted in their arrangement; the courses are very irregular in their widths, and apparently arranged upon no systematic rule. The opposite (east) side of the Broletto is very similar, but one of its windows is remarkable for the way in which the shafts are knotted together in the centre. This is not at all an uncommon feature in Italian pointed, and I have often wondered how it is that the eye is not at once disgusted with it, instead of being, as it usually is, pleased. I take it to be a justifiable device on some such ground as this: it takes much labour and skill to cut several shafts out of one block of marble, but all this labour and skill is unthought of, if they are entirely separated, or held together by a band which might perchance be made of some other material; this knot therefore is devised as the only means of explaining to us that the shafts so carved have really been accomplished with a very great expenditure of time and patience and skill, and do not depend upon any artificial band for the firmness with which they are all united in one. The capitals of all the columns in this Broletto are very well carved.

By the side of the Broletto stands the Duomo, the bad character of whose west front, even though it is of late Gothic, hardly tempted me to go in to see the effect of the interior. I did so, however, and found a large but uninteresting church, with groining of pointed section, which gives considerable character to an otherwise insipid work. The west front has doorways of Lombard character, and above them a large rose window; but every part of the exterior and interior seems to have been so much altered that little remains of the original work.

Internally works of restoration were going on, and these permitted me to see that the whole church had a great deal of colour introduced on the walls and over the groining, though I was unable to ascertain anything satisfactorily as to its age or character.

---

[78] I think no apology is necessary for the omission of this modern stage in my view of the Broletto.

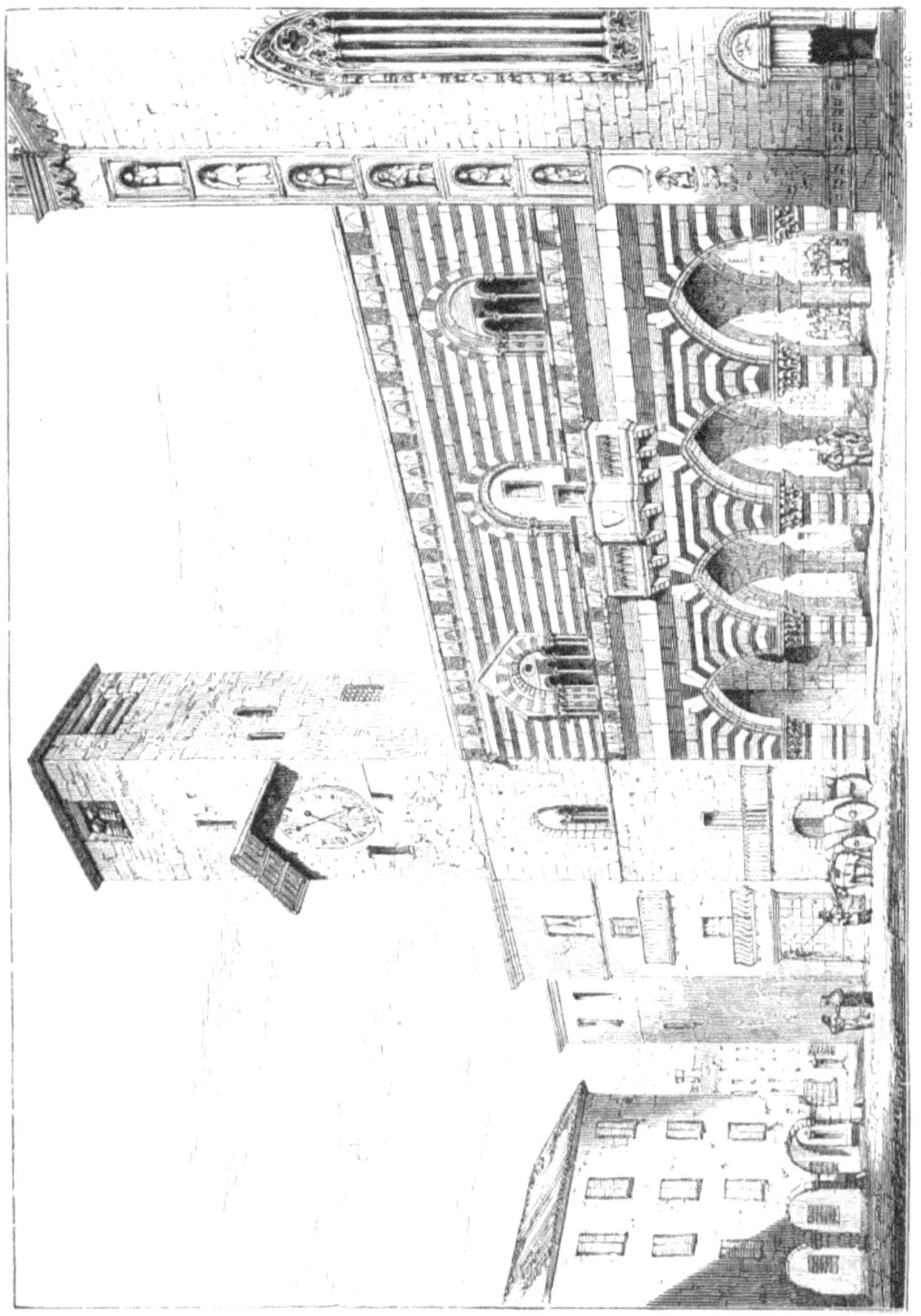

63.—Broletto. Como.

64.—Sta. Maria, Como.

About ten minutes' walk from the cathedral is the fine Lombard church of
Sta. Maria. This has unfortunately been much modernized, but its east end with
an apse arcaded outside, and finished with a fine eaves-cornice rich in shadow, is
still extremely striking and almost unaltered. It is built of black and white stone.
Here, alas! I remember that I thought at the time of my first visit, ends my hurried
study of Gothic architecture in Italy. But if at that day it was somewhat sad to

leave Como after an all too rapid journey, it has been my happiness to revisit the quaint old town again and again since, and each time with increased pleasure. Italian scenery, Italian art, Italian travel, afford some of the happiest recollections of well-spent days of travel, which, if they have never been able to exceed in pleasure or to approach in profit the remembrances of travels in my own and other lands, undertaken for the same purpose, are nevertheless full to overflowing with lessons in art which no true architect could afford to despise or wish to forget.

CHAPTER XIII.

Departure from Como—Varese—Lake of Varese—Italian Boatmen—
Intra—Laveno—Lago Maggiore—Magadino—Road to Hospenthal—The Dazio Grande—Airolo—Hospenthal—Ascent of the
Furca—Valley of the Reuss—Lake of Luzern—Luzern—The Unter Hauenstein—Strasburg.

"And now farewell to Italy—perhaps
For ever! Yet, methinks, I could not go,
I could not leave it, were it mine to say
'Farewell for ever!'"

Rogers.

THERE was great delay in leaving Como; the passport officer was asleep, and
no one dared to awaken him for our convenience; at last we determined to start,
and went off to the passport office, and, after waiting nearly half an hour, the dila-
tory clerk arrived, and our passport having been stamped with the "Buon per par-
tire," so uncivilly glad to get rid of you as it seems to be, I mounted the carriage,
and we were soon on our way.

All Como was astir, and bedecking the houses and churches, and building
triumphal arches across the roads, for some religious fête whose nature we did
not discover; but we soon left its streets and hills behind, and began to look out
anxiously for our first view of Monte Rosa and its attendant Alps; but, alas! the
weather, instead of clearing, rapidly became more and more cloudy, and ere long
we felt that we must give up all hope of getting even the most distant glimpse of
the monarch of this portion of the Alpine chain.

Without this view, from which we had promised ourselves so much pleasure, the road is tame and uninteresting all the way to Varese, where we changed
our horses and carriage. It is an uninteresting town, with a good many villas and
gardens, belonging, I believe, to inhabitants of Milan, who come out here for the
mountain air. None of their houses are free from that general look of dreariness
and lack of care which seem to afflict most Italian villas. Passing through Varese,
we soon saw on our right a very famous pilgrimage church crowning the summit
of a considerable hill, and approached by a succession of chapels, somewhat as in
the still more famous pilgrimage church of Varallo, and so popular that round it
there seems to have grown up a small town for the accommodation of the pilgrims.

Farther on we passed the lake of Varese, and from one point in the road had a view of no less than about five different lakes, one of which was Lago Maggiore. The Lago di Varese is a tame, uninteresting sheet of water, surrounded by low flat woody country, except at one point on the north, but even there the hills do not rise immediately from the lake.

The only approach to old buildings that we saw were one or two brick campanili of early date, and the remains of a castle, near Varese, finished at the top with the favourite forked battlement.

We had much ado to make our driver understand our desire to reach Lago Maggiore without delay, and, to say the truth, there was something too much like cruelty in the attempt to compel our poor steeds to any such feat of speed and strength as the performance of some six miles an hour really appeared to be. As we neared the lake the scenery improved; and woody hills, with here and there a dashing streamlet finding its way down the hill-side, and a glimpse now and then of the blue water of the lake, made the way pleasant. At last we reached the outskirts of the village of Laveno, and were immediately chased by all the male population of the place, who explained their eager pursuit when at last we stopped on the beach, by vying with one another for the privilege of conveying us across the lake to Intra, where we had to join the steamer. I asked their charge, and they rather astonished me by demanding twelve francs and a buono-mano; of course I blandly offered them five francs, much to their disgust, and with shrugs of their shoulders and grand looks of contempt they turned away. However, I was determined not to submit to so palpable an imposition, so, when I was having my passport *visé*, I asked the courteous passport-officer what the fair charge might be? "Four and a half lire," was the answer. "But how am I to compel the rascals to take me?" — "Oh! bring them up to me," he replied; so down I went to where all the boatmen were discussing together the atrocity of my offer, and, taking two of them by the arm, I quietly walked them up to the friendly officer; the rest followed, and then commenced one of the most amusing scenes I ever witnessed. The passport-officer told them to take me for the four and a half lire, upon which, they all, standing with their right arms extended towards him, answered with a furious volley of Italian ejaculations, quite unintelligible to me, but sufficiently absurd when contrasted with the quiescent state of their antagonist. Their eloquence was, however, all in vain; for, after a short attempt to reason them into submission, my friend sent them off, and threatened to send a soldier with us if they did not start at once. Before I could reach the beach again the luggage was all in the boat, and in another minute we were afloat, propelled by three sturdy fellows, who, after having tried in vain to make me pay fourteen lire and a buono-mano, were really not apparently much annoyed when I paid them the legal fare, being about one-fourth less than at a guess I had first of all offered! They were evidently true philosophers.

I fear that my experience of travelling in Italy obliged me to look upon the proceedings of these men as by no means unusual or peculiar to boatmen; wherever you go it is the same, and, unless you wish to pay much more than the rest of the world ever thinks of paying, you must make a point of disputing hotel accounts, shop charges, and voiturier's charges; the result always is, that you pay about twenty per cent less than you otherwise would, and are evidently looked up to with infinitely more respect.

About half an hour sufficed to take us to Intra, the Sardinian port opposite to Laveno, just a glimpse being obtained of the famous Isola Bella as we crossed. A Sardinian soldier welcomed us to his liberal Majesty's dominions, and, as we told him that we were going on by the steamer, allowed us to go into the town without shewing our passports. There was, however, nothing to see, except the pretty view of the opposite hills—they are scarcely mountains—and of the long sheet of water stretching up and down for many a mile, and commanded almost more completely hence than from any other place in its whole extent.

We dined at a very miserable inn, with a pretty lookout, and, as it happened to be a *jour maigre*, could get nothing fit to eat; the landlord took, however, a convenient view of the matter, and, assuring us that he never made any difference on this account, charged us as though we had eaten all the delicacies of the season. Here, again, as I had time on my hands, I amused myself with lowering my host's demands, and finally paid him a fair valuation for a very *maigre* dinner.

This business was no sooner satisfactorily finished, a sketch of the opposite coast having been secured during the argument, than the steamer arrived, and in a few minutes we were ploughing our way along the fair expanse of water, leaving the not very honest people of Laveno and Intra behind us and forgotten, all our attention being devoted to the gradually developing beauties of the upper end of the lake.

We were amused at Laveno by the warlike demonstrations of the Austrians, who had there a very smart little war-steamer for the protection of their interests on the lake, besides a small fort. They had, in fact, less territory on the lake than either Sardinia or Switzerland; luckily, however, for the peace of the water, these two last states seemed not to think it necessary to keep up a rival force, and so the little war-steamer at Laveno remained, untouched and uncared for, and her officers passed their lives in smoking cigars and longing for some change of place and duty, which was provided for them at last by the abrupt conclusion of Austrian rule in these parts a few years after the time of this visit.

Our steamer kept very much to the Sardinian shore of the lake, and, as there are two or three great bends in its course, a view of one small portion only of the lake is obtained, until, upon reaching a promontory, and rounding it, as it were a new lake and new scenery are disclosed; and happily, as the water is ascended towards Magadino, each turn brings more beautiful scenery than the last, until, as the head of the lake is neared, the view is very grand—not equal, certainly, to the head of Lake Como—but still exceedingly beautiful. The sun was just setting as we reached Locarno, and then our steamer, skirting along the sedgy shores of the lake—where the Ticino, at its entry, brings down a continually increasing deposit of mountain refuse—brought us in a few minutes to Magadino.

Our principal companions on the steamer were a large party of English, whose travelling-carriage and horses blocked up half the boat, and a very pleasant old Italian woman, whose elaborately neat hair and magnificent array of pins, each filigreed at the end, and all radiating like arrows from a central knot of hair, through which two larger and more magnificent pins were passed horizontally, forced upon our notice—but not more strongly than it had been forced before—this wonderful smartness and elaborate treatment and get-up of the hair, so common among the middle and lower classes in the North of Italy, and so unlike the customs of a similar class in England: I am bound to say, though, that the result of the elaborate straining and dressing of the hair seems generally to be, that, by the time women are fifty, they have no hair at all, or, at best, some two or three stray locks, which are then brought carefully together, and tied up, with a bold disregard of effect, in a knot at the top of the head.

When we landed at Magadino we found a diligence waiting, and, securing the *coupé*, jumped in, and were soon trotting off rapidly on the road to Bellinzona; in little more than an hour we passed through its gateway without having our passports demanded (how pleasant a change after Italy!), and were soon comfortably ensconced at the very respectable Albergo dell' Angelo.

We started from Bellinzona very early the next morning, determined, if possible, to surmount the worst part of the road and to sleep at Hospenthal, on the northern side of the pass. The view of Bellinzona on leaving it is very striking; three old castles perched on crags above give it an air of picturesque antiquity, and these, with the mountains rising grandly on either side of the Ticino, and sloping down in the distance to the bosom of Lago Maggiore, make a most beautiful picture. The situation is not, however, to be compared to that of Chiavenna, whose wall of mountains, clothed with Italian luxuriance of foliage, is pierced here and there with a chasm only, for the passage of some headlong river dashing down into the broad valley below the town; here the valley continues to be of considerable width for some miles above the town, whilst there one scarcely sees in what way any road is to escape across the mountains.

The first portion of the road is not very interesting. The pass of the Bernardino soon turns off to the right up a valley which allows a partial view, and from this point the S. Gothard road is sole possessor of the valley. Our first change of horses was at Bodio; and from thence the road gradually became much more beautiful. Many churches are seen scattered here and there on the summits of the inaccessible-looking mountains on either side of the valley, all of them whitewashed and generally distinguished by their tall campanili, and sometimes by the small cluster of houses and the patches of cultivated ground around them, betokening man's labour as well as man's religious love, on the summit of these forbidding-looking steeps. And whilst the distant prospect was so fair, the scenery close to the road was embellished by vineyards and magnificent chestnuts, growing in some places among great rocks shivered from the mountain-side above, and, in others, in groves on either side of some beautiful stream descending in a silver fall over the grey precipices which overhang the road.

The villages through which we passed were pretty and picturesque, and the villagers all very busy in the fields bringing in their hay, and gathering their grapes, which are always trained here over rocks and roofs in the most picturesquely irregular way; and altogether the valley, rife with so many signs of industry and activity, bore thoroughly the appearance rather of a Swiss than of an

Italian district. The upper slopes of the mountains, on either side, were clustered with fir-trees, and the deep blue water of the Ticino, here gently murmuring, there hastily dashing over some rocky impediment, made grateful music in our ears and imparted additional beauty to the way.

At Biasca and Giornico there are ancient churches, the exteriors of which are, however, of no interest; though the interior of the latter, with its crypt and curious paintings, well deserves a passing visit; but besides these all seemed new, and the houses as well as the people and the scenery soon began to remind us of Switzerland. There were those particularly large well-to-do looking inns in every village, with white walls and windows resplendent with green wooden shutter-blinds which are so common throughout this country; and here and there were to be seen houses with a display of well-carved or craftily-framed woodwork, which gave proof of our rapid approach to the land *par excellence* of carpentry.

But it was not till Faido had been passed, and the increasing barrenness of the hills, the entire absence of vineyards, and the only occasional appearance of some grand old chestnut-tree, weatherbeaten and rugged from conflict with many a storm, or, may be, some frightful inundation such as the Ticino loves at times to indulge in, shewed how rapidly we were rising into mountain regions, that the scenery became really striking. Then the road seems suddenly to arrive at the end of the valley, but presently as we advance, a narrow gorge in the mountain is perceived, and we enter this, the most magnificent portion of the Val Levantina, called Dazio Grande. The road is admirably engineered, carried through two or three short tunnels, and in excavations in the rocks above the torrent; the dark blue water leaps from rock to rock, and here and there dashes down in a fine waterfall; and the scenery is altogether so striking that, on the whole, I am much inclined to give the preference to this portion of the valley—that is to say, from the commencement of Dazio Grande to within a short distance of Airolo—over any portion of similar length in the whole course of the Splügen. The first narrow defile passed, the valley opens out again, and, with occasional glimpses all the way of the old road winding below near the margin of the stream, and destroyed some years since in a storm, ere very long we reach another defile as beautiful as the last, but much shorter; for here, after crossing the stream and mounting a short distance, a projecting rock is pierced, the river finds its outlet beneath through a chasm not twenty feet in width, and then, the valley opening out again, Airolo is seen just before us, and beyond the little cluster of houses which marks the village rise the mountains, so grandly and abruptly closing in the head of the Val Bedretto, up which our course now lies, whilst every here and there on their rugged sides or summits some snowy peak or glacier edge tells not uncertainly of their grand elevation.

We arrived at Airolo by about two o'clock, and here we had a rest of an hour and a half for dinner, followed by a ransacking of a collection of Swiss woodwork, ending—as such an operation always does—much to the advantage of its proprietor.

With fresh horses we were soon on the road again, and now the weather, which had been unpromising and occasionally wet, seemed inclined to improve, and we commenced the real ascent of the mountain under rather more promising circumstances than we had at first anticipated. The road soon leaves the river, and, turning to the right, winds and twists about in the serpentine fashion known only to Alpine roads, and quite incomprehensible until one has seen them, keeping the church and village of Airolo in view, first on the right, then on the left, for hours. Here and there a straight bit of road gives hopes that the zig-zagging is over, but the thought is no sooner expressed than it is contradicted by another ascent worse than before, and one begins to envy the electric telegraph carried here in straight lines from point to point, where one would have thought it impossible to gain footing for its supports, and giving fair idea of the directness and speed of the communications of which it is the channel. The head of the Val Tremola, as the valley along which the road finds its way is called, is nearly reached, and the last glimpse of the mountains, at the head of Val Bedretto, is caught, when a stream is crossed and the last flight of zig-zags is commenced; these are both numerous and intricate, and as one looks down upon them from above, their interlacings produce a most singular effect. At last, however, these are surmounted, greatcoats and plaids are in requisition, and we all begin to feel uncomfortably cold. The cold grey colour of the wild mountains of granite, great blocks from whose sides strew the ground thickly on either side, seems to harmonize well with the scene, and when presently we pass the Capuchin hospice our driver tells us that we are at the summit. Two or three dark deep-looking pools or tarns stand close to the hospice, and reminded me in their gloomy and cold aspect of the tarn which gives so much character to the hospice of the Grimsel. The same kind of scenery accompanied us on the now rapid descent; the sun went down, and the stars were soon out shining brilliantly upon the mountain road, when at last a sudden turn brought us in sight of lights, and then, descending a few zig-zags, we saw below us the roofs of the houses of Hospenthal, and, in less time than it takes to describe, were standing on the steps of one of the best inns even in Switzerland, the Goldner Löwe, and superintending the unpacking of our goods.

In such an inn as this everything proves forcibly that one is in Switzerland; the rooms are all very clean and very small, and there is a certain homely air about everybody and everything which is the especial charm of the better class of Swiss country inns, and in which they excel, perhaps, all but the very best English inns of the same kind.[79]

We spent an amusing evening, having for companions a Frenchman with his wife and two daughters, all very lively and exceedingly loquacious: the walls of the modest *salle à manger* rang with hearty laughter until after the time at which early travellers generally go to bed, and so we paved the way doubtless for a hearty night's rest.

The first thing to be done in the morning, after the discussion of the excellent trout and honey put before us, was to take a stroll up to the old castle which lends so much picturesque character to the village. The weather was glorious; the

---

[79] This old inn is a thing of the past. A large, bustling, and much smarter hotel has taken its place; and a magnificent carriage-road has put a stop to all need for walking by pleasant field-paths to the Furca.

perfectly blue sky overhead, the bright green of the valley, the luxuriance of the lower slopes of the mountains, and the view up the pass of the Furca closed in with a white line of snow, combined together to make us all regret our determination to push on rapidly for Luzern; and no sooner was the regret felt than—like idle school-children enjoying themselves while they may—we made up our minds to ascend the Furca, sleep on the summit of the pass, and return early the next morning. No sooner said than done; our horses were taken out of the carriage, and in half an hour, with a guide and horses for the ladies, we were on our way for a mountain excursion, full of that elastic feeling which the treading of a Swiss mountain-path always gives, and bent upon enjoying ourselves to the full.

The contrast with the flat dusty roads and the sultry weather to which you are so often forced to submit in Italy made the walk especially pleasant; and though, compared to many other mountain excursions, it was of slight interest, under the circumstances it presented more than common attraction to us. The path was one of those pleasant ways so common in Switzerland—a paved narrow road between banks of fields or low walls, gradually rising and falling, now crossing the dry bed of some glacier torrent, and now bridging the stream which descends the valley to feed the Reuss. The fields were rich in colour, and bright with various and lovely flowers, and the lower slopes of the mountain were tinted a rich purple with the bloom of herbs, cropped gratefully here and there by small and melancholy looking sheep.

The small village of Realp is soon reached, and then the ascent begins; this is rather stiff, and it has taken us, when we reach the summit, just four hours and a half of hard walking from Hospenthal. We found dinner going on at the little hostelry at the top, and, after partaking of it, started again to ascend the Furca-Horn, a mountain rising above the summit of the pass, and, as we had been told, quite worth the trouble of the ascent. There was no kind of path, and in places the mountain-side was so steep that I began to think it was no place for ladies to scramble up; however, they thought otherwise, and after divers tumbles in the snow, and surmounting rather formidable-looking obstacles, we reached the summit at last, and, sitting down on the edge of a great rock, spent a long time in enjoying the glorious view.

Just under us was the vast glacier of the Rhone, and then beyond it we looked down the long valley of the same river until its shape was obscured by mist, and traced the path by which we had walked in a previous journey up the steep Meyenwand to the Grimsel. Immediately in front of us were the vast peaked mass of the Schreckhorn, the whole course of the glaciers of the Aar, and the peaks of the Finster-Aarhorn, the Jungfrau, and the Mönch; above our heads rose the Galenstock, and opposite us the Mutthorn and Monte Fiudo; whilst the summit of Monte Rosa, discerned with difficulty among a marvellous array of distant peaks, completed one of the finest views of snow-covered mountains which it has ever been my good fortune to behold.

Long time did we keep our elevated seats, scanning again and again the glorious panorama, and at last, most unwillingly, commenced the descent; this was more difficult, though much more speedy, than the ascent, as the side of the mountain was both steep and slippery. We reached the summit of the pass, itself about eight thousand three hundred feet above the sea, in little more than an hour, the ascent to the Horn having occupied about two hours and a half; and here we found our French friends of the previous evening, who had in vain endeavoured to follow us in our ascent, but had been one and all obliged to give up the attempt.

Late at night we all went out again to look at the most glorious moonlight effect it is possible to imagine; the peaks of the mountains and the vast fields of snow or glacier lighted up by the bright light of the moon had a charm about them peculiarly fascinating.

Very early the next morning we started again on our way back to Hospenthal, and got down to the inn in good time, had breakfast, and then, mounting our carriage, we were soon off again down the valley of the Reuss. The Devil's Bridge was ere long reached, and the glorious scenery with which it is surrounded amply redeemed the expectations I had always formed of its extreme beauty; indeed for grandeur, combined with luxuriant cultivation of the lower slopes of the mountains, and for the wild beauty of the course of the river itself, nothing even in Switzerland surpasses the narrow valley through which the turbulent Reuss finds its way from Andermatt to Amsteg.

Here the valley widens considerably, and orchards full of fruit-trees, covered with bright-looking apples, spread half over the valley, on each side of which the mountains are very grand in their outline. Before long Altdorf is reached, and all the scenes so dear to Swiss freemen are rapidly passed, until at last our carriage sets us down on the very edge of the lovely Lake of Luzern, where the half-hour which we have to wait for the departure of the steamer is spent in attempting a sketch of the rocks which descend so precipitously into the deep recesses of the lake.

Much harm is done by overpraising beautiful scenery, and even the Lake of the Four Cantons suffers from this; for so much has been said and written about its unmatched loveliness and grandeur, that the result is perhaps a slight disappointment with the reality. One great beauty, no doubt, is the succession of entirely distinct views which different portions of the lake afford, though at the same time the irregular outline of the water very much diminishes its apparent scale; I doubt, too, whether there is any one view so grand as that at the head of Lake Como, though otherwise I know no lake which can be preferred to it.

On the voyage down the lake, Tell's Chapel and the famous Grütli were of course seen; a distant view was caught of the old cradle of Switzerland, the little town of Schwytz, with the grand peaks of the Mythenberg rising proudly behind it; the Righi, and the black-looking Pilatus, were each in turn passed; and as evening drew on, the flat shores of the lower part of the lake were neared, and presently the spires and turrets of Luzern came in sight. In a few minutes the bustle of landing being over, the immense Schweizer Hof received us within its capacious walls, just in time for one of those accommodating late tables-d'hôte so acceptable after a long day's travel.

Three or four hours spent the next morning in strolling about served only to convince us that there was not very much of architectural interest in the city itself. A line of old wall, broken at short intervals by picturesque and irregular towers, and a very long covered bridge across the lake just where the Reuss runs out of it, are the only noticeable features. The bridge is ornamented with an immense number of oil-paintings—two to each principal rafter—illustrative of the history of the place and country, not valuable as works of art, but curious in themselves, and giving much additional interest to the structure.

The principal church has two western towers and spires; the latter are of metal and managed in the way so common in this part of the world, though never, so far as I know, attempted in England,[80] with the angles of the spire over the centre of the cardinal sides of the tower. The whole of the rest of the church is modernized; and there is a singular modern cloister, which nearly surrounds the churchyard, and contains an immense array of graves and grave-crosses.

We left Luzern at eleven for Basel, in the diligence, and had a very pleasant ride over often-travelled ground, of which, therefore, the less said perhaps the better. The rich luxuriance of the crops, the careful farming, the vast barns, and the great loads of produce which are constantly met upon the road, remind the traveller more of England than any other portion of the Continent ever does. The Lake of Sempach was soon passed on our right, and at last a pause was made in the good old-fashioned way, for a very comfortable dinner at the little old town of Zofingen. At Aarberg the dashing Aar was crossed, and soon the ascent of the Unter Hauenstein range was commenced; and here we enjoyed the most extensive of all the day's views of the Alps—the last and grandest. Gradually as the summit is reached peak after peak is seen rising up above the mist which shrouds the lower slopes of the mountains, their white outlines tenderly relieved against the blue sky: we recognized one after the other almost the entire range of the grandest mountains in Europe, seen before nearer but not in fairer guise, but wherever seen leaving the same lasting impression upon the mind. Suddenly we overpassed the summit, and began rapidly to descend the northern slope of the hills; but the last link that bound us to the land in which we had been voyaging, as we hope, not for the last time, is never to be remembered but with affectionate regard, touched, as every one must be, in viewing such a panorama, with the extreme glory of the scene.

We had now done with mountains and with mountain scenery, though the road was still interesting and very pretty, and at last late in the evening we reached Basel. The moon was shining brightly on the Rhine as we went to our beds for the last time, in this journey at least, in Switzerland.

We were amused, on our way to Strasburg, by the comparative insignificance in our minds of the chain of the Vosges, which, on our outward journey, had impressed us as really very striking in their outline. So much for the effect of a recent acquaintance with grander mountains!

Strasburg Cathedral was visited, not for the first time and with a consequent

[80] The famous steeple of Antwerp is arranged in the same way. The spires of S. Elizabeth at Marburg, and the metal spires of the churches at Lübeck and Luneburg, are also somewhat similarly treated.

increase of pleasure. Such magnificent architecture as that of its most exquisite nave is truly refreshing after Italian work, and, small as its scale is compared to that of Milan, it in no way lost its effect upon my mind. I was particularly struck by the vast difference between the delicate art shewn in the design of the traceries, in the softly rounded contour and dark recesses of the mouldings, and in the vigour and beauty of the carving of all the capitals, heightened as they are by the flood of coloured light let into the interior by its immense windows filled with some of the noblest stained glass in Europe, compared with that shewn in the rude traceries, heavy carving, and plainness or absence of moulding, which characterize almost all Italian Gothic work. No more strong or decided example need be desired of nearly all the points of contrast between the best work, north and south of the Alps, than this, the first great northern Gothic church seen on the homeward way, presents, when compared with all the work which has nevertheless been studied with so much pleasure and advantage on the southern side of the Alps.

It is only fair to say that the first impression produced by the west front of Strasburg was one—felt, indeed, before, but much more strongly now—of the smallness of scale and narrowness of the whole. I have not at any time had any especial love for this front, but, just after seeing the simple unbroken façades of Italian churches, with their grand porches and their simple breadth of effect, there is something so entirely destructive to all repose in a front covered as this is with lines of tracery, panelling, niches, and canopies in every direction, that it leaves, I confess, a painful feeling upon the mind, of the restless nature of its designer's thoughts. But this is true only of the west front, for, on entering by the door into the nave, all such thoughts are banished on the instant, and you stand awestruck at the beauty and solemnity of the art in which hitherto Northern architects alone have ever approached at all nearly to perfection, and convinced at the same time that, with such a work to refer to, we need never doubt, between the comparative merits of Gothic architecture north and south of the Alps.

CHAPTER XIV.

Concluding Summary—Classic and Gothic Architecture—Italian Gothic—Shafts—Cornices—Monuments—Cloisters—Windows—Brickwork—Colour in Construction—Truth in Architectural Design and Construction.

"Alas! of thousand bosoms kind,
That daily court you and caress,
How few the happy secret find
Of your calm loveliness!"

Christian Year.

I PROPOSE in this chapter to sum up, as shortly as I can, the information which I have gathered in the course of my tours in the North of Italy, on the subject of mediæval art. In doing this I shall have to remark, not only on the beauties, but also on the failings of Italian Gothic architecture, and to give expression to the thoughts which arise in examining its remains as to developments which are possible to us in the same direction, as well as to suggest some of the lessons which may be learnt from them.

I think it may be gathered, from what has been already said, that it will be useless to look for anything like the completeness in the development of the style in Italy which our ancestors attained to in England; and this is easily accounted for. In England there were no Classic buildings to find here and there an admirer, or perhaps a cluster of disciples, as in Italy; and men worked, therefore, when the Gothic style was thoroughly established, freely, and in their own way, and apparently quite untrammelled with a suspicion even that there had ever been another style brought to perfection by people above most others civilized and refined in their habits and tastes, and one moreover which was distinguished by certain broad and strongly marked lines of separation from the style which they inherited from their fathers, and practised and brought, as nearly as they could, to perfection. In England, therefore, in the Middle Ages, we may look in vain for any evidence of active sympathy with a more ancient and venerable style than that which was then in the fulness of vigour, life, and constant development; and consequently, if it be likely that any infusion of the art practised by the ancients could have aided the Northern architects in their work, we must not expect to find here any trace of such assistance or such advantages. But in Italy the case was far different: the love for the remains of earlier ages was never dead, but only slept, ever and anon to break forth in some new appropriation of ancient materials, or some imitation and reproduction of an ancient form or idea. So in Venice, in the thirteenth century, whilst pointed arches were being reared by some to support the walls, not only of the churches, but of the houses also, other hands were busy with the task of raising aloft those two Classic shafts, with their antique capitals and detail, which, even to the present day, stand peculiar and well-remembered features of the Piazzetta of S. Mark; standing proofs, if such are indeed wanted, that there had been artists in earlier days whose art was noble and well worthy of the emulation of men in all ages.

And this Classic seed fell into not ungrateful soil; for though there, as else-where throughout Europe, the value of the pointed arch as a feature in construc-tion — independently, that is, of its intrinsic beauty — must have been well known, and was boldly recognized where it could not be avoided, there were nevertheless in a hundred ways proofs that men still remembered the lessons and traditions of the past, and used it with a certain degree of caution and unwillingness, and associated with features which, rightly or wrongly, were at the time eschewed by all Northern architects, either as being contrary to its spirit, or through ignorance of their existence. This fact would seem, therefore, to place the Italian works of the Middle Ages in the ranks of hybrid and mixed styles, and to debar them from competition with the more pure contemporary works of Northern Europe.

There will, however, always be much profit in the careful examination of such works as these in Italy, because their authors stood in the same position that we do now, and, conversant to some extent with the beauties of the best Gothic archi-tecture of the North and the best Classic examples of Italy, took what they deemed best from each, and endeavoured to unite the perfections of both.

Classic architecture is that of the lintel and impost, involving the idea of rest: Gothic is that of the arch and the flying buttress, involving the idea of life and motion. The two ideas are absolutely opposed to each other. Classic architecture, directly it admits the arch, ceases to be true to itself in any real artistic sense; yet if it refuses to use, and to exhibit the use of the arch, it denies itself wilfully the use of the best known mode of construction. Gothic architects may still, on the other hand, as they always have done, gain much from the teachings of Classic buildings. And if sometimes there is too great liveliness and want of repose in their works, they may usefully study those of their predecessors who undoubtedly ob-tained more breadth and repose in them by some knowledge of Classic examples, than they would have had if they had not known them.

Gothic architecture was essentially the work of scientific men; the most con-summate skill being displayed in arranging thousands of small blocks of stones, any one of which might be carried upon a strong man's shoulders, into walls rising far in height above anything ever dreamt of by the Greek, bridging great openings, and providing by the exactest counterpoise of various parts for the perfect security of works whose airiness and life would seem to have lifted them out of the region of constructive skill; and yet all these wonderful works were executed in materials as ponderous in their nature as those which the Greek had handled so rudely in construction, and so delicately in ornamentation.

The natural result of this excess of science was, perhaps, that less delicacy and beauty of detail became necessary; for when the plain rough walls, without carving and without ornament, were nevertheless of necessity so beautiful in their intricacy of outline and delicacy of structure; and when, too, so little (comparatively) plain surface remained to be looked at or dwelt upon, men cared less for the choicest examples of the sculptor's art, and were less obliged to satisfy the eye with them. Much, therefore, as Art gained in most ways by the invention of the arch, she at the same time lost something which had been until then possessed, and which, too, was essential in the highest order of work.

This was the case, speaking generally; but, as need hardly, I suppose, be said, there are examples scattered here and there throughout the North of Europe, and particularly in France and England, which shew distinctly enough that their artists had grasped this necessity in its very fullest extent; and were in no degree satisfied with anything less than the greatest perfection in the sculpture, and other decorations with which they adorned their works.

Italian architects stood, in the thirteenth and fourteenth centuries, in a position in many respects very different from that held by their Northern contemporaries, and the marks of this difference are everywhere to be seen. It was natural to them to reconcile in their works, so far as they could, the principles of two styles which we are too prone to deem irreconcilable; and where they have achieved a real success, it ought to be a lesson that the course which they pursued is still open to us, though with larger opportunities and greater knowledge. At the same time they committed faults which we ought especially to beware of imitating in any respect.

They ignored, as much as possible, the clear exhibition of the pointed arch, and, even when they did use it, not unfrequently introduced it in such a way as to shew their contempt for it as a feature of construction; employing it often only for ornament, and never hesitating to construct it in so faulty a manner that it required to be held together with iron rods from the very first day of its erection. This fault they often found it absolutely necessary to commit, because they scarcely ever brought themselves to allow the use of the buttress; and this reluctance was a remarkable proof of their Classic sympathies. Classic architecture was as distinctly symbolic of rest as Gothic was of life; the column and lintel of the one were as still and symbolical of perfect repose, as the arch of the other, sustained by the strong arm of the flying buttress, was of life, vigour, and motion. Italian Gothic architects then, in never resorting to the buttress, avowed their feeling that a state of perfect rest was the only allowable state for a perfect building, and they preferred almost always to use the arch for its beauty only, and avowedly not for its constructional value, which they evidenced by tying it together with iron bars at its base, which there was no intention of disguising, and therefore no shamefacedness in the use of. From this, I believe, at least one beauty arose. It is obvious that the pointed arch, descending upon the capital of a shaft without any visible stay or buttress to retain it in its place, would look weak and thin; and it was soon perceived that, in order to overcome this difficulty, the only course was to add to its substance by cusping it on the under side. Thence came the trefoiled arches so frequent in Italy, and always so very lovely. As so much depended upon them, no pains were spared in bringing their outline into the very purest form. To this we owe the absolute perfection which characterizes some of the trefoiled arches in early Italian work; of this we have an example (to take one instance among many) in the tombs of the Scaligers, at Verona, in which the mass of the trefoil descending from the arch conveys to the eye the impression of a firmness which, in part, it certainly gives, but which would nevertheless be insufficient in reality for the stability of the work, without the aid of the connecting rod of iron below.

In northern Gothic architecture, arches invariably tell their own story, and do their own work, avowedly and without any disguise; in Italy this is the exception, not the rule, and the commonest exception is seen in the arcades dividing the aisles from the naves of churches, and in the large open arches forming the arcades upon which public and private buildings so often stand, though even these are sometimes (as in the second stage of the Ducal Palace at Venice) formed of continuous traceries in place of arches, and are dependent for their stability, like the single arches of tombs and monuments, upon the assistance of iron ties.

Another proof of the reverence for ancient tradition in art is furnished by the extent to which, throughout the time of the prevalence of pointed architecture in Italy, the round arch was also used. Examples of this are very frequent, and of the most capricious kind. At Cremona, e.g., the south transept has semicircular arches throughout, and the north transept pointed arches; the date of both being, however, as nearly as possible the same. At Verona, in the old house given in plate 14, some of the bearing arches are pointed, some round; and again, in some buildings the main arches are round, and the ornamental pointed. Again, one of the most common cornices in all the mediæval brickwork of Italy is a continuous arcade of round arches intersecting one another, and forming at their intersections pointed arches; and in the Ca' d'Oro, one of the most elaborately ornate late Gothic buildings in Venice, some of the entrance arches are pointed and some round. It needs not, however, that examples should be multiplied, for almost every building exhibits some trace of this kind of confusion.

The Venetian love for the ogee arch, which spread thence to Verona, Vicenza, and Ferrara, has been already mentioned; no doubt we must look to the East for the very early introduction of this feature in Venice, and I only incidentally refer to it here as proving, from the way in which it was perpetually used, that its adopters had no peculiar love for the form of the pure pointed arch, of which it is certainly a most vitiated perversion.

With this, by way of preface, let us now go on to look at the features of these Italian works in detail. We shall find that we have two influences brought out, even more strongly than in most mediæval works, in Italian buildings. These are, first, local, and next, personal influences. The Venetian, the Bolognese, and the Veronese, for instance, are all distinctly local styles, in which early traditions were preserved, to some extent, from first to last; and to these might be added the Florentine, the Genoese, and the Pisan. On the other hand it is impossible not to notice the very great personal influence exercized over their descendants, as well as over their contemporaries, by some of the greater Italian architects, of whom I may adduce Nicola Pisano as the most eminent example.

There is a third influence which must not be overlooked—that of foreign architects. Milan Cathedral, designed by a German, is very unlike any other Italian building in style; San Francesco at Assisi was also the work of a foreigner; and the western front of Genoa Cathedral owes much of its peculiar and extremely beautiful character to contact with, and knowledge of, French art; whilst Vercelli is another instance, as far as its interior is concerned, which may be included in this list. Generally speaking, however, the influence of the foreigner seems to have been confined pretty much to the particular church designed by him.

In the Middle Ages the Italians led a life more akin to our own, at the present day, than other people. The country was populous, the cities numerous and rich, and the people full of emulation and individuality. This was precisely the condition of things that would lead, most certainly, to the employment of artists from a distance, and to the establishment of a professional practice of the art earlier than elsewhere. It led to the employment of the family of the Pisani, of the Campione clan, the sculptors of Como, the Cosmati in Rome, and many others. In England and in France it is much more difficult to point to any facts proving the employment of the same architects in various parts of the country, and there is, at first sight, therefore, less of what is obviously personal in their art in the Middle Ages.

The history of our old architects in England and France is very peculiar; they were, as a rule, each confined to a certain district, in which they wrought in what was in fact a merely local variety of their national style. In point of artistic talent, they were very equally matched, so that it is difficult to assign the pre-eminence to any one over the rest, though in England we may point to our Yorkshire abbeys, and in France to the buildings in the Isle de France as being on the whole the finest examples. We have had no Nicola Pisano here; our old architects' work is singularly equal in its character in each period; and whether it was displayed in the little village church lying concealed on the banks of a rippling stream, or in the vast abbey of some sequestered valley, or in the cathedral church of the busy city, there seems to be matter for equal admiration in all. In Italy, on the other hand, we see a number of individual architects exercizing each his peculiar influence, varying very much in their skill and power, and having, moreover, the doubtful advantage of a constant recollection of the works of a different style of art, from whose traditions they never escaped. Placed, in short, very much in the position that we are at the present day, they never wrought with the same absolute and joyous freedom that marks their contemporaries' work in France and England; and thus, though their architecture may be inferior, it is of very special value to us; for we may, perhaps, see better the cause of some of our own shortcomings, when we investigate theirs, and so we may hope to excel the works which they executed under conditions so similar to those under which we labour, even if we cannot quite rival the complete perfection of the greater mediæval architects of the North. And, seeing that all the faults of Italian Gothic artists arose from their incomplete devotion to the new art, and their lingering fondness for the old Classic forms, we shall be led probably to recognize the paramount importance of throwing ourselves heartily and entirely into the study and practice of the one great and national division of our art, and then, not venturing to attempt to design in some base imitation of Classic one day, or in a pretended Gothic the next, as is only too much the custom, we shall make our sense of art so completely a portion of our inmost selves, as never to do anything new in any but our own one special style. We shall, in short, recognize, as the greatest danger to the progress of real art, that eclectic spirit which the Italians never escaped from, and which, in our own day, leads men to design their work in the style which they or their clients fancy for the moment, and not in that which is the truest result of previous experience, and most fitted to the country in which it is to be executed.

In examining the features of any national school of architecture, it is worthy of notice how distinctly some of its peculiarities and prejudices are marked from the very first, even in the ground-plans of the buildings it produced. This is notably the case in the ecclesiastical edifices of France, England, and Germany. Each country, after the art had become settled and, so to speak, acclimatized, had its special arrangement of plan, which was seldom departed from and was handed on from age to age as a precious heirloom. And, going to Italy, we shall find that the same feature strikes us there in almost all the buildings of the pointed style, and that the buildings from which they were directly derived are the same as those from which we indirectly derived our own. Their plans are all derived from two ancient types, both of which are of venerable antiquity. It was from the basilica, converted into a church, with its nave and aisles terminated at the end, by an apsidal projection from a sort of transept, that all of one class of the Italian Gothic churches with transepts were copied. Indeed, if we look at the ground-plan of S. Paul without the walls, at Rome, and compare it with the fully developed church of Sta. Anastasia, at Verona, we shall see that absolutely the only difference is the addition of small chapels on the east side of the transept; so that in place of the one apse, which marks the former, we have the central apse and subsidiary chapels on each side of it. The church of San Clemente, at Rome, with its three aisles ended with parallel apses at the east end, is a variety of this type, followed in such churches as the Cathedral of Torcello, and indeed in all later Italian Gothic churches without transepts. And even when, as in the thirteenth and fourteenth centuries, the Italian architects endeavoured to secure an immensely wide unbroken area of nave, they still looked back fondly to these old precedents, and finished them at the east, with three parallel apsidal chapels.

The other model was the Byzantine plan of S. Mark's at Venice, itself imported from the East, which was copied closely in the south-west of France, and produced no slight effect in modifying the simple Romanesque plan, until it assumed all the characteristics of the complete Lombard style, and from the North of Italy sent out vigorous off-shoots, of which the most important were those which we trace all along the valley of the Rhine, and throughout the centre of France.

Thus, the ground-plans of Italian Gothic buildings were simply a natural development from those of earlier date, and adhering, as they always did, very closely to the older plan and arrangements, afford us scarcely an example of those later developments of prolonged choirs, of which our English cathedrals and abbeys afford perhaps the most magnificent examples, or of the splendid French *chevet* with its surrounding aisle and chapels. The traces of Classic influence on the plan are indeed so many and so clear, that it is hardly speaking too strongly to say that Gothic planning was never developed by Italian architects, so shackled were they by the ever-present influence of buildings in another style. Hence, the more we study their peculiarities, the more we see how curious a mixture there is in them of the character of Classic and Gothic buildings, and how essentially clumsy all their planning is when compared with the scientific work of the more thoroughly Gothic architects of the North. If we compare an ordinary Italian groined church with a French or English example, we shall find one very marked difference in them. In the former each bay of the nave is square, and hence each bay of the narrower side aisles is oblong, with the greatest width towards the nave; in the latter, on the contrary, the aisle compartment is square, and that of the nave oblong, with its narrowest side towards the aisle. Hence, in the former, the points of support are farther apart, and the plan loses much of its intricacy, and at the same time, no doubt, the whole building loses much of its apparent scale. The enormous church of San Petronio at Bologna, for instance, has but six bays in the length of its vast nave, and the eye refuses to be convinced by the practical measurement of the foot of the real dimensions of the building. The object of the Italian architect always was to obtain as few points of support as possible in a given area; but there is little if any real gain in this. The points of support in the Italian churches were larger, and the cost in the end was probably much greater than in the apparently more intricate and complex plans of the French and English architects. The science displayed in their planning was therefore of a superficial and mistaken description, and not really equal to that which marks the work of their Northern competitors.[81]

The same absence of subdivision is seen in the elevation of each bay of an Italian church, where in place of the triple division in height of our great Northern churches, with their well-accentuated proportions and beautiful variety of detail, we have a singularly meagre design perpetually repeated, and consisting generally of simple broad arches, with a small circular clerestory window above them, and no other kind of decoration, save where the painter has come with his ever-ready art to the rescue of the apparently incompetent architect.

How this plainness and severity was corrected we have already seen in the interior of Sta. Anastasia, at Verona—a church which, though it is simple and unadorned in its construction almost beyond any large church with which I am acquainted, has been made remarkable, owing to the skill of its decorator, for being more than usually ornate and magnificent.

The invariable simplicity of Italian groining has been often noticed in these pages, and need only be referred to here as illustrating the love of simplicity upon which I have dwelt. No one feature gains so much by it as this, and I can fancy the horror with which an Italian, or indeed any other architect, in the thirteenth century, would have viewed such fine works in their way, as our own examples of complicated fan-traceried groinings. The painting of this simple groining at Vero-

[81] The usual plan is sometimes deviated from and improved by having two bays of aisle opening with two arches into each bay of the nave, so that every bay of groining throughout the church is very nearly square. This is a common plan in early German churches, and is one of the many indications of similarity between German and Italian work, which might be adduced were we to enter on this interesting question.

na, at Lodi, and still more at Assisi, proves how it ought always to be treated; and happily in England we have still more than one example of the same kind, as, for instance, two chapels in the Cathedral at Winchester.

So far for the plan. When we look at single features of the building we shall find another peculiarity meeting us at every turn, and of the good effect of which it is impossible to speak too warmly. This is the constant use of the detached shaft or column. This is the one great and lasting beauty which was derived from Classic examples. The Italians, finding it used with luxurious profusion in their Classic and Byzantine buildings, persevered in its use throughout the whole Gothic period. It is true that, as time wore on, there was a somewhat less free use of it than at first, but it was never altogether ignored. We cannot say as much for our own ancestors: so long as the influence of Lombard and Romanesque art is visible in French, German, and English Gothic, so long the detached shaft was used, and just in proportion as in course of time that influence decreased, so did the frequency of its use decrease. Our fourteenth and fifteenth century buildings present nothing in its place but combinations of mouldings, in themselves very beautiful, but by no means so beautiful as to reconcile us to the loss of that which they so entirely supplanted. One consequence of their introduction, to the exclusion of the detached shaft, was, that the art of sculpture deteriorated just in proportion as the art of moulding was developed. There is no place in which architectural sculpture can be more fittingly displayed than in the capital of a column. It is the most convenient, and at the same time the most conspicuous, position for it. It is, too, the most important feature in every design in which the detached column is used. The gathering together of all the arch mouldings into one above the capital, in order that their forces may be collected before being transmitted to the ground, leads naturally to the laying of a special emphasis on this point above all others; and it is one of the strongest among the many reasons in favour of earliest Gothic, and against the later varieties of the style, that in the former the use of shafts involved the use of forcible and elaborately-cut capitals, so that this point might be most distinctly marked, whilst in the latter, by the disuse of the shaft and the constant practice of carrying the mouldings of the arch down to the ground without any interruption, it was made as little of as was possible.

In this respect, therefore, above all others, Italian Gothic artists—having given way to change less than their contemporaries—are worthy of our highest admiration. The love of variety, which is characteristic of all good Gothic art, is conspicuous in the Italian treatment of the shaft just as much as in the northern Gothic variation of mouldings. When they are plain cylinders, and not banded (and the band occurs but seldom in Italian work), they often taper slightly, and with very beautiful effect. This was distinctly a relic of the Classic entasis, and the examples given in a note will suffice to shew the extent to which the shaft is reduced in proportion to its height.[82] Wherever, however, the shaft is spiral or decorated with

[82]	Height. of Shaft		Diameter at Base.	Diameter at Neck.
	Ft.	in.	In.	In.
Cloister, San Zenone, Verona	3	11½	5⅛	4¼
Cloister, Genoa Cathedral	4	5	6	5¼

carving, or when the occurrence of a band destroys the idea of its continuity from base to capital, its monolithic character needs not to be marked, and the shaft is then always made of the same diameter throughout. The ornamentation is of various kinds. Circular shafts are inlaid, carved, diapered, or made of marbles selected for their beauty of colour. Lucca Cathedral affords, perhaps, the best examples of decoration by inlaying: there the shafts are of white marble inlaid with dark green; some have a diaper, others are girt with a succession of simple chevrons, others with spiral lines, others with crosses, flowers, fleurs-de-lis, or foliated circles; and one, at least, with a succession of imitations of arcades one over the other; but I remember no example of the same kind in the buildings described in these pages. At Lucca these inlaid shafts are frequently alternated with sculptured shafts, of which examples are common all over Italy. They are deeply cut with spiral lines of mouldings, occasionally adorned with sculpture of flowers, as in the doorways at Bergamo and Modena, and are often also inlaid richly with mosaic.

The best examples of the richer kinds of shafts are seen frequently in Italian Gothic buildings and monuments south of the Apennines. Such, for instance, as those which, with rich iron work between them, form the screen round the altar under the "crossing" of Sta. Chiara at Assisi, or in the monument of Pope Benedict X. at Perugia, where the shafts are of white marble, the spiral lines formed with a bead and fillets, and at the base and neck of the shaft the beads are all connected together with small arches, in the spandrels of which vine leaves are delicately carved; whilst to add to the extraordinary richness of the work, small figures are carved in the marble creeping round the shaft in the hollow formed by the spiral construction, and the spaces between the mouldings are filled in with glass mosaic patterns in red, green, and blue on a gold ground. The shafts of Orcagna's shrine in Or' San Michele, Florence, are of the same character, but these extraordinary decorations occur generally only in the best and richest internal work, executed under the direct influence of Florentine, Neapolitan, or Roman artists.[83]

The arrangement of spiral shafts was generally, but not always, symmetrical. In the Campanile of Florence, where they occur in pairs on each side of a window, they are always arranged with the spiral lines curving in opposite directions. In the porch of Sta. Maria Maggiore, Bergamo, the three shafts in each jamb are all different: the first spiral and carved, but not moulded; the second moulded with chevrons; the third spiral and moulded only, and the central shaft is red whilst the others are all white. In the spirally designed string-courses of the Venetian palaces the spiral lines are always worked in opposite directions right and left of the centre.

Another bold variety is seen in the beautiful coupled shafts at the entrance to the crypt of San Zenone, Verona, where both the shafts are quatrefoil in section, but entirely different in character, one of them being quite straight, the other slightly, but yet conspicuously, spiral. In a monument in the south aisle of the

Cloister, San Stefano, Bologna   2   8½   4⅜   4⅛

[83] The shafts used in the shrine of S. Edward at Westminster are of the same description, and shew that in one of the most exquisite works in England our early architects saw no incongruity between their beautiful but foreign character and the otherwise, at that time, purely national architecture.

same church, four shafts are cut out of one block of marble; and in order that this may be realized they are knotted together in the centre; and a similar example exists in the porch, of which I have given a view, at Trent, and in one of the windows of the Broletto at Como. The shafts round the lower basin of Nicola Pisano's beautiful fountain at Perugia are in clusters of three, chevroned, spiral, and fluted in the greatest possible variety; and in later works, in which we find that the error of continuing arch mouldings to the ground, instead of stopping them on the capital, was occasionally committed—as, e.g., in the archway to the baptistery in the church of the Frari, at Venice—we see an instance of a moulded imitation of such a cluster of shafts as these of Nicola Pisano's, chevroned and spiral, forming jamb and arch alike. In the later doorways, such as those of the western front of the cathedral of Como, and many of those at Monza, Pavia, and in most of the Venetian churches and buildings, the jambs and arches are identical in section; but even in these cases there is always a capital interposed, and I hardly remember an example of a continuous moulding without an impost, which at least marked—if often in an incomplete manner—the line of the springing of the arch.

I must not forget that which is, after all, the most charming of all arrangements of shafts, viz. the use of them in couples, set generally one behind the other, so that, in elevation, extreme delicacy is secured, whilst, in perspective, there is beautiful light and shade, and ample effect of strength. This is a favourite arrangement in cloisters and in belfries; and, wherever it occurs, one regrets, as one looks at it, that though in old days French, Spanish, German, and even Irish[84] architects gladly followed the Italian example, it was so seldom that an Englishman condescended to do the same.[85]

In the treatment of mouldings the Italian Gothic work is quite peculiar. An Italian architect would have been surprized, could he have seen the dark and piquant recesses of the mouldings in which his Northern brethren in the thirteenth and fourteenth centuries so much delighted. He rarely, if ever, indulged in a deep hollow, but made a point rather of shewing the hard sharp outline of the square edges of his stones or bricks, relieved only by the interposition of simple round members, alternated with flat hollows; his mouldings, even when designed for such grand works as the Ducal Palace, being bald and crude in design, though they conduced no doubt to that breadth of effect to which he always desired that everything should be sacrificed. There is but little skill shewn in the way in which their contours are drawn, and the carelessness with which they are fitted to the size of the capital that carries them is a constant source of disgust to any one who has been trained by the study of the exquisite English mouldings of the same period. The architectural carving was designed with the same idea; for when it was introduced elsewhere than in the capitals of columns, it was always very flat and delicate, severe in outline, and not much relieved, and often very decided in its direct imitation of nature. This, however, is mainly seen in the earliest examples, for I am bound to say that later Italians never rivalled the Byzantine capitals of S. Mark's, or some of those in the early church of San Zenone, Verona. Indeed, as

[84] Jerpoint and Cong Abbeys are Irish examples.

[85] English examples may be seen in the western porch of Fountains Abbey, and among the extensive fragments of Egglestone Abbey, near Barnard Castle.

time wore on, the carving in Italian buildings became steadily worse and worse. Most of the later Venetian capitals are bad in their outline, confused and purposeless in all their lines, and shew no sense of that vigorous petrifaction of the elements of natural growth and form, which was so sensitively felt and expressed by French and English artists.

Cornice—San Francesco, Brescia.

And, next, we come to the cornice, the feature which above all others must most startle men who, for the first time, make acquaintance with Italian work, and which most recalls in its idea its Classic prototype; for, though its treatment in detail is as unlike that of the ancients as it can well be, it is, nevertheless, so decidedly marked and so prominent a feature (crowning not only the summits of walls, but even running up the gables, and returning round buttresses), that it is impossible not to regard it as another evidence of admiration for, and imitation of, earlier work.

The ordinary northern parapet is never used, the eaves almost always finishing with the common Italian tiles projecting slightly over the deep cornice of the walls. We have nothing at all parallel to these cornices in England, and I remember but few examples of anything of the same kind in the North of Europe, save in the transept of Lübeck Cathedral, and such churches as those of Bamberg and the Rhine country; which last seem to be derived from the Lombard churches of Pavia, and to have nothing in common with later pointed work, and to have exerted little, if any, influence on its development.

I have said enough, I hope, to explain the grounds for my opinion that, with the single exception of their use of shafts, we never find the same kind of perfection in Italian Gothic buildings as in French or English works of the same date; but I am not slow to allow, nevertheless, that they do contain features of extreme beauty and purity; and many of them peculiar to themselves. There is perhaps no country in the world which excels Italy in the buildings which were erected for civic and domestic purposes. The Doge's Palace, and many of the other palaces at Venice, the Broletto of Como, the other houses or palaces of which I have given illustrations throughout this volume, are some only among many which might be enumerated, any one of which would have not only an advantage over very many of our own buildings, as a model of good architecture, but at the same time the merit of fitness for the purposes for which our domestic buildings in towns are at the present day required. Then again, there are, as I have shewn, the exquisite porches; the peculiar, and generally noble, campanili; the many-shafted cloisters; the perfect monuments; the use of brickwork of the best kind; and, finally, that in which Italian architecture of the Middle Ages teaches us more than any other architecture since the commencement of the world—the introduction of colour in construction—which is managed generally with such consummate beauty, refinement, and modesty, that oven where it accompanies faulty construction and unworthily sham expedients, it is impossible to avoid giving oneself up altogether to admiration of the result.

It will be seen that I am not by any means a blind enthusiast about Italian architecture. Who, indeed, that has studied on the spot, as I have done, not only a vast number of buildings in England, but also nearly all of the best examples in France, Spain, and Germany, could do otherwise than profess his truest allegiance to be due to the truthful beauties of his own national variety of the style? I should think that most students would agree with me, if they found themselves able to institute such a comparison.

The first view of an Italian Gothic church, whatever its date, is startlingly and, I think, disagreeably unlike anything that we are accustomed to in our own old buildings. You may go to a great English cathedral and find that from every point of view, inside and outside, every feature is well proportioned to its place, and beautiful in itself, whilst the *tout ensemble* is also perfect in proportion and mass.

This can never be said of Italian work. It never produced anything perfect both in detail and in mass; and one always finds it necessary to make excuses for even the best works, such as one never finds necessary, or allows oneself to think of making, for English works. There is something really absurd in comparing even the best of the Italian churches with such cathedrals as those of Canterbury or Lincoln, so superior are the latter from almost every point of view. The Italian church is usually a long, broad, rather low building, lighted with but few windows, having but a small, if any, clerestory, and with scarcely any irregularity in shape or plan; it has scarcely ever more than one tower, and this is never combined with the rest of the design in the manner common to us in England or France. There is no approach, therefore, to such combinations of steeples as are familiar to us at Canterbury, Wells, Laon, Reims, or Rouen, and undoubtedly there is very much less external grandeur. The steeple, when it does occur, is often detached; and when it is engaged, it does not open into the church, but is placed in some irregular and abnormal position, where it is at once felt that it is purposely not intended to be looked at in conjunction with the main façade of the building. There is no attempt even to secure a tolerable sky-line. The only relief to the monotonous outline of the main building is at the crossing, where something in the way of a low, mean dome is occasionally introduced, but this is always of but slight elevation, and not intended to produce any good external effect, such as was aimed at in our own central steeples. So also if we look at their façades, we have a feature on which, in common with ourselves, they often lavished considerable expense, and probably the greatest pains. The treatment is very similar in its idea throughout the whole period during which the style prevailed; and the effect produced is undoubtedly oftener very disappointing than attractive. The commonest type of façade is one in which the cornice, which is generally of slight projection, but deep and marked in character, is carried up the flat gable of the building, whilst the whole front, divided by vertical pilasters into three or five divisions in width, is lighted either by a series of circular windows, or by one large and important rose in the centre. This class of front is common to most of the Gothic churches in Lombardy.

At Ferrara, we see another and very different design in the grand front to the cathedral, which, save that it is entirely and shamelessly a sham front, might vie even with that of a Northern cathedral in beauty, intricacy, and richness of character; but this design is not really very Italian in style, and is a solitary example. When an Englishman sees the tympanum of the principal doorway of such a church filled with a sculpture of S. George and the Dragon, he may be pardoned for recollecting that our royal family have sprung from the same stock as the D'Estes, once Lords of Ferrara, the front of whose cathedral is almost the finest in Italy.

Other portions of Italian churches are even less satisfactory than their façades. I have already explained that the clerestory is rarely lighted by anything more elaborate than a succession of circular windows of small size. The church of Sta. Anastasia, Verona, gives us the best example of these, the windows there being of brick, filled in with very good early plate tracery in stone. The east end is often more picturesque than the west; and that of the church of San Fermo Maggiore, Verona, affords a good example. The east ends of the churches of the Frari and SS.

Giovanni e Paolo, at Venice, are perhaps the two finest examples of this portion of the building to be seen in Italy, and are worthy of very high praise.

If we descend from generals to details, we shall find much more to admire, and altogether much more to interest us. The doorways and the porches, which protect without concealing them, are often especially beautiful. I have already mentioned the doorways of Sta. Anastasia and San Zenone at Verona, of S. Mark's, Venice, the cathedral at Modena, and the north porch of Sta. Maria Maggiore, at Bergamo, all of which are full of beauty and full of national character. Another favourite and beautiful type is that of the porch on the north side of San Fermo, at Verona, which is arched on each face, and roofed with a flat-pitched roof, gabled both ways. In the doorways, inclosed within these porches, we shall hardly find so much to admire, and must not expect anything like our own or the great French examples. Generally the opening is square-headed, with a lintel often formed by an ingenious dovetailing of stone together,[86] and the mouldings of the jambs are too often continuous and very small and badly marked in their sections.

The exquisite monuments which so often occur against the walls or by the sides of Italian churches are somewhat similar in idea to these porches. Of these I have said so much that I only refer to them here, as among the most charming features of Italian art. I think that our own monuments, rich as our country is in them, will only be considered much superior to the best of these by those whose patriotism warps their judgment! One of the most perfect examples of the class is to be seen in the Castelbarco monument close to the church of Sta. Anastasia, Verona. Here the pointed trefoiled arch, on each face of the canopy over the tomb, springs from four detached shafts, and fits very closely under flat gables or pediments, above and from between which rises a perfectly plain pyramidal mass of stone. The very simplicity of the design of these monuments is their greatest charm; and so conscious were their designers of this, that they seem to me to have lavished all their care and refinement upon them. There are of necessity iron ties at the springing of the arch; but it was felt necessary to give the eye a sense of security beyond what the existence of these ties could afford, and this was accomplished by adding on the under side of the arch a simple and rather heavy cusp, generally proportioned with a degree of delicate skill of which modern architects appear to me (if I may dare to say it) never to dream. I believe that good architecture may generally be detected at once, by the excellence of such apparently small matters as the shape of a cusp. I am certain that good Italian architecture invariably has cusping, which is both nervous in its curve and yet delicate; and I believe that most modern cusps are drawn by the hundred as a mere matter of routine, without care and without pleasure, and consequently without good effect.

Not less beautiful than the porches and monuments is another feature which occurs in Italy, as often as, and perhaps more perfectly than, anywhere else—the cloister. This consists generally of an open arcade supported on detached shafts, and is very frequently of two stages in height. Notwithstanding their extreme simplicity and moderate amount of enrichment, these Italian cloisters are always cap-

---

[86] Numerous examples of masonry arranged in the same way occur in old English examples. The openings of fireplaces in particular are often so constructed.

ital in their effect. They owe this very much to the number of shafts which support their arches; these are generally of marble, coupled together except at the angles, where there are usually four. Some of the cloisters which still remain in Verona, are among the most beautiful examples. Nor are those of San Stefano, Bologna, nor at a later date those of the church of Sant'Antonio at Padua and at Brescia, less worthy of study. They never have the beautiful traceries of our Northern cloisters, for the sufficient reason, that the climate rendered less protection from the weather necessary; and the consequence of this is, that their arcades, being always severely simple in design, no effort was ever spared to make them as perfect as possible in their proportions.

The cloisters of the cathedral at Aosta are interesting as affording an instance of the lavish richness of illustration which some of the mediæval sculptors bestowed on their work; the capitals throughout being sculptured with illustrations of subjects, all of which are made fully intelligible by inscriptions incised in the stone—a favourite practice not only of early Italian sculptors, but of their brethren in Germany and France. In the cloister of San Gregorio, Venice, we have another variety in which the shafts support the woodwork of the roof in a very picturesque fashion, without any arches. This is a type of cloister which might often be most useful in modern work, and is an evidence of the extent to which a Gothic artist may, when necessity requires it, trench boldly on what is ordinarily supposed to be the exclusive province of Classic art—the use of the shaft and lintel; but here the Gothic artist with his usual reality made his lintel of wood in place of stone.

The Italian treatment of windows is especially worthy of note. The drawings which I have given will shew how generally the tracery, commonly called plate-tracery, was used. It is, indeed, a very beautiful mode of treatment, but quite distinct from all fully-developed systems, inasmuch as it deals only with the piercings here and there in the block of stone which forms the window-head, and not with the intricate combinations of lines which mark out the outlines of the spaces to be pierced. The difference is great—the one kind giving that exquisite depth and mystery and admitting of the infinite variety so characteristic of northern Gothic, the other giving breadth and flatness of effect, and leaving space on its broad surfaces for the play of the brilliant sunshine, save where the black piercing of some simple form—quatrefoil or trefoil—gives life to the otherwise monotonous window-head. Of the two the former admits of infinitely more variety and display of fancy and ingenuity; though the latter, perhaps, when seen at its best, is really the more beautiful. Both of them are, however, so good as to be equally usable, and neither of them to the exclusion of the other.

In Italian Gothic traceries, it is difficult to shew the progression or regular development which marks every stage of northern Gothic. There are numerous examples of simple lancet windows, of cusped lancets, of combinations of lancets cusped or uncusped, and oftentimes of windows of plate-tracery, and then of more developed tracery which, however, was still treated as plate tracery with the addition of mouldings. In the later windows an unsightly effect is produced by the wide and bald plain splay or reveal which is usually formed round the window, outside as well as inside, and also by the placing of glazing behind the traceries in a separate wooden frame, so that they are completely concealed from view on the interior. The tracery of the second stage of the Doge's Palace at Venice is probably equal to any that has ever been executed, and may well be the pride of the country. It has also the special peculiarity, common to all Venetian domestic work, of being sufficiently strong in its section and construction to bear an enormous weight of wall without the aid of any discharging arch above it. There is another class of traceries which seems to have been essentially an Italian invention, and which is as objectionable as any tracery that I know. Examples of this may be seen in the south transept of SS. Giovanni e Paolo, at Venice. They give the idea of having been cut out to order, from an enormous mass of ready-made tracery, kept in slab, sold by the superficial yard, and cut to fit any opening required. There is no attempt to finish the tracery where it meets the inclosing arch, and the effect is consequently always rude and unskilful.[87]

Another feature is, the constant use at all dates of shafts in place of moulded window monials; and another, the very frequent insertion of a transome of tracery, across the middle of the height of the window. The use of the shaft instead of the moulded monial does not seem to be so admirable in ecclesiastical as in domestic work. It generally accompanied the system already mentioned of fixing the glazing in wooden frames, behind the stonework, and hence seldom looks well in church-windows except on the outside. The deep transomes pierced with tracery are of common occurrence. They are seen in almost all the Venetian Gothic churches, but their utility and beauty are alike doubtful.

No country affords more frequent examples of circular windows than Italy. They occur in almost every church, and are of stone, marble, and brick. The best example I know, of very early pointed character, and one which is unsurpassed anywhere, is in the west front of the church of Sta. Maria, Toscanella. Here there is an inner wheel, and the space between the two wheels is divided by shafts, between each of which is pierced a quatrefoil. The little window in the gable of the oratory of San Zenone, Verona, is a favourable example of a smaller window. It is of eight lights divided by shafts, and well moulded and proportioned in all its parts. Other circular windows as at S. Mark's, Venice, and in the church of Sant'Antonio, Padua, are of the class already described, where the tracery seems to have been inserted, without reference to, or connection with, the inclosing circular line.

I have now, I think, exhausted the distinguishing features of an Italian church, with the exception of its campanile. This, as I have said before, is always a single steeple (with the perhaps unique exception of Genoa Cathedral, which has two), generally detached from the main fabric, planted wherever it happened to be most

[87] There is a very curious example of Italian tracery in the church of San Giacomo, in Bologna. This is a two-light window, composed of a series of slabs of stones, pierced with geometrical figures and supported by shafts. It has, beginning at the sill and reckoning upwards—1, two lights divided by a shaft monial; 2, a slab pierced with two trefoiled heads to the lights; 3, a large transome panel of stone pierced with a quatrefoil and two trefoils; 4, same as 1st; 5, same as 2nd; 6, the arch, whose tympanum is filled in with another pierced slab of stone. It will be seen that the construction of such a window as this is altogether unlike that of any English window.

convenient; sometimes as at Vercelli, not even at right angles to the building to which it is attached, and with but little reference to its effect upon the remainder of the building. There are no features of Italian buildings which are so universally remembered with pleasure; and similar as they are in their general scheme, there is nevertheless a considerable variety in their treatment in detail. The first thing to be noted is, that they are never supported by buttresses, and that the usual mode of ascent was by a staircase in the thickness of the wall, and not by any such excrescence as a staircase turret. The outline is severely square and simple, and, unlike as it is to most of our English steeples, generally exceedingly striking. No doubt the apparent height of these towers is enormously increased by the absence of buttresses. The originals of all Italian campanili seem to be the early steeples of the Roman churches, divided into a series of stages of equal height, pierced with windows not varying much in design throughout. The most exact reproductions of these steeples may be found so far from the centre of Italy as at Susa at the foot of the Mont Cenis, and in other very similar erections all over the North of Italy. With certain broad general features of resemblance there are, however, several local variations, which may be divided roughly into the following separate classes or schools:—(1) The Pisan: (2) the Venetian and Veronese: (3) the Genoese: and (4) the Florentine: of which I need here only speak of the Venetian and Veronese, which are undoubtedly among the finest. In the Veronese there is a very distinct imitation of the pure Romanesque examples, whilst in the Venetian there is generally less subdivision into stages, the walls being arcaded with very slightly recessed lofty arcades, and the horizontal divisions being much fewer in number. Of these, San Giacomo del Rialto is one of the best examples; it is executed, as all the Venetian examples are, in brick. In all these examples the pilasters at the angles are carefully marked. But there is another variety of distinctly Italian towers in which this is not the case. The finest example of this is the tower of the Scaliger Palace, at Verona, where the simple unbroken mass of masonry and brickwork shoots up into the sky all but unpierced until the belfry stage. Of this kind of tower the examples are not unfrequent in the smaller churches in Lombardy, and in the public halls and private houses of many of the cities described in these pages. The tower at Asti is one of the best of these.

There remain two other subjects which, more than any others, meet us at every stage of our study of Gothic architecture in Italy. These are, first, the use of brick; and secondly, the introduction of coloured materials in construction, of both of which, as we have seen, there are so many valuable examples.

It has been by far too much the fashion of late years to look upon brick as a very inferior material, fit only to be covered with compo, and never fit to be used in church-building, or indeed in any buildings of any architectural pretension, so that I suspect many people, trusting to their knowledge of pointed architecture in England, would be much surprized to find that, throughout large tracts of the Continent, brick was the natural, and indeed the popular material during the most palmy days of architecture in the Middle Ages. Yet so it was that in Holland, in the south-west of France, in Northern Germany, and the Low Countries, in large tracts in Spain, and throughout Northern Italy, stone was either scarce or not to be obtained, and brick was therefore everywhere and most fearlessly used.

In all these countries, just as in Italy, it was used without any concealment, but each country developed its practice in this matter for itself, and there is therefore considerable diversity in their work. They are all unlike, and far superior to what remains to us of ancient brickwork in England, for I need hardly say that, with a rare exception here and there, and in comparatively small districts, brick was not used in England between the time of the Romans and the fifteenth century, and, when used afterwards, was seldom remarkable either for any singular beauty or originality of treatment. In this matter, therefore, we are obliged to go to the Continent for information.

String-course—Palace of Jurisconsults, Cremona.

Italian brickwork is remarkable as being almost always executed with nothing but red bricks, with occasional but rare use of stonework; the bricks for the ordinary walling are generally rather larger than ours, in no way superior in their quality, and always built coarsely with a wide joint of mortar. Those used for windows, doorways, and generally where they were required to attract attention and to be ornamental, were made of much finer clay and moulded with the greatest care and skill. The transepts and campanile of Cremona Cathedral are instances of red brick used without any intermixture of stone save in the shafts of the windows, and their effect is certainly very grand. The mouldings are elaborate, and the way in which cusping is formed singularly successful. This, it must be observed, was not usually done by means of bricks moulded in the form of a cusp, but with ordinary bricks, built with the same radiating lines as those of the arch to which they belonged, and cut and rubbed to the necessary outline. Sometimes, as, e.g., in the windows at Mantua,[88] which are some of the very best I have ever seen, the points of the cusps and key-stones of the arches are formed in pieces of stone, the alternation of which with the deep-red hue of the bricks produces the most satisfactory effect of colour. This sort of treatment is common at Brescia, Verona, Mantua, and Venice, but unknown at Cremona.

[88] See plate 40, p. 190.

Window in North Transept, Cremona Cathedral.

In nearly all cases where brick is used for tracery, it is in the shape of plate-tracery. The tympanum of the arch is filled in with a mass of brickwork, through which are pierced the arches over the several lights of the window, and these are supported on marble or stone shafts with carved capitals, instead of monials:[89] and above these sometimes, as in the windows of Sant'Andrea, Mantua, are three cusped circles; sometimes, as in the palace at Mantua, only one cusped circle; or else, as in a beautiful example at Cremona, the plain brick tympanum is relieved by the introduction of a panel of terra-cotta, bearing the cross on a shield, whilst round its outer circumference delicately treated though large cusping defines the outline of the arch.[90]

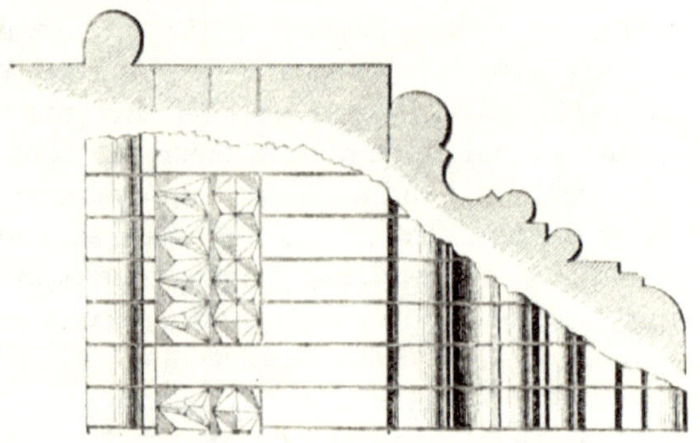

Detail of Window-jamb—Cremona.

[89] The windows in the Castle of S. Angelo, between Lodi and Pavia, are the only examples I met with of the use of brick for monials. In Northern Germany, on the contrary, where the shaft was almost unknown, brick monials are universal, and generally unsatisfactory in their effect.

[90] See preceding page.

The windows at Coccaglio[91] and at Monza[92] are examples of tympana left quite plain, or, as in the former case, pierced only with a small opening of a few inches in diameter, which nevertheless gives much effect to the design. In the latter case there is a feature which is well worth notice, because it is remarkable in the best Italian brickwork, and always very effective. Labels are exceedingly rare, but their place is usually supplied by a course of very narrow deep red bricks which surrounds the back of the arch. In the window in Monza Cathedral there are two such courses—one about 4½ inches wide, the other not more than 2½. They serve to define the arch and keep it distinct in effect from the walling around it. Sometimes, as in the Vescovato at Mantua, and in the houses at Asti, these narrow bricks are introduced between a succession of rims of brickwork on the same face, alternated very picturesquely with squares of stone, and sometimes, as in some beautiful arcading outside San Fermo Maggiore at Verona,[93] to define and enliven the lines of stonework; for in this case, though the work is all in stone and no brick was really required, so great was the appreciation of colour, that it was gladly and most successfully introduced. In the early cloister of San Zenone we see it again,[94] as also in all the very beautiful arches which still remain in the Broletto of Brescia.[95]

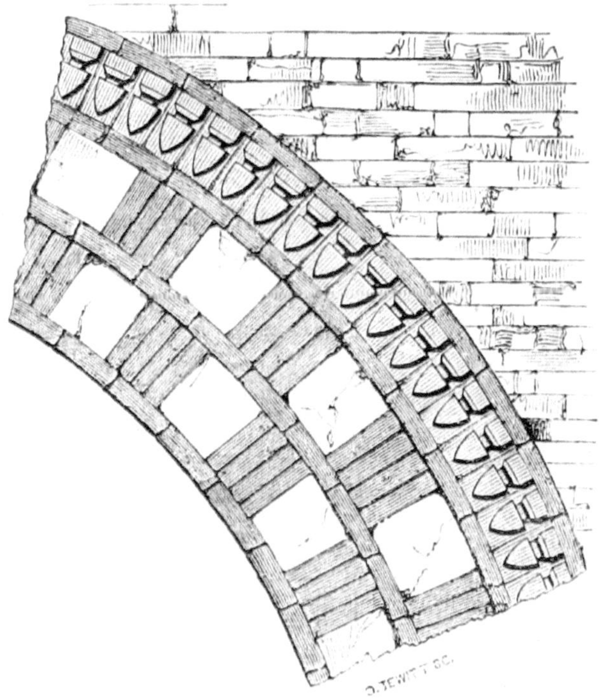

Brick Archivolt, Vescovato—Mantua.

[91] See pp. 43, 44.
[92] See p. 261.
[93] See plate 18, p. 91.
[94] See plate 15, p. 82.
[95] See plate 9, p. 53.

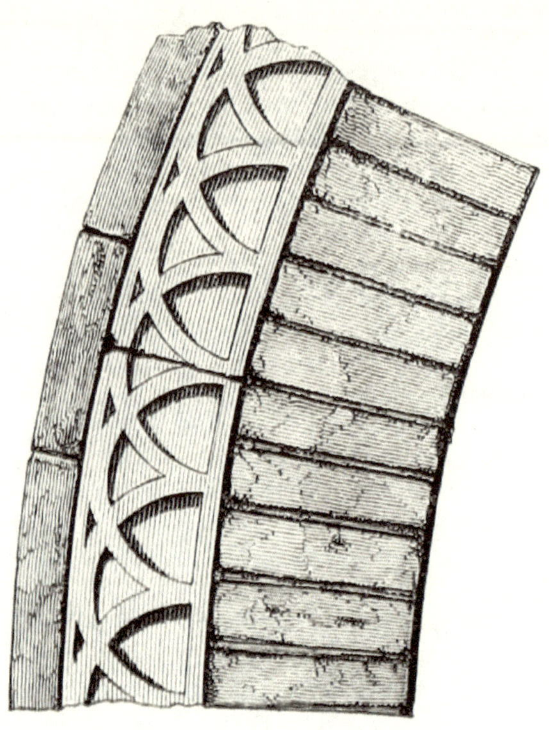

Arch-mould — Cremona.

But beside this there was another way in which Italian architects produced a very beautiful effect: this was in the alternation of stone and brick. We have one of the first examples of this in the magnificent walls of San Zenone at Verona, in which a deep red brick is used in courses alternating with a very warm-coloured stone. The brick is used very irregularly: beginning at the base of the walls over the cloisters, we have alternately with courses of stone, first a band of three courses of brick, after this one course of brick, four courses, five courses, two courses, one course, and then the cornice, which is mainly of stone, but relieved by two courses of narrow bricks; in spite of the variation in the height of the brick courses, those of stone in this case are nearly uniform in depth. In the west front of San Fermo Maggiore[96] we have brick and stone used in alternate and regular courses all the way up; in this case the brick is used rather for colour than for any other reason, though the side walls of this church are entirely of brick and crowned with excessively deep brick cornices.

The churches at Asti afford examples of the worst kind of counterchanging of stone and brick; in them the jamb of a window is treated like a chess-board, being chequered with alternate red and white both horizontally and vertically. To accomplish this the construction is ingeniously twisted, and it need hardly be said that the effect is not at all good.

---

[96] See plate 17, p. 89.

The interior of San Zenone, Verona, is lined with brick and stone, arranged just as it is outside, and the effect is most satisfactory; indeed, this and the interior of the baptistery at Cremona, still left in their original state, shew how noble an effect of colour may be given by brick internally, and how mistaken we are when we cover our walls with undecorated plaster. I have seen it maintained by men who possibly had never seen such old works as these in their old state, that such colour as this is savage and fit only for uncultivated men. If, however, there is refinement in whitewash or plaster, I am unable to see it, and I can see no more inconsistency in honestly shewing the real materials of the wall inside than in doing so outside. This at any rate is beyond all doubt what these old Italian architects did.

Window — Verona.

The east end of the church of the Frari at Venice is another example of coursing with stone.[97] There, however, the courses are far apart, and seem to be intended to define the lines of the springing of arches, of transomes, and the like; and this they do very satisfactorily. But, perhaps, the very best example of mixed stone

[97] See Plate 24, p. 132.

and brick is that which we have in the window-heads of the church by the side of the Duomo at Verona,[98] in which the arrangement of the two colours is quite perfect. In this case the cusped head of the light is executed in stone, not in brick; and this is, I think, as a general rule, by far the better plan; for if an attempt is made to execute tracery in brick, we have the example of the Germans before our eyes as a warning. They rarely (S. Katharine, Lübeck, is almost a solitary exception) used stone in their window tracery; and as they never developed the kind of brick plate-tracery which is so characteristic of the best Italian work, they built windows which were either bald and ugly in their simplicity, or else, endeavouring to execute elaborate traceries by the use of bricks, moulded into the forms of component parts of tracery, they produced what are even more distasteful than any other kind of window; in part because they consist of an endless repetition of small reticulations, and in part because they lead naturally to the constant reproduction of the same window for economy's sake.

Brick Window, Sant'Andrea—Mantua.

There can be no doubt that the best windows for brick churches are either those beautiful Italian developments of plate-tracery in which all the bricks are carefully cut and rubbed for their proper place, or those in which, within an inclosing arch of line upon line of brickwork, a small portion of stone is used for the traceries. And this last has the advantage of giving much more opportunity for variety of form and beauty of effect than any brick traceries can ever give.

There is one point in which a curious practical difference exists between our old work and most old Italian. Here it was not the custom to have keystones to pointed arches, whilst there it is quite the rule to have them; this may have been partly, perhaps, because it was a matter of convenience to mark the central stone in arches composed of alternate voussoirs of brick and stone, and it may have been partly some relic of Classic traditions: not only, however, is there a keystone, but sometimes, as in the Broletto at Brescia, this is additionally distinguished, above

[98] See Plate 18, p. 91.

the rest of the stone voussoirs, by some small ornament carved upon it. With one more fact I think I may end what I have to say on this head: this is with reference to the mode in which some of the Italian brick arches very beautifully follow the fashion, not so uncommon in stone, of increasing in depth as they approach the centre. In this manner, one sometimes sees an arch whose outer circumference is pointed, whilst its inner line is a semicircle. This was a fashion most popular in Florence, and not so common in Northern Italy; still it is to be seen at Monza, Verona, and elsewhere. The effect is always very good, and, though quite unknown to our forefathers in England, may well be introduced in our works, as it gives great appearance of strength, and is no doubt, at the same time, the strongest possible form of arch.

No one can deny that the study of Italian brickwork must be useful to those who are compelled, as we so often are, to use the same material in buildings for whose good architectural effect and character we are anxious. But, far as it is in advance of most ancient brickwork in England, there are points in which we must refuse to follow it; we need not, for instance, in attempting to rival its beauties, confound them with faults which were essentially those of the whole Italian style, and not specially of Italian brickwork. We may with the greatest advantage emulate the Italian system of brick-window tracery, whilst we take care never to imitate the equally common custom in Italy of erecting sham fronts in order to display our traceries. Again, though they never used any but red bricks, there is no reason why we should not enliven our work with the contrast of other colours. Germany gives us examples of green and black bricks, and, indeed, Italy affords some (e.g., Sant'Antonio, in Padua, Murano, and Torcello) of a yellowish brick; and, no doubt, the effects producible by these contrasts of colour are such as Italian architects were always ready to avail themselves when they had the opportunity. This their parti-coloured works in marble sufficiently prove; but at the same time it was seldom that they ventured upon such works in brick; and as it must be admitted that there is no sort of work which so much requires skilful handling, or which is so liable to degenerate into vulgarity, as this, it is probable that they advisedly abstained from it.

As to the question whether it be desirable or not to introduce brick at all in ecclesiastical edifices, or generally in public buildings, one might, a few years ago, have been anxious to say somewhat. I trust, however, that the ignorant prejudice which made many good people regard stone as a sort of sacred material, and red brick as one fit only for the commonest and meanest purposes, is fast wearing out, and that what now mainly remains to be done is to shew how it may most effectively be used, not only in external, but also in internal works.

One word only as to its colour, for I think that we ought as much as possible to insist upon this being taken into consideration. We do not, as a general rule, I suppose, adopt any material in good works of architecture simply because it is the very cheapest that can be obtained; sometimes, indeed, we must, and then I should be the last to contend against what is simply an act of necessity, not of choice; but ordinarily, before, for economy's sake, we determine to sacrifice the colour of our work, and to use those detestable-looking dirty yellow bricks in which London so much indulges, we ought to consider whether, by some economy in other respects, we may not save enough to allow of the use of the best kind of red brick for the general face of our walls.[99]

At the present day there is, I think, absolutely no one point in which we fail so much, and about which the world in general has so little feeling, as that of colour. Our buildings are, in nine cases out of ten, cold, colourless, insipid, academical studies, and our people have no conception of the necessity of obtaining rich colour, and no sufficient love for it when successfully obtained. The task and duty of architects at the present day is mainly that of awakening and then satisfying this feeling; and one of the best and most ready vehicles for doing this exists, no doubt, in the rich-coloured brick so easily manufactured in this country, which, if properly used, may become so effective and admirable a material.

The other mode of introducing colour in construction, by means of the use of marbles, deserves also some notice. In my notes upon the buildings as they were passed in my journeys, I have described two modes in which this kind of work was treated: the first was that practised in Venice—the veneering of brick walls with thin layers or coats of marble; the other, that practised at Bergamo, Cremona, and Como—in which the marble formed portion of the substance of the wall.

These two modes led, as would naturally be expected, to two entirely different styles and modes of architecture.

The Venetian mode was rather likely to be destructive of good architecture, because it was sure to end in an entire concealment of the real construction of the work; the other mode, on the contrary, proceeded on true principles, and took pleasure in defining most carefully every line in the construction of the work. It might almost be said that one mode was devised with a view to the concealment, and the other with a view to the explanation, of the real mode of construction.

I have already described, at some length, the main features of these old works in marble, and I feel, therefore, that all that need now be done is to point out the degree to which they afford matter for our imitation with the coloured materials and marbles which we fortunately have in Great Britain fit for the purpose, though not in very great variety.

There appears to me to be a certain limited extent to which we may safely go in the way of inlaying or incrustation: we may, for instance, so construct our buildings as that there may be portions of the face of their walls in which no strain will be felt, and in which this absence of strain will be at once apparent; obviously, to instance a particular place, the spaces inclosed within circles constructed in the spandrels of a line of arches can have no strain of any kind. They are portions of wall without any active function, and may safely be filled in with materials the only object of which is to be ornamental. All kinds of sunk panels inclosed within arches

---

[99] It would be difficult to give stronger evidence of the intrinsic effect of a good coloured material than is afforded by the fact that designs so really ignorant in their architectural detail as, e.g., most of the buildings of the time of William III. and Queen Anne should nevertheless have a certain charm for us, solely derived from the beautiful colour of the bricks with which they are built.

or tracery would come under the same head; the spaces between string-courses might also do so very frequently, if, as in old examples, the string-courses were large slabs of stones bedded into the very midst of the wall, and so capable of protecting the thin, weak slabs of marbles incrusted between them.

In Venice we have some grand examples, at S. Mark's, of this system of incrustation filling in the whole of the space within large arches; here it is lawful, because there is no weight upon it to thrust it out of its place or disjoint it, as the least pressure most certainly always will. So far in praise of the Venetian system. But in other parts of the same building we have this system carried to a length which I cannot but think most mistaken, and which, I most heartily trust, may never find imitators here. In these the arches were constructed in brick, and then entirely covered with marble. Of course there was some difficulty in doing this, and the way in which the difficulty was met was extremely ingenious; a succession of thin slabs of marble was placed round the soffeit of the arch, having perhaps enough of the cohesion given by the form of the arch to enable them to support their own weight, and further supported by metal staples let into the joints of the brickwork. The edges of these thin slabs projected sufficiently in advance of the face of the brickwork to allow of their being worked with some kind of pattern—generally, as has before been said, a sort of dentil—and of their giving some support to the thin slices of marble with which the walls were then covered. The whole system was excessively weak; and this can nowhere be better seen than in the Fondaco de Turchi, where almost the whole of the marble facing and beautiful medallions, in which it was once so rich, have peeled off, and left nothing but the plain and melancholy substratum of brick. Few architects, I should think, would like to contemplate their work perishing in this piecemeal manner, any more than they would enjoy the thought of a west front left unfinished, like that of Sta. Anastasia at Verona, and prepared only for marble with rough, irregular, and unsightly brickwork.

It would be unjust not to say that often, very often, this system of incrustation, even when carried to the extreme limits of what seems to be lawful, wins upon our love by the exquisite delicacy and taste of the sculptured patterns, worked in low-relief, with which it is covered. The men who did this work were, perhaps, more of sculptors than of architects; and certainly it must be confessed that never in buildings in which the construction is mainly thought of, is there, so far as I know, so much elaborate thought and skill exhibited in the decorative part of the work as in buildings such as these.

Sometimes, the sculptured medallions set in the centre of a plain surface of marble are of exquisite taste and beauty; whilst here and there, as e.g. in S. Mark's and in one or two spots in the water-front of the Ducal Palace, are examples of great beauty, of medallions formed of marbles of various colours, arranged with great refinement in some kind of geometrical pattern, which shew another and equally beautiful mode of relieving plain spaces of walling.

The plain surfaces of the walls in Venetian work were commonly either entirely inlaid, or else inlaid within a square inclosing border of projecting moulding. The inlaying was composed of a number of rectangular slabs of marble, not by any means always of the same size, supported to some extent by the projections of the inclosing marbles or by those of the archivolt, but always dependent mainly on metal cramps let into the fabric of the wall; and, when possible, these marbles were slabs cut out of the same block, and put side by side, so as to produce a kind of regular pattern wherever the veining of the marble was at all positively marked.

The other mode of introducing constructional colour in marble commends itself to one's reason as that which is most likely to endure for ages, and as that, therefore, which ought, wherever it may be, to be adopted. The first idea of the architects of these buildings seems to have been to arrange their material with as much regard to strong contrasts of colour as was possible. The first thing they did, therefore, was to alternate the colours of every course of masonry, either simply as in the Broletto at Como[100] and in Sta. Maria Maggiore at Bergamo,[101] or as in the west front of the cathedral at Cremona, where very narrow layers of white marble are laid between each of the other courses, which are of course so much the more defined.

The description which I have already given of these works, as well as of the porch at Bergamo, will shew how regular is the way in which this system of counterchanging the colours was carried out by the purely constructional school; this is, in fact, the great mark of difference between the constructional and the incrusting school of Italian architects, the whole arrangement of coloured materials by the two schools being quite different, and producing singularly different results. The most common fault of the Venetian system of incrustation must have been that upon a general surface of plain wall you had here and there a square patch of marble surrounding a window opening; that of the other system would be, in the opinion of many, that you have too stripy an effect of colour, and that all the divisions, moreover, are horizontal.

The former must certainly have been the case wherever the incrustation did not extend over the whole surface of the walls, which was very frequently the case; but the latter is not really a fault; it was only an elaboration in a more beautiful material of the same system which we have seen pursued with such happy results by the builders of Verona in brick and stone,[102] and which we find adopted by the architects of Northern Germany in the frequent alternation of courses of red and black brick, and sometimes by our own forefathers in the coursing of flint work with stone, or in the counterchanging of red and white stones which we see in some of the Northamptonshire churches. The system was a thoroughly sound one, because it not only proceeded from and depended on the natural arrangement of the material, but afforded the best possible means for displaying the various colours which were to be used.

Probably all these systems are mainly useful now as shewing us certain principles which we may work out and apply to our own somewhat different circumstances; and surely one of our first objects ought to be the discovery of the extent

---

[100] See plate 63, p. 267.

[101] See plate 1, frontispiece.

[102] Some of the mediæval buildings in Greece have small patterns carved in low relief all round the walls in occasional courses, which are evidently intended to produce the kind of effect referred to above.

of our means and opportunities, which in this matter are at the present day far beyond what is generally imagined.

It must never be forgotten by us that our forefathers had very limited means of obtaining materials from one locality and transporting them to another; and were moreover, to a great extent, unacquainted with the materials which might, if necessary, be obtained. We have not this excuse; we not only know what materials we may obtain, but we have at the same time marvellous facilities for their conveyance between all parts of the country; and we know also how much has been done of old in other countries by using them in a proper way.

No excuse therefore can be found for us if we continue to neglect to avail ourselves of them as though they were still undiscovered. We have alabaster, which may be wrought at a really trifling expense; large fields of marbles, of which those of Devonshire and Ireland are particularly valuable for architectural decoration, and those of Derbyshire and Purbeck for the formation of shafts and columns: we have, moreover, an exhaustless supply of granites of various colours; of serpentine; and, lastly, of building-stones of many tints, many of which may be very effective when contrasted. In addition to these natural materials we have every facility for making the most perfect bricks; and, owing to the excellence already achieved by our manufacturers of glass and pottery, we have no difficulty in making mosaics and tiles, either for roofing, flooring, or inlaying, of any degree of beauty, either of colour or form.

With such advantages we ought long since to have effected far more than we have ever attempted, or apparently ever thought of. Our buildings should, both outside and inside, have had some of that warmth which colour only can give; they should have enabled the educated eye to revel in bright tints of nature's own formation, whilst to the uneducated eye they would have afforded the best of all possible lessons, and, by familiarizing it with the proper combination of colour and form, would have enabled it to appreciate it.

And then, if ever the day shall come when our buildings thus do their duty and teach their proper lesson to the eye, we may hope that we shall see a feeling, more general and more natural, for colour of all kinds and for art of every variety in the bulk of our people. At present it is really saddening to converse with the majority of educated men on any question of colour. For them it has no charms and no delight. The puritanical uniformity of our coats and of all our garments is but a reflection from the prevailing lack of love of art or colour of any kind. A rich colour is thought vulgar, and that only is refined which is neutral, plain, and ugly.

Perhaps in all this there may be something more than art can ever grapple with; it may be ingrain, and part of the necessity of the present age; but if so, oh for the days when, as of yore, colour may be appreciated and beloved, when uniformity shall not be considered beauty, nor a hideous plainness be considered a fit substitute for severity! Oh too, for the days when men shall have cast off their dependence on other men's works, and the customs of their own days, and, like true men and faithful, shall honestly and with energy, each in his own sphere, set to work to do all that in them lies to increase the power of art and to advance its best interests. All these aims and objects are more or less bound up with the best interests of a people, however old and however powerful, because they depend for ultimate and real success upon the thorough belief, on the part of all its votaries, in certain great and eternal principles, which, if always acted upon, would beyond all doubt sometimes make great artists and always good men.

The principle which artists now have mainly to contend for is that of TRUTH; forgotten, trodden under foot, despised, if not hated for ages, this must be their watchword. If they be architects, let them remember how vitally necessary truthfulness in construction, in design, and in decoration, is to any permanent success in even the smallest of their works; or sculptors, let them recollect how vain and unsatisfactory has been their abandonment of truth in their attempted revival among us of what in Classic times were—what they no longer are—real representations and natural works of art; if painters, let them remember how all-important a return to first principles and truth in the delineation of nature and natural forms is to them, if they are ever to create a school of art by which they may be remembered in another age.

Finally, I wish that all artists would remember the one great fact which separates by so wide a gap the architects, sculptors, and painters of the best days of the Middle Ages from us now—their earnestness and their thorough self-sacrifice in the pursuit of art, and in the exaltation of their religion. They were men who had a faith, and hearts earnestly bent on the propagation of that faith; and were it not for this, their works would never have had the life, vigour, and freshness which even now they so remarkably retain. Why should we not be equally remembered three centuries hence? Have we less to contend for, less faith to exhibit, or less self-sacrifice to offer than they, because we live in later days? Or is it true that the temper of men is so much changed, and that the vocation of art has changed with it? I believe not. There have been evidences enough that there is no lack of liberality on the part of our employers, where there is any evidence of skill and enthusiasm for his work on the part of the artist. The English architect of to-day has opportunities as great as those of any of his predecessors, if he will but use them. But he must use his art as one who respects both himself and it. There is no real respect for an art when it is treated, as it always has been by the Renaissance architects and their followers, as a mere affair of display. No good building was ever yet erected in which the architect designed the front, and left the flanks or internal courts to take care of themselves. So also no good building was ever seen, in which the exterior only was thought of, and the internal decoration and design neglected. But this is almost universal now, except in the few buildings in which the Gothic style has been carefully revived. In such treatment of art as this, there is an ingrain falseness, which is as demoralizing as it is ruinous. If architecture is only an affair of outside display, no one will take any real interest in it, for from the first it is the evidence of the architect's love for his work which has given the human interest which is all in all to it.

It is this truthfulness only, in every line and every detail of every part of a building, which can ever make great architecture—it is this only which one would wish to extract from the works of our forefathers—and this only which I have desired to discover in the works of those Italian artists whose labours I have been considering, and whose efforts I have endeavoured to set before my readers; and it is this desire which can alone be my excuse for having undertaken the work which I have now brought to a conclusion.

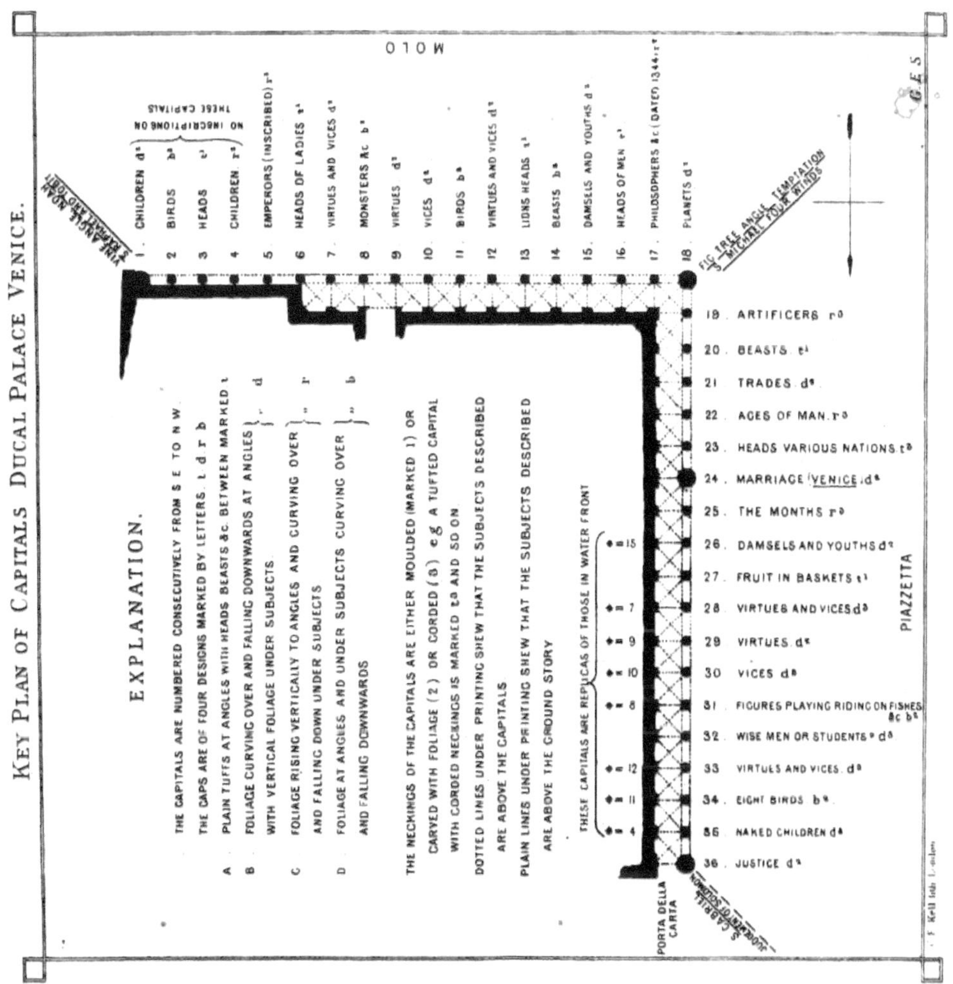

65.—Key Plan of Capitals in Ducal Palace (Doge's Palace), Venice.

EXPLANATION.

THE CAPITALS ARE NUMBERED CONSECUTIVELY FROM S E TO N W.

THE CAPS ARE OF FOUR DESIGNS MARKED BY LETTERS. t d r b

A . PLAIN TUFFS AT ANGLES WITH HEADS BEASTS &c. BETWEEN MARKED t

B . FOLIAGE CURVING OVER AND FALLING DOWNWARDS AT ANGLES ⎫
WITH VERTICAL FOLIAGE UNDER SUBJECTS. ⎬ " d

C . FOLIAGE RISING VERTICALLY TO ANGLES AND CURVING OVER ⎫
AND FALLING DOWN UNDER SUBJECTS. ⎬ " r

D . FOLIAGE AT ANGLES AND UNDER SUBJECTS CURVING OVER ⎫
AND FALLING DOWNWARDS ⎬ " b

THE NECKINGS OF THE CAPITALS ARE EITHER MOULDED (MARKED 1) OR
CARVED WITH FOLIAGE (2) OR CORDED (3) eg A TUFTED CAPITAL
WITH CORDED NECKINGS IS MARKED t3 AND SO ON.

DOTTED LINES UNDER PRINTING SHEW THAT THE SUBJECTS DESCRIBED
ARE ABOVE THE CAPITALS.

PLAIN LINES UNDER PRINTING SHEW THAT THE SUBJECTS DESCRIBED
ARE ABOVE THE GROUND STORY

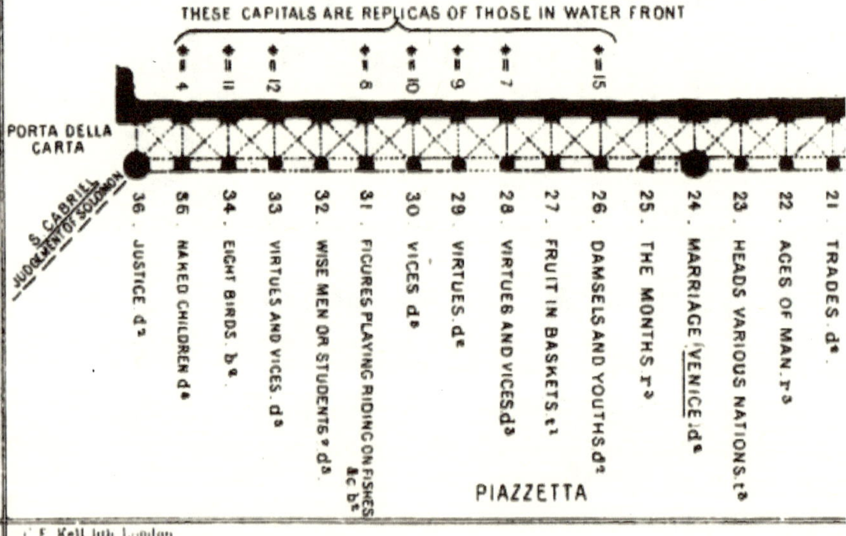

Key Plan (Enlarged - Left)

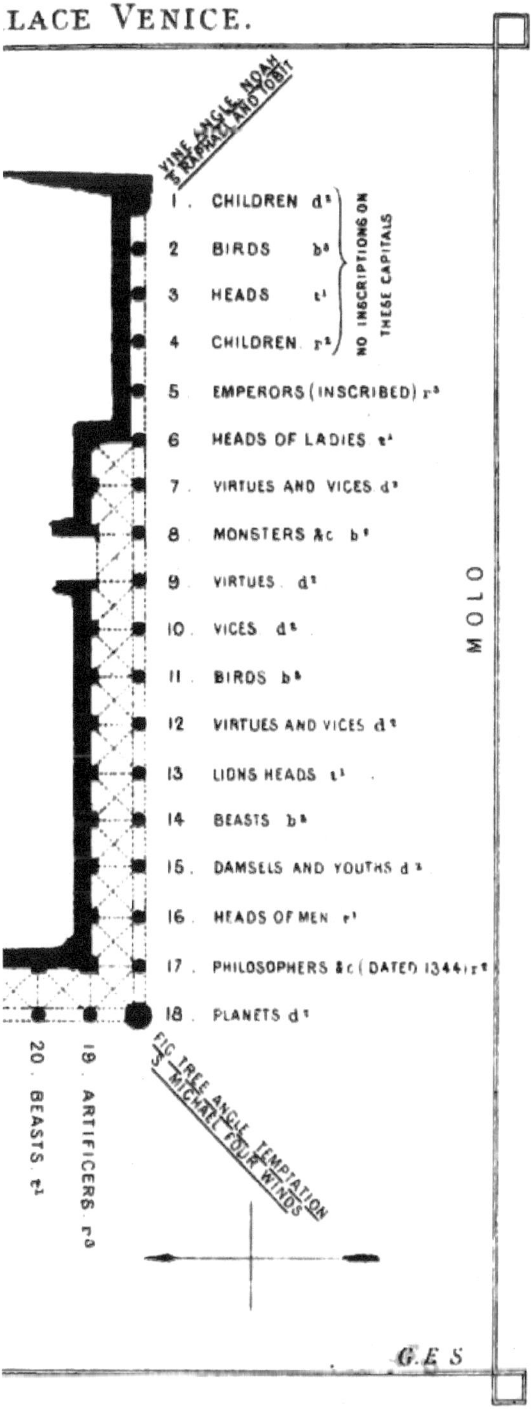

Key Plan (Enlarged - Left)

APPENDIX.

Catalogue of the Subjects of the Sculptured Capitals in the Lower
Stage of the Doge's Palace, Venice.

THE capitals are numbered as in the accompanying key-plan, beginning at
the south-east angle on the Molo front, and going from right to left until the last
capital, near S. Mark's, is reached. For those who wish for something more than
a catalogue, I need hardly say that in the latter portion of the second volume of
the 'Stones of Venice,' Mr. Ruskin has given all that can be desired, with his usual
felicity and beauty of verbal illustration.

In the 'Annales Archéologiques,' vol. xvii. (1857), Mr. Burges has given a very
full and careful account of all the capitals, to which M. Didron Ainé has added
some supplementary notes.

Zanotto ('Il Palazzo Ducale di Venezia,' vol. i. pp. 209-355) has given a still
more full description, accompanied by rather rude outlines of all the lower range
of capitals. There is small need, therefore, for anything more than a mere catalogue
here, which it seems to me may be of service to some of those who are able to look
at the Ducal Palace, but unable to carry with them any of the weighty volumes to
which I have referred.

South-east Angle.—Above the capital is the Drunkenness of Noah. Above this,
on a level with the traceries of the upper arcade, the archangel Raphael, with Tobit,
who bears a scroll with these words—

EFICE Q̄
SO. FRE
TV̄. RAFA
EL. REVE
RENDE
QUIETŪ.[103]

CAPITAL I. Partly built up. Has three figures of nude children, one with a comb
and shears, another with a bird. The foliage is good; but the nude figures have the
appearance of semi-Renaissance work.

II. Partly built up. Large birds—one devouring a serpent, another a fish, and
the third pluming its feathers. The foliage here is not very good, and the design of
<u>the capital in no</u> way first-rate, the birds being treated in a very naturalesque way.

[103] "Oh, venerable Raphael, make thou the gulf calm, we beseech thee!" This figure
looks towards the sea and the port.

III. Partly built up. Large heads, male and female. The man has a helmet, partly of plate, but with chain mail round the neck.

IV. Partly built up. Children, nude, holding (1) a bird, and (2 and 3) fruit.

V. Partly built up. Emperors. This is the first capital which has inscriptions. Those visible are (1) TITUS VESPASIAN IPAT; (2) TRAJANUS INPE; and (3) (OCT)AVIANUS IPATO.

VI. Partly built up. Large heads, alternated with tufts of foliage, badly carved.

VII. Virtues and Vices. (1) Liberality; inscribed LARGITAS. ME. ONORAT. (2) Constancy; COSTANCIA. SU. NIL. TIMĒS. (3) Discord; DISCORDIA. SU. - - - DISCORDANS. (4) Patience; PATIENTIA. MANET. MECUM. (5) Despair; DESPERACIO. MORS. CRUDELIS. (6) Obedience; OBEDIENCIA.A.DNO.EXIBEO. (7) Infidelity; INFIDELITATE.—ILI.GERO. (8) Modesty; MODESTIA.ROBŪ OBTINEO. This capital should be compared with No. XXVIII. The foliage here is very beautiful; but the execution of No. XXVIII. is best.

VIII. Monsters, generally with musical instruments. A riding figure here wears chain armour. There are no inscriptions on this capital, and its intention is very obscure.

IX. Virtues. (1) Faith; FIDES.OPTIMA.IN.DEO. (2) Fortitude; FORTITUDO.'SUM.VIRILIS' (Mr. Ruskin), or 'INVINCIBILIS.' (3) Temperance; TEMPERANTIA. SUM. IN. OMIBU. (4) Humility; HUMILITAS.ABITAT.I.ME. (5) Charity; KARITAS.DEI.MECŪ.EST. (6) Justice; REX.SUM.JUSTICIE. (7) Prudence; PRUDENTIA.METIT.OIĀ. (8) Hope; SPĒ.HABE.IN.DNO. The differences between this capital and No. XXIX. are very slight. In the latter, Prudence has a book, which she has not here; and Temperance has a jug here in addition to the chalice which the other carries.

X. Vices. (1) Luxury; LUXURIA. SUM. IMENSA. (2) Gluttony; GULA. SINE. ORDINE. SŪ. (3) Pride; SUPERBIA.PREESSE.VOLO. (4) Anger; IRA. CRUDELIS. Ē. IN. ME. (5) Avarice; AVARITIA. ANPLECTOR. (6) Idleness; ACCIDIA. ME. STRĪGIT. (7) Vanity; VANITAS.IN.ME. HABUNDAT. (8) Envy; INVIDIA.ME.CŌBVRIT. This capital is very finely sculptured.

XI. Birds. Some web-footed, some not so; and with no inscriptions.

XII. Virtues and Vices. (1) Misery; MISERIA. (2) Cheerfulness; ALACRITAS. (3) Folly; STULTICIA.. E. REGNAT. (4) CASTITAS (CE)L(EST)IS.Ē. (5) Honesty; (HO) NEST(ATEM. DILIGO). (6) Falsehood. (7) Injustice; INJUSTICIA. SEVA. SŪ. (8) Abstinence; ASTINĒCIA.OPTIMA.E.. This capital is so much damaged as to be hardly intelligible without comparison with No. XXXIII.

XIII. Lions' heads, large and coarse, and with very poorly carved tufts of foliage between them.

XIV. Wild animals. The whole of the beast, not the head only, is given. They are poorly carved and designed.

XV. Damsels and Youths. Considered by Selvatico, and after him by Mr. Ruskin, to represent Idleness. There are no inscriptions. More probably they represent the youth of the higher class with marks of their sportive occupations. This is an extremely well-carved capital.

XVI. Eight large heads alternately with tufts of foliage. The whole finely carved and designed. Supposed by Zanotto to represent the foreigners who traded with Venice. Selvatico describes it as representing Latins, Tartars, etc., and as being in fact a repetition of No. XXIII. (*vide infra.*)

XVII. Philosophers. This is very much damaged, and the inscriptions are nearly destroyed. (1) Solomon. (2) Triscian. (3) Aristotle. (4) Tully. (5) Pythagoras. On a label carried by this figure Mr. Burges reads the date 1344. Mons. Didron interprets it 1399; this is a date, however, which he will not admit, believing the real date to be 1299. Mr. Ruskin does not appear to have seen these figures, and I have been unable to satisfy myself about them.

XVIII. This is the angle capital. Above it is the Temptation of Adam and Eve; and on the second stage, the four winds on the capital of the arcade, and the Archangel Michael above. The whole is a perfectly beautiful group of sculpture, of an equally beautiful and well-selected story.

Planets. (1) Creation of Man; DE.LIMO.Ds.ADA.DE.COSTA.FORMAVIT.ET.EVA. (2) Saturn; ET.SATURNE.DOMUS.EGLOCERUNTIS.ET.URNE. (3) Jupiter; INDE.JOVI.DOMA.PISCES.SIMUL.ATQ.CIRONA. (4) Mars; E—ARIES.MARTIS.ET.ACU—E.SCORPIO.PARTIS. (5) The Sun; EST. DOMU. SOLIS. TU. QUOQ.SIGNE.LEONI. (6) Venus; LIBRA. CŪ. TAURO. VENUS.—T. PURIOR. AURO. (7) Mercury; OCCUPAT.ERIGONE.STILBONS.GEMIUQ.LACONE. (8) The Moon; LUNE CANCER.DOMUT.PBET.Ī.ORBE SIGNORIO. The whole of the sculpture of this capital deserves careful study. Mars is a figure in chain mail. Venus, seated on a bull, and the Moon—a female figure in a boat, with a crescent in one hand and a crab in the other—are both of them exquisitely treated.

XIX. Artificers. Figures alternately crowned and uncrowned working at parts of a building. The foliage is admirable. The pieces of stone on which the artificers are at work are inlaid with porphyry. Mr. Ruskin points out that all the architectural details represented are such as would be found in the early part of the fourteenth century. It is certainly very curious that among the workers one has 'DISCIPULUS OPTIMUS;' another—'DISIPŪLS INCREDŪL,' over the head: a reference to S. John and S. Thomas, which is not intelligible to me.

XX. Beasts. Eight large heads, well carved and set as knops below masses of rather heavily treated leaves. The beasts have their names inscribed: LEO. LUPUS. URSUS. MUSIPUL. CHANIS.[104] APER. GRIFO. VULPUS.

XXI. Trades. Finely carved. Inscriptions over the heads of the workmen: (1) LAPICIDA SUM. (2) AURIFICES. (3) CERDO SUM. (4) CARPENTARIUS SUM. (5) MENSURATOR. (6) AGRICHOLA. (7) NOTARIUS SUM. (8) FABER SUM.

XXII. The Ages of Man. A very interesting capital. (1) + LUNA. DNAT. IFANCIE. P. ANO. IIII. (2) MECUREŪ. DNT. PUERICIE. P. ANO. X. (3) ADOLOSENCIE. (VEN)US. P. AN. VII. (4) INVENTUTI.DNT.SOL.P.AN.XIX. (5) SENECTUTI.DNT.MARS.P. AN. XV. (6) SENICIE. DNT.JUPITER.P.ANN.XII. (7) DECREPITE.DNT.SATN.UQ.AD.MŌTE. (8) ULTIMA.E.MORS.PENA PECATI.

---

[104] Mr. Ruskin founds an argument on the introduction of an H in this way in what he calls one of the Renaissance capitals of the Piazetta (the 33rd). He omits to notice its use in this undoubtedly early capital.

XXIII. Nations. This is treated in the same way exactly as No. XX. The heads are inscribed, Latini. Tartari. Turchi. Ongari. Greci. Goti. Egicy. Persii. It will be found that, counting from the south-west angle, the second and fifth capitals on each front are of the same description, i.e. Nos. XIII. and XVI. on the west side, and XIX. and XXIII. on the Piazzetta front. I think this militates against Mr. Ruskin's view that this capital is not old, as it shews how very regularly they are placed; and I do not see much to choose between in these four capitals. It is worth notice here that this capital is, to a considerable extent, a replica of No. XVI.; but the latter has no inscriptions.

XXIV. Love and Marriage. This is a much larger column than the others. It carries a cross wall above, so placed as to allow of rooms on the sea-front, about sixty-three feet in width. It is one of the most exquisite of all the series. The subjects are: (1) A young man with his hand on his heart, admiring a damsel. (2) They meet and converse. (3) She puts a crown on his head, and presents him with an apple. (4) They embrace. (5) The marriage bed. (6) They hold their bambino wrapped in swaddling clothes between them. (7) The child grows, and enjoys life. (8) The child is dead, and his parents mourn over his body. The change in character from the extreme smartness of dress in the earliest subject to the carelessness about it in the last, should be observed.

Above this capital is a figure of Venice personified, in one of the divisions of the tracery. She is seated on lions' backs, with her feet above the sea.

XXV. Labours of the Months. This is not a replica. (1) March; Marcius. Cornator. (2) April and May; Aprilis + Magius. (3) June; Junius.cū.cerisis. (4) July and August; Julius + Augustu. (5) September; Septebe. Supeditat. (6) October and November; Octobē + Novembe. (7) December; Decem - - - cat suum. (8) January and February; Janvarivs + Februaru.

XXVI. Sports and Employments of damsels and young men. This is a replica of No. XV. The foliage here is exquisitely carved. There are no inscriptions. The figures, as in the other, hold: (1) A horse. (2) A bird, and the leg of a larger bird (hawking?). (3) A distaff. (4) A dog. (5) A flower. &c. &c.

XXVII. Fruit in baskets. This is not a replica. It is the finest of the "knop" series of capitals. The fruit is admirably carved, and here the exact imitation of nature in the fruit, combined with foliage in the knops between the baskets, which is quite conventional and architectural in its character, is extremely interesting and instructive, as shewing how distinctly the sculptor knew the proper limits of conventional and realistic representation. The fruit are described: (1) Cherries; Serexis. (2) Pears; Piri. (3) Cucumbers; Chocumeris. (4) Peaches; Persici. (5) Gourds; Cuche. (6) Melons; Moloni. (7) Figs; Figi. (8) Grapes; Huva.

XXVIII. Virtues and Vices. This is a replica of No. VII. The differences are very small. Here II is prefixed to the "ONORAT" of the other capital.

XXIX. Virtues. A replica of No. IX.

XXX. Vices. A replica of No. X., but well deserving study.

XXXI. Monsters. A replica of No. VIII., but very rudely carved, and very inferior to the next.

XXXII. Students. This is *not* a replica of No. XVII. The figures are admirably treated, all looking thoughtful, and some holding foliage. It seems to represent the more thoughtful side of youth as compared with the idle side, represented in the capitals XV. and XXVI. Zanotto supposes the figures to be the Seven Wise Men of Greece; but the eighth figure — a woman speaking — does not lend itself to this. Mr. Burges most ingeniously suggests that it refers to Nouvella d'Andrea, who, in her father's last illness, lectured from behind a curtain to his pupils; her father died in 1348.

XXXIII. Virtues and Vices. This is a replica of No. XII.

XXXIV. Eight birds. A replica of No. XI.

XXXV. Nude children. A replica of No. IV. They have birds, fruit, etc., in their hands.

XXXVI. Justice and Lawgivers. This is the north-west angle column. The capital has the following subjects: (1) Justice; JUSTITIA. (2) Aristotle; ARISTOTEL. CHE. DIE. LEGGE. (3) Moses; - - - L.PUOLO.D.L.SUO.ISEL.RITA.[105] (4) Solon; SAL.UNO.DEI. SETE.SAVI.DI.GRECIA.CHE.DIE.LEGGE.(5)Scipio;ISIPIONE.ACHASTITA.CHE — E.LA.FIA.ARE.[106] (6) Numa Pompilius; NUMA POMPILIO.IPERADOR.EDIFICHADOR.DI.TEPI.E.CHIESE. (7) Moses receiving the tables of the law; QUADO.MOISE.RICEVE.LA.LEGE.I. SUL.MONTE. (8) Trajan; TRAINO.ĪPERADORE.CHE.DIE.JUSTITIA.A.LA.VEDOVA.

The carving of foliage in this capital is, I think, simpler, and on the whole better than that on the other great angle, capital No. XVIII., with which it invites comparison; but the carving of the figures is quite inferior, and later in character. The foliage above this capital, which supports the Judgment of Solomon, is inferior to that on the capital itself, and is, I believe, considerably later in date, being no doubt of the same age as the figures in the Judgment, i.e. not earlier than 1430-1450. Above this angle is the figure of the Archangel Gabriel.

THE END

---

[105] Unintelligible; but explained by Zanotto to be: "Mosè che die' legge al suo popolo Israelita."

[106] Zanotto reads this: "Scipione a castita che rende la figlia al padre."

Lector House believes that a society develops through a two-fold approach of continuous learning and adaptation, which is derived from the study of classic literary works spread across the historic timeline of literature records. Therefore, we aim at reviving, repairing and redeveloping all those inaccessible or damaged but historically as well as culturally important literature across subjects so that the future generations may have an opportunity to study and learn from past works to embark upon a journey of creating a better future.

This book is a result of an effort made by Lector House towards making a contribution to the preservation and repair of original ancient works which might hold historical significance to the approach of continuous learning across subjects.

HAPPY READING & LEARNING!

LECTOR HOUSE LLP
E-MAIL: lectorpublishing@gmail.com